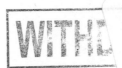

 Rob

Perspectives on Trade and Development

PERSPECTIVES ON TRADE AND DEVELOPMENT

Anne O. Krueger

HARVESTER WHEATSHEAF
New York   London   Toronto   Sydney   Tokyo   Singapore

First published 1990 by
Harvester Wheatsheaf,
66 Wood Lane End, Hemel Hempstead,
Hertfordshire, HP2 4RG
A division of
Simon & Schuster International Group

Printed and bound in Great Britain by
BPCC Wheatons Ltd, Exeter

British Library Cataloguing in Publication Data

Krueger, Anne O. (Anne Osborn)
   Perspectives on trade and development
   1. Foreign trade
   I. Title
   382

ISBN 0-7450-0615-9

---

1 2 3 4 5 94 93 92 91 90

CONTENTS

ACKNOWLEDGEMENTS

I should like to acknowledge the permissions received to include in this book the following of my papers originally published elsewhere.

Chapter 2 *Growth, Distortions, and Patterns of Trade Among Many Countries*, Princeton Studies in International Finance, no. 40, February 1977, pp. 1–19 and 44–45. Copyright © 1977. Reprinted by permission of the International Finance Section of Princeton University.

Chapter 3 'Comparative Advantage and Development Policy Twenty Years Later', in M. Syrquin, L. Taylor and L. Westphal (eds), *Economic Structure and Performance: Essays in Honor of Hollis B. Chenery*, 1984. Copyright © 1984 by Academic Press, Inc. Permission granted by Academic Press.

Chapter 4 'Factor Endowments and *per capita* Income Differences Among Countries', *Economic Journal*, vol. 78, September 1968. Permission granted by Basil Blackwell Ltd.

Chapter 5 'Trade Policy as an Input to Development', *American Economic Review, Papers and Proceedings*, May 1980. Permission granted by the American Economic Association.

Chapter 6 'The Relationships Between Trade, Employment and Development', in T. Paul Schultz and Gustav Ranis (eds), *The State of Development Economics: Progress and Perspectives*, New York, Basil Blackwell, 1988, pp. 357–83. Permission granted by Basil Blackwell Ltd.

Chapter 7 'The Political Economy of the Rent-Seeking Society', *American Economic Review*, vol. 64, no. 3, June 1974, pp. 291–303. Permission granted by the American Economic Association.

Chapter 8 'Interactions Between Inflation and Trade Regime Objectives in Stabilization Programmes', in William R. Cline and Sidney Weintraub (eds), *Economic Stabilization In Developing Countries*, 1981. (Prepared for Brookings conference on Economic Stabilization in Developing Countries, 25/26 October 1979, Washington DC.) Permission granted by The Brookings Institution.

Chapter 9 'Problems of Liberalization', in Arnold C. Harberger (ed.), *World Economic Growth, Case Studies of Developed and Developing Nations*, 1984. Permission granted by ICS Press.

Chapter 10 'Some Economic Costs of Exchange Control: The Turkish Case', *Journal of Political Economy*, vol. 74, no. 5, pp. 466–80, October 1966. Copyright 1966 by the University of Chicago. Permission granted by University of Chicago Press.

Chapter 11 'An Empirical Test of the Infant Industry Argument', with Baran Tuncer, *American Economic Review*, vol. 72, no. 5, December 1982, pp. 1142–52. Permission granted by the American Economic Association.

Chapter 12 'The Importance of Economic Policy in Development: Contrasts Between Korea and Turkey', in Henryk Kierzkowski (ed.), *Protection and Competition in International Trade: Essays in Honor of W. M. Corden*, 1987. Permission granted by Basil Blackwell Ltd.

Chapter 13 'The Role of the World Bank as an International Institution', in Allan H. Meltzer and Karl Brunner (eds), *Carnagie-Rochester Conference Series*, vol. 18, 1983, pp. 281–312, Elsevier Science Publishers. Permission granted by Elsevier Science Publishers B. V.

Chapter 14 'Aspects of Capital Flows Between Developing and Developed Countries', in Assaf Razin and Ephriam Sadka (eds), *Economic Policy in Theory and Practice*, Academic Press, 1987. Permission granted by Macmillan Press Ltd. and St. Martin's Press.

Chapter 15 'Development Thought and Developmental Assistance', Chapter 2 of *Aid and Development*, with C. Michalopoulos and V. Ruttan. Permission granted by Johns Hopkins University Press.

Chapter 16 'The Developing Countries' Role in the World Economy', in J. Frenkel and M. Mussa (eds.), *World Economic System: Performance and Prospects*, 1984. Permission granted by Auburn House Publishing Co.

PART I

INTRODUCTION

1 · PERSPECTIVES ON TRADE AND DEVELOPMENT

This volume contains selected papers that were written over the period 1965–85, focusing on the relationship between trade and exchange rate policies and overall economic development. I had long since intended to write a book, analyzing systematically the theory, evidence, and policy implications of what has been learned about the trade–development relationship, but other professional commitments always seemed to take precedence. When Harvester Wheatsheaf approached me about this volume, it seemed to me that I could take advantage of much I had already written and provide a reasonably systematic account.

In the volume itself, the chapters are organized according to their theme: the two chapters of Part II provide discussions of the relationships between trade strategies and development; the next four chapters of Part III then focus on links between factor endowments (the traditional stuff of international trade theory), developing countries' policies, and trade strategies in terms of their growth; Part IV contains five studies which amplify, through empirical and other means, the role of economic policy in development, and the four chapters constituting Part V focus on the international economic environment in which development efforts are taking place.

Most of the chapters are self-explanatory. It may help the reader, however, to understand the context in which each one was written, which itself reflects something of the change in thought regarding development that has taken place over the past several decades.

When I was a graduate student in the late 1950s, some of the most exciting events in the world were the efforts of newly independent countries to raise living standards and achieve economic development. My primary focus in graduate school was on international economics, with its emphasis on the factor proportions explanation of trade, the welfare costs of protection, and the optimality of free trade under most circumstances. However, ideas for appropriate means to achieve rapid economic growth in developing countries focused on contributions such as Nurkse's balanced growth, Prebisch's call for import substitution, and the need for planning models.

On the one hand, international economics seemed to provide important tools of analysis, but, on the other, policy-makers concerned with development appeared to be rejecting those tools. The apparent contradiction was uncomfortable, but I left it alone for several years. Then, in the summer of 1965, I accepted an assignment with the US Agency for International Development to work on issues of trade policy and development. That opportunity included a chance to try out ideas in a particular instance, and the one that was chosen was Turkey.

Travel there, and discussions with businessmen and others were sufficient to convince even a casual observer of some of the problems associated with import substitution regimes. The experience reinforced my view of the importance of the traditional tools of analysis and led to the article 'Some Economic Costs of Exchange Control' (Chapter 10).

The Turkish experience led me to question, to some degree, the factor proportions explanation of trade, which implies that factor prices may (under certain conditions) be equalized throughout the world. The natural question was: if prices were equalized, how much difference in per capita incomes among countries would we observe? The resulting estimates appeared as 'Factor Endowments and Per Capita Income Differences Among Countries' (Chapter 4), which demonstrated that a considerable proportion – possibly as much as half – of observed differences are explicable by differences in factor endowments, if one includes human capital as an important factor of production.

The conviction that Turkey was not achieving as much as might have been accomplished with her import substitution regime, coupled with the notion that factor endowment differentials are important, then led to a questioning of the conventional wisdom as to the costs of inappropriate economic policy mistakes. At about that time, I had the opportunity to spend some time in India, analyzing the costs and benefits of its import substitution policies. Within a short period of time, it was evident to me that businessmen were devoting much of their time to circumnavigating government regulations and controls, and that the focus of economic activity was to profit by regulations, rather than to produce goods and services, a phenomenon that also took place in Turkey. The upshot was 'The Political Economy of the Rent-Seeking Society' (Chapter 7), which demonstrated that in addition to the traditional welfare triangle of losses associated with tariffs, price controls, and other non-optimal interventions, deadweight losses could occur as individuals allocated resources to seeking out the rents associated with controls.

During that same period, Jagdish Bhagwati and I were directing the National Bureau of Economic Research (NBER) project on Foreign Trade Regimes and Economic Development. There were altogether ten countries covered by excellent researchers in that project, and the cumulative impressions gleaned by the simultaneous research results were much stronger for all project participants than the conclusions of any one study individually. A number of important insights emerged for all project participants. One of the countries covered by the project was Korea and the very rapid growth of that country – associated with a spectacular rate of growth of exports – was impressive.

Shortly thereafter, I was invited by the Korea Development Institute and the Harvard Institute of International Development to participate in their project on the Modernization of Korea, analyzing the trade and payments regime, and foreign aid, from 1945 to 1975. That experience was invaluable in demonstrating practically what international economics had taught theoretically: by using comparative advantage, Korea's growth rate had been far in excess of that earlier deemed feasible.

The intellectually challenging question was why Korea should have grown that much faster. A first effort was contained in 'Growth, Distortions, and Patterns of Trade among Many Countries' (Chapter 2), which was presented as the Graham Lecture at Princeton University in 1977. It sketches out a role for trade policy – based on comparative advantage in labor-intensive manufactured goods in a three-factor, multi-sectoral framework – that is much greater than that implied by the traditional 'two-by-two-by-two' model of international trade. Some of the same ideas were advanced further – especially the importance of markets in providing competition and incentives – in 'Trade Policy as an Input to Development' (Chapter 5).

As the evidence – from the NBER study already mentioned, and also from the Little, Scitovsky and Scott OECD study (1970), and the ongoing success of Korea and Taiwan – continued to mount that countries promoting exports fared better than their counterparts relying on protection and import substituion, an important problem arose: once protection has been in place for a period of time, it becomes difficult to dismantle it, but increasingly important to do so. An early effort to grapple with this issue was 'Interactions between Inflation and Trade Regime Objectives in Stabilization Programs' (Chapter 8), which focused on some of the problems associated with reforming trade regimes in the context of rapid inflation – a surprisingly modern theme in light of some of the difficulties of developing countries in the late 1980s. At a later date, 'Problems of Liberalization' (Chapter 9) carried the argument somewhat further.

By the late 1970s, it was widely accepted that the outer-oriented trade regimes of the East Asian newly industrializing countries (NICs) had played a major role in their rapid growth. Some critics, however, alleged that that growth was at the expense of domestic economic objectives, and, in particular, that it was incompatible with employment growth, itself a prerequisite for spreading the fruits of economic growth to the large majority of the population. This led to my directing the NBER project on Trade and Employment in Developing Countries, which attempted to trace out more carefully the linkages between trade strategies and domestic economic variables of importance, especially employment. Some of the major findings of that study are reported in 'The Relationships between Trade, Employment, and Development' (Chapter 6).

The results of the project, together with further evidence from both the rapidly growing NICs and from the more slowly-growing countries, provided further stimulus, which was reflected in 'Comparative Advantage and Development Policy Twenty Years Later' (Chapter 3), which surveyed the ways in which thinking had changed over the twenty years after Hollis Chenery had written his famous article on the trade–development relationship.

Even in traditional international economics, it had always been recognized that there could be a case for temporary protection if an industry would generate sufficient externalities and experience falling costs over time. Despite the evidence, and an excellent theoretical article by Robert Baldwin, many advocates of protectionist policies in developing countries continued to rely on the infant industry argument to defend those policies. No amount of theory can ever definitively resolve an issue, and I was fortunate enough to persuade a Turkish colleague, Baran Tuncer (now at the World Bank) to collaborate in studying what had happened to protected industries in Turkey. The result was 'An Empirical Test of the Infant Industry Argument' (Chapter 11) which shows that, in the Turkish case, there was little evidence to support the notion that these industries had deserved protection.

Finally, by the early 1980s, the contrasts between Turkey and Korea were becoming more pronounced. It had always struck me that their two economies had a great deal in common – wedged between two giants in each instance, and with unique histories. Turkey had a much more favorable natural resource endowment and per capita income in the 1950s, but Korea's growth had been so much more rapid that Turkey looked like the much poorer country in the 1980s. 'The Importance of Economic Policy in Development: Contrasts Between Korea and Turkey' (Chapter 12) once again analyzed, this time empirically, the role of economic policy in affecting development.

From the early 1970s onward, it has been evident that outer-oriented countries will grow more rapidly than highly protectionist ones whatever the state of the international economy, but all will grow more rapidly in the context of a healthy, supportive international economy. The four chapters constituting Part V of this volume reflect on various aspects of those links. 'The Role of the World Bank as an International Institution' (Chapter 13) considers the role of the World Bank as an institution dealing with official capital flows to developing countries. 'Aspects of Capital Flows between Developing and Developed Countries' (Chapter 14) was written shortly after the onset of the debt crisis of the 1980s, and attempted to sort out many of the issues raised by the crisis and its aftermath. 'Development thought and Development Assistance' (Chapter 15), written jointly with Vernon Ruttan, traces changes in thinking about economic development and the role of policy, and the ways they affect foreign aid.

It is always easy to dwell on those things that are not going as well as might be hoped, and certainly the growth of the developing countries could and should be more rapid. None the less, it is a mistake to conclude that development efforts have been a failure. The book concludes, therefore, with 'The Developing Countries' Role in the World Economy' (Chapter 16), an effort to put into perspective the growth of the developing countries since the Second World War. On balance, the record is somewhat better than most observers believe. Hopefully, with accumulated knowledge and understanding of the development process, the next forty years will witness an even more rapid rate of growth and closing of the gap between developed and developing countries.

As these chapters should make clear, a healthy international economy will provide an appropriate environment. Thus, it will be up to developing countries' governments to undertake policies and provide incentives that are conducive to economic efficiency and reward the accumulation of the appropriate types of physical and human capital.

REFERENCES

Baldwin, Robert E. (1969). 'The Case Against Infant – Industry Tariff Protection', *Journal of Political Economy*, vol. 77 (May), pp. 29–305.

Chenery, Hollis B. (1961). 'Comparative Advantage and Development Policy', *American Economic Review*, vol. 51, no. 1 (March), pp. 18–51.

Little, Ian M.D., Tibor Scitovsky and Maurice Scott (1970). *Industry and Trade in Some Developing Countries: A Comparative Study*, Development Centre of the OECD. London: Oxford University Press.

PART II

LINKS BETWEEN TRADE AND DEVELOPMENT

2 · GROWTH, DISTORTIONS, AND PATTERNS OF TRADE AMONG MANY COUNTRIES

2.1 INTRODUCTION

The basic question to be explored in this study is the way in which the factor-proportions explanation of trade, as developed by Heckscher, Ohlin, and Samuelson, can be stated as a testable hypothesis or series of hypotheses. Three strands of thought are central to the argument: (1) it has long been recognized that developing economies have large agricultural sectors and that trade in primary commodities cannot be explained by the countries' endowment of labor and capital; (2) given the observed difference in factor endowments between developing countries and the industrialized world, it seems reasonable to develop a model of complete specialization rather than one of factor-price equalization; and (3) while numerous theoretical reasons have been advanced in attempts to explain the Leontief paradox – that American exports were more labor-using than American import-competing production – the effects of distortions in goods and factor markets have not been systematically explored in the context of empirical testing of the

First printed in 1977. It is a great honor to have been invited to give the Frank D. Graham Memorial Lecture. Graham's contributions to the field of international trade are widely recognized. His ideas serve as the basis for much of the modern theory of trade as developed by McKenzie and others. Many of his insights still hold strong appeal and are the subject of ongoing research. Indeed, in some respects the model developed in this study is one for which Graham's contributions can be regarded as a precursor.

The reasearch underlying this study was financed in part by the Agency for International Development through the National Bureau of Economic Research. I am indebted to Stephen P. Magee and to members of the Trade and Development Workshop at the University of Minnesota, especially T. Paul Schultz, for helpful discussions when the research was in progress. William Branson, Carlos Díaz-Alejandro, James Henderson, Ronald Jones, Peter Kenen, Sir Arthur Lewis, Fritz Machlup, and Richard Snape all commented on the original version, and many of their suggestions led to significant improvements.

Heckscher–Ohlin–Samuelson (HOS) factor-proportions explanation of trade. While such an omission may be acceptable in dealing with some developed countries, it is surely not so for the developing countries, where market imperfections are thought to be the rule rather than the exception.

It is convenient to develop the argument in stages. First, a simple model of comparative advantage is developed for n commodities, m countries, and two factors of production, under the usual competitive assumptions. Next, the model is amended to incorporate the existence of a primary commodity, or agricultural sector. Finally, distortions in the goods and factor markets are introduced into the model.

2.2   THE FACTOR-PROPORTIONS HYPOTHESIS

Two issues arise in connection with the hypotheses emanating from the HOS model. The first relates to the question of whether predictions pertain to the pattern of production or the pattern of trade. For reasons that will become evident below, it will prove useful throughout this study to discuss patterns of production, although it will be seen that there is a close, logical link between production and trade patterns in the n-commodity model.

The second issue relates to alternative interpretations of the predictions arising from the model. On the one hand, they can be interpreted positively, as predictions about the actual pattern of production, in which case they would constitute a set of hypotheses about the observable production patterns. Alternatively, the factor-proportions model can be interpreted normatively, as predictions about the properties of an efficient production pattern that will provide society with the largest attainable consumption bundle for any given inputs allocated to traded-good production. The latter interpretation corresponds, up to a point, to a hypothesis about the nature of an efficient pattern of production. Predictions can then be interpreted as forecasting what would happen under efficient resource allocation.

The two alternative interpretations coincide, of course, if the structure of production is efficient, but they might not coincide under inefficient allocations. Since one purpose of this exercise is to consider the effect of market distortions on the observed pattern of trade, it will be useful to regard the HOS model and hypotheses as being normative. Under this second interpretation, as will be demonstrated, the HOS hypotheses could be correct, while observed production patterns ran counter to them owing to inefficient production patterns. Although the model developed in this chapter assumes a well-functioning competitive market, it can readily be shown that the HOS hypotheses would also be borne out given the assumptions about technology under any economic structure that provided an efficient allocation of resources for production of tradable goods.

2.2.1   Assumptions and Statement of the Basic Model

As indicated above, there are assumed to be n commodities, m countries, and two factors of production in the basic model considered here. Later, the model will be extended to incorporate an agricultural sector, and the n industries under consideration here will then be understood to be those producing n separate commodities within the manufacturing sector. For the moment, however, it is simplest to start by regarding the n commodities, each produced with two factors of production, as constituting the entire economy. Each of the n production functions displays constant returns to scale, with diminishing marginal product to each factor of production.

Consider now the cost-minimizing labor–capital ratio associated in each industry with a particular arbitrarily chosen wage–rental ratio. Order the commodities so that commodity 1 has the highest labor–capital ratio (at that wage–rental ratio), commodity 2 has the next highest, and so on down to commodity n, which has the lowest labor–capital ratio. It will be assumed that, for all wage–rental ratios, repetition of this procedure would result in exactly the same ordering of commodities – i.e. there are assumed to be no factor-intensity reversals. A sufficient condition for this ordering of commodities to be the same throughout the entire range of wage–rental variation is that all production functions have the same elasticity of substitution. The exclusion of factor-intensity reversals implies something fairly important: with undistorted factor markets, one would observe the same ordering of factor intensities across industries in every country, regardless of whether goods prices were the same or not. This proposition will be seen below to be of some importance for testing for the effects of factor-market distortions.[1]

We now have a labor-intensity ordering of production functions across countries and a specification of technology which is common to all m countries. In addition, it is assumed that within each country perfect competition prevails in every industry in which there are positive production levels, with perfect factor mobility among all producing industries. The wage rate equals the value of the marginal product of labor, and the rental on capital equals the value of the marginal product of capital for all industries with positive production levels. These assumptions assure that each country will be producing efficiently on the boundary of its production-possibility set and that the domestic marginal rate of transformation between any pair of produced commodities will equal the price ratio.

These specifications of the nature of the market within each country, and of the production technology, are the same for all countries. What distinguishes each country is its labor–capital endowment. For purposes of simplicity, it is assumed that each country has its own fixed and inelastic supply of labor and of capital. Full employment of both factors prevails in every country. On that basis, one can compute the ratio of the labor to the capital endowment in each country. The countries can then be so numbered that country 1 has the highest endowment of labor to capital, country 2 the next highest, and so on to country m, which has the lowest labor–capital endowment. Thus, commodities are numbered so that a higher number implies a higher capital–labor ratio in production: countries are numbered so that a higher number is associated with a greater abundance of capital relative to labor.

The assumptions made so far are sufficient that, for any given set of prices confronting producers in a particular country, the area along the boundary of the production-possibility set in which competitive equilibrium can occur will be fairly closely circumscribed. For a particular country and set of prices, there are three possibilities. First, it is possible that it will be profitable to produce only one commodity, in which case all labor and capital within the country will be employed in that industry, the wage–rental ratio being determined by the production function for that industry. Second, it may be profitable to produce exactly two commodities, in which case the wage–rental ratio will be determined by the price ratio between the two goods, and the precise composition of output will be such that factors are fully employed at the factor proportions implied by the wage–rental ratio. Third, it may be that it is equally profitable to produce three or more commodities, in which case the precise composition of output is indeterminate, although the wage–rental ratio will be determined by the prices of any two of the commodities.[2]

So far, the production side of the model has been specified. To develop a full general equilibrium model of trade, it would now be necessary to add some demand relations to the model, and then to establish some properties of the resulting equilibrium price, production, and trade constellation. For purposes of exploring the implications of the HOS model, however, it can be assumed that international prices are given. Hypotheses can then be formulated in terms of the structure of production (and later transformed into hypotheses about the factor intensity of trade). As is well known, the only way in which demand patterns may influence the HOS predictions is through the possibility that they might offset differences in production patterns. It will be seen below that the only role demand patterns can play in this $n \times m \times 2$ model is to determine whether, when more than one commodity is produced by a particular country, produced commodities are exports or import-competing goods.

One way to interpret the assumption that international prices are determined outside the system is to assume that each country under consideration is small relative to the rest of the world and thus does not influence international prices by its production and consumption behavior. It is more satisfactory, however, simply to postulate that there is in the background a price-determining mechanism, via demand and supply relations, that results in the establishment of some constellation of equilibrium prices. The setting, then, is that international prices are given and there are no transport costs or other impediments to trade. Therefore, prices are the same in all countries (as there can be no home goods in the absence of transport costs). The zero-transport-cost assumption will be relaxed below, and the implications of the HOS model for factor proportions in the presence of transport costs will be examined.

2.2.2 Implications of the Basic Model

For any particular country, given international prices, either only one commodity is produced or the domestic wage–rental ratio is determined by the commodity–price ratio when two or more commodities are produced. For a pair of countries, the implications of this proposition are straightforward. If both countries produce two or more goods in common (or, at the limit, if producers in both countries are indifferent between their existing production pattern and an output bundle that would entail producing two or more goods in common), there will be a common wage–rental ratio between those two countries. All that can be said about production patterns is that factor proportions in each country will be the same in each industry (with the same wage–rental ratio) and the more labor-abundant country will have a production bundle more heavily weighted toward the labor-intensive commodities. It is possible that the more labor-abundant country might produce a commodity more capital intensive than some commodity produced by the capital-abundant country: as Bhagwati (1972) has shown, only the overall weighting of factor intensities can be predicted when factor-rental equalization occurs.

For present purposes, let us assume that there is no factor-rental equalization. This does no violence to the basic model: if two countries have overlapping production patterns and factor-rental equalization, they can be regarded as one country in an economic sense. Such may be the case, for example, for some of the European economic community countries.

In effect, the assumption of no equalization of factor rentals implies that no pair of countries produces two commodities (or more) in common: specialization must result.[3] What, then, can be said about the production patterns for two countries between which factor rentals are not equalized? It follows immediately that the more labor-abundant country will specialize in producing more labor-intensive (lower-numbered) commodities than the more capital-abundant country. The more labor-abundant of any pair of countries cannot produce any commodity more capital-intensive than the least capital-using commodity produced in the other. The two countries might produce a commodity in common (if they are adjacent to each other in factor endowments), but the wage–rental ratio would be lower in the more labor-abundant country and it would produce the common commodity using a more labor-intensive technique.

That the wage–rental ratio must be lower in the labor-abundant country follows immediately from the fact that, if the ratio were higher, it would be profitable to produce more capital-intensive goods with more capital-intensive techniques in the labor-abundant country, an impossibility under the assumption of full employment in both countries.

It is evident that the foregoing statements hold independently of the number of commodities under consideration. In a world of 100 commodities and 2 countries, it would be quite possible for the more labor-abundant country to specialize in the first 49 commodities, while the other country produced 51 or 52.[4]

Figure 2.1 illustrates the possible sorts of production pattern that might emerge under the assumptions set forth above. In Figure 2.1, $m = 11$ and $n = 9$, although other numbers are equally plausible. Commodities are listed in the columns and countries in the rows. An × in the ith row and jth column indicates that the production of commodity j is positive in the ith country, and a blank means there is no production of the commodity in question. For expository convenience, it is assumed that there are no cases with zero production levels where producers are indifferent as to whether they produce or not.

Inspection of the combinations of production patterns between pairs of adjacent countries illustrates the properties of the model. Country 1 produces commodities 1 and 2, and produces commodity 2 in common with country 2. There is, however, no presumption of factor-rental equalization between countries 1 and 2, as country 1 may have a considerably lower wage–rental ratio than country 2. Country 2 also produces commodities 3 and 4 (and must be endowed with a higher capital–labor radio than country 1), producing commodity 4 in com-

		1	2	3	4	5	6	7	8	9
	1	X	X							
	2		X	X	X					
	3				X					
	4				X					
	5				X	X				
Country	6				X	X				
	7					X	X			
	8					X		X		
	9						X	X		
	10							X		
	11								X	X

Commodity

Figure 2.1 Possible production patterns for eleven countries and nine commodities

mon with countries 3, 4, 5, and 6. It is apparent, however, that capital intensity of production of commodity 4 is greater in each higher-numbered country. Note that country 2 produces one commodity in common with country 1 and one commodity in common with country 3: there is no factor-rental equalization because there are not two commodities produced in common. Countries 5 and 6 produce two commodities in common and therefore must have equal wage–rental ratios. Likewise, countries 7, 8, and 9 must have factor-rental equalization between them, although at a higher wage–rental ratio than countries 5 and 6. The fact that country 8 does not produce commodity 6 illustrates the remote possibility of factor-rental equalization in a circumstance where a more labor-abundant country (number 7) produces a more capital-intensive commodity (number 6) than a more capital-abundant country (number 8, which produces commodity 5).[5] Country 10 also produces commodity 7 but uses more capital-intensive techniques than do the three countries with factor-rental equalization. As drawn here, country 11 is the only country producing the two most capital-intensive commodities, 8 and 9, although it could happen that factor-rental equalization took place among the most capital-abundant countries, with more than one country producing the most capital-intensive commodity.

Obviously, other constellations of production patterns are also possible, but Figure 2.1 sufficiently illustrates the basic possibilities. Generalizing, when there is no factor-rental equalization (or when all geographic units with the same wage–rental ratio are treated as a single country), the following conclusions emerge:

1.   Production in the most labor-abundant country will be concentrated on the most labor-intensive commodity or commodities, and production in the most capital-abundant country will include production of the most capital-intensive good. Country 1, in other words, is certain to produce commodity 1, and country m is certain to produce commodity n. For countries 2 to $m - 1$, those with higher capital–labor endowments will produce higher-numbered commodities than those with lower capital–labor endowments. It will never be so that a relatively more capital-abundant country will produce a more labor-intensive good than any less capital-abundant country (since it is assumed that factor-rental equalization cannot occur).

2.   If a country produces more than one commodity, the produced commodities will lie adjacent to each other in the factor-intensity ordering. Whether the additional commodities produced are import substitutes or exports will depend on the country's factor endowment (in the absence of transport costs) and on demand conditions. It is clear that at least one produced commodity will be exported and that all non-produced commodities will be imported. It is quite possible that all commodities domestically produced will be made in sufficient quantities to satisfy domestic demand and to export. It is also possible that imports of one or more commodities would result. Except for the most and the least capital-abundant countries, therefore, import-competing industries can lie on either or both sides of the factor intensity of export industries.[6] There will be no essential commodity characteristic that distinguishes import substitutes from exports. The key distinction is between produced and non-produced commodities.

3.   If any two countries produce a common commodity without factor-rental equalization between them, the more capital-abundant country will be found employing a more capital-intensive technique of production than the labor-abundant country, and the wage–rental ratio will be higher than in the labor-abundant country.

4.   In general, the factor-proportions explanation of trade will show up in the pattern of specialization of production rather than in the factor intensity of exports and import-competing goods. Countries in the middle of the factor-endowment ranking will tend to specialize in producing commodities in the middle of the factor-intensity ranking. They will import labor-intensive commodities from more labor-abundant coun-

tries and capital-intensive commodities from countries with relatively higher capital–labor endowments.

The implications of these propositions for empirical testing of the factor-proportions explanation of trade are immediate. However, it is preferable to analyze the effects of extending the model and of relaxing various assumptions before spelling out the empirical propositions that emerge.

2.2.3 Growth in One Country

As a first step in extending the model, it is instructive to examine how the pattern of production and factor prices would change if one relatively labor-abundant country started accumulating capital more rapidly than the rate of growth of its labor force, while international prices and other countries' factor endowment were constant.[7]

Straightforward application of the factor-rental-equalization and Rybczynski theorems yields the results. It will be recalled that there are three possible initial conditions: (1) the country is specialized in the production of one commodity; (2) the country produces two or more commodities but no more than one in common with any single country; and (3) there is factor-rental equalization with another country and two or more commodities are produced in common. Consider the first case – complete specialization in one commodity. As capital accumulates relative to labor, the production process becomes more capital-intensive, with an increase in the wage–rental ratio but continued complete specialization in the single commodity. As accumulation continues, the rental on capital continues to decline until it is profitable to produce the next higher-numbered commodity. After production of that commodity has started, continued capital accumulation results in shifting the composition of output toward the more capital-intensive commodity. At some point, production of the commodity initially produced ceases. During the period of producng both goods, the wage–rental ratio is constant, as international prices are given. When production becomes concentrated on the next-higher commodity, the wage–rental ratio starts rising again and continues until it is profitable to produce the next commodity.[8]

There is, then, a two-phase progression up the commodity chain.[9] In the phase when only one commodity is produced, the wage–rental ratio increases with capital accumulation but the pattern of production remains unchanged. In the phase when two goods are produced, the wage–rental ratio is constant, but the structure of production is shifting among commodities. It is easy to see that starting from the initial position described in case 2 does not essentially alter the argument: initially, the composition of production would shift until the time when continued production of the more labor-intensive commodity was inconsistent with full employment at the existing wage–rental ratio; the wage–rental ratio would then start increasing and production techniques would become more capital-using.

Finally, there is the third case – that of factor-rental equalization. Starting in such a position, output of the capital-intensive commodity would increase relatively faster than capital accumulated until production of the labor-intensive commodity ceased, and the story would then be the same as for the first two cases.[10] In all three cases, as the country accumulating capital shifts its production structure to more capital-using goods, it must 'meet' and 'pass' some other countries along the way. During times when it begins producing new goods, there may be a period when factor rentals equal those of the country whose factor endowment is next most capital-intensive to the country in question. Once that country is passed, specialization can rule again, but at some point the next country must also be met and passed. Indeed, in the context introduced above, with one country accumulating capital and all other countries unchanged, the accumulating country would eventually become the most capital-abundant and would specialize in the production of one or more of the most capital-intensive commodities.

The two-stage progression here has strong implications for the pattern of trade and its changes over time that would be observed for a rapidly growing country: exports of labor-intensive commodities would gradually be replaced by exports of more capital-intensive commodities as the changing factor endowment altered the country's comparative advantage. Whether a commodity was an export or an import substitute would depend on the factor endowment and the demand pattern, and there is no prediction about relative factor intensity at a point in time.

2.2.4   An Agricultural Sector

Although the n-commodity model spelled out above may be a useful first approximation for trade in manufactured commodities, it is surely unsatisfactory for agricultural and other primary commodities, especially in the context of a discussion of developing countries' comparative advantage. Moreover, everyone knows that one of the key features of low-per-capita-income countries is the very high proportion of national income, and even higher fraction of population, in the agricultural sector.

Jones (1971b) has developed a two-good, three-factor model of trade that can be adapted to take into account this aspect of reality. To avoid confusion later, I shall speak of sectoral outputs as being 'goods', in contrast to the n 'commodities' produced within the manufacturing sector. One of Jones's goods will be regarded as food, the only output of the agricultural sector, and the other will be the n-commodity output of the manufacturing sector. The distinctive feature of Jones's model is that each good requires only two factors of production as inputs: one factor is specific to each sector and one factor is mobile between the two sectors. For present purposes, labor is regarded as the mobile factor, employed in both manufacturing and agriculture, land is treated as the factor employed only in agricultural production, and capital is the factor specific to manufacturing.

It is useful to begin by considering the case with only one manufacturing commodity. For given (international) prices of the manufacture and food, an equilibrium is described by the following conditions: (1) equality of the wage between the two sectors; (2) full employment of all three factors of production, with the services of capital and land valued at their marginal products; and (3) competition among cost-minimizing firms within each sector. Unlike the 2×2 HOS model, factor rewards are not independent of factor endowments: for a given labor force, the wage, which is uniform, will be higher the greater the endowment of either capital or land, holding the other specific factor constant. For a given stock of land, the fraction of the labor force in agriculture will be greater the smaller the stock of capital. These results follow from the assumption of labor mobility and competitive factor rewards: if the stock of either land or capital increases, the marginal product of labor in that sector must rise. Maintenance of wage equality between sectors therefore implies that some labor must migrate from the other sector, which, with a given amount of the specific factor, implies a higher marginal product of labor in that sector, as well as reduced output.

We now wish to consider what happens over time to a country faced with fixed international prices, still retaining the assumption of only one manufactured commodity. It is simplest to start by assuming an initial equilibrium with a zero capital stock and to investigate what happens if capital accumulation begins with a constant stock of land and an unchanging labor force.

In the initial no-capital-stock equilibrium, the wage will be determined by the land–labor ratio. The greater the labor force relative to the land, the lower will be the marginal product of labor. Presumably, some agricultural output would be exported in return for imports of manufactures. If a small amount of saving takes place, some labor must move from agriculture to manufacturing in order to maintain wage equality between the sectors. The wage must rise from its initial equilibrium as the labor–land ratio falls with the shift of workers to the manufacturing sector. Note that if two different countries started capital accumulation with very different man–land ratios, the initial choice of techniques in their manufacturing sectors would differ, with the country having the more favorable endowment of land using, even initially, techniques that require more capital per worker. That, in turn, implies that the increment of manufacturing output per unit of capital would initially be smaller in the land-rich country.

Once a manufacturing sector is started, further increases in the capital stock imply a rising wage–rental ratio, an increasing marginal product of labor in agriculture, and reduced agricultural output as the same quantity of land is combined with fewer workers. In the two-sector model, the country would initially be a food exporter and a manufactures importer, regardless of the land–man ratio. With capital accumulation, there would inevitably (at constant world prices) come a point where the country shifted from being a net exporter of food to being a net exporter of manufactures.[11] The higher the initial land–man endowment, the greater would be the capital accumulation necessary to reach the crossover point and the higher would be the wage at which such a point was reached. For present purposes, however, the precise location of the crossover is largely irrelevant: the pattern of production within manufacturing will be independent of whether the country is a net exporter of food or of manufactures.

This can be seen by joining the basic two-sector, three-factor model to the *n*-commodity, two-factor model outlined above. In particular, let there be *n* manufacturing production functions, each of which uses labor and capital with constant returns to scale and diminishing marginal products to either factor, while the agricultural sector produces food, using labor and land in its production process, again with constant returns to scale and diminishing returns to either factor. World prices are again given, equality of the wage between industry and agriculture is assumed, and all factors are fully employed.

Diminishing marginal product of labor in agriculture implies that more labor will be supplied to the manufacturing (urban) sector the higher the urban wage. To see the properties (and comparative statics) of an equilibrium, let the urban capital stock be given and consider the circumstances under which the country would produce manufactured commodities 1 and 2; the wage–rental ratio is implied by the relative prices of the two manufactured commodities (given by world prices). If, at that wage, the quantity of labor supplied from the agricultural sector is such that the urban capital–labor ratio lies between the factor proportions associated with the wage–rental ratio in the first and second industries, both commodities will be produced. By construction of the ordering of commodities, the country's labor–capital proportions within manufacturing will be relatively high, and the country will have relatively low wages.

We now have a situation in which there is a capital–labor ratio for the country as a whole *and* a capital–labor ratio for the manufacturing sector. One might find two countries with comparable overall labor–capital ratios but very different wage–rental ratios, if one country was considerably more land-abundant per man. The land-abundant country would have a higher capital–labor ratio in the manufacturing sector and a higher wage–rental ratio than the land-poor country. Conversely, identical wage–rental ratios might be observed if one country's overall capital–labor ratio was greater and its land–labor ratio less than the other's. In that case, similar commodities would be produced by the two countries, despite the diversity in their overall factor endowments. Paradoxically, for any given country-wide capital–labor endowment, the manufacturing sector's capital–labor ratio depends on the country's land–man ratio: the more land there is, the higher will be the wage for any given capital stock.

Suppose now that the wage–rental ratio implied by prices of manufacturing commodities 1 and 2 elicited an urban labor supply such that the overall manufacturing labor–capital ratio (given the fixed capital stock) exceeded the factor proportions that would be used in the first industry at that wage–rental ratio. It is clear that there would be an excess supply of urban labor. The equilibrium wage would therefore be below that associated with positive production levels for commodities 1 and 2. That would result in somewhat less labor being supplied to the first industry, but, even more important, it would imply that commodity 1 is the only manufacture produced.

Consider, then, an equilibrium with wage equality between the urban and rural sectors, and manufacturing production specialized in the first commodity. The quantity produced might be insufficient to supply the domestic market, in which case it would be an import substitute (and the economy would necessarily export food), or it might exceed domestic demand, in which case it would be an export. Either way, it would be labor-intensive relative to other manufactured commodities, which would be imported and not produced domestically.

Now consider what would happen if, from that initial equilibrium, an increment of capital were acquired. Capital deepening in the first industry would occur, thereby tending to raise the wage (inducing more workers to migrate to the urban area) and lower the rental on capital.

The net effect would always be some degree of capital deepening within the first industry, because additional workers would migrate only at a higher wage. Thus, capital accumulation would necessarily increase both the urban and the rural wage and lower the return on capital (and on land).

If capital accumulation continued, a point would be reached at which the wage–rental ratio rendered profitable the production of the second, as well as the first, commodity. At that point, continued capital accumulation would result in increased output of the second commodity and reduced output of the first commodity, following the Rybczynski theorem, and constant factor prices (with a constant urban labor force, also). At some point, the capital–labor ratio would reach that found in the second commodity's production, specialization would be complete in the second commodity, and the wage–rental ratio would once again start increasing as further capital accumulation occurred.

In a world of constant prices with one country accumulating capital, one can readily extend the model to show that the country could 'progress' from specialization in agriculture with no manufacturing activity to a situation in which the most capital-intensive manufactured commodities were produced. Note that the production of some food would continue throughout the process, although, as stated, the model implies decreasing food output throughout the capital-accumulation process (and, perhaps, a shift from food exports to food imports).[12]

It is also simple to consider the situation in which the marginal product of labor in agriculture is high enough so that, instead, specialization is somewhere further up the commodity ordering: even at an early stage of development, comparative advantage within manufacturing need not lie in labor-intensive commodities.

Several points should be noted before scrutinizing the implications for empirical testing. First, the distinction between poor and underdeveloped countries emerges clearly from the model. A 'poor' country is one with an unfavorable land–man endowment. An underdeveloped country is one with a relatively small endowment of capital per person. An underdeveloped country, however, could conceivably have a higher per capita income and real wage than a 'more developed' but poorer country. Second, a country abundantly endowed with land and therefore with a relatively high wage would not necessarily have a comparative advantage in labor-intensive manufactures even in its early stages of capital accumulation: the real wage at which persons would leave agriculture might be too high. In such an instance, the capital–labor ratio in manufacturing would be higher in the early stages of development than in a poorer country, while output per unit of capital and the rate of return on capital would be lower than in a lower-wage country. The apparent paradox of a high-wage, land-rich underdeveloped country or a land-poor, low-wage developed country may thus be explained: Carlos Díaz-Alejandro suggests that Argentina and Japan in the 1920s may be prototypes.

Third, the supply of labor to the urban sector (quite aside from the issue of population growth, which can readily be incorporated into the growth implications of the model) will be relatively more elastic, the smaller is the urban sector relative to the rural sector and the more elastic is the output of the agricultural sector with respect to labor.[13] Thus, one would expect comparative advantage to shift slowly in the early stages of growth, as small changes in the manufacturing wage would elicit a relatively large change in labor supply from the large agricultural sector. For a constant rate of capital accumulation, therefore, one would expect to observe an increasing rate of increase in the urban real wage (and a commensurate change in the rate of change in the return on capital) and a decreasing rate of increase in the rate of growth of manufacturing output. An increasing rate of capital accumulation resulting from higher incomes would reinforce the tendency. 'Early' development would therefore consist of the growth of the manufacturing sector with relatively slow changes in the composition of output and the wage–rental ratio. 'Later' development would witness a much slower rate of transfer of labor to the urban sector but more rapid changes in the wage–rental ratio and in the composition of manufacturing output.

2.2.5 Transport Costs and Home Goods

Despite the many appealing features of the model spelled out above, a troublesome aspect is that it forecasts the production of relatively few manufacturing commodities at each stage of development. That may, of course, be an accurate prediction. How many constitute 'few' depends on the number of commodities relative to the number of countries. If there are 200 countries and 5,000 commodities, failure of production patterns to overlap might still imply the production of a sizeable number of individual manufacturing commodities in each country.

Incorporation of transport costs into the model provides a partial basis for believing that a somewhat greater overlapping of production patterns is possible without factor-rental equalization than is implied by the basic model. It also suggests that the process of growth will entail continuous shifting of output compositions and an increasing wage–rental ratio, rather than the two-phase progression spelled out above.

Assume that transport costs are a constant percentage of international price for all manufactured commodities. Domestic prices of exportables would be less than their international prices by the percentage which transport costs constitute of international price, while the domestic price of imports and domestically produced import-competing commodities would be an equal percentage above the international price.[14]

When domestic price can vary at a constant world price – within a range, of course – two things change. First, it is no longer necessary that production be concentrated in one or two manufacturing commodities only and an import-substituting sector becomes much more likely. The factor intensity of domestic production of import-competing goods will still be similar to that of exportables: for the country with the lowest manufacturing capital–labor ratio, import-substituting production will generally be more capital intensive than export production, and conversely for the most capital-abundant country. For countries in the center of the endowment range, however, import-substituting industries' factor proportions are likely to lie on either side of that of the export industries.

Second, when domestic prices can vary within the range set by transport costs, there will be a slight change in the way the pattern of production will alter with increases in the capital stock. In particular, the prices of commodities will be free to change somewhat as capital accumulation occurs. To see this, return to the example given in Section 2.2.4, where it was assumed that a country with a low land–labor ratio (and therefore a low wage) began accumulating capital. It was asserted that such a country would initially produce commodity 1, the most labor-intensive manufacture, and then the wage rate would increase as capital accumulation continued until it became profitable to produce commodity 2. While that analysis remains correct, there would be an additional aspect to the process of capital accumulation: initially, the domestic price of commodity 1 could exceed the world price by the margin of natural protection afforded by transport costs. With capital accumulation, the wage would rise relative to the rental but, in addition, the price of the commodity would decrease. Moreover, import-substituting production of the second manufactured commodity could start relatively sooner than was implied by the cycle of rising real wages followed by constant wages as production shifted between industries. This is because the domestic price of the second commodity could exceed its world levels. Thus, the phase pattern described above would not be quite so pronounced; instead, relative price changes of domestically produced goods could absorb some of the alterations resulting from changed factor endowments in the urban sector.

With proportionate transport costs for all manufactured commodities, there is likely to be a range of commodities, on either side of the factor intensity of the country's exports (except where the country itself is in an extreme position), for which it would be profitable to produce for domestic consumption. Thus, a moderately labor-abundant country exporting a commodity or commodities in the middle of the factor-intensity range might produce import substitutes on both sides of the factor intensity on its export. It remains the case, however, that the goods it did not produce would require more extreme factor proportions than those it did produce.

If transport costs differ significantly among commodities, of course, the preceding analysis no longer holds. Some possibilities can, however, be dealt with. Suppose, for example, that labor-intensive commodities have higher transport costs as a percentage of international price than do capital-intensive goods. The following ought then to be the case: (1) for commodities more labor-intensive than those exported by any particular country, the height of transport costs (as a percentage of international price) should be correlated with the labor–capital ratio in the industry; (2) one would expect to observe relatively less specialization in countries with capital-abundant manufacturing sectors than in countries with labor-abundant manufacturing, as the former would tend to have more import-substituting activity; and (3) world exports would constitute a greater proportion of the world supply of capital-intensive commodities than of labor-intensive commodities.

Of course, if transport costs are sufficiently high, a commodity can become a 'home good', as international trade is virtually ruled out in all but exceptional cases. Many services, such as haircuts, medical care, and retail delivery of commodities, are generally thought to be labor-intensive. However, there are other items, such as financial services, communications, and the like, which are probably equally location-tied, and which seem to be capital-intensive. The existence of home goods does not basically alter the propositions set forth above except in the ways in which it affects the basic two-commodity-model predictions.[15] If home goods' factor proportions are at the world average for all commodities, home goods would tend to be capital intensive in labor-abundant countries and labor-intensive in capital-abundant countries. When home goods are present, price–output responses of traded goods could become perverse, and thus some of the comparative-statics propositions set forth above would not necessarily hold. Propositions about the comparative advantage of a country within manufacturing industries would still be valid, however, for any allocation of labor and capital to the production of traded goods.[16]

2.3   THE IMPACT OF COMMODITY- AND FACTOR-MARKET DISTORTIONS UPON THE COMMODITY COMPOSITION OF TRADE

Thus far, attention has been centered upon the factor-proportions explanation of trade as a hypothesis about the determinants of the production pattern for goods not based on natural resources under efficient resource allocation. If resource allocation were always efficient, the task would be accomplished. The model developed above could be elaborated in numerous directions, but the basic propositions have emerged and empirical tests of it could be undertaken.

In some countries, such as South Korea and probably most of the industrialized world, there is reason to believe that markets function fairly efficiently and that the model can therefore be tested along the lines sketched above.[17] A disturbing question arises, however, in cases where it is believed that distortions in the commodity and factor market may significantly affect the commodity composition of trade: how can one interpret the outcome of any examination of that pattern? To illustrate the difficulty, assume that, for a particular country where distortions are believed to be important, a pattern of trade in manufacturing emerges that does not conform to the specialization patterns set forth above. How can one distinguish between the possibility that the HOS model does not apply and the hypothesis that distortions so alter the trade pattern as to produce the observed result? The question is of considerable importance for policy purposes in a host of developing countries: if those countries' 'true' comparative advantage lies in labor-intensive manufactures, policy makers may be able to promulgate measures that encourage such exports even if they cannot remove the distortions directly. If, however, the HOS model is inappropriate, attempts to promote such exports might make the situation worse rather than better.

Research to date has thrown considerable light on what would happen if particular distortions were, in fact, observed. In this section, those results will be reviewed in order to ascertain whether direct empirical observations can make it possible to distinguish between the impact of distortions and the efficient pattern of trade.[18]

The procedure is as follows. It is assumed that the model developed in Section 2.2 holds for a particular country.[19] To make exposition simple, it will be assumed that this country would, under efficient resource allocation, produce food and the first several manufacturing commodities: it is thus the country with the lowest capital–labor endowment in manufacturing, and would, under an efficient allocation of resources, be a low-wage country. The question then is: given particular distortions, what would be the observed pattern of production, and how would that pattern differ from the efficient one? In most cases, the reader can readily generalize the results to cover countries elsewhere in the capital–labor-endowment ranking. When application to countries in the middle of the endowment range may not be obvious, a footnote gives the relevant line of argument.

The questions now under consideration are the impact upon the structure of production of (1) distortions in the goods market so that domestic prices diverge from international prices by more than transport costs, and (2) distortions in the factor market so that domestic factor prices do not reflect the opportunity cost of employing those factors.

2.3.1 Goods-Market Distortions

The effects of goods-market distortions are well known and can be spelled out briefly.[20] In general, one can readily devise testable hypotheses about the systematic relation between those distortions and the shifts in patterns of production that will result if factor markets function efficiently.

The production structure that would result from efficient resource allocation can be altered by tariffs or subsidies to industries that would otherwise be unprofitable domestically. A variety of devices can provide the needed protection: credit allocations or tax exemptions to the favored industries, public enterprises operating at losses financed through tax revenues, tariffs, quotas, and so on. The exact form of the incentive for domestic production can make a difference for a variety of issues, but, for present purposes, the key distinction is between tariffs and other measures. Subsidies can make any industry an export industry, even one that would not produce at all in an efficient allocation. Similarly, taxes can be levied on an industry that has comparative advantage which will penalize it enough to render domestic production entirely unprofitable.[21]

When taxes and subsidies are used, therefore, it is possible not only to distort the structure of production, but to distort it so much that the 'wrong' commodities are exported. This must sometimes occur in countries with large import-substitution sectors built up under high levels of protection in circumstances where 'export subsidies' are accorded only to new industries. In such cases, industries that would be exporting under an efficient allocation may not produce at all, while others that might not be operating may be exporting.[22]

If all the incentives and market imperfections that result in distortions and inefficient production patterns are concentrated within the goods market, it still seems possible to devise a test as to whether the HOS model of *efficient* production is valid: the net protection equivalents of all the various incentives, disincentives, and market imperfections should be positively correlated with the capital–labor ratios of the protected industries.[23] This is because, for the most labor-abundant country, which is the one on which the discussion is centered, the HOS model predicts that higher rates of protection will be needed to render domestic production possible, the higher the capital intensity of the industry. The fact that the 'wrong mix' of industries was producing would, of course, alter the equilibrium wage–rental ratio but production of commodities that were too capital-intensive for an efficient pattern of production would result in a decline in the equilibrium wage–rental ratio, thereby rendering the cost disadvantage of capital-intensive industries even greater than they would be at the wage–rental ratio associated with an optimal allocation of resources.[24]

When tariffs (and tariff equivalents) are the only distortion in the system, the correlation between protection and factor intensity should still hold. However, reversal of commodities is not possible, and thus the predictions of the HOS model would be observable. Under tariff protection, some industries would be producing that would not produce under an efficient allocation. It is not possible, however, to render an industry that would be an exporter under an efficient allocation into a non-producing industry. Protection can cause some resources to be used in import substitution that would otherwise have been employed in producing the commodities for export. However, the most that production can be diverted is to the point of autarky: tariffs can raise the internal price of commodities and thereby render their production for the domestic market profitable, but they cannot induce exports of those commodities at the lower world prices.

Thus, in the absence of subsidies, trade patterns could not be reversed as long as factor markets were functioning efficiently. One could therefore test the HOS model, as long as exporting industries were not receiving subsidies: the factor intensity of non-produced commodities would be contrasted with the factor intensity of exportables and import substitutes not receiving protection. One would observe the manufacturing sector of the labor-abundant country producing the most labor-intensive commodities for export. In addition, of course, one could test for the relationship between the capital intensity of industries and the height of protection.[25] In the event that the labor-abundant country was not exporting labor-intensive manufactures, one could reject the factor-proportions explanation of trade even though tariffs were used to protect domestic industry. Likewise, if the height of protection necessary to induce domestic production was not positively correlated with the capital intensity of the protected industries, that again would constitute grounds for rejection of the HOS model.[26]

Of course, with subsidies to particular exports (or, as in some countries, requirements that firms export certain portions of their output in return for import licenses), comparison of the factor intensity of a country's exports with that of non-produced commodities might reveal that either exports or non-produced commodities were more capital-intensive. However, the correlation between the height of the protective equivalents and the capital intensities of the various industries should still be positive and one should be able to test the HOS model directly against observable data within the country.

2.3.2 Factor-Market Distortions

We now wish to consider the case in which commodity prices are undistorted, i.e. equal to world prices, while the prices of factor services differ from those that would prevail under perfect competition in factor markets.[26] The case is the precise opposite of that for commodity-market distortions: when the distortions in factor markets are firm- or industry-specific, as with credit rationing, bureaucratic allocation of licenses for importing capital goods, and case-by-case decision-making on tax exemptions and subsidies, it is usually not possible to infer anything about the efficient pattern of trade from direct observation of the data. Firm- or industry-specific variations in factor prices are equivalent to subsidies and taxes; when such specificity occurs, the observed pattern of trade need not bear any relation to an efficient one.[27]

However, when the factor-market distortion can be characterized in some systematic way, under some circumstances inferences can be drawn that make it possible to ascertain how the observed pattern of trade is related to an efficient one, and thus to test the HOS model even in the presence of distortions. By 'systematic characterization' I mean a departure from only one of the efficiency conditions for the allocation of factors of production among alternative uses. For example, if payment to one factor is uniform across all activities, while there are two different returns to the other factor with one subset of all activities paying a higher return than the other subset, the effects of that differential on resource allocation can be analyzed. Another systematic type of distortion occurs if the return to one factor is pegged above the level that would prevail under competitive conditions, with the result that the factor is not fully employed.

It may be that a distortion model is the appropriate one for analysis of economic behavior in some countries. It is widely believed that there are countries in which the wage–rental ratio, at least within some part of the economy, is constrained to a higher level than would prevail in the absence of distortions.

Currencies are often overvalued and propped up by import licensing, with differential exchange rates for different categories of commodities. Usually, imported capital goods are permitted at the most favorable exchange rate, so that recipients of licenses to import capital goods receive a sizeable implicit subsidy on capital services. In addition to permitting importation of capital goods, governments often extend credit on exceedingly favorable terms, well below market interest rates, to producers of certain types of commodity. Credit subsidization, combined with overvalued exchange rates, can reduce the cost of capital services to some domestic entrepreneurs below their opportunity costs. The difference in cost of capital services for those entrepreneurs and for others without access to import licenses and scarce credit can be quite substantial.[29]

Such practices in the pricing of capital goods and the extension of credit would, by themselves, introduce a distortion between the factor prices confronting the favored producers and others. However, there are grounds for believing that, in many of the same countries, the price of labor to the same favored entrepreneurs may be above that which would prevail in a distortion-free market. Minimum-wage laws, training requirements, legislation dictating the construction of housing and other facilities for workers, union agreements, and even the 'guilty' consciences of multinational corporations may all result in the payment of higher effective wages to workers than would obtain in a competitive market.[30]

Since, within the manufacturing sector, only the wage–rental ratio affects resource allocation, the effects of the capital- and labor-market distortions can be analyzed as an increase in the wage–rental ratio above its efficiency level.

Factor-market distortions may significantly affect observed patterns of trade. When certain types of systematic factor-market distortion are present, a finding that production and exports are concentrated in a capital-intensive industry or group of industries by a labor-abundant country is no longer prima facie cause to reject the factor-proportions explanation of trade. Nor, for that matter, is a finding of a labor-intensive pattern of production sufficient to accept it. Indeed, in the context of the standard two-commodity, two-factor HOS model, it has been shown that a difference in the wage–rental ratio paid by two industries may bring about any of the following results: (1) the 'right' commodity will be produced and exported with the 'right' factor intensity; (2) the 'right' commodity will be produced and exported with the 'wrong' factor intensity; (3) the 'wrong' commodity will be exported with the 'wrong' factor intensity; and (4) the 'wrong' commodity will be exported with the 'right' factor intensity. Suppose one observed a production and export bundle of highly capital-intensive commodities in a labor-abundant country in which factor-market distortions were thought important. One could not determine without further investigation whether this pattern was observed because capital–labor substitution had occurred in the export industry, causing it to be more capital-intensive than it would be at a common wage–rental ratio with other sectors; because import-competing industries or non-producing industries were the ones that should be exporting under an efficient allocation; or because the HOS model was inappropriate.

In this section, I discuss the effects of various types of factor-market distortions on the pattern of production one would observe if the model spelled out in Section 2.2 truly described an efficient allocation. The positive predictions that emanate from the various models of behavior under factor-market distortions are then evaluated to ascertain the circumstances under which inferences can be drawn about efficient patterns of trade in the presence of distortions.

One of the interesting lessons of the distortion literature is that it is not enough to say 'distortion': three separate types of distortion have so far been analyzed. Each case has been developed in the context of a two-commodity model, as the authors have had in mind an urban and a rural sector, and application of these analyses to the model of Section 2.2 requires identification of the source of the distortion. In the first case, an exogenously imposed real minimum wage applies over the entire economy (with open unemployment when the real minimum wage is binding). This case readily extends to the n-commodity model by assuming a wage floor across the entire economy.[31] In the second case, based upon the Todaro (1969) and Harris and Todaro (1970) model of labor markets, the urban wage is above the rural wage, and the unemployment rate clears the labor market; in effect, the expected urban wage (equal to the actual urban wage, times the probability of finding work, adjusted for the length of time it takes to do so) is equal to the rural wage. In applying this distortion model to the n-commodity, two-sector case, the natural interpretation is that there is a minimum real wage in the urban sector and thus a variable differential in the wage between the rural and urban sectors, with open unemployment. In the third, and probably most thoroughly explored, case, a two-commodity, two-factor economy with full employment has a wage–rental ratio in one industry that differs by a constant multiplicative factor from the wage–rental ratio in the other industry. Two alternative interpretations of this case are possible: (1) the wage differential in question can be between the urban and rural sectors; or (2) there is an organized, large-scale sector within manufacturing in which wages are equal to those in the rural sector. This latter interpretation would correspond somewhat to the notion of a 'modern' and a 'traditional' sector within manu-facturing.[32]

The task at hand is to apply the results obtained in the literature for the two-commodity, two-factor case to the two-sector, n-manufacturing-industries, three-factor model for a single country. Consideration of the empirical applicability of any of these cases is well beyond the scope of this chapter. In practice, of course, great care is needed to ascertain whether a distortion exists and, if so, which form it takes.[33]

An economy-wide real wage floor

It is simplest to start with the case in which there is an economy-wide wage–rental ratio above that which would prevail under competition and perfect factor markets.[34] It is immaterial whether the distortion results from minimum-wage legislation, union behavior, or other causes. Brecher (1974) has explored this case in the two-by-two context in terms of a real minimum wage, a practice that is followed here. The analysis holds equally, however, should the rental on capital somehow be pegged above its equilibrium level.

In the Brecher model, the locus of competitive outputs coincides with the transformation curve until the point at which the wage implied by the relative price of the two commodities equals the real minimum wage; it then becomes a Rybczynski line from that point to complete specialization in the capital-intensive commodity; finally, it moves back toward the transformation curve as output of the capital-intensive com-modity increases. Naturally, employment decreases from the point at which the locus of competitive outputs deviates from the transformation curve until the point of specialization in the capital-intensive commodity, and then increases until full employment is reached at the point at which the transformation curve and the locus of competitive outputs coincide with specialization in the capital-intensive good.

The situation is depicted in Figure 2.2a. The set of efficient production possibilities is the transformation curve AD. If an initial, efficient free-trade equilibrium is at point B, where production is concentrated in X, the labor-intensive commodity, the set of other outputs that can be produced under profit-maximizing behavior by firms with the commodity prices implied by the slope of the tangent to point B (not drawn) is the line BC. Along BC, both commodities are produced, and employment declines as the output of the labor-intensive commodity decreases. At point C, there is complete specialization in the capital-intensive com-modity, Y. Curiously enough, as production of Y increases from C to D, employment is increasing and the production technique employed in Y is increasingly labor-intensive.

To understand the Brecher model, it is useful to imagine that a

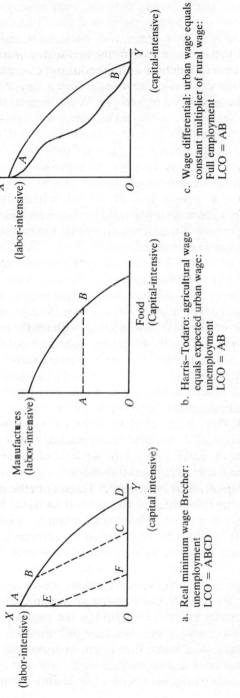

Figure 2.2 Locus of competitive outlets under differing assumptions about the nature of distortions

minimum-real-wage law is passed with the real wage denominated in terms of the labor-intensive good. The Rybczynski line must shift to the left. A sufficiently high real wage will make full employment with specialization in the labor-intensive commodity impossible. Such a situation is illustrated in Figure 2.2a by the locus of competitive outputs described by *EFD*. That locus is associated with a higher real minimum wage than the locus described by *ABCD*. With the minimum real wage associated with *EFC*, full employment could be attained only with specialization in the capital-intensive commodity, and that could occur only if there were a sufficiently high price for the capital-intensive good to maintain the real wage in terms of the labor-intensive commodity. Of course, if the real minimum wage were increased without any change in commodity prices, production of the labor-intensive commodity would decrease, but the economy would not become specialized in producing the wrong commodity and unemployment would simply increase as the real minimum wage was increased.

Three features of the model are especially relevant for present purposes: (1) within this model in its two-commodity form, it is possible that the 'wrong' commodity will be produced and even that there will be specialization in it; (2) the higher the real wage, the greater is the likelihood of wrong specialization; and (3) at a sufficiently high real wage, full employment is possible only if the price of the capital-intensive good is sufficiently high *and* the real wage is fixed in terms of the labor-intensive commodity.[35]

Applying the Brecher model to the two-sector, three-factor manufacturing commodities model developed in Section 2.2 is relatively straightforward. If there is an economy-wide real wage and the stock of capital is independent of the level of real output, a higher real wage will be associated unequivocally with a smaller level of urban employment *and* a lower level of agricultural employment.[36] At given international prices, a given capital stock and a real wage entirely determine the industry (or industries) in which it will pay to specialize. The higher the real wage, the more capital-intensive the industries of specialization will be, and the lower will be the real return on capital.[37] From this, it follows immediately that employment must be less than in the absence of the distortion.

Several consequences of the fixed-real-wage model are immediately apparent. First, since both agricultural output and manufactured output must fall with increases in the real wage, it is not clear what will happen to the agricultural–manufactures balance of trade: it could either increase or decrease. A country that might be a net importer of food under an efficient allocation of resources might becomes a net exporter, or conversely. There is no a priori basis on which to assign likelihoods to either outcome. Within manufacturing, however, it is clear that the higher the real wage, the more capital-intensive will be the industries within which production will take place, and, as long as relative prices of manufactures remain at free-trade levels, the more capital-intensive will be the techniques of production used within those industries. It is not possible for the factor intensities of produced commodities to reverse; that is, it is not possible that an industry that would be labor-intensive under an efficient allocation could become capital-intensive with a higher minimum wage.

It would thus appear that when the entire economy is operating subject to a minimum-real-wage constraint, there is no possibility of industries reversing factor intensities. Therefore, if the most labor-abundant country was found to be exporting the most labor-intensive goods when it was subject to a minimum-wage constraint, one could be confident that the same outcome would apply under an efficient allocation. If that country was exporting manufactured commodities that were not the most labor-intensive, however, there would be a question about whether the distortion changed the pattern of production or whether the HOS model did not described an efficient allocation. One could not ascertain whether the failure of the factor-proportions hypothesis to hold called into question the validity of the model or was due to the real minimum wage, and direct observation of data would not provide a means to distinguish between hypotheses. Simulation of optimal allocations, examination of changes in production patterns prior to the imposition of the real-wage constraint, or other means would have to be devised in order to test whether the HOS theorems would hold under optimal resource allocation.

Fixed urban real wages
The second model, with a fixed real wage in the industrial sector above that in the rural sector, can have the same effects within the manufacturing sector as the economy-wide fixed real wage. The production pattern actually observed might be one in which the manufacturing sector was specialized in the wrong commodities. The higher the fixed urban wage, the more the production structure would shift toward more capital-intensive commodities, given international prices. As with the uniform wage, however, commodities that were capital-intensive under the real-wage constraint would also be capital-intensive at free trade.

However, the fact that the Harris–Todaro model posits a difference in the wage–rental ratio between the urban (manufacturing) and rural sectors adds a twist to the model: it is possible that the labor intensity of agriculture and manufacturing might be reversed. Suppose, for example, that industry were labor-intensive at free trade.[38] As the real minimum wage applying to the manufacturing (urban) sector rose, the quantity of labor employed in the urban sector would decline. At some critical wage, the labor intensity of the manufacturing sector would equal that in the rural sector.[39] How soon this happened would depend on what happened to rural employment as the urban wage rose. If total workers in the city, employed plus unemployed, increased as the wage increased, then the 'crossover' would be relatively slow in coming; agriculture, as well as industry, would become less labor-intensive with increases in the real wage. If, however, urban employment fell sharply with increases in the real wage, it is possible that agricultural employment would increase as urban employment fell. In such a case, agriculture would become more labor-intensive while manufacturing was shifting to production of more capital-intensive commodities (and substituting capital for labor within each producing industry) and the point at which the two labor intensities crossed would be attained more quickly.

The locus of competitive outputs under an urban wage constraint is illustrated in Figure 2.2b. There, it is assumed that manufacturing would be labor-intensive in the absence of a real-wage constraint, but that the fixing of the real wage sets the manufacturing output level at OA. The locus of possible output points is therefore the line AB, and the point B would be infeasible unless the real wage in agriculture happened to equal that in industry there. An increase in the urban real wage would shift the line AB downward. Thus, the Harris–Todaro model differs from the fixed-real-wage model in its implications for the possibility of reversing factor intensities between agriculture and manufacturing. That may be of considerable importance in a number of contexts if it is believed that the Harris–Todaro description of labor-market conditions is valid. Even if it is appropriate, however, the analysis of comparative advantage and the effects of the distortion within the manufacturing sector can be carried out as in the Brecher model: a manufacturing wage rate above that under an efficient allocation could easily lead to concentration of production in commodities that were more capital-intensive than the country's situation would render optimal. Such a circumstance could not, however, lead to a reversal of factor intensities, and if the country's production and trade appeared to conform to the HOS model, this would confirm the HOS hypotheses.

Wage differential within manufacturing
The most analytically interesting of the three cases of distortions is the two-commodity, two-factor model in which the wage–rental ratio in one industry is a constant multiple of that in the other, while full employment of both factors always prevails. For application to the n-manufacturing-industries model, the case is of interest if one subset of the n industries

has the same wage as the agricultural sector, while the other subset pays a different, presumably higher, wage.[40] If, for example, the chemical, basic-metal, and machinery industries are favored industries, then the constant-wage-differential model, developed by Johnson (1965), Jones (1971a), Herberg and Kemp (1971), and others would apply.[41]

The locus of competitive outputs in the two-commodity, two-factor model is represented in Figure 2.2c by the line AB, which must lie everywhere, except at the two complete specialization points, inside the production possibility curve. This follows immediately from the fact that the marginal rate of substitution among the two factors of production is different in the two industries, and it would therefore be possible to attain more of both outputs by reallocating factors between them at any point at which both commodities are produced.

The problem, in the full-employment, constant-differential case, lies in the fact that it is no longer possible, with such a distortion, to identify the direction of the change in output that will result from a change in relative prices of the two commodities. It is possible, for example, that the price of one commodity might increase, and that the competitive response would be for output of that commodity to decrease and output of the other commodity (whose relative price had fallen) to increase.

The reason for this can be most easily understood with the aid of Figure 2.3.[42] The Edgeworth box drawn there is based on the production

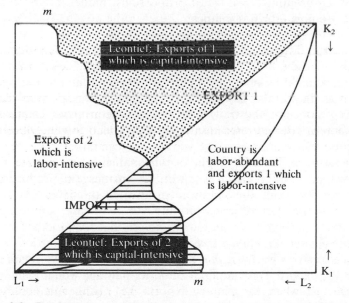

Figure 2.3   Production possibilities between two countries with a constant stock of labor and capital

possibilities between two commodities, 1 and 2, with a constant stock of labor and capital. In the absence of wage differentials (i.e. under conditions of efficient production), commodity 1 is assumed to be labor-intensive. The locus of efficient output points (the curved line) lies below the diagonal representing equal factor proportions in both industries. Every point in the Edgeworth box corresponds to a particular set of input combinations and outputs. Moving to the east and to the north represents greater output of 1, and there is a given real income associated with each output point. For the sake of exposition, assume that demand patterns associated with those output points and real income levels mean that commodity 1 will be exported to the right of the *mm* line and will be imported to the left of the *mm* line.

Two distinct cases must be analyzed. In the first, the labor-intensive industry must pay higher wages than the capital-intensive industry. In the second, the lower wage-rental rate applies to the labor-intensive industry. Taking the first case, start with wage-rental equality and then introduce a differential. The labor intensity of industry 1 will diminish and that of industry 2 will increase. As the differential increases and commodity prices adjust, at some point, industry 1 will become capital-intensive in the physical sense; i.e. it will employ more capital per worker than industry 2. At that point, the physical factor intensities are reversed, so that production will take place somewhere above the diagonal representing equal factor proportions.[43]

There are now four possibilities:

1. The wage differential might not be sufficient to reduce production below consumption or to reverse factor intensities, so that the country might be operating below the diagonal and to the right of the *mm* line. In that case, the differential would not be sufficient to alter production and trade patterns away from 'true' comparative advantage. This corresponds to the white area below the diagonal in Figure 2.3.

2. The wage differential might not be sufficient to reverse factor intensities, but it might result in an increase in production of commodity 2 and a reduction in production of commodity 1, to a point to the left of the *mm* line. In that case, the country's production would have altered enough so that commodity 2 became the export commodity. Inspection of the factor proportions of the two industries would reveal that the capital-intensive commodity was the export. The finding of Leontief paradox would result. This is the case where the country exports the 'wrong' commodity with the 'right' factor proportions. It is the horizontally striped area of Figure 2.3.

3. The wage differential and accompanying price changes could be sufficient to move the country across the diagonal but leave production to the right of the *mm* line. In that case, commodity I would be exported, but empirical estimation would show that commodity I was the capital-intensive commodity, and thus the 'perverse' factor intensity of exports would be found – another Leontief-paradox area – in which the 'right' commodity is exported with the 'wrong' factor proportions.[44] This is the case illustrated by the shaded area of Figure 2.3.

4. The distortion could be sufficient to render commodity 1 capital intensive and to reduce output sufficiently so that commodity 2 was exported and labor-intensive. In this final case, one would find that exports were indeed labor-intensive, and thus confirm the HOS comparative-advantage model! This corresponds to the unshaded area above the diagonal in Figure 2.3. Here, the 'wrong' commodity is exported with the 'wrong' factor proportions!

It thus appears that, in the two-commodity, two-factor model with full employment and a constant differential in factor rewards, anything can happen. The question, of course, is how these results can be extended to the *n*-manufacturing-commodities, two-sector model of efficient production developed in Section 2.2. As already noted, the differential must lie within the manufacturing sector, so that some manufacturing industries are confronted with a higher wage–rental ratio than the rest. If that is the situation, few conclusions are possible unless the factor-market distortion is somehow systematically related to the factor-intensity ordering of the manufacturing industries. If it is, two cases can be analyzed.

1. Suppose that capital-intensive industries pay a higher wage–rental ratio than labor-intensive industries.[45] Then, if a country's comparative advantage under an efficient allocation lay in production of commodities in the middle of the factor-intensity ordering, say commodity 5, one should observe specialization of production in commodities with disparate factor proportions on either side of the 'natural' specialization point. It might be, for example, that the lower wage–rental ratio that would result for labor-intensive industries would enable industry 3 to become more profitable than industry 5, while the lower rental–wage ratio confronting capital-intensive industries caused industry 7 to bid resources away from industry 5. Thus, one would expect to observe a production pattern where industries of dissimilar factor intensities were profitable.

2. Suppose that labor-intensive industries pay a higher wage–rental ratio than capital-intensive industries.[46] If countries specialized in

the commodities forecast by the HOS model, one could accept that as verification of the model: this is the case in which reversals could lead to the Leontief-paradox results even when the HOS model was correct, but in which specialization in production of the 'right' commodities could not result from distortion if the HOS model was valid.

Beyond these cases, little can be said, although one can hope that examination of specific distortion patterns that did not conform to either of those two cases might provide ways of testing the HOS model.

Summary

What emerges from consideration of the literature on distortions is an entirely new set of possibilities that must be evaluated when examining the factor-proportions explanation of trade: the empirical measures appropriate for testing the HOS model under efficient allocation cannot be uncritically accepted as constituting a test in the presence of distortions. It is probably a valid first approximation that most industrialized countries' factor markets may not be sufficiently distorted to affect production and trade patterns and factor proportions significantly. The same may or may not be true for the developing countries.

The presence of tariff interventions and export taxes does not create fundamental difficulties for testing the factor-proportions model. Indeed, some testable hypotheses about the relationship between factor proportions and the height of protection emerge to provide yet another way of testing the factor-proportions explanation of trade. Subsidies to exports can influence the trade pattern in any conceivable direction and thus prevent testing. When factor-market distortions are significant, all sorts of possibilities arise: a labor-abundant country, which would be exporting labor-intensive commodities under an efficient allocation, might in fact export commodities whose capital intensity was substantially higher than that. Other patterns, also at variance with the efficiency model, are possible, too.

In general, when there is a distortion between the manufacturing and rural sectors, some means of testing for the separate effects of distortion and efficiency influences on trade patterns are available. When the factor-market distortion is within the manufacturing sector, however, no single set of observations can enable identification of the separate contributions of each factor. The important lesson is that, in the presence of factor-market distortions that are thought to affect resource allocation significantly, one cannot draw any inferences about the efficient commodity composition of production and trade and its factor proportions solely from observation of the actual pattern of production and trade.

NOTES

1. Note that, even with factor-intensity reversals, *all* industries would employ more labor-intensive techniques at a lower wage–rental ratio under any efficient allocation. This implication would be useful empirically were it not for the impossibility of identifying homogeneous factors across countries.

2. For a given price set, it can never be more profitable to produce three commodities than two. This is what makes the composition of output indeterminate.

3. In the context of a multi-commodity model, specialization takes on a different meaning from the one it has in two-commodity models. In the latter, specialization implies a positive production level for only one commodity. With many commodities, specialization means the failure to produce at least as many commodities in common as there are factors of production.

4. If commodity prices were truly imposed at random, it would be highly improbable that either country would have positive production levels for more than a few goods (and there is no assurance whatsoever that the commodities at either factor-intensity extreme would be produced at all). In reality, prices are determined in the market and are related to production costs via supply and demand: at the wage–rental ratio associated with a particular commodity's production, there *are* prices at which other commodities can also be produced at competitive equilibrium; if the factor demands derived from the output mix demanded at those prices are not equal to factor supplies, the wage–rental ratio can adjust as commodity prices alter.

5. The empirical likelihood of such an outcome is open to question, especially if one takes into account the existence of transport costs. A simple proof that it could happen in the model set forth above is as follows. If the wage–rental ratio in country 8 were lower than in 9, then commodity 6 would be cheaper to produce in country 8 than in country 9 at prevailing factor prices and the competitive profit conditions would not be met. Therefore, the wage–rental ratio in 8 and 9 must be the same. The reverse reasoning can then be used between countries 7 and 8, as a higher wage–rental ratio in 8 than in 7 would imply that commodity 5 could not be competitively produced (see Bhagwati, 1972, for a fuller discussion).

6. Whether an industry is an import substitute or an export is simply a matter of the precise nature of the factor endowment relative to other countries and, of course, demand conditions. Consider, for example, country 1 in Figure 2.1. It must export commodity 1 and may export commodity 2, depending on whether production is greater or less than domestic demand. It could, however, be using virtually all its resources in the production of commodity 1, so that demand for commodity 2 exceeded domestic production. In that case, commodity 1 would be exported, and commodities 2 through 9 imported.

7. In effect, this is the 'small country' assumption, and it could not be valid indefinitely, as continued growth, with the rest of the world of constant size, would eventually make the country in question very large. Many of the statements in this section can, however, be interpreted to apply to a situation in which all but one country is accumulating capital relative to

labor at a common rate and the country in question is growing more rapidly. Formal extension of the model to that case is difficult and not attempted here. The problem lies in the fact that, as shown by the Rybczynski (1955) theorem, if a country is producing two commodities and its capital–labor endowment increases, output of the capital-intensive commodity must increase more rapidly than the proportional change in the capital stock, while output of the labor-intensive commodity must change less than the proportional change in the quantity of labor (so that, if there were no change in the quantity of labor, output of the labor-intensive commodity would have to decrease). To attempt to describe growth of the world economy would therefore require consideration of demand conditions, as price changes would surely have to be incorporated explicitly into the model.

8. It could happen that production of one commodity ceased simultaneously with the start of the other. In that event, there would be no period with a constant wage–rental ratio.

9. It is shown below that introducing transport costs probably smooths the stepwise progression described here.

10. Strictly speaking, the assumptions made are insufficient – if the labor force is growing – to ensure that such an outcome will occur: output of the more labor-intensive commodity could be growing but at a slower rate than the growth of the labor force. This is where the 'small country' assumption becomes inadequate.

11. A necessary condition for the validity of the assertion is that food is a normal good.

12. Strictly speaking, this statement is valid only if it is assumed that there is no upper limit to the marginal product of labor in agriculture.

13. If there is disguised unemployment in the rural sector, so that persons leave at some fixed wage as urban jobs are available, the real wage would remain constant for a greater interval of capital accumulation and output would increase more rapidly in the urban sector. The composition of output would not start changing until the urban real wage began rising. For an excellent discussion of the issues involved in identifying the nature of the urban labor supply, see Sen (1975).

14. Once import-competing production is adequate to satisfy the domestic market, the domestic price of the good is free to vary within the range determined by transport costs. It could even be less than the international price, but by an amount insufficient to enable exports with competitive profit levels. Thus, the domestic price of exportables must be exactly equal to their international price less transport costs; the domestic price of importables can be anywhere from the international price less transport costs to the international price plus transport costs. It must exactly equal the latter only when imports and domestic production are both sold in the domestic market.

15. For a summary of the basic theorems of the HOS model when home goods are present, see Batra (1973, chap. 12).

16. Likewise, if it were assumed that production of home goods required only labor as an input, the analysis would not be affected. It should be noted that intermediate goods also do not affect the analysis in so far as they are all tradable; when they are home goods, the complications discussed above arise.

17. But see the interesting paper by Hufbauer and Chilas (1974), who attempted to estimate the impact of protection on the extent of specialization among the Western European countries compared with regions of the United States: the authors found that American regions were more specialized than comparable European countries, thus providing another piece of indirect evidence in support of the view that specialization patterns and not comparison of import-competing and export coefficients are the appropriate forms for empirical work.

18. It is always possible, of course, that simulation models can be developed which attempt to ask what would happen if maximization took place. The purpose here is to ascertain the effects of distortions and to determine whether direct testing is possible. The possibility of employing other techniques is beyond the scope of this chapter.

19. To attempt to formalize an n-country model in which there are distortions in more than one country is an incredibly complex task that will not be attempted here.

20. Travis (1964) has expounded the position that it is trade impediments which prevent the realization of the HOS predictions.

21. Of course, if subsidies were granted to all exports on a comparable basis, reversal could not happen. What is required is the creation of a change in the relative prices of exportables.

22. This seems clearly to have been the case in India (see Bhagwati and Srinivasan, 1975; Krueger, 1975). Partly for that reason, as well as for the reason given in Section 2.2, it is difficult to interpret the Bharadwaj and Bhagwati (1967) results on Indian trade.

23. Intermediate goods have not been explicitly dealt with here. If they were, then it would be effective rates of protection that should be correlated with capital intensity.

24. For the most capital-abundant country, protection rates should be positively correlated with the labor intensity of the industry. For countries in the middle, one would have to partition commodities into those more capital-intensive and those less capital-intensive than the manufacturing sector's factor endowment. The hypothesis is that the height of protection needed to induce domestic production is positively correlated with labor intensity for the commodities on that side of the sector's endowment, and positively correlated with capital intensity for commodities on the other side.

25. The presence of protection and the fact that it would induce production in more capital-intensive industries than would occur under an efficient protection pattern increases the likelihood that there would be greater capital intensity in the import-competing commodities than in export industries. This result holds only for the countries with extreme manufacturing endowments, however.

26. Of course, one would have to use the appropriate protection measure, including the tariff equivalents of quotas and the subsidy equivalents of credits and the like, and omitting all tariff redundancy. In addition, appropriate measures of capital and labor would, as always, be necessary.

27. Strictly speaking, if factor markets are distorted, the price of home goods will in general diverge from that which would prevail under competition in all markets. It must therefore be assumed in this section that there are no home goods. Since transport costs do not affect the results, as international

prices are assumed given, they, too, will be assumed absent. The world under discussion is therefore one in which there are n manufactured goods and food, with all prices given to the country under consideration by the international market. There are, as before, three domestic factors: land, which is always fully employed in agriculture; capital, which is always fully employed in manufacturing; and labor, which is used in both sectors. It will be seen that there are a number of possible distortions, each of which can be characterized by a set of conditions on the wage and employment of labor. Full employment may or may not be assumed, and the wage may or may not be common between agriculture and manufacturing or within manufacturing.

28. Of course, if one knew the subsidy and tax equivalents of these measures, they could then be treated as protective rates, and empirical work could proceed in the same manner as described for the commodity-market distortions.

29. For a discussion of the effects of these practices, see McKinnon (1973).

30. Thorough empirical examination of labor-market conditions must take into account differences in skill levels. Such considerations are well beyond the scope of this chapter.

31. If one regards the 'real wage floor' as applying only to the manufacturing sector, the case merges with the full-employment, constant-differential case discussed next.

32. A difficulty with this interpretation is that there are generally commodities, such as textiles, produced in both sectors.

33. See Sen (1975) for a careful discussion of the issues that arise in analysis of labor markets.

34. It should be recalled that it is assumed initially that domestic prices equal international prices. The effects of introducing tariffs in the context of the factor-market distortion are examined below.

35. If a labor-abundant country did specialize in producing the capital-intensive good and was on its transformation curve (at D in Figure 2.2), it would be using more labor-intensive techniques of production than other countries whose 'true' comparative advantage lay in producing that commodity. It should be stressed again that this could happen only if the distortion-ridden country somehow managed to increase the relative price of the capital-intensive commodity enough to make production profitable at a high real wage with labor-intensive techniques of production. One can doubt whether there are many instances of wrong specialization and full employment.

36. That employment (and output) in agriculture will fall follows immediately from the fact that the real wage increases from its distortion-free level.

37. This can be seen most easily by thinking of the 'dual' of the undistorted case. Consider the wage rate that would prevail with complete specialization in commodity 1. Let the wage rise to the point where it pays to produce commodities 1 and 2, i.e. to the wage–rental ratio implied by the prices of the first two commodities. Then, production of both commodities will be profitable, and, with total capital stock the same, employment must be smaller. Let the wage increase a little more. Now production only of commodity 2 will be profitable; as the real wage rises (for a given price of output and capital stock), employment in the second industry will be smaller. At some point, the wage will be that implied by the prices of goods

2 and 3, and production of both will be profitable, and so on. It should also be noted that the value of production of manufactured goods, evaluated at international prices, will decrease with increases in the real wage.

38. The straightforward definition of 'labor intensity' in this context is clearly the hours of labor employed per unit of international value added in a given sector.

39. If agriculture is labor-intensive relative to industry, and the real wage is higher in industry, the reversal could never happen in physical terms, although it might be that labor's share became higher in industry than in agriculture.

40. If the wage differential were between all manufacturing, on the one hand, and agriculture, on the other, the analysis would be the same as for the Harris–Todaro case.

41. For a survey of the literature, see Magee (1973); Corden (1974, chap. V) has a good exposition of the basic model and its implications.

42. I am indebted to Stephen Magee, who called this representation to my attention.

43. Note that the relative price of the labor-intensive commodity must increase or production would simply become completely specialized.

44. It should be stressed that this result could not be observed unless the relative price of the commodity was above the level that would prevail at free trade. If, for example, textiles are the 'efficient' export for a particular country and are observed to be capital-intensive relative to other produced commodities, one could rule out the proposition that they were naturally labor-intensive unless their relative price was higher domestically than in international markets. This could happen, of course, but would require subsidization of exports *and* factor-market distortion so that the wage–rental ratio facing the export industry was higher than that facing the other industry.

45. One could presumably test whether there had been a reversal of the factor intensities in response to the differential by contrasting the factor-intensity ordering of the country with that of other countries thought to be unaffected by the distortion.

46. The comment in footnote 45 applies again.

REFERENCES

Batra, Raveendra N. (1973). *Studies in the Pure Theory of International Trade.* New York. St. Martin's.

Bhagwati, Jagdish N. (1972). 'The Heckscher–Ohlin Theorem in the Multi-Commodity Case'. *Journal of Political Economy*, vol. 80 (September/October), pp. 1052–5.

Bhagwati, Jagdish N. and T.N. Srinivasan (1975). *Foreign Trade Regimes and Economic Development: India.* New York: Columbia University Press.

Bharadwaj, R., and Jagdish N. Bhagwati (1967) 'Human Capital and the Pattern of Foreign Trade: The Indian Case'. *Indian Economic Review*, vol. 3 (October), pp. 117–42.

Brecher, Richard (1974). 'Minimum Wage Rates and the Pure Theory of International Trade'. *Quarterly Journal of Economics*, vol. 88 (February), pp. 98–116.

Corden, W.M. (1974). *Trade Policy and Economic Welfare*. London: Oxford University Press.

Harris, John R. and Michael P. Todaro (1970). 'Migration, Unemployment and Development: A Two-Sector Analysis'. *American Economic Review*, vol. 60 (March), pp. 126–42.

Herberg, Horst and Murray C. Kemp (1971). 'Factor Market Distortions, the Shape of the Locus of Competitive Outputs, and the Relation between Prices and Equilibrium Outputs' in Jagdish N. Bhagwati *et al.*, *Trade, Balance of Payments and Growth*. Amsterdam: North-Holland.

Hufbauer, Gary C. and John G. Chilas (1974). 'Specialization by Industrial Countries: Extent and Consequences' in Herbert Giersch (ed.), *The International Division of Labour Problems and Perspectives*. Tübingen: Mohr.

Johnson, Harry G. (1965). 'Optimal Trade Interventions in the Presence of Domestic Distortions' in Robert E. Baldwin *et al.*, *Trade, Growth and the Balance of Payments*. Amsterdam: North-Holland.

Jones, Ronald W. (1971a). 'Distortions in Factor Markets and the General Equilibrium Model of Production', *Journal of Political Economy*, vol. 79 (May/June), pp. 437–59.

Jones, Ronald W. (1971b) 'A Three-Factor Model in Theory, Trade, and History' in Jagdish N. Bhagwati *et al.*, *Trade, Balance of Payments and Growth*. Amsterdam: North-Holland.

Krueger, Anne O. (1975). *The Benefits and Costs of Import Substitution in India: A Microeconomic Study*. Minneapolis: University of Minnesota Press.

McKenzie, Lionel (1955). 'Equality of Factor Prices in World Trade'. *Econometrica*, vol. 23 (July), pp. 239–57.

McKinnon, Ronald W. (1973). *Money and Capital in Economic Development*. Washington, DC: The Brookings Institution.

Magee, Stephen P. (1973). 'Factor Market Distortions, Production and Trade: A Survey'. *Oxford Economic Papers*, vol. 25 (March), pp. 1–43.

Rybczynski, T.M. (1955). 'Factor Endowment and Relative Commodity Prices'. *Economica*, vol. 35 (November), pp. 336–41. Reprinted in Richard E. Caves and Harry G. Johnson (eds), *A.E.A. Reading in International Economics*. Homewood: Irwin, 1968, pp. 72–7.

Sen, Amartya (1975). *Employment, Technology and Development*. London: Oxford University Press.

Todaro, Michael P. (1969). 'A Model of Labor Migration and Urban Unemployment in Less Developed Countries', *American Economic Review*, vol 59 (March), pp. 138–48.

Travis, W.P. (1969). *The Theory of Trade and Protection*, Cambridge, MA: Harvard University Press.

3 · COMPARATIVE ADVANTAGE AND DEVELOPMENT POLICY TWENTY YEARS LATER

3.1 INTRODUCTION

In most developing countries, the early efforts of politicians to raise growth rates and living standards almost always included high trade barriers and a set of policies to foster industrialization through import substitution. These efforts were based largely on an instinctive rejection of the doctrine of comparative advantage, which was understood to imply laissez-faire in all matters pertaining to the trade regime and domestic economic policies. In addition, that rejection was often associated with the policy prescription that developing countries should forever specialize in the production and export of primary commodities in exchange for manufactures. Because of these associations, attacks on the doctrine of free trade served as a focal point for the debate over the applicability of principles of rational resource allocation to developing countries.

Over almost four decades of research and experience with development policies and their effects, the range of the debate over trade policies has been greatly narrowed. Although initial arguments were more emotional than rational, analyses of the theoretical issues and empirical evidence gradually increased understanding of the issues involved and reduced the range of disagreement.

If one were to pinpoint the landmark contribution to this advance in understanding, Chenery (1961) would stand out. His seminal paper provided a carefully reasoned statement of the tensions between trade theory and development policy. He advanced the dialogue by a quantum leap in his dispassionate and careful analysis of the issues, and in his identification of the many empirical questions that required

First printed in 1984. This essay was written while visiting the Industrial Institute for Economic and Social Research in Stockholm, for whose support I am grateful. It was published in a Festschrift in honor of Hollis Chenery. Comments by Larry Westphal were useful for revision.

investigation. His essay stood for well over a decade as the definitive statement of the profession's understanding of the trade-policy and growth relationship. Only with additional research, prompted in part by his analysis, has the profession been able to move beyond it. Thus, it seems appropriate that the relationship between trade policy and development should be re-examined in the light of the theoretical advances and empirical evidence amassed since the 1960s.

It is useful to start by reviewing the issues as Chenery set them forth in the early 1960s. Thereafter, the experience of some developing countries is briefly reviewed to motivate the reassessment of trade policies and their impact which follows. Then, in the section on inner- and outer-oriented growth, the alternative strategies are contrasted. Then follows an analysis of factors that may have accounted for differences in growth rates under alternative strategies. A final section summarizes the progress of the past two decades.

3.2   TRADE POLICY VERSUS GROWTH, *CIRCA* 1960

Chenery set forth the criteria for the optimality of free trade in terms of market structures and pricing mechanisms, as was then conventional.[1] He then noted (Chenery, 1961, p. 21) that

> Growth theory contains at least four basic assumptions about underde- veloped economies that differ strongly from those underlying comparative advantage doctrines: (1) factor prices do not necessarily reflect opportunity costs with any accuracy; (2) the quality and quantity of factors of pro- duction may change substantially over time, in part as a result of the production process itself; (3) economies of scale relative to the size of existing markets are important in a number of sectors of production; (4) complementarity among commodities is dominant in both producer and consumer demand.

Chenery then considered productivity changes over time, 'dynamic external economies', and 'uncertainty and flexibility' as considerations that might militate against the optimality of the free trade outcome even of a perfectly competitive market allocation.

Chenery was careful to note that market imperfections did not neces- sarily imply that a departure from laissez-faire was clearly justified. None the less, the basic arguments he evoked were widely used by others as the reasons for departures from free trade, and especially for the encouragement of import-substitution industries, on the grounds that they possessed the dynamic characteristics that warranted intervention.

Theoretically, of course, there is no way to resolve the argument: there might in principle be dynamic external economies, various infant industry mechanisms, and other phenomena whose presence destroys the optimality of laissez-faire and free trade. At a theoretical level, it is possible for trade theorists to point out that many of the stated bases for departures from free trade are really the basis for alternative, and potentially Pareto-superior, interventions. Thus, as Fishlow and David (1961) noted, in the case of factor-market imperfections, policies other than a trade intervention would lead to an outcome superior to that attainable with a trade intervention: correction of the distortion at its source is first best.

For present purposes, it is important to note that advocates of relatively unfettered trade and liberal economy were essentially on the defensive in 1960: they questioned the size of the presumed dynamic factors and noted the static costs that were incurred. Essentially, the argument for protection, quantitative controls, and economic planning in general was an argument of market failure in a laissez-faire economy and a contrasting of that presumed failure with the performance of an ideal command economy (where it was left to the economist to decide how much detailed intervention was ideal). Nowhere in the discussion did the advocates of liberal trade policies suggest that the dynamics of growth were in their favor; on the contrary, there was a presumption that growth considerations were in at least potential conflict with the efficiency of static resource allocation.

3.3   EXPERIENCE WITH EXPORT-LED GROWTH

While the debate over resource allocation and dynamic factors proceeded, some developing countries were abandoning or substantially reducing their trade barriers and other controls on economic activity. The results were far more spectacular than even the most ardent of proponents of free trade would have forecast. Growth rates rose to heights that had previously been regarded as unattainable. South Korea achieved a rate of growth of real GNP in excess of 10 per cent a year over the entire decade from 1960 to 1970 and weathered the oil price increase of 1973 to 1974 better than almost any other oil-importing country. Taiwan, Hong Kong, Singapore, and Brazil also thrived on outer-oriented trade policies to an extent not previously deemed feasible. Although special circumstances were at first thought to have been responsible for each success story, it soon became apparent that the export-oriented countries had enough in common so that there was something more to their success than apparently lucky circumstances and specific factors.

This is not the place to review the circumstances of each successful export-oriented strategy. Many cases have been intensively scrutinized elsewhere,[2] and numerous analyses of cross-section and time-series

Table 3.1   Experiences of the successful exporters

Country	Period	Rate of growth (%) of: Real GDP	Rate of growth (%) of: Dollar value of exports	Ratio to GDP of: Exports	Ratio to GDP of: Investment
Brazil	1960–67	4.1	3.7	0.07	0.14
	1968–73	11.5	16.5	0.08	0.23
Hong Kong	1963–78	8.2	9.2	0.99	0.28
Korea	1953–60	5.2	5.7	0.03	0.11
	1960–78	9.6	28.4	0.29	0.35
Singapore	1965–78	8.6	8.7	1.87	0.39
Taiwan	1960–76	8.7	20.9	0.47	0.28

Sources: United Nations, *Yearbook of National Accounts Statistics*, 1966, Table 4A; 1975, Volume III, Tables 2A and 4A; 1979, Table 6A; World Bank, *World Development Report*, 1978 (for Taiwan) and 1981.
Note: Ratios are from the last year in the interval indicated.

performances of groups of countries confirm the surprisingly strong relationship between export growth and over-all growth of real GNP.[3] Table 3.1 gives a few pertinent data simply as a reminder of the success. As can be seen, Brazil and South Korea dramatically altered their growth rates and economic structures after their changes in strategy. Taiwan adopted unified exchange rates, a liberalized outer-oriented trade regime, and policies geared to improving resource allocation in the 1950s – so a contrast between performance under alternative incentive structures is not possible. Nor are data available for Singapore and Hong Kong to contrast performance.

For present purposes, three points are important: (1) no observer of any of these countries can doubt that the remarkable rates of growth were somehow closely related to factors associated with the rapid growth of exports; (2) for all countries where it was possible to contrast performance before and after policy changes, there could be little doubt that the growth rate jumped sharply after adoption of export-oriented strategies; and (3) the fact that the high growth rates of real GNP were sustained for a long period suggests strongly that the accelerated growth was not due simply to static gains from improved resource allocation. Indeed, to attribute all the increase in the growth rate directly to increased exports would imply an implausibly large multiplier. The unresolved question is this: What is it about an export-oriented strategy that brings about such a remarkable economic transformation?

In a sense, therefore, the tension between growth-theory and resource-allocation precepts of the early 1960s has been turned around.

Whereas theory suggested that there might be dynamic factors that contravened the static optimizing resource-allocation principles, the empirical evidence suggests that there are dynamic factors at work along an export-oriented growth path. From a theory without any evidence in the early 1960s suggesting departures from free trade for dynamic reasons, the tables are turned: empirical evidence strongly suggests dynamic factors that may be associated with export-led growth. The rest of this chapter explores the possible links between an export orientation and overall economic performance. As will be seen, there are numerous hypotheses, some of which may simultaneously be valid, some mutually contradictory. To suggest that a number of mechanisms may generate dynamic factors is not to quantify their importance. Indeed, the success of the export-oriented countries has raised a host of questions, especially about microeconomic behavior, that require empirical investigation to further understanding of the growth process.

3.4   INNER- AND OUTER-ORIENTED STRATEGIES CONTRASTED

The terms *outer-oriented*, *export promotion*, *export substitution*, and *export-led growth* have all been used interchangeably to describe the policies adopted in the successful exporting countries. That practice is continued here. It should not, however, be interpreted to mean that there is complete agreement as to what an export-oriented strategy is.[4]

3.4.1   What Is Export-oriented Growth?

- A first question is whether an export-oriented set of policies is anything other than the absence of policies discriminating in favor of sales in the domestic market.[5] The criterion for optimal resource allocation, it will be recalled, is that the marginal rate of transformation in production domestically should equal the ratio of prices in the international market (i.e. the international marginal rate of transformation) in the absence of monopoly power in trade.[6]

In principle, a government could protect some industries in the domestic market while simultaneously providing sizeable export subsidies to other industries.[7] In practice, however, the scope for such two-way protection is limited; (1) protective devices or export subsidies are meaningful only if they discriminate against some other activities; (2) protection of any sizeable number of activities is generally inconsistent with encouraging exports, because exporters require relatively easy access to international markets for their imports of raw materials and intermediate and capital goods; and (3) protection at the heights deemed necessary to induce import-substitution activities usually requires a degree of control (to prevent smuggling, false invoicing, and so on) that deters exports and makes the security of a protected domestic market sufficiently profitable to pull resources into import-substitution activities at the expense of potential exports.

Thus, most analysts would agree that an export-oriented strategy is one in which there is no bias of the incentive structure toward favoring production of import substitutes. Although some industries may be encouraged by special incentives, those incentives would be at least as great, if not greater, to production for exports than to production for sale in the domestic markets. What is probably not agreed on is whether an export-led growth strategy is one that has no bias of the trade regime (and other incentives) or whether it is one that has a bias making production for export even more profitable than it would be under free trade. As is seen below, there are a number of bases for believing that an export-oriented strategy generally entails less of a departure from free trade and equalized incentives than does an inner-oriented strategy.

Indeed, in what follows, there are two interpretations of almost every aspect of the discussion. On one hand, the factors that have apparently favored higher growth under export-oriented policies can be interpreted as having been precisely those that have resulted in the economy's being closer to a static optimal resource allocation. Alternatively, they can also be interpreted as having been the result of encouraging the dynamic factors previously thought to be associated with protectionist policies and departures from free trade.[8]

3.4.2 Salient Characteristics

The essential characteristics of import-substitution and export-oriented regimes have been examined elsewhere.[9] As is well known, no two regimes are identical and each must be analyzed in the context of all prevailing conditions, especially those in factor markets. None the less, some features are fairly uniform, and for present purposes what is required is to establish a few stylized facts that will be used in the discussion that follows.

The following differences will be assumed to exist between import-substitution and export-oriented regimes:

1. Import-substitution regimes generally have licensing procedures for imports of manufactured producer goods, and importing is generally not possible until an application for an import license has been made and acted on. This process inevitably entails delays and paperwork. By contrast, export-oriented regimes permit ready access to imports of intermediate and capital goods, at least to exporters.

2. Import-substitution regimes are characterized, *inter alia*, by over-valued exchange rates so that there is excess demand for foreign exchange (demand held in check by the licensing already discussed). One important consequence is that domestic producers of import substitutes would receive a substantially lower price for their product in the world market than they do behind the wall of tariff and quantitative-restriction protection that is the hallmark of import-substitution regimes. Because of this, it rarely pays an import-substitution firm to expand its production beyond that which can be sold in the domestic market. By contrast, export-oriented regimes have fairly realistic exchange rates and provide at least as much incentive to sell abroad as to sell domestically, if not more, with the consequence that most firms base their capacity on expected domestic and foreign sales.

3. Generally, it requires virtual prohibition of imports to induce continuing import substitution. Either imports are prohibited by the licensing system once domestic production capacity is in place, or a tariff is imposed at a level sufficiently high to make the import alternative uneconomic. This results in widely differing tariffs and tariff equivalents (nominal and effective) for different import-substitution industries. Under export promotion, by contrast, most incentives are couched in such a way that they apply to all exporters and are based on either the dollar value of export sales or the value added in export sales. This results in a considerably greater degree of uniformity in the incentives confronting producers of different products, at least in the export markets.

4. Whereas import-substitution regimes are characterized by quanti-tative restrictions or prohibitive tariffs for many commodities, export-oriented policies generally entail the avoidance of quanti-tative restrictions and the use of (generally low) tariffs with relatively simple procedures to permit exporters access to the international market at international prices for their inputs.

3.4.3 Relationship to Industrialization

One way in which import-substitution and export-oriented trade strategies do not greatly differ is that the rate of industrial growth exceeds that of the rest of the economy under either strategy. In fact, output of primary commodities seems to grow more rapidly under export promotion than under import substitution, but the industrial growth rate is also higher. In some instances (notably Brazil), the switch to an export orientation has witnessed the emergence of major new primary commodities as exports, as well as the rapid expansion of manufactured exports. But the chief reason for import substitution in many developing countries is to stimulate industrial growth, and it is for the industrial sector that arguments over the alternative strategies are set forth here.

3.4.4 Disadvantageous Import Substitution or Advantageous Export Promotion?

An unresolved question concerns the degree to which export-oriented trade and growth strategies led to superior performance because of their advantages or because of the drawbacks of an import-substitution policy. It is possible to defend either view, and in a sense the two propositions are opposite sides of the coin. One can, for example, argue that import-substitution policies very quickly resulted in the exhaustion of easy import-substitution opportunities and that growth was retarded as saving rates did not increase as rapidly as the capital intensity of additional import-substitution ventures. Thus, import substitution slows down. Alternatively, one can argue that exporting permits concentration in low-cost activities and becomes easier as entrepreneurs gain experience in international markets. Either way, what is really important is the contrast between the two. In what follows, the focus is on the difference between alternative strategies.

There are some apparent paradoxes, however. Import substitution, which was rationalized in many countries as a means of reducing dependence on the international economy, seems to increase that dependence because import-substitution activities are import-intensive and require imports of intermediate and capital goods to sustain production and growth. Thus, the economy becomes vulnerable to declines in foreign exchange. By contrast, export promotion seems to reduce dependence in the sense that foreign exchange earnings grow rapidly, markets become increasingly diversified, and the economy becomes increasingly flexible.

Similarly, import substitution is relatively easy to launch, because such initially simple and administratively straightforward measures as protection or import prohibitions provide adequate incentives for initial ventures. It becomes increasingly difficult and costly over time, however. By contrast, starting an export-oriented growth strategy is difficult and requires a combination of policies and a determination by the government that is difficult politically to achieve. Once started, however, an export-oriented growth strategy seems to have a number of self-reinforcing features. For example, under import substitution the profitability of producing for the domestic market, combined with the import intensity of import substitution, seems to shift the demand for foreign exchange rapidly outward while simultaneously discouraging exports and thus shifting the supply of foreign exchange inward.

Currency overvaluation in turn encourages intensification of import restrictions and further foreign exchange shortage; further import substitution requires increased supplies of foreign exchange to maintain flows of imported intermediate goods and raw materials and to permit new investments. Conversely, successful export promotion implies an upward shift in the supply of foreign exchange, thus permitting additional liberalization of the import regime and thus furthering the bias of the regime toward exports.

3.5   WHY IS PERFORMANCE DIFFERENT?

Three constellations of factors bear on performance differences. Their relative and absolute importance probably varies considerably between countries, because of their different circumstances (such as size and resource endowment) and because of political and cultural differences that under either set of incentives affect both the ways in which politicians and bureaucrats behave and also the relations between government and business.

The three sets are technological factors, determinants of economic behavior, and political–economic interactions. By *technological factors* are meant such considerations as the nature of production functions, including the extent of indivisibilities and economies of scale, the presence of infant-industry considerations, and the spread in factor intensities across activities. *Economic factors* refer to such phenomena as people's responses to incentives and direct controls, the impact of industry structure on behavior, and the flexibility of the economy. *Political-economic interactions* relate to the determinants of policy, the factors that influence decision makers to alter their course, and the pressures which bear upon policy-makers.

3.5.1   Technological Factors

Several properties of production functions may be important in leading to different payoffs between export promotion and import substitution as strategies for industrialization and growth. These include the possibilities of exploiting scale economies and indivisibilities under alternative strategies, the differences in factor intensity between different production processes, infant-industry considerations, and possibly even the interdependence among industrial activities.

Small size of the domestic market
Casual inspection of population statistics can give a misleading impression of the size of domestic markets for manufactured products in

Table 3.2   Illustrative calculation of relative size of markets, 1979

Country	Population (millions)	GNP ($ millions)	Non-agricultural income ($ millions)	Value of industrial output ($ millions)
Tanzania	18.0	4,680	2,152	608
Ethiopia	30.9	4,017	2,169	603
Bangladesh	88.9	8,001	3,520	1,040
Egypt	38.9	18,672	14,377	6,535
Philippines	46.7	28,020	21,295	9,807
Indonesia	142.9	52,873	37,011	17,448
South Korea	37.8	55,944	44,755	21,818
Turkey	44.2	58,786	45,265	17,048
Nigeria	82.6	76,322	59,531	34,345
India	659.2	125,248	77,653	20,966
Sweden	8.3	115,536	112,069	36,972
Brazil	116.5	207,370	184,559	78,801
Canada	23.7	228,468	219,329	75,394
United Kingdom	55.9	353,288	346,222	127,183
Germany	61.2	717,876	703,518	351,759
Japan	115.7	1,019,317	968,351	425,113
United States	223.6	2,376,868	2,305,571	808,135

Source: World Bank, *World Development Report*, 1981.

developing countries. Since many of the technological and economic factors considered below are essentially based on the proposition that markets in developing countries are usually too small to make import substitution policies an economically viable alternative (for various reasons to be considered below), it is useful to start with some calculations to show how small those markets are. Table 3.2 contains some computations. The third and fourth columns are intended to provide some indication of the size of the market for various industrial products. To be sure, no indicator of 'size of market' is perfect for all industrial products. For some (e.g. fertilizers), the size of agricultural output may be preferable. But for many commodities either the size of non-agricultural GNP (possibly as a measure of potential consumer demand taking into account Engels' Law) or the size of the industrial sector (possibly as an indicator of the size of market for investment goods and intermediate goods) may be crude proxies. Only for some consumer non-durables, such as matches, candles, clothing, and footwear, can population size alone play a significant role.

As can be seen, even some populous developing countries have markets, however measured, that are small in contrast with the developed countries. Bangladesh, for example, is estimated to have a non-agricultural income approximately 3 per cent of that of Sweden and less than 2 per cent of that of Canada, neither of which is regarded as an economy large enough to forego the benefits of specialization and international trade. Even Brazil, which has a large population and is in the middle-income country group, has a market apparently similar in size to that of Canada. Despite a large population, the Indian market is estimated to be just over a quarter that of Brazil, based on the value of industrial output. Obviously, for low-income countries with smaller populations, the size of the domestic market is even smaller than that indicated for those included here.

The important consideration here is that import-substitution policies inherently tend to encourage expansion of any industry only up to the size of the domestic market (which may be smaller when commodities are higher-priced). Because of the properties of import-substitution regimes (as outlined above), expansion of an activity beyond the amount sold in the domestic market is seldom profitable. Many of the technological, economic, and political–economic considerations discussed below hinge crucially on this proposition. It is of interest that one of the four features of growth theory that Chenery noted was the small-size-of-domestic-market proposition.

How important are indivisibilities and scale economies?

For processes and activities that are highly divisible and have constant returns to scale, the size of production run does not matter.[10] And there are industries, especially among consumer non-durables, in which there do not appear to be significant indivisibilities and in which small size of production may not be a barrier to economic viability.

There are other processes, however, where one or more indivisibilities are important, or where there are sizeable scale economies. There are often essential pieces of capital equipment (e.g. heavy presses) for which a substantial volume of production is required before they are fully utilized. Likewise, there are many processes for which there is a minimum efficient size of plant (e.g. fertilizer, tires) or for which there are significant indivisibilities. In most metal casting, pressing, and shaping activities, for example, the die or mold must be changed whenever a new shape or form is to be produced. The longer the length of the production run for a metal product, the smaller the fixed costs relative to variable costs. Obviously, the importance of this consideration diminishes with the length of the production run, but, given modern technology, the variety of shapes and forms is almost unlimited. With small sizes of domestic markets, the lengths of production runs can frequently be so small that the time changing dies and molds exceeds the time they are in operation before another change must be made. Producers naturally offer a smaller variety of specialty shapes and sizes than would be profitable with larger markets.

Import-substitution policies generally entail reliance on sales in the domestic market for most output and thus lead to short production runs and high average variable costs. But an export-oriented strategy permits a developing country, regardless of the size of its domestic market, to establish economically efficient sizes of plants and to maintain long production runs. Thus, the limitations of a small domestic market can be largely overcome, at least for traded goods, in an export-oriented economy. And under an export-oriented strategy, producers in a small developing country can obtain specialized products that are not produced domestically at internationally competitive prices. By contrast, under import-substitution regimes, either delays are substantial in obtaining items not domestically produced or producers must obtain their items (possibly of less than optimal specification) from high-cost (possibly monopolistic) domestic sources.

Differing factor intensities

It is widely recognized that developing countries are usually relatively well endowed with unskilled labor and that the rate of human and physical capital formation (broadly defined) is the constraint on expanding the industrial sector. If most industrial activities had fairly similar factor proportions, this constraint would act equally to limit industrial growth under both trade strategies unless one resulted in more rapid factor accumulation than the other. But when factor proportions differ significantly among industrial sectors, export promotion permits a more rapid growth of value added and employment of unskilled labor in industry for the same rate of human and physical capital formation. In particular, if there is a wide range of factor intensities for industrial processes, countries whose economies are oriented toward the international market will witness fairly rapid expansion of the relatively unskilled-labor-using industries. Under import substitution the limits of expansion of those industries will be largely determined by the rate of growth of domestic demand once production has expanded sufficiently to replace imports. Thereafter the growth of output can proceed only at the rate of growth of real income times the income elasticity of demand for the commodity in question (unless costs and prices are falling).

The wide variation in incremental capital–output ratios (ICORs) across countries suggests that there may be significant differences in either factor proportions or efficiency under alternative trade regimes. For the 1960–73 period, ICORs ranged from 1.7 to 2.5 for Korea, Singapore, and Taiwan, to 5.5 and 5.7 for Chile and India (see Balassa, 1978b, for details). When Brazil switched trade strategies, the ICOR fell from 3.8 for 1960–6 to 2.1 for 1966–73. Although there are many possible reasons for these differences,[11] significant differences in factor proportions and exporters' abilities to expand production of items with appropriate factor intensities are undoubtedly important.

Infant-industry considerations
The infant-industry argument has a long history in economic thought and is well known. It rests on the proposition that new, or infant, industries may generate externalities and exhibit decreasing costs over time in such a way that (1) it will not pay any individual firm to undertake the 'learning investment' and incur the initial losses under laissez-faire conditions, but (2) the early losses in these activities will be repaid to society with an adequate rate of return if they are undertaken.[12] Thus, whereas the factors considered earlier in this section are consistent with static optimization, the infant-industry argument points to dynamic factors.

The infant-industry argument, in one form or another, has been extensively used as a basis for defending intervention, and especially protection, in developing countries, on dynamic grounds. Trade theorists long ago pointed out that protection was an inefficient instrument, even in relation to infant-industry considerations. But they based their case on the proposition that production could be encouraged through the use of a production subsidy (or a tax on non-infant industries) with the same benefits and without the consumption costs necessarily incurred with protection. Given the experience of the export-oriented developing countries, there are important grounds for believing that infant industries, once developed, can be expanded well beyond the size of the domestic market. Indeed, if the infant-industry argument were valid, expansion of the infants well beyond the size of the domestic market would generally be crucial to realizing the available returns from the infants.

Stated another way, if there were infant industries whose development could result in large-scale cost reductions, restriction of their output to the quantities demanded in the domestic market would reduce the dynamic gains from development of the industry to far smaller magnitudes than would be possible if the industry could be induced to export. Viewed in this light, there is nothing in the infant-industry argument that indicates that import substitution, or more generally protection, is preferable to an unbiased or export-oriented strategy for trade and growth.

The experience of successful exporting countries suggests that there were gains, well beyond the size of the domestic market, from expanding many industries. If the resources devoted to increasing the size of production run in firms had instead been devoted to other undertakings, it need not be argued that those activities would necessarily have been ones with comparative disadvantage in the long run; it would suffice if additional output in industries already started could have achieved further scale economies or exploited further indivisibilities in the production process. To be sure, if the source of dynamic gains lay in the learning process, the argument would apply with less force. But one would then expect to have observed smaller differences in growth performance between export-oriented and import-substitution regimes.

Interdependence and quality
Efficient production of most manufactured goods entails the use of a wide variety of inputs. For all but the simplest processing activities, production depends on inputs with exact specifications, and gradations in quality or deviations from specifications raise producers' costs in important ways. Countries adopting inner-oriented trade strategies have generally (because of foreign exchange shortage and to enforce protection) required producers to obtain their intermediate inputs from domestic producers if at all possible. The mechanism to ascertain whether domestic sources were available has usually been sufficiently restrictive to cause long delays in obtaining import licenses. The consequence has been that domestic producers have generally been restricted under import-substitution regimes to obtaining many of their inputs domestically. This in turn has led to a negative sort of interdependence: in so far as individual producers have not achieved satisfactory standards of quality control, their products have raised costs in using firms and lowered the quality of other producers' output.

The fact that the demands for intermediate inputs are generally fairly specialized has in turn implied that there were few domestic producers of any particular item. So, the interdependence of the economy has resulted in a situation where production stoppages (or even inadequate quality of inputs) in one sector very quickly affect other firms and industries. These phenomena, in turn, lead to high costs for users of the intermediate goods.

Under a liberal trade regime, exporters have access to international markets for their intermediate inputs. Their freedom of choice permits them access to the cheapest source (including considerations of quality, reliability, and delivery date), thus reducing their own production costs. That this may be important is suggested by the fact that in South Korea, even with its relatively labor-intensive consumer-goods exports in the 1960s, about 50 per cent of the value of exports represented inputs of imported intermediate goods and raw materials (see Krueger, 1979).

3.5.2 Economic Behavior

If the technological factors just discussed were of sufficiently large magnitude, they alone could explain differences in performance under alternative policies. Little evidence is available about their relative importance, however. The same can be said for the influences on economic behavior discussed here.

The point of departure is once again the relatively small size of most domestic markets. That size implies that, when industries are encouraged by protection, there will either be few firms producing a given product line or that firms will be small. Any policy encouraging competition by increasing the number of firms in a line of activity will result in reduced size of each firm and hence loss of scale economies.[13] Moreover, many import-restricting mechanisms preclude entry and reduce the possibility of competition among firms, regardless of the number in the industry. To cite one example, a frequently encountered licensing mechanism allocates imports of intermediate goods and raw materials to firms in proportion to their share of industrial capacity or output. To the extent that outputs and inputs are in more or less fixed proportions and the resale of inputs is either costly or prohibited, these mechanisms tend to render market shares fairly rigid, thus inducing a lack of competition among firms. That, together with the small market and the limitation of expansion of industries to the rate of growth of the domestic market, generally implies fairly uniform growth rates for most firms and industries: changing shares come about more slowly than they would in a more competitive environment.

The absence of competition probably cuts down the concern of entrepreneurs about engineering and economic efficiency: some part of their monopoly rents may be taken in the 'quiet life'. Moreover, to the extent that competitive mechanisms are weakened, relatively high-cost firms will lose their market share more slowly than they would under alternative market structures while low-cost firms will expand more slowly. And, in so far as each industry's growth is linked to the growth of the economy and differs only when income elasticities of demand differ, there is little scope for changing the shares of individual industries in overall output.

By contrast, when industrial growth is based on the international market, competition is provided in that market, and firms can be of optimal economic size whatever the size of domestic market. Low-cost firms can expand at their desired rate unconstrained by raw-material availability or the price elasticity of domestic demand for the product, thus leading to cost reductions and output expansions for industries greater than observed under more slowly changing shares even for *given* costs in individual firms. Moreover, industries with comparative advantage can increase their shares of industrial output faster when they can profitably export than when their growth is restricted to their share of the (slowly growing) domestic market.

Thus, to the extent that competitive markets induce lower-cost activities in firms, an export-oriented trade strategy will presumably induce greater economic and engineering efficiency. For any given distribution of costs within an industry, the possibility of exporting permits more rapidly changing market shares. Finally, changing the shares of industries in industrial output can further accelerate the average rate of increase of factor productivity and of the industrial sector.

Acquiring evidence about the quantitative importance of these components of industrial growth will be difficult and time-consuming. None the less, in seeking to understand the reasons why outer-oriented trade strategies have resulted in more rapid growth of output, it seems clear that they warrant further investigation.

3.5.3 Policy Formulation

It is widely recognized that government policy instruments that seek to regulate and control through negative means are less likely to achieve the intended results than those that create incentives for individuals to carry out desired courses of activity. None the less, there seems to be a universal temptation for politicians to want to regulate economic activity and to pass laws rather than to create incentives.

There are, however, a number of obvious limits to the extent to which quantitative controls can be imposed in the context of export-oriented policies. Moreover, the feedback to policy-makers signaling that mistakes may be being made is almost certainly much stronger under an export-oriented policy stance than it is under import substitution.

For example, if the exchange rate is permitted to become overvalued, lagging exports are far more visible under export promotion than are rising premiums by import licenses under import substitution. It is possible that the constraints on the policies, and the quicker feedback to policy-makers about the effects of their policies, are at least as important in explaining the success of outer-oriented regimes as are the economic and technological factors considered above. But quantifying their role would provide a much greater research challenge.

About the limits of quantitative restrictions, it was already stated that exporters must have ready access to the international market for their purchased inputs. Provision of that access substantially reduces the scope for quantitative restrictions on any category of imports: if quantitative restrictions are highly restrictive, the reward for evading them will be substantial. When the reward is substantial, enforcement is possible only with fairly detailed scrutiny of all incoming goods. That scrutiny, in turn, is inconsistent with the ready access required for exporters. Thus, the fact that some imports are intermediate goods used by exporters imposes a limit on the amount of protection accorded to any productive activity.[14]

Moreover, an export-oriented set of policies by its nature rewards those who export and is non-discriminatory among exportables. In and of itself, that feature implies that there will be considerably less variation in the protective or subsidy equivalents of export incentives than usually arises from the incentives for import substitution. Since rewards are inherently based on performance, which in turn is highly correlated with the social profitability of the activity, there is a greater built-in tendency toward less variability in incentives under export promotion than under import substitution.

In addition to the added constraints on the size of mistakes under an export-oriented strategy, there is also a greater likelihood that mistakes will be rectified sooner. The reason is that there is likely to be quicker and more self-evident feedback. Since even the most unrealistic policy-maker recognizes that foreigners cannot be forced to accept domestically produced goods, any decision to encourage a line of exports that happens to be uneconomic will be accompanied by large losses, either to the exporter, who will then contract production, or to the government, if it is inducing exports by subsidies. Either way the costs are highly visible and provide feedback that policy is inappropriate, feedback that is far stronger than an implicit or explicit tariff of comparable magnitude under import-substitution regimes, where firms have captive markets.

These considerations pertain to broader classes of policy as well. In particular, the maintenance of an unrealistic exchange rate is possible under an outer-oriented regime only if export subsidies continue to make exporting profitable. But if overvaluation of the currency increases, the cost of the subsidies also grows. As with other measures, these self-evident costs provide feedback and incentives for some government officials (those in the treasury and those attempting to expand their expenditures on other items) to support moves toward a realistic exchange rate.

One other potentially important, but probably unmeasurable, aspect of feedback should be noted: under import substitution and direct controls over imports, firms have built-in incentives to misrepresent their activities in ways that will induce the receipt of more import licenses and other permissions and privileges. Government officials naturally must suspect information presented to them, and thus require verification or check producers' claims before acting on their applications. Under an export-oriented regime, the incentive to misrepresent performance is far smaller, as is the scope for so doing: surrender of foreign exchange proceeds is sufficient proof of exports and a fairly realistic exchange rate provides little incentive for misrepresenting performance. Moreover, since most developing countries are relatively small in the world market, there is a smaller tendency for government and industry to view each other with suspicion, and a greater tendency to view their joint efforts as a positive-sum game *vis-à-vis* the rest of the world. This, in and of itself, seems to generate relatively more straightforward relations between government and business in export-oriented economies.

3.6   SUMMARY AND CONCLUSIONS

Ironically, the same dynamic factors thought earlier to be the basis for a 'growth theory' prescribing divergences from free trade appear on inspection to be factors that, if they exist at all, favor reliance on the international market in the process of economic growth.

Whether there are dynamic factors, and how important each of them may be, is still an open question. The growth rates of the outer-oriented countries suggest that something more than the direct impact of exports was at work in accounting for the superior growth performance. When one examines critically some of the bases on which that superior performance may have rested, most of the factors earlier thought to have justified protectionist regimes are arguments, if for intervention at all, for a bias toward exporting as contrasted with production for a protected domestic market.

Whether that 'something more' emerges because export-oriented regimes are *de facto* closer to a free-trade resource allocation optimum, or whether their superior performance is instead the result of their ability to capture the dynamic gains associated with an export-oriented strategy, is still unresolved. Its investigation will require careful empirical analysis of the hypotheses sketched out above. What seems certain is that the existence of dynamic factors in no way creates a presumption that growth induced by protecting the domestic market will be in any way superior to growth under neutral or outer-oriented trade strategies.

In so far as the superior results achieved under an export orientation have been the result of the behavioral differences sketched out in the previous sections, rather than the technological factors, openness itself, rather than export growth, is a critical ingredient for rapid increases in output and productivity. This consideration is significant in evaluating the prospects for future growth of developing countries in the context of a potentially slower expansion of world trade: if openness conveys benefits due to competition and the nature of policy instruments used, the gains from an export orientation will be almost as great (if the world economy remains open) with slower growth of world trade as with more rapid growth. To be sure, the growth potential of developing countries will inevitably be even greater with more rapid growth of the international economy. None the less, if the major gains from an outer-oriented trade strategy come about because of the effects of that strategy on the domestic economic structure, the costs to developing countries of a deceleration in the growth of world trade will be far smaller than if the technological hypotheses explaining the difference in growth performance under alternative strategies are correct.

Obviously, the technological and behavioral hypotheses (as well as those about economic policy) have relevance, and the important questions center on their quantitative magnitude. Although much remains to be learned, the interrelationships of an export-oriented trade strategy with the entire structure of domestic economic activity warrant the conclusion that far more is at work in bringing about rapid growth under an outer–oriented trade strategy than simply the increased share of exports in GNP.

In the light of twenty years of experience, how do the four factors enumerated by Chenery now stand? Distortions in factor prices remain a focal point of concern, though they are more likely to be regarded as the result of government policies than as a constraint on governments. That the quantity and quality of productive factors increases still plays a central role in development thinking. Economies of scale may be important, but cannot be viewed as a source of tension between growth and trade theory. Complementarities may exist, but do not take center stage in most analyses. If something has been added to our understanding, it centers on economic behavior, the role of incentives, and the failure of economic policy likely to arise when that behavior is not taken into account.

NOTES

1. Trade theory has proceeded in three stages. In the first stage, the gains from free trade were demonstrated almost without qualification. In the second stage, theorists derived the conditions in terms of perfect markets under which free trade would be optimal. In the third stage, theorists derived optimality conditions in terms of equality between domestic and international marginal rates of transformation and then proceeded to show circumstances under which a trade intervention might improve welfare contrasted with laissez-faire in the presence of inequality between transformation rates. In general, it can be shown that if domestic and international marginal rates of transformation are not equalized due to domestic market imperfections, intervention in the trade sector will always be at

most a second-best welfare solution contrasted with a domestic intervention directed toward the source of the distortion.

2. For analysis of the South Korean experience, see Frank *et al*. (1978), Krueger (1979), and Westphal and Kim (1977). South Korea moved away from the export-oriented model and began developing heavy industry in the late 1970s. The consequences for the economy were disastrous and, at the time of writing, the government was attempting to move back to the earlier growth path.

   For Taiwan, see Fei *et al*. (1979) and Liang and Liang (1981). For Hong Kong, see Lin *et al*. (1980), Riedel (1974), and Sung (1979). For Brazil, see Carvalho and Haddad (1981) and Langoni (1972).

3. See, among others, Balassa (1978a; 1982), Michaely (1977), and Krueger (1978, Chap. 11).

4. There is, however, agreement on what an export-oriented strategy is not. In particular, it is not a set of *ad hoc*, specific policies encouraging designated industries that are highly protected in the domestic market to sell some (usually small) fraction of their output abroad in return for continuing to receive their privileged position. Most highly protectionist countries adopt some incentives to induce their protected industries to export at least to some extent. That specific inducement, often nothing other than a tax charged on domestic producers to offset part of their monopoly position in the domestic market, is at best a partial offset to the overall discrimination of incentives in favor of selling in the domestic market.

5. In practice, several distinctions need to be drawn. There is, first, discrimination by product that occurs when some commodities receive higher protection or larger subsidies than others. There is, second, discrimination by place of sale, even for the same commodity. Although both types of discrimination occur (with the export-oriented countries having discriminated in favor of overseas sales contrasted with home sales of the same commodity) the discussion in this chapter proceeds as if the only form of discrimination was that of import barriers (which would discriminate against exportable commodities) or export subsidies (which would discriminate against import-competing commodities). Of course, if an exportable were protected in the domestic market and subsidized in like amount, there would be discrimination in favor of the commodity and no discrimination by geographic destination.

6. It is improbable that developing countries have monopoly power in their imports of manufactured goods, the ones subject to protection. The practice of regarding international prices as correctly reflecting the international marginal rate of transformation will be followed throughout this chapter. If the readers believe there are instances of monopoly power in trade, the statements can easily be amended to provide for optimal tariffs.

7. Assume that all exports were accorded subsidies as a percentage of the f.o.b. price at the same proportionate rate as the *ad valorem* uniform rate of protection on all imports. Then, the resulting resource allocation would be the same as with free trade at a unified exchange rate, if no distortions were introduced by capital flows at a different rate. In practice, exports are encouraged by a variety of devices (tax exemptions, favored access to rationed credit, and so on) but the subsidy equivalent of these devices can

be calculated, so that it simplifies exposition to refer to these as subsidies. There are also interesting questions about the side-effects of some export inducements, including credit rationing, in inducing non-optimal choice of techniques. These issues are ignored here.

8. There is an interesting contrast in the economic policies of the successful exporters. Singapore appears to have been interventionist, Hong Kong genuinely laissez-faire, and Brazil, Taiwan, and South Korea somewhere in between. As is discussed below, however, to the extent that there was intervention, it generally was in providing incentives rather than in imposing direct controls. Likewise, all the successful countries seem to have provided most incentives across the board so that eligibility for rewards was determined by total export performance and was not differentiated by commodity groups.

9. On import-substitution regimes, see Bhagwati (1978); on export-oriented regimes, see Balassa (1978a).

10. Even here, the statement must be qualified in so far as failure to expand one group of activities may require that resources be used in other, less viable, activities.

11. Some of the economic-behavioral factors suggested later in this section point to the possibility that productivity may increase more rapidly in all industries under export promotion than under import substitution. To the extent that those factors are empirically important, they, too, would result in a lower observed ICOR.

12. See Baldwin (1969) for an excellent analysis of the conditions under which the infant industry argument might be valid.

13. It is in principle conceivable that, with highly elastic price elasticity of demand, the reduction in price accompanying the elimination of monopoly power might permit an increase in the average size of firm, production run, or whatever the relevant unit for achieving economies was.

14. A partial exception to this statement is luxury consumer goods that are not domestically produced. Some countries, most notably Korea, have imposed relatively high duties on imports of those goods with the intent of taxing luxury consumption heavily. Since those goods are not usually used in production, and domestic production is not undertaken, protection or import prohibitions on those items seems not to have a high cost.

REFERENCES

Balassa, B. (1978a). 'Export Incentives and Export Performance in Developing Countries: A Comparative Analysis', *Weltwirtschaftliches Archiv*, vol. 1, pp. 24–61.

Balassa, B. (1978b). 'Exports and Economic Growth: Further Evidence', *Journal of Development Economics*, vol. 5, no. 2, pp. 181–9.

Balassa, B. (1982). 'Policy Responses to External Shocks in Sub-Saharan African Countries', Development Research Department Report no. 42, World Bank.

Baldwin, R.E. (1969). 'The Case against Infant Industry Protection', *Journal of Political Economy*, vol. 77, no. 3 (May/June), pp. 295–305.

Bhagwati, J. (1978). *Foreign Trade Regimes and Economic Development:*

Anatomy and Consequences of Exchange Control Regimes. Cambridge, MA: Ballinger, for the National Bureau of Economic Research.

Carvalho, J. and C. Haddad (1981). 'Trade and Employment in Brazil' in A. Krueger, H. Lary, T. Monson and N. Akrasanee (eds), *Alternative Trade Strategies and Employment, Vol. 1: Individual Studies*. Chicago: University of Chicago Press, for the National Bureau of Economic Research.

Chenery, H.B. (1961). 'Comparative Advantage and Development Policy', *American Economic Review*, vol. 51, no. 1 (March), pp. 18–51.

Fei, J., G. Ranis and S. Kuo (1979). *Growth with Equity: The Case of Taiwan*. London: Oxford University Press.

Fishlow, A. and P. David (1961). 'Optimal Resource Allocation in an Imperfect Market Setting', *Journal of Political Economy*, vol. 69, no. 6 (December), pp. 529–46.

Frank, C.R., Jr., K.S. Kim and L. Westphal (1978). *Foreign Trade Regimes and Economic Development: South Korea*. New York: Columbia University Press, for the National Bureau of Economic Research.

Krueger, A.O. (1978). *Foreign Trade Regimes and Economic Development: Liberalization Attempts and Consequences*. Cambridge, MA: Ballinger, for the National Bureau of Economic Research.

Krueger, A.O. (1979). *Studies in the Modernization of Korea: The Developmental Role of the Foreign Sector and Aid*. Cambridge, MA: Harvard University Press.

Langoni, E. (1972). 'Distribuição da Renda e Desenvolvimento Econômico do Brasil', *Estudos Econômicos*, Vol. 2, pp. 5–78.

Liang, K.S., and C.I.H. Liang (1981). 'Trade and Incentive Policies in Taiwan', mimeo.

Lin, T.B., V. Mok and Y.P. Ho (1980). *Manufactured Exports and Employment in Hong Kong*. Hong Kong: Chinese University Press.

Michaely, M. (1977). 'Exports and Growth: An Empirical Investigation', *Journal of Development Economics*, vol. 4, no. 1 (March), pp. 49–53.

Reidel, J. (1974). *The Industrialization of Hong Kong*. Tübingen: Mohn.

Sung, Y.W. (1979). 'Factor Proportions and Comparative Advantage in a Trade-Dependent Economy: The Case of Hong Kong', Ph.D. dissertation, University of Minnesota.

Westphal, L., and K.S. Kim (1977). *Industrial Policy and Development in Korea*. Washington, DC: World Bank Staff Working Paper no. 263.

PART III

DETERMINANTS OF INCOME LEVELS AND GROWTH

4 · FACTOR ENDOWMENTS AND PER CAPITA INCOME DIFFERENCES AMONG COUNTRIES

The days when a single factor – capital, skills, entrepreneurship – was believed to be the key to economic development (and hence the single explanatory variable in explaining income differences) have long since passed. There is widespread agreement that all these factors, and many others, contribute to low per capita incomes in the less-developed countries. Despite this agreement, little has been done to quantify the importance of each of the explanatory variables, much less their interaction.

It would be highly useful to know how much of the difference in per capita incomes between a developed and a less-developed country is attributable to less capital (or land and natural resources) per head, how much to lower skill levels and how much to other factors. Although all may affect relative income levels, it is important for analysis and policy whether disparities in resources account for 20 per cent of the difference, or whether they account for 90 per cent. For if most of the disparities are attributable (at least in a proximate sense) to uneven resource endowments per head, models of resource accumulation should be the basis for analyses of development. If, however, resource disparities explain little of the differences in income levels between countries, economists must search anew for a theory of output determination, for the central question of economic development must then become the reason for differences in outputs with comparable inputs.

First printed in 1968. The research for this paper was partially supported by a grant to the author from the National Science Foundation. The computer work was done at the Social Science Research Facility of the University of Minnesota with the assistance of Marsha Masucci and Peter Greenston. I am indebted to Professors Edward M. Foster, John C. Hause, James M. Henderson and T.W. Schultz for helpful discussions and comments at various stages of the research.

Models focusing upon technology differences, 'dual' economies and the like would then appear appropriate.

Moreover, the relative importance of various resource differences is of considerable interest. Should natural resources account for most of the difference in output per head, the prognosis for economic growth would be rather dim. Likewise, should physical capital disparities be negligible in explaining income differences and human capital differences important, significant policy implications could be drawn for development planning.

Definitive answers for these questions are beyond the scope of this chapter. A generally agreed methodology would be required, as well as a variety of data that is not presently available. This chapter is meant to go part of the way, however. It is assumed that all countries are subject to a uniform production function, and empirical estimates of the importance of some selected resource differences are derived under fairly widely accepted assumptions. It is shown that three variables, normally associated with the concept of human capital, can explain more than half the difference in income levels between the United States and a group of the less-developed countries for which data are available.

At the outset, in Section 4.1, it is assumed that all countries are subject to a uniform constant-returns-to-scale aggregate production function. This implies a uniform per capita production function with decreasing returns to increments of non-labor resources per head. It is then shown that weighting per capita resource differences by the marginal products of factors in an advanced country will result in an underestimate of the difference in per capita income that is attributable to those resource differences. Moreover, this method of weighting will result in an underestimate of the quantitative importance of any subset of factors. That is, it can be shown that even if the poorer country had as much of all remaining resources per head as the developed country, its per capita income would be even less than the figure obtained by using the developed country's marginal products to estimate output in the less developed country.

In Section 4.2 the method is used to estimate the degree to which three human-resource attributes – educational attainment, age structure and urban–rural distribution – account for per capita income differences. In Section 4.3 estimates are presented for each attribute separately, and some inferences about their contribution to development are drawn. In Section 4.4 some hypotheses are put forward with regard to the importance of resource differences in accounting for variations in per capita income.

4.1   ESTIMATING THE IMPORTANCE OF
RESOURCE DIFFERENCES

4.1.1   The Production Function

Assume that all countries are confronted with an identical aggregate
constant-returns-to-scale production function of the general form

$$Y = f(X_0, X_1, X_2, \ldots, X_n) \qquad (4.1)$$

where Y is total income at international prices, and the X_is are
quantities of $(n + 1)$ factors of production. The marginal products of all
factors are assumed positive and diminishing, and are denoted by f'_i.

The problems of defining an aggregate production function are well
known, and require little comment here. It is worthwhile to note,
however, that if the aggregate production function concept is useful in
one country and if the underlying assumption of trade theory that each
production function is identical between countries is accepted, then
there are no more difficulties for an aggregate production function over
many countries than there are for a single-country function.[1]

Let X_0 be the number of persons in the labor force. Then the per
capita income version of expression (4.1) will be

$$y = Bf(x_1, x_2, x_3, \ldots, x_n) \qquad (4.2)$$

where $y = Y/P$, $B = X_0/P$, $x_i = X_i/X_0$ and P is the total population. B is
the fraction of the population in the labor force. The per capita
production function is homogeneous of degree less than one with strictly
diminishing marginal products to each factor.

In the absence of complete information about the parameters of the
production function and the resource endowments of all factors in any
pair of countries, the problem is to ascertain how much per capita income
will differ with any known disparity in per capita factor endowments. It
is useful, in what follows, to identify the United States with a developed
country and India with a less-developed country. The method, however,
is general, and will be applied in the next section to a variety of other
countries.

Let $x^0 = (x_1^0, x_2^0, \ldots, x_n^0)$ be the Indian per capita factor endowments,
and x' be a corresponding vector of the United States factor endowments
per head. Suppose first that India had the same endowment of all factors
per head as the United States, except for factor i. In that event, it is
easily shown that, if $B' \geqslant B^0$,

$$y' - y^0 \geqslant f'_i(x'_i - x_i^0) \qquad (4.3)$$

where y' is United States per capita income, y^0 Indian per capita income and f'_i the marginal product of the ith factor in the United States.[2] That is, use of the American marginal product times the difference in the ith factor will understate the difference in income resulting from the resource disparity. If, then, Indian and United States per capita factor endowments were known, and were the same for all but one factor, the marginal product of that factor in the United States could be used to give a lower bound estimate of the resultant difference in per capita income.

It is an unlikely case in which the per capita endowments of all factors but one are the same. It is a plausible first approximation that the less-developed countries have less of almost everything on a per capita basis. Assume that $x' \geqslant x^0$. We now wish to ascertain the importance of known resource differences in the absence of data about some endowments. In this case for the production function (4.2) it is generally the case that

$$y' - y^0 > \sum f'_i(x'_i - x^0_i) \qquad i = 1, \ldots, m \qquad (4.4)$$
$$m \leqslant n$$

where the first m resources are those for which quantitative information is available.[3]

Relation (4.4) gives the following information. For any subset of factors m, the resource differences per head times the marginal products in the advanced country will understate the quantitative importance of differentials in any subset of resources. That is, with the poorer country's resources per head of the m factors it would be impossible to attain a per capita income of $\sum_{i}^{m} f'_i x^0_i$ unless the poor country accumulated more of other resources. Not only is something known about the relative importance of the resources for which data are available but some information can be gleaned about the relative importance of those factors for which quantitative information is unavailable. For, if it is known that actual income is $\bar{y}$, American income y' and that y_i is attributable to a deficiency of resource x_i, then it must follow that all other factors can account for no more than $y' - \bar{y} - y_i$.

That the per capita income difference would be at least $\sum_{i=1}^{m} f'_i(x'_i - x^0_i)$ because of the difference m in resources does not mean that if the m resources per head were increased to the United States level income would rise by an amount equal to or greater than that sum. For, if some other resource endowments were smaller the marginal products of the m

resources would be less in India than in the United States, if Indian resources of the m factors were increased to the United States level.

While relation (4.4) suggests a means of estimating the quantitative importance of any given factor-endowment difference, it is based upon the assumption that the advanced country has at least as much of all resources per head. This assumption is probably acceptable for physical capital and natural resources for the United States *vis-à-vis* the less-developed countries. It would, however, appear open to the objection that the less-developed countries at least have more unskilled and semi-skilled labor per head than do the Americans. Closer inspection, however, reveals that this depends upon the definition of a factor of production. The process of investing in education and training adds to the stock of human resources. All college graduates are high-school graduates, grammar-school graduates *and* unskilled labor. The fraction of the labor force with a college education is less than or equal to the fraction with a high-school education, and so on.

Defined in this way, countries with more human capital have as much unskilled labor per head and more skilled labor per head than do countries with less human capital. Viewed in this light, the productivity of a college graduate will be at least as great as that of a high-school graduate (since the college graduate can always do the work of a high-school graduate). The restriction upon the production function, that all marginal products be positive, is sufficient to ensure this.[4] Hence, it is possible to allow for a widely varying substitutability of more and less skilled workers with skilled workers always receiving a higher income (since they receive the sum of the marginal products of all lower skill classes plus their own). This specification, empirically, is consistent with the United States having no less of any factor of production. While it is possible that the United States has less of some specific resource than one of the less-developed countries, it is doubtful whether this consideration is of importance for the class of countries included below.

4.1.2   An Example

A simple example may make the properties of the estimation method clearer. Suppose all countries are subject to a Cobb–Douglas production function of the form:

$$Y = X_0^{\alpha_0} X_1^{\alpha_1} X_2^{\alpha_2} X_3^{\alpha_3} \qquad (4.5)$$

and its per capita version:

$$y = B x_1^{\alpha_1} x_2^{\alpha_2} x_3^{\alpha_3}$$

where X_0 is the total labour force, x_1 the fraction of the population having completed eight years of school or more, x_2 those having completed high school or more and x_3 is capital per man. For estimation by the method presented above it is not necessary to know the parameters of the production function. However, we wish here to contrast the results with the 'true state' of the world. Plausible estimates of the αs are $\alpha_1 = 0.25$, $\alpha_2 = 0.20$ and $\alpha_3 = 0.33$. Implicitly, $\alpha_0 = 0.22$. These guesses are based on casual inspection of relative shares among countries: the Indian labor share appears to be about 0.4, and there is surely a return to skill in it; the American labor share is about 0.65 with more of a return to skills; the capital share is about 0.33. For simplicity, set the United States factor endowments at unity (since choice of units is arbitrary). About one-fifth of the Indian labor force has completed (approximately) elementary school or more, and about one-twelfth secondary school or more. The Indian capital stock is probably some small fraction of the American. Say it is 3 per cent. Then, Indian per capita income would be

$$y^0 = (0.2)^{0.25}(0.08)^{0.20}(0.03)^{0.33} = 0.1269$$

or one-eighth that of the United States. The United States marginal products are 0.25 for elementary-school graduates, 0.2 for secondary-school graduates (and the high-school graduate wage 0.45) and 0.33 for the services of capital. If account were taken of the smaller fraction of Indians than Americans in the labor force the income disparity would be even greater. This is considered below, but would complicate the example unnecessarily.

If the underlying production function were unknown, but Indian factor endowments were known, the difference in output per head, estimated at American wages, would be

$$0.25(0.8) + 0.2(0.92) + 0.33(0.97) = 0.70$$

which is less than the true difference of 0.8794. Moreover, if no information were available about the Indian capital stock, but the labor force data were available, the use of American marginal products to estimate the importance of skill differences would yield an estimate of 0.38 (i.e. so long as skill differences remained, Indian per capita income could not rise above 0.62). In fact, skill differences account for 0.593 of a total per capita income difference of 0.879, in the sense that even if the Indian capital stock per head were increased to the American level, Indian per capita income would be 40.7 per cent that of the United States.

4.1.3   Skills as Efficiency Units

A special case of relation (4.4) is where skill classes are perfect substitutes. The relation is powerful, because even without knowing the exact form, or parameters, of the production function, quantitative information about the minimum importance of any resource difference can be obtained. In the event that there were perfect substitution among some subset of factors of production, relation (4.4) would hold with equality. For present purposes, that subset is skill levels. If persons of different skills were perfect substitutes, investment in man could be regarded as increasing the number of efficiency units of labor, and the aggregate production function could be written $Y = f(E, X_{m+1}, \ldots, X_n)$, where E is the number of efficiency units of labor and $X_{m+1}, \ldots, X_n$ are the endowments of non-human resources.[5] Investment in human capital could be viewed as the process of adding to society's stock of efficiency units of labor, just as investment in machines increases the stock of physical capital. If all labor classes were perfect substitutes the ratio at which they could be substituted would be the same in all countries, since wage differentials would reflect efficiency differentials unambiguously. While the present value of the human capital stock would be a function of the physical capital endowment, the interest rate, etc., the measurement of efficiency units of labor would be invariant with respect to these variables, with any given class of labor chosen as the unit of measurement. While relation (4.4) indicates that use of an advanced country's marginal products will underestimate the difference in income attributable to factor-endowment variations, it would provide an exact measure of the difference in human capital stocks if skill groups were perfect substitutes. Hence, in Section 4.2 the estimates of the difference in attainable income attributable to human capital differences can also be viewed as an estimate of the difference in the human capital stock per head.[6]

4.2 THE IMPORTANCE OF HUMAN CAPITAL DIFFERENCES

4.2.1 The Data

For empirical estimation, focus is on three attributes of the human capital stock – years of school, which is the best available cross-section proxy for investment in man; age distribution; and urban–rural distribution of the population. Age is included, in part to assess the effects of population growth and in part because age is a determinant of productivity for a variety of reasons, to which attention will return in Section 4.3. Sectoral distribution is included largely because it is widely held to be a factor in determining income per head.

These factors were selected for two reasons: first, data on population distribution by this classification are available for a range of countries, and the United States Census provides income data for a comparable breakdown; second, quantification of the economic significance of these human capital variables is important for its own sake. The low average educational attainments of the labor forces in most less-developed countries are well known. The economic importance of these phenomena, however, has been the subject of impressionistic evaluations. Quantification of the economic significance of illiteracy, adverse age structure and the like is important in itself. It is, of course, to be hoped that data will become available so that the effects of other resource endowment differences can also be assessed.

The 1960 United States Census of Population presented median income data for persons in 1959, classified by age, years of school completed and place of residence. These data were used as United States marginal products. Although earnings data would have, in principle, been preferable, the form in which they were presented in the Census creates a number of problems. Most important, perhaps, was the inclusion of only experienced members of the labor force aged eighteen and over,[7] and the lack of appropriate cross-classification.[8] Although income data suffer in principle from the inclusion of non-human capital rentals, the use of median data probably offsets part of the inclusion.[9] The

Table 4.1 Sector-specific incomes by age and education, United States, 1959 (dollars per person)

Age	Years of school completed			
	0–4	5–8	9–12	13+
		Urban		
15–19	307	221	452	609
20–24	1,307	1,508	2,041	1,719
25–34	1,629	2,370	2,700	4,140
35–44	1,837	2,656	3,204	5,379
45–54	1,825	2,756	3,392	5,662
55–64	1,636	2,491	3,064	5,182
65+	893	1,139	1,485	2,744
		Rural		
15–19	225	208	274	354
20–24	546	1,011	1,537	1,663
25–34	913	1,793	2,188	3,393
35–44	1,077	1,992	2,577	4,273
45–54	1,026	1,921	2,525	4,062
55–64	851	1,562	2,034	3,408
65+	640	880	1,097	1,862

Source: US Bureau of the Census, *United States Census of Population 1960. Subject Reports. Educational Attainment*, Final Report PC(2)-5B (Washington, DC: US Government Printing Office, 1963), Tables 6 and 7.

Census figures imply a United States per capita personal income of $1,696 in 1959, contrasted with the National Income Accounts estimate of $2,166. Some sources of discrepancy are obvious: the inclusion of incomes in kind in the National Income Accounts (which is about 4 per cent of national income, and not included in Census returns), imputed interest payments (3 per cent of personal income), failure of respondents to report irregular income and non-wage and salary income (5 per cent of personal income), and use of 1960 population data with 1959 income data (new births and death of those with income in 1959 prior to the 1960 Census – about 3 per cent). The remainder of the difference (7 per cent) must be attributed to the use of median, rather than mean, figures, and, it is hoped, reflects the lack of inclusion of persons with high non-wage and salary incomes. Use of personal income as a base implies the exclusion of undistributed corporate profits and corporate taxes. This also helps eliminate the influence of physical capital.

Table 4.1 presents the incomes assigned to individual classes on the basis of United States Census data. These data were derived by summing over individual census classes as follows:

$$y_j = \frac{\sum_i N_{ij} y_{ij}}{\sum_i P_{ij}}$$

where N_{ij} is the number of persons with income in the ith subclass of j in the United States distribution, y_{ij} the median income of those persons with income in the subclass and P_{ij} is the number of persons in the subclass.[10]

The subclasses were aggregated to conform to the distributions available for other countries. For example, United States data present individual medians by age, education and sex for persons residing in central urban cities, the urban fringe, other urban, rural farm and non-farm places. Since data are classified for other countries only for urban–rural residence, the United States medians were aggregated to this level.

Data for other countries' population distributions were drawn from the 1963 *Demographic Yearbook of the United Nations*. In order to render population classifications comparable, several adjustments had to be made. In general, an effort was made to make the adjustments in such a way as to underestimate the skill differential, although the error in so doing cannot be estimated precisely. The two most important problems were the allocation of respondents in other countries where either age, or education, or both were unknown, and the decision as to comparability of educational attainment. The unknowns were allocated to individual cells in proportion to the fraction of those reporting in that cell. The *Demographic Yearbook* data show a very high fraction of unknown, especially for educational attainment. The suspicion is that a higher fraction of the unknown belong in the lower educational group-ings; to allocate them proportionately undoubtedly results in an over-estimate of educational attainments.

Comparability of educational attainments also presented great diffi-culty, and again it was decided to err in the direction of overestimating the less-developed countries' human capital structure. Persons in the less-developed countries reporting no education were assumed compar-able to those in the United States with four years or less of education. Persons with any elementary school at all in the less-developed countries were assigned the income of persons in the United States with between five and eight years of school. All those with any secondary education (as classified by the United Nations) were assumed comparable with Americans completing between nine and twelve years of school. Lastly, all those with any higher education were assigned to the groups with more than thirteen years of education in the United States. These allocations create two sources of bias: (1) the education is probably less than comparable; and (2) the proportion of persons completing each level of education in the United States is probably higher than the proportion in countries with less human capital.

4.2.2 The Estimates

Table 4.2 presents the results of the computation $y^0 = \sum_i f_i' x_i^0$, where f_i' the median income in the United States in the ith class, and x_i^0 is the fraction of the population in the ith class in the country in question.[11] The index i ranges over all age–sex–educational attainment-sector classifications. Column 1 presents the United Nations estimate of the country's per capita gross domestic product as a percentage of the United States per capita gross domestic product. Column 2 presents the estimate of $\sum_i f_i' x_i^0$, as a percentage of United States income.

The figures in column 2 may be interpreted as follows. Mexico's per capita income in 1959 (or, in general, the year closest to 1959 for which data were available) was reported to be 14.2 per cent that of the United States. Even if Mexico had had the United States endowment per head of land, capital and other resources, Mexican per capita income would have been less than 45.6 per cent that of the United States. If Mexico and the United States have the same aggregate production functions Mexico could not hope to increase her per capita income above 45.6 per cent of that of the United States unless her stock of human resources

Table 4.2 Estimated per capita products and estimates of importance of human-capital variables

Country	Per capita GDP as a percentage of US per capita (1)	$\dfrac{\sum_t f_t' x_t^0}{\sum_t f_t' x_t'} \times 100$ (2)	Percentage difference explained $(100 - (2))/(100 - (1))$ (3)
Canada	72.6	100.5	−1.8
El Salvador	7.5	45.5	58.9
Ghana	7.7	38.0	67.2
Greece	12.5	71.8	32.2
Honduras	7.5	36.6	68.5
India	3.0	34.1	67.9
Indonesia	3.1	37.3	64.7
Iran	7.2	39.8	64.9
Israel	38.3	83.8	26.2
Jamaica	16.2	56.7	51.7
Japan	14.4	93.2	8.0
Jordan	6.9	38.7	65.8
Malaysia	7.9	44.2	60.6
Mexico	14.2	45.6	63.4
Panama	15.0	51.5	57.1
Peru	7.3	51.0	52.9
Portugal	11.6	67.1	37.2
Puerto Rico	23.2	59.8	52.3
South Korea	4.7	44.3	58.4
Taiwan	3.9	48.5	53.6
Thailand	3.6	46.5	55.5

were improved. Further, even if data were available on capital, land, etc., smaller Mexican endowments of these factors would turn out to be far less important than the human capital stock differential. That is, if Mexico had the United States human capital stock and inquiry were made about the importance of other factors of production the resulting computation would show that Mexico could achieve something in excess of 69.4 per cent of United States per capita income (since it has been shown that the sum of the factor differences times their marginal product will be less than the income differences). To state the same proposition another way, of the 85.8 per cent difference in per capita income, 54.5/85.8, or 64 per cent is explained by the differences in human capital stock.

In Table 4.2 the United States estimates of per capita income are treated as 'true' per capita income data. In fact, there is considerable evidence to support the proposition that the poorer the country, the higher the degree of underestimate of its income.[12] If the actual income figures in column 1 are underestimated, the explanatory power of the human capital differences, given in column 2, becomes even greater.[13] The countries in the sample that could attain even half the United States per capita income with their existing human capital stock are Canada, Greece, Israel, Jamaica, Japan, Panama, Peru, Portugal and Puerto Rico. For Canada, per capita income is 72.6 per cent of that of the United States, and the difference does not lie in the human capital stock. For every country except Canada, Greece, Israel, Japan and Portugal, more than half the difference between their reported per capita income and United States per capita income is accounted for by differences in their human capital stock. Again, with the exception of Canada, these countries are generally regarded as being endowed with a small natural resource base, and information about their endowment of other resources might well explain much of the difference.

Column 3 of Table 4.2 presents the percentage of the observed per capita income difference explained by the differences in human capital stock. When it is remembered that column 2 presents a maximum estimate of the attainable level of income with existing human capital resources (both analytically and because of biases in estimation) and that the reported per capita incomes are probably underestimates, it appears incontrovertible that the shortage of human capital is the major explanatory variable in the low per capita incomes of the countries in the sample.

4.3   THE IMPORTANCE OF AGE, EDUCATION AND SECTOR

Even if India had the same education-sector distribution in each age group as the United States, attainable per capita income would be lower than in the United States because of the Indian age distribution. Similarly, even if the age-sector distribution were the same as the American, the lower Indian educational attainment would result in a smaller attainable income. Clearly, there is also interaction, in the sense that given both age and education, the attainable income is lower than the sum of the age and educational discrepancies would indicate.

In order to sort out the influence of the three factors, calculations were made of what the attainable per capita income of the countries in the sample would be (1) if each age group had the United States educational sector distribution; (2) if each education group had the United States age-sector distribution; and (3) if the age–education distribution in each sector were the same as in the United States. The first factor indicates the upper estimate of attainable income if age were

Table 4.3   The separate importance of age, education and sectoral distribution

Country	Percentage by which attainable income is lower due to:				Attainable income as percentage of US
	Age	Education	Sector	Interaction	
Antigua	15.8	13.2	3.9	9.5	58.2
Canada	− 7.9	8.1	− 0.5	− 0.3	100.5
Cyprus	6.5	18.2	5.6	7.7	61.7
El Salvador	14.2	24.1	3.2	12.7	45.5
Ghana	10.5	30.3	6.9	14.1	38.0
Greece	− 6.5	28.6	4.2	2.4	71.2
Honduras	15.6	23.9	4.8	18.8	36.6
India	7.5	32.6	8.4	13.3	38.2
Indonesia	8.1	32.2	8.9	13.1	37.3
Iran	7.8	33.2	5.3	13.6	39.8
Israel	5.4	13.6	− 3.5	0.6	83.8
Jamaica	10.9	16.0	5.8	10.2	56.7
Japan	0.1	3.7	1.7	1.2	93.2
Jordan	19.1	23.3	2.5	15.9	38.7
Malaysia	12.9	25.0	4.7	12.9	44.2
Mexico	15.1	22.9	3.0	13.1	45.6
Netherlands	11.2	14.8	5.7	10.4	57.6
Panama	18.2	16.0	3.0	11.0	51.5
Peru	18.2	18.3	2.2	10.0	51.0
Portugal	− 2.6	29.9	2.9	2.7	77.1
Puerto Rico	16.3	12.6	3.1	7.8	59.8
Sabah	9.8	28.7	8.5	15.3	62.6
Sarawak	10.9	28.0	8.3	16.5	35.9
Seychelles	7.3	22.1	7.4	11.1	51.9
South Korea	12.6	24.8	6.1	11.9	44.3
Taiwan	14.5	21.6	3.9	11.2	48.5
Thailand	14.0	21.4	5.5	12.3	46.5
USSR	− 2.4	22.8	3.6	4.2	71.8

the only difference, the second education and the third sector. These estimates are presented in Table 4.3.

The first column gives the percentage by which income would be lower if the marginal product of each person in a given age group were the same in the country in question as in the United States. For some countries – notably the Latin American – attainable per capita income would be at least 15–20 per cent less than in the United States, even if the education-sector distribution within each age group were the same as the American. A comparable interpretation of columns (2) and (3) may be made. Column (4) presents the interaction between the three variables.

It remains to consider the implications of these results. The concept of human capital has proved fruitful in considering a variety of economic phenomena. Meaningful interpretation of, and new insights into, empirical phenomena as seemingly diverse as formal education, on-the-job training, information in the labor market and migration have resulted from use of the view that persons invest in themselves in large part because of the expected return on the investment. One of the recurring findings has been the importance of age, in a variety of contexts. For any given difference in wages, a person of younger age will anticipate a higher rate of return for additional education, migration or search for higher wages than will an older person. This implication of the age distribution has been extensively investigated by Becker (1962). In addition, it has long been recognized that the 'economically active' population, as a fraction of the total population, is a relevant statistic for many purposes. The higher is this fraction, not only is the 'productive' population larger but the fraction of the society's resources necessary to invest in any given average amount of training for the young will be smaller.

Equally obvious, but less frequently mentioned, is that the expected return on investment in human capital depends on the probability of survival to any given age. Increases in the rate of population growth attributable to declining mortality rates for individuals over ten years of age are undoubtedly very different in their effects from reductions in infant mortality rates. The former would tend to increase the expected rate of return on investment in human capital, and alter the age distribution in a way such that the older age groups become an increasingly larger fraction of the population; increases in survival rates for those under ten will probably leave the return on investment in oneself unaffected and will, in addition, increase the fraction in the younger age groups. If the elasticity of output with respect to labor is about one-half, an increase in the rate of population growth of 1 per cent will, if generated by reduced mortality rates for those in the labor force, increase per capita income if more than one-half of the population is under the minimum age at which their marginal product is positive. Conversely, a drop in the infant mortality rate will lead to a decline in per capita income by the full amount of the percentage increase in the population.[14]

Since the rate of return on investment in human beings is a function of initial costs, the income differential between levels of skills and the probability of survival to any given age, efficient allocation of investible resources between human and non-human wealth will be a function of these factors. Since, in general, the gestation period for investment in human beings is probably longer than that for physical capital, it is apparent that raising the survival rates of those over fifteen will increase the optimal ratio of human to non-human wealth, by increasing the expected rate of return on investment in human capital. As such, the optimal amount of human capital is also a function of survival rates, and therefore of the age structure of a society. Just as the percentage rate of growth of capital stock is too simple a variable to characterize the variety of effects of different kinds of capital formation, so the rate of population growth is evidently far too naïve a variable for adequate characterization of growth of the labor force.

In Table 4.3 the relative and absolute importance of differences in age structure varies markedly among countries. For most (the exceptions are Japan, Greece, Portugal, Israel, the USSR and Canada), even if the training and sectoral distribution at each age were the same as in the United States and specific incomes the same, per capita income would be lower than in the United States by more than 10 per cent, and frequently almost 20 per cent. For Iran, Indonesia and India the decline in infant mortality rates is fairly recent, and available evidence suggests that the age distribution will, over the next ten years, become even more unfavourable. In this regard, the rate of change in the rate of population growth, because of its impact on the age structure of the population, may be as important as the rate of population growth itself.

While the interrelationship of age and education is fairly obvious, the rationale for inclusion of the sectoral distribution of the population is far less straightforward. For, while age structure and the stock of human capital for persons above twenty-five, at least, are in the short run fairly fixed, migration between sectors is feasible. Sectoral distribution was included because it is so widely regarded as an important explanatory element in the difference between the developed and less-developed countries, and because the data were available. It is of interest that census data overstate the income differential between United States rural and urban residents (because of exclusion of income in kind, including imputed interest on owner-occupied dwellings), and yet only in a few isolated cases do United States income data suggest that sectoral redistribution would have an important effect on 'attainable' income.[15] It is possible that the potential for raising income per head through urban in-migration is vastly greater than the computations of Table 4.3 indicate. However, the relatively small difference generated by sectoral structure, contrasted with the sizes of the educational and age disparities, suggests that more rapid urbanization (with the implied shift in industrial distribution of the labor force) has its large visible effect because of differences in the skill compositions of the urban and rural labor force.

With regard to use of years of schooling as an indicator of investment in human capital, little need be said. It is well known that there are wide differences in the quality of education, and that it is difficult to estimate the extent to which ability and years of schooling are correlated. If part of the difference in United States incomes is a function of differences in ability, the degree to which incomes would be lower in other countries is overstated, because (presumably) the average ability of the less well educated is higher. It is difficult to estimate the importance of this qualification. However, some allowance for this was made by assuming that those in other countries with no education had the same income as Americans with up to four years of education.

At this point it should be noted that nothing in this chapter sheds any light on the degree to which investment in human capital is efficiently allocated in the countries under consideration. It is widely held that there are too many liberal arts and not enough technical students in many less-developed countries. To the extent that the distribution within educational categories, or the allocation of persons among classes, is non-optimal, it is evident that, once identified, the appropriate strategy is to alter the allocation of new resources invested in human capital. The data presented above provide no insight into this class of problems.

4.4   SOME HYPOTHESES

4.4.1   The Importance of Resource Differences

A method has been developed to estimate the contribution that factor-endowment differentials make to varying levels of per capita income. Of the vast differences in income levels between the United States and the less-developed countries, more than half the disparity can, on conservative assumptions, be explained by differences in the three variables investigated here. While many other factors, including the endowments of other resources, are undoubtedly very important, the explanatory power of the human capital constellation of factors is impressive. Estimation of the contribution of human capital is, however, a first step towards answering the questions raised at the beginning of this chapter. Considerable additional data and research will be required before a final judgment can be rendered on the explanatory power of resource differences.

None the less, speculation upon the outcome of that research raises several interesting questions. While no firm verdict can be reached, resource differences surely account for a substantial part of income differences. There is, indeed, some question as to whether 'technology differences', low productivity per man and other similar characterizations of the less-developed countries do more than describe the low level of per capita resource endowments.

Perform the mental experiment of categorizing non-human wealth (homogeneous land, machines, etc.) and obtaining data on its distribution and return in the United States, and its distribution in physical units in other countries. How much more of the disparity in income levels would be explained? Using United State income figures, there would not only appear the *direct* reduction in income (increase in column 2 of Table 4.2) but also an interaction term with education, sectoral redistribution and age as reflected in Table 4.3. All these resource differences, taken together, could not account for as much of the difference in income levels as do the variables examined in Section 4.2. The compelling question is how much of the difference could not be explained in these terms.

The conceptual and empirical difficulties of finding and measuring homogeneous categories of land, capital, etc., are obvious. But the significance of the human capital variables is sufficiently great at least to put forward the hypothesis that resource disparities account for per capita income differences. Were this hypothesis borne out, growth models focusing upon resource accumulation would provide a frame of reference for analysing economic development. The view, expressed by Hicks (1965, p. 3), that growth theory and development economics have no connection would, in that event, be invalid, although two-factor models may be an inadequate basis for capturing the essentials of a multi-factor world.

Extending these models to incorporate efficient human and non-human accumulation would raise a number of problems; and the issues are too complex to discuss here. Some implications of the human capital models can, however, be briefly noted. Since investment in human beings undoubtedly has a longer gestation period than investment in most types of physical capital, it is probably the case that the optimal ratio of human capital to physical capital is a decreasing function of the interest rate. The greater income differential between more and less skilled occupations in less-developed countries may reflect this phenomenon, as well as differing life expectancies. For any given interest rate, the optimal stock per head of human resources will be positively related to the stock of physical capital, for reasons analysed by Kenen (1965). As indicated above, it will also be related to life expectancy. A planning horizon of five to ten years would almost certainly result in few, if any, resources devoted to education. On the other hand, the choice of physical capital investments (and their productivity) will depend on the current skill level of the labor force. The well-known sensitivity of planning models to the choice of terminal dates would become magnified in models with widely varying gestation periods for different types of investment.

4.4.2 Factor-Price Equalization

Speculation about the additional explanatory power of other resource differences raises a second question. That is, how far is the trading world from factor-rental equalization? Certainly the evidence presented here is not proof that the world is close to factor-rental equalization. However, the views expressed by Travis (1964, p. 246), that 'the ability of trade to equalize factor returns and thus to allocate world production optimally is limited, even if transport costs are zero', and Caves (1960, p. 92) that 'one may well wonder why the arid factor-price equalization theorem has attracted so much attention.... The whole discussion is, for better or worse, a supreme example of non-operational theorizing' appear to be virtually universal. Indeed, Kemp (1964, p. 45) goes so far as to claim that 'the "factor price equalization theorem" is important if only because it focuses attention on the obstacles to equalization'.

The model of Section 4.1 demonstrates that if factor prices differ measurement of differences in factor endowment will provide an *underestimate* of the importance of the resource differences. However, if factor-rental equalization existed the measure would be exact. While transport costs, tariffs, complete specialization and the host of other conditions which will prevent full equalization[16] certainly exist in the trading world, the search for exceptions to the theorem seems to have been based on the implicit belief that factor prices are far from equalized. That more than half the difference between United Nations estimates of per capita income of each of the less-developed countries in the sample and that of the United States is explained by demographic variables alone must surely cast some doubt on the degee of conviction with which the factor-price equalization model is held to be unrealistic. When it is further considered that the available evidence suggests considerable understatement of the less-developed countries' per capita incomes, and that there is less capital and land per person, there is certainly some room for questioning the degree to which even highly restrictive commercial policies, transport costs and unequal factor endowments have prevented the tendency for factor-rental equalization (or for that matter, whether factor prices might not be fairly similar in the absence of trade, in such a way that other factors would be important in explaining trade patterns).

If, for example, knowledge of capital and land per head led to the result that India could not attain even, say, 20 per cent of United States per capita income with her prevailing factor endowment, the divergence in factor rentals could not be very large. Without the data, it is impossible to assess the degree of factor-price differences. However, it is also undesirable to dismiss the possibility of equalization or near-equalization without such a test.

The conclusion that emerges from the foregoing is that the difference in human resources between the United States and the less-developed countries accounts for more of the difference in per capita income than all other factors combined. Nothing has been said, however, to 'explain' the differences in human capital stocks. Such an explanation may lie in a variety of factors, such as low savings rates, institutional patterns, tradition and the interdependence of low life expectancies, high interest rates, the return on such investments. Similarly, the demonstration that human capital variables are very important does *not* imply that optimal development strategy consists of investing in human beings with all available resources. On the contrary, there almost certainly exists an optimal ratio of human to non-human capital, and concentration on investments of either type would result in less than the attainable rate of economic growth for any given savings rate.

NOTES

1. Factor-price equalization can occur if factor endowments are not too disparate. In that event, the result derived below is exact. To the extent that countries are specialized, and earn rents through international trade, the degree of underestimation is reduced.

2. The proof is as follows: $y' - y^0 = \int_{x_i^0}^{x_i} f_i' \, dx_i$ evaluated at the (equal) endowments of the other factors. Since f_i' is strictly decreasing in x_i $\int_{x_i^0}^{x_i^0} f_i' \, dx_i > f_i'(x_i' - x_i^0)$.

3. I am indebted to my colleague, Professor Thomas Muench, for the following proof.

   Define: $f(x_1, x_2, \ldots, x_n) = f(x)$ as a homogeneous function of degree $a \leqslant 1$, and concave in $\{x_i \geqslant 0\}$. P is the convex production set $\{(y, x) : y \leqslant f(x), x_i \geqslant 0\}$.

   Theorem: Let $y' = f(x')$. If the first derivatives f_i all exist and are finite at the point x', then $y' - y^0 \geqslant \sum_{i=1}^{n} f_i'(x_i' - x_i^0)$ for all $(y^0, x^0) \varepsilon P$.

   Proof: Rewrite as $y^0 - \sum_{i=1}^{n} f_i' x_i^0 \leqslant y' - \sum_{i=1}^{n} f_i' x_i' = c^*$. Then the assertion is equivalent to the statement that $L(y^0, x^0) = y^0 - \sum\limits_{i=1}^{n} f_i' x_i^0$ is a tangent functional to P at the point (y', x'). Such a functional exists (Dunford and Schwartz, 1958, p. 447, Theorem 6). Since the first derivatives of $f(x)$ and $\sum f_i' x_i^0 + c^*$ are equal at x', $y^0 - \sum\limits_{i=1}^{n} f_i' x_i^0 = c^*$ is the unique tangent hyperplane at x'. Finally, since $(y', \lambda x')$ ε P, where $\lambda > 1$ (because $y' = f(x') \lessgtr \lambda a f(x') = f(\lambda x')$) and $y' - \lambda \Sigma f_i' x_i' < c^*$, $L(y^0, x^0)$ must be the (unique) tangent functional at x'. QED.

4.   Suppose that skilled and unskilled labor were considered as separate factors of production, with the sum of the fractions in each class equal to unity. Then, some sort of restriction upon the range of factor proportions would have to be made in order to ensure that the marginal products of the more educated were not less than of the less educated. If, for example, a Cobb–Douglas function were specified and converted into a per capita form there would be a distinct maximum attainable output and optimal population distribution among educational classes.

5.   Arrow (1962, p. 173) has suggested that increasing labor efficiency can be incorporated into growth theory by treating the growth rate of the labor force as the sum of its quantitative and qualitative growth. Such a formulation is consistent with an efficiency-units view of man, but ignores investment in man.

6.   In this regard, it is interesting to note that the human capital stock of India, Indonesia and a few other countries is about one-third that in the United States (see Table 4.2); this was the estimate chosen by Leontief (1963, p. 334).

7.   After the computations were completed, Hanoch's (1965) work came to my attention. He used data drawn from the 1 in 1,000 Census sample, which undoubtedly have many advantages over the published Census data.

8.   Median earnings by age and education are presented only by occupation groups. See US Bureau of the Census, *US Census of Population, 1960. Subject Reports. Educational Attainment.* Final Report PC(2)-5B. Washington, DC: US Government Printing Office, 1963.

9.   It should be observed that the use of income rather than earnings data creates a bias in the estimate only if the ratio of human to non-human wealth varies with human capital. If the non-human to human capital ratio increases with education the return to education is overstated. If it decreases, the return is understated.

10.   Implicitly, those with no income were assigned a median income of zero. This is equivalent to allowing for differences in the labor-force participation rates, denoted by B, in Section 4.1. Since women are included in the sample, the lower participation rates of women in the labor force in less-developed countries are not taken into account except in so far as women with lower educational attainment have lower participation rates in the United States.

11.   The table includes only those countries for which both the population distribution and the per capita income estimates are available. Countries for which calculations of the age–education-sector components were made, but in which no per capita income statistic is available, are included in subsequent tables.

12. See Gilbert and Kravis (1954). For a recent survey of the attempts to estimate 'true' differences, see Beckerman (1966).
13. While there is some reason for believing that the ratio of GDP to personal or national income is probably higher in the developed countries than in the less-developed countries (because capital stock per man, and therefore depreciation per man, is higher in the more developed countries), the difference in the two ratios is a second order of smallness, given all the other problems of international comparisons of per capita income.
14. There seems to be widespread acceptance of the view expressed by Bruton (1965, p. 278) that 'the age distribution – and hence the dependency ratio – is more or less independent of changes in the mortality rate of the kind that usually occur'. The empirical basis for this belief is not obvious.
15. Average (of the medians) rural income in the Census data was $1,170, compared with $1,830 for urban residents. Had all rural residents in the United States received the same income as their age–education specific urban counterparts, rural income would have been $1,620, or 88 per cent of the urban average. In view of the neglect of income in kind, it is questionable what the magnitude of the differential really is.
16. See Chipman (1966, pp. 35–7) for an analysis of all the possible violations of the assumptions on which the theorem is based.

REFERENCES

Arrow, Kenneth (1962). 'The Economic Implications of Learning by Doing', *Review of Economic Studies*, January.

Becker, Gary S. (1962). 'Investment in Human Capital: A Theoretical Analysis', *Journal of Political Economy*, October.

Beckerman, Wilfred (1966). *International Comparisons of Real Incomes*. Paris: Organization for Economic Co-operation and Development.

Bruton, Henry J. (1965). *Principles of Development Economics*. Englewood Cliffs, NJ: Prentice Hall.

Caves, Richard E. (1960). *Trade and Economic Structure*. Cambridge, MA: Harvard University Press.

Chipman, John C. (1966). 'A Survey of the Theory of International Trade: Part 3, The Modern Theory', *Econometrica*, January.

Dunford, Nelson and Schwartz, Jacob (1958) *Linear Operators, Part I: General Theory*. New York: Interscience.

Gilbert, Milton and Kravis, Irving (1954). *An International Comparison of National Products and the Purchasing Power of Countries*. Paris: Organization for European Economic Co-operation.

Hanoch, Giora (1965). 'Personal Earnings and Investments in Schooling', unpublished doctoral dissertation, University of Chicago.

Hicks, Sir John (1965). *Capital and Growth*. New York Oxford University Press, p. 3.

Kemp, Murray (1964). *The Pure Theory of International Trade*. Englewood Cliffs, NJ: Prentice Hall.

Kenen, Peter B. (1965). 'Nature, Capital and Trade', *Journal of Political Economy*, October.

Leontief, Wassily (1963). 'Domestic Production and Foreign Trade: The American Capital Position Re-examined'. *Proceedings of the American Philosophical Society*, September.

Travis, William P. (1964). *The Theory of Trade and Protection*. Cambridge, MA: Harvard University Press.

5 · TRADE POLICY AS AN INPUT TO DEVELOPMENT

What difference does the set of commercial policies chosen by a developing country make to its rate of economic growth? Three points are salient. First, in its present state, trade theory provides little guidance as to the role of trade policy and trade strategy in promoting growth. Second, the empirical evidence overwhelmingly indicates that there are important links between them. Third, a number of hypotheses as to the reasons for these links have been put forward, but there is not as yet sufficient evidence to enable us to estimate their relative importance.

Turning first to theory, there are many static propositions but few useful theorems about the effects of alternative trade policies on growth. Clearly there are gains to be achieved through trade in the development process. Even the trade and growth models along Corden–Johnson lines (see Corden, 1971; Johnson, 1971) are based upon differential rates of change in capital–labor ratios in two-country, two-commodity worlds under assumptions of free trade. They provide little indication of the quantitative importance of trade as a contributor to growth, and still less insight into the probable orders of magnitude of the losses in attainable growth rates that may be incurred with departures from free trade.

To be sure, once the assumption that there are only two goods is abandoned, theory suggests that activity in production of tradables should be undertaken to the point where the international marginal rate of transformation ($IMRT$) equals the domestic marginal rate of transformation ($DMRT$), with no production in lines where domestic opportunity cost exceeds the international price ratio. An allocation of

First printed in 1980. University of Minnesota. I am indebted to James M. Henderson for helpful suggestions on a first draft of this chapter. The research underlying the chapter was supported in part by the National Science Foundation, under grant No. NSF/SOC 77-25776.

resources satisfying this criterion would be optimal in the absence of any dynamic considerations.

Theory does not, however, indicate how many activities are likely to be undertaken. Nor does it suggest the relative importance of exporting and import-competing activities in an optimum allocation, or how that allocation would change with growth. Worse yet, there is nothing in theory to indicate why a deviation from the optimum should affect the rate of economic growth. Most growth models suggest that there are once-and-for-all losses arising from non-optimal policies with lower levels of income resulting from them but no change in growth rates.

Turning from theory to practice, developing countries' trade policies have fallen into two distinct categories. One group of developing countries has adopted trade policies which diverge from the optimality criterion, often by a large amount, by protecting their domestic industries. These 'import-substitution' policies have been employed to stimulate domestic production on the theory that non-agricultural sectors must grow at a rate above the rate of growth of domestic demand, and can do so only in so far as additional production substitutes for imports. The other category, 'export promotion', has consisted of encouragement to exports, usually beyond the extent that would conform to the IMRT = DMRT criterion. Countries adopting an export-oriented trade strategy have generally experienced rapid growth of traditional exports, but even more rapid growth of non-traditional exports.

Experience has been that growth performance has been more satisfactory under export promotion strategies (meant as a general bias toward exports and not as a package of specific measures to encourage selective exports of particular items themselves induced by a bias toward import substitution) than under import-substitution strategies. While it is impossible to specify a particular model of the growth process that will simultaneously satisfy all observers, the relationship between export performance and growth is sufficiently strong that it seems to bear up under many different specifications of the relationship. It has been tested over many countries for: (1) rates of growth of real GNP and of exports (see Michaely, 1977); (2) for real GNP net of exports and exports (see Balassa, 1978); and (3) for rates of growth of GNP as a function of rate of capital formation, aid receipts, and export growth (see Michalopoulos and Jay, 1975). Time-series and cross-section data have been pooled, so that deviations of countries' growth rates from their trends have been estimated as a function of the growth of export earnings (see Krueger, 1978, pp. 271ff.). In all of these specifications, rate of growth of exports has turned out to be a highly significant variable. While the 'success stories' of Korea, Taiwan, and Brazil are well known, there are enough other observations, both for different time periods in the same country (for example, Turkey and the Philippines) and of countries (including on the positive side Ivory Coast, Colombia, and Malaysia, and on the negative side India, Argentina, and Egypt), to leave little doubt about the link between export performance and growth rates.

Moreover, it seems clear that export performance is a function in large part of governmental policies. While an export promotion strategy will not always be successful in generating more export growth (especially if policies affecting the domestic market are inappropriate), certainly policies adopted to encourage import substitution, especially when they include overvalued exchange rates and quantitative restrictions upon imports, retard the growth of exports. Moreover, in instances where exports have fortuitously risen (for example, through favorable terms-of-trade changes as in Chile in the mid-1960s) or where other sources of foreign exchange such as foreign aid have grown (as in Egypt), economic performance has not matched that attained when exports have grown rapidly.

The central question, then, is why such a difference in growth performance should be associated with export promotion contrasted with import substitution. There are three major hypotheses, and each undoubtedly contains some explanatory power. Their relative importance probably varies from country to country, and of course they are not entirely independent. Elaboration of these hypotheses provides an indication of the many ways in which the choice of trade strategy and its implementation can significantly affect the rate of economic growth. In view of the fact that empirical testing of alternative hypotheses has not yet been undertaken, there can be legitimate differences in opinion.

The first hypothesis is that technological-economic factors imply an overwhelming superiority for development through export promotion. These factors include such phenomena as minimum efficient size of plant, increasing returns to scale, indivisibilities in the production process, and the necessity for competition. According to this hypothesis, failure to take advantage of the opportunities to exploit these phenomena through trade significantly impairs the attainable rate of growth. A second hypothesis is that differences in growth rates have resulted, not from the choice of trade strategy *per se*, but rather from excesses in the ways in which import-substitution policies were administered. The third hypothesis is that policies adopted in pursuit of an export-promotion strategy are generally far closer to an optimum, both in the DMRT = IMRT sense and with respect to the domestic market, than are those adopted under import substitution. Under this interpretation, the role of trade policy is to constrain policy-makers in such a way that they do not impede the growth rate as much as they otherwise would.

Both the first and second hypotheses are consistent with the notion that the non-agricultural sector of most developing countries is, in some sense, an 'infant industry', and requires some stimulus for growth. The third, by contrast, essentially takes the negative view, that markets would function well and provide satisfactory growth if only policy-makers would abstain from counterproductive intervention.

The first hypothesis really amounts to an assertion that the gains from trade, especially for developing countries, are so sizeable that the losses associated with import substitution significantly reduce the rate of return on factor accumulation. On the negative side, domestic markets are extremely small in most developing countries, and attempts to replace imports result in the construction of plants of less than efficient minimum size, while simultaneously generating an oligopolistic or monopolistic market structure. As import substitution proceeds, new activities are increasingly capital-intensive and inefficiencies from below minimum efficient size increase. On the positive side, so the argument runs, export promotion permits entrepreneurs to base their plans on whatever size plant seems appropriate: size of domestic market is no longer a virtually binding constraint, as it is when the activity is profitable only because of very high rates of effective protection. Moreover, monopoly positions arise less frequently under export promotion, as exporters face competition from abroad as well as from other domestic producers.

Export promotion may also be more efficient in permitting rapid expansion of profitable activities; by contrast, under import substitution, most activities are constrained to expanding at approximately the same rate: inefficient firms and sectors expand approximately as rapidly as efficient ones. In this view, potential export lines consist of a number of industrial products (girls' sneakers, wigs, tennis rackets, engine parts, plywood, and so on) and it is as much a matter of the right entrepreneur, and the right specialized product, as choosing the 'right industry' that is necessary for rapid growth. To be sure, factor proportions and comparative advantage may result in greater profitability of relatively labor-using industries, but the basic notion is that there are thousands of industrial products, and that, among relatively labor-intensive activities, the ones which will develop into exports will be those in which there are firms with good management and an ability to utilize factors of production efficiently.

A final aspect of the technology-related view of the advantages of export promotion has to do with factor proportions. Given the vast disparity in capital–labor ratios of the industrial sectors of the developed and developing countries, the opportunity for trade represents a means for shifting the demand for labor outward more rapidly than the import-substitution strategy permits. If there are differences of, say, two-to-one and six-to-one in capital–labor ratios between activities at the prevailing wage–rental ratio, while the rate of capital accumulation is the binding constraint on expansion of employment in the urban sector, an allocation of additional capital to the labor-intensive activity for export will permit an upward shift in the demand for labor three times as great as that which would occur if import substitution dictates the start of the more capital-intensive activity. To be sure, the expectation is that the more rapid rate of growth of demand for industrial labor would drive up the urban wage once the demand for labor was rising more rapidly than the labor force, but this is precisely a desired outcome of policy.

Even within the 'technology' view of the superiority of the export-oriented policy, it is important to learn the extent to which gains accrue because of indivisibilities, competition, and minimum-efficient-size considerations, and the extent to which they are the result of the ability to trade 'surplus' factors. For, if the first set of factors is of preponderant importance, regional trading arrangements among LDCs may offer some hope for increasing gains from trade. However, if gains result primarily from 'factor proportions' trade, the scope for intra-LDC trade as a substitute for LDC–DC trade is far more limited. There is already evidence that 'factor-proportions' trade is important (see Krueger 1983), although its relative weight, contrasted with other technology considerations, is not known.

The second hypothesis focuses upon the costs of import substitution policies as in fact carried out, and suggests that alternative means of achieving import substitution might have avoided them. According to this view, the failure of import substitution resulted from the excesses of the particular ways in which domestic industries were encouraged: extreme currency overvaluation combined with quantitative restrictions provided the equivalent of prohibitive tariff protection; techniques of allocating import licenses were employed which prevented competition among domestic firms and rewarded entrepreneurs for license-getting abilities rather than their cost-minimizing performance; and excessive and detailed quantitative controls were employed over many aspects of economic activity. One of the costs was the failure of export earnings to grow as much as they would have under 'better' import-substitution policies; that in turn led to 'stop-go' patterns with their attendant costs. Simultaneously, the emerging 'foreign exchange bottleneck' had both direct and indirect impacts upon the structure and growth of the economy. In particular, efforts at 'import substitution' stopped being geared toward development of economic new industries, and became focused upon 'foreign exchange saving', often in highly irrational and indiscriminate ways, which further distorted the system.

The third view denies the need for any bias toward exports and implicitly or explicitly asserts that growth would be optimal in the absence of intervention. A bias toward exports is therefore better than one toward import-substitutes only because policies are less distortive. In this view, an export-oriented strategy imposes constraints on policy-makers, both in what they can attempt to do, and in making them aware of the costs of mistakes. Policy-makers receive feedback in a relatively short time period as to the costs of their policies. Also, it is infeasible to rely upon quantitative controls: the international price, at least, cannot be administered and, to that extent, more generalized forms of incentive, including a relatively realistic exchange rate, must be employed. Indeed, it is argued that incentives cannot be as biased toward export promotion as they can be toward import substitution. This is precisely because to do so would require either export subsidization (whose costs would be immediately evident through the drain on the budget) or such a degree of currency undervaluation that a current account surplus would absorb much of the country's savings potential.

According to this third line of argument, constraints upon policy-makers go well beyond the inability to impose too great a bias toward exports. For example, it is virtually impossible to administer any highly protective system for intermediate and capital goods imports if exporters are expected to compete in international markets: they must be per-mitted ready access to imported raw materials, intermediate goods, and capital equipment. To impose any comprehensive system of licensing or controls would entail delays and other costs inconsistent with the export strategy. Thus, the commitment to an export-oriented development strategy implies a fairly liberal and efficient trade regime, and thus pre-vents paperwork, delays, bureaucratic regulation, and other costs that can arise under import substitution. This in turn limits the restrictions that can be imposed on capital account. More generally, under an export promotion strategy, there is an international market in the background: it functions as a constraint upon economic behavior, both of entre-preneurs and of government officials, and simultaneously provides feedback to them as to the success or failure of policies in terms of their objectives.

Undoubtedly, all three approaches to the differential in economic performance contain elements of truth. There are export opportunities that are passed up under import substitution where indivisibilities or increasing returns within a range would permit sizeable gains in output. There are also high-cost import-substitution activities which, if never undertaken, would have freed resources for considerably more productive use, even within an import-substitution strategy. Likewise, the international market has served to constrain policy-makers and induce them to abandon uneconomic policies sooner than they otherwise would have done. Knowledge is not yet far enough advanced to determine the relative importance of the alternatives. It will not be until we have far more information than is currently available about the order of magnitude of indivisibilities and minimum-size plant contrasted with size of markets in LDCs, and also about the determinants of politicians' and bureaucrats' behavior. Moreover, it is certain that the primary sources of growth are internal, and that there is no magic formula, or single policy change, that can by itself account meaningfully for differences in economic performance.

None the less, experience has clearly demonstrated the importance of access to international markets in providing a means of permitting more rapid growth than would otherwise be feasible. Given the enormous difficulties and costs of achieving the institutional and other changes that economic growth requires, it is probable that trade policy changes have a higher rate of return to LDCs than most other feasible policy changes. It is, of course, to be hoped that protectionist pressures in the developed countries do not result in fewer opportunities for the LDCs. If such protectionist measures are taken, they will lower the rate of return to outward-oriented trade strategies. They will however, for the foreseeable future, still leave that rate distinctly above the returns from a policy of persisting with inward-oriented growth

REFERENCES

Balassa, B. (1978). 'Exports and Economic Growth: Further Evidence', *Journal of Development Economics*, vol. 5, no. 2, pp. 181–9.
Corden, W.M. (1971). 'The Effects of Trade on the Rate of Growth' in Jagdish Bhagwati *et al.* (eds), *Trade, Balance of Payments, and Growth*. Amsterdam: North Holland.
Johnson, H.G. (1971). 'The Theory of Trade and Growth: A Diagrammatic Analysis' in Jagdish Bhagwati *et al.* (eds), *Trade, Balance of Payments, and Growth*. Amsterdam: North Holland.
Krueger, A.O. (1978). *Foreign Trade Regimes and Economic Development: Liberalization Attempts and Consequences*, Cambridge, MA: Ballinger, for the National Bureau of Economic Research.
Krueger, A.O. (1983) *Trade and Employment in Developing Countries 3, Synthesis and Conclusions*, Chicago: University of Chicago Press.

Michaely, M. (1977). 'Exports and Growth: An Empirical Investigation', *Journal of Development Economics*, vol. 4, pp. 49–53.

Michalopoulos, C. and K. Jay (1975). 'Growth of Exports and Income in the Developing World: A Neoclassical View', US Agency for International Development discussion paper no. 28, November.

6 · THE RELATIONSHIPS BETWEEN TRADE, EMPLOYMENT, AND DEVELOPMENT

Of the various subspecialities that comprise the academic field of development economics those of trade and development, on one hand, and of labor markets and development, on the other hand, are probably the two most emotive. Trade issues, ranging all the way from empirical assertions about the terms of trade to policy issues such as the straw man of 'import substitution versus export promotion' (when, in fact, the real question is what impact alternative policies have on the efficiency of both), have been extensively and hotly debated. No less contentious were earlier assertions with respect to 'disguised unemployment' and the nature of labor markets in developing countries.

In both of these fields, knowledge has evolved remarkably rapidly, and lengthy surveys have been and can be written on each (see Krueger, 1984, and Spraos, 1980, on trade policy issues; and Squire, 1981, and Binswanger and Rosenzweig, 1984, on labor markets). However, until recently, the question of the relationship between trade and employment was at least as much neglected as the two individual fields were researched. In part, this was because an improved understanding both of labor markets and of the implications of alternative trade strategies was required before questions about the relationship could be meaningfully addressed. In part, too, the relative neglect of questions concerning the relationship between trade and employment emanated from the very different focuses of the two subfields, and hence, the reluctance of scholars in each specialty to trespass on the other field.

In this essay, an effort is made to set forth what has been learned about the relationship between trade and employment in the development process and to indicate areas where future research is likely to contribute significantly to knowledge. To do so requires first a brief review

First printed in 1988. I am indebted to Eric Manes and Susan Hume for valuable assistance with the empirical work reported upon in Section 6.3, and to participants in the Yale Growth Center symposium for helpful comments.

of some of the important aspects of the evolution of thought with respect to trade and labor markets separately. Thereafter, attention turns to what (little) is known, or thought to be known, about the relationship between trade and employment. A final section then sets forth areas in which future research is needed.

6.1 TRADE AND DEVELOPMENT

As is well known, early thought on development tended to equate 'industrialization' with development, and then to focus on the role that international trade might play in industrialization. The key question, clearly, was the type of trade regime that would be most conducive to industrialization.

At least two strands of thought led many development economists to advocate protection. The first was based on the premise that developed countries had such a head start (due, perhaps, to infant-industry reasons) that 'industrialization' would not proceed at a satisfactory rate in the absence of protection. The second was based on the belief that developing countries' comparative advantage lay in highly specialized, primary commodity lines, that an open trade regime, therefore, would result in each country's continuing specialization in a few primary commodities, and that the demand for these commodities was both price- and income-inelastic. That being the case, it seemed self-evident that developing countries could not hope to attain rates of growth above the world average through maintaining their specialization; the income elasticity of demand for importable goods would exceed unity, and hence the relative price of importables could be expected to rise.

'Import substitution' then seemed to be the logical solution: protecting domestic infant industries would encourage them to become 'leading growth' sectors and simultaneously their growth would satisfy upward shifts in demand for importables as incomes rose, thereby simultaneously removing pressures that would otherwise arise on the balance of payment.

A first point to note is that, in this view of appropriate trade policies for development, there would be little or no direct linkage between trade and employment.[1] Protection, by its nature, would cut off the domestic economy from the international marketplace, and issues pertaining to employment, therefore, could be addressed in the context of a relatively closed-economy model. Hence, early concerns with trade strategies were of a kind that provided an analytical separation between trade and employment. With hindsight, this is especially surprising in light of the Heckscher–Ohlin model of international trade, which essentially posits a very strong link between employment and comparative advantage (see Section 6.3).

The 'import-substitution, elasticity-pessimism' view of the role of trade in development was virtually universal in the 1950s. Practice went even further than theory, however. Most developing countries experienced a marked deterioration in their terms of trade at the end of the Korean War commodities boom, and imposed or tightened import restrictions sharply in response. The resulting level of protection to domestic industry was probably far greater than might have been decided upon, had the policy objective remained solely that of fostering domestic industrial development. In many, if not most, developing countries, the extremes to which the trade regime went were far beyond what had originally been intended and imposed significant economic losses upon entire economies. It took some time, however, for the consequences of these policies to play out, and longer for them to be recognized.

The first departure from the import-substitution, elasticity-pessimism view of trade policy and its role came with the recognition of two related realities. First, the gains from trade were simply too great to be passed up. Secondly, 'foreign exchange shortage' rapidly became a virtually independent constraint to growth in the context of trade and payments regimes employing exchange control, import licensing, and usually prohibitive protection to import-competing industries. Gradually, too, the failure of exports to grow even as much as expected and losses of shares in a rapidly expanding international economy served to highlight the fact that exchange-rate overvaluation and protection both discriminated against exports, and that a negative supply response was significantly larger and more quickly forthcoming than had been anticipated.

For present purposes, two other negative consequences of industrialization behind high protective walls may be mentioned. One was the fact that the growth of industry, which was supposed to be a leading growth sector, was not accompanied by significant growth of employment. As noted first by Prebisch (1964), then by Baer and Herve (1966), Morawetz (1974), and others, industrial growth was accompanied by very little employment growth, and the capital intensity of industry rose quickly.

Although it was not recognized at the time, this failure of import substitution to be accompanied by rapid employment growth was part of a negative side of the link between trade and employment, to which attention will return in Section 6.3. The other related negative consequence was the rapid increase in observed incremental capital–output ratios (ICORs) over time. While rising ICORs are to be expected as savings rates rise and capital stock per employee increases, the actual increases were far beyond those that might reasonably have been expected. In part, this was because further import-substitution activities of necessity had to be in more capital-intensive lines, and in part it was because of rising costs of further import substitution as the small size of domestic markets, and other factors, led to ever-higher capital requirements for additional output.

Although the negative consequences of import substitution as actually practiced were becoming increasingly evident, there does not seem in the 1960s to have been a great deal of recognition that slow employment growth, increasing foreign exchange shortage, and other difficulties were at least in significant part a consequence of the import-substitution policies.

However, by that time, some developing countries were altering their trade strategies – and meeting a much greater measure of success than even the advocates of those changes had anticipated. That there was success is not in dispute (see Balassa, 1978; Bhagwati, 1978; and Krueger, 1978), although there is some disagreement as to whether the successful trade strategies were 'laissez-faire, free trade', or whether instead they were biased toward exports. Nor is there any question that a necessary if not sufficient condition for that success was a different trade strategy. However, the extent of the success was so great that, unless one has an export theory of value, the question immediately turned to the phenomena associated with or accompanying the trade regime that might explain it. The questions still requiring research center largely on the quantitative importance of the various factors that contributed to success.

Here, some of the key hypotheses regarding the reasons for success under the outer-oriented trade strategy are examined, because they affect analysis of the linkage between growth of trade and employment. For most of them, there are suggestive pieces of evidence supporting the hypothesis, some of which are cited, although an exhaustive survey of the evidence to date would require a separate paper exclusively on that subject. Attention returns to some of these hypotheses in Section 6.4, where directions for future research are considered.

There are two broad classes of hypotheses on or explanations of the success of outer-oriented trade regimes.[2] On the one hand, there are explanations which focus on the way trade regimes affect macroeconomic variables. Under these explanations, growth proceeds more rapidly because of changes in the macroeconomic environment. Díaz-Alejandro (1976), for example, attributed much of Colombia's faster growth after it altered strategy to the cessation of the 'stop-go' cycle, which had earlier centered around sharp shifts in domestic monetary and fiscal policies in response to periodic balance-of-payments crises and foreign exchange shortage. More generally, countries with outer-oriented trade regimes are able to use the international market to counter adverse shifts (such as crop failure) that would otherwise lead to bottlenecks and slower domestic growth.

To the extent that it is the macroeconomic impact of trade strategy that permits more rapid overall growth, the link to employment can be analyzed in a manner similar to that of any other growth-enhancing policy. For analyzing the links between trade and employment, therefore, it is the second, or microeconomic aspects of the link that deserve review. Here, focus is on industry structure (including firm size and size of individual production runs), the degree of competition, and incentives. The effects of different trade strategies on these microeconomic variables is the result both of some negative consequences of highly protective trade regimes and of the positive benefits of a more open trade regime. Later on, in Section 6.3, attention turns to the ways in which incentives can affect export prospects and capital–labor ratios of individual industries.

For present purposes, the question – of whether an outer-oriented trade regime is neutral, as between exportable and import-competing domestic production, or whether there is some bias (although much smaller in magnitude than that toward import-competing production under an import-substitution strategy) toward exportables – can be ignored. The crucial differences, for purposes of analyzing employment, center upon the incentives provided for individual producers, the scope they have for expanding production in individual product lines and for altered market shares, and the ways in which they affect output and growth.

A few stylized facts about import-substitution and outer-oriented regimes will set the stage for discussion. An import-substitution regime is usually characterized by provision of virtually prohibitive protection, most often outright bans on imports, to domestic producers for any product sold on the domestic market; this immediately provides reduced incentives for sale abroad relative to the domestic market. There is typically an overvalued exchange rate, and licensing of all imports and other purchases of foreign exchange is the mechanism through which the balance of payments is constrained. Import licenses, usually only for 'essential' intermediate goods and capital goods employed in production, are allocated to producers of commodities for the home market. This directly provides an implicit subsidy to production of these commodities, as the importers receive the implicit premium on the licenses. Both exchange rate overvaluation and the high cost of domestically produced inputs typically serve as disincentives to exporting.

As has been extensively analyzed, the consequences of this sort of trade regime vary somewhat depending on the precise nature of the regime, including the mechanism employed for allocation of licenses, and the offsets, if any, to the disincentives to exporters (such as duty drawbacks or free importation of inputs used in production for re-export).

But in almost all cases, domestic markets are sufficiently small that the protective mechanisms used under import-substitution regimes provide a great deal of monopoly power to producers of commodities competing with importables. They also lead to strong incentives to expand into new import-competing lines (because of the usually automatic protection available and because entry into a new line provides monopoly power for a new activity, whereas expansion into activities competing with other domestic procedures is necessarily more competitive).

These characteristics have a number of consequence. First, because new investment is largely directed to new activities, the capital intensity of new investment in the manufacturing sector rises over time as 'easier' import-substitution activities have already been undertaken. The opposite side of the coin for an export-oriented regime, of course, is that firms producing labor-intensive goods can, if successful, expand beyond the size of the domestic market. The capital intensity of production can, therefore, rise much more slowly under an outer-oriented trade regime. This, of course, has immediate implications for employment, as a given savings rate will finance more new jobs at a given real wage. Secondly, because of sheltered positions in the domestic market, the normal market mechanisms that create incentives for lowering costs and that punish inefficient producers and reward efficient producers are much weaker, if they exist at all, under import substitution. Market shares are to a great extent 'guaranteed' by the licensing regime whenever intermediate goods are employed in more-or-less fixed proportions to output, both because low-cost producers cannot readily obtain more inputs[3] and because high-cost producers receive the premium on import licenses. Thus, the normal entry and exit mode that provides incentives for efficiency and penalizes those who cannot achieve it is weaker, if it exists at all, under import-substitution regimes. The implications of this set of considerations on labor markets are considered in Section 6.3. Here, it should only be noted that there have been few empirical studies of industrial organization in developing countries that have set about testing the proposition that changes in market shares are less volatile the more restrictive the trade and payments regime. Thus, while it can be stated that the effects are present, further research will be needed to ascertain the quantitative significance of them.

Yet another significant difference between import-substitution and export-oriented regimes lies in the scope that exists for direct controls over domestic markets and in the feedback policy-makers receive as to the consequences of their decisions. This consideration pertains to a wide variety of matters, including the extent to which exchange-rate overvaluation can arise and persist, the degree of divergence between international and domestic price relativities, and the impact of tax structures and controls on interest rates and financial institutions on savings and on resource allocation. But of particular relevance for considering the link between labor markets and employment is the scope for labor-market interventions. Clearly, when prohibitive protection is provided to a large component of domestic industrial activity, producers can compensate for higher labor costs through exercising their monopoly power better than when they are competing in international markets. To that extent, the scope for intervention in labor markets is linked to the trade regime in important ways. It has often been asserted that countries such as Korea could not have succeeded in their export-oriented development strategy if their labor markets had not been left to function fairly freely in response to market forces. But the opposite is also true: the fact that Korea followed an outer-oriented strategy left policy-makers with less scope for intervention in labor markets, had they considered doing so, than they would have perceived under an alternative trade regime.

One final point deserves mention: for many developing countries, unskilled labor is the abundant factor of production, and comparative advantage within industry (and probably in other economic activities) probably lies in producing and exporting some reasonably labor-intensive goods and services. It is highly misleading to think of comparative advantage in terms of 'industries': the number of products within each industry is vast, and the particular subset of commodities that may advantageously and profitably be produced within any one country will depend on the flair of the particular entrepreneur as well as more conventional 'trade-theoretic' factor supplies. There is nothing in theory to predict that Hong Kong would produce more ladies' short-sleeve cotton blouses, while Korea would produce more ladies' long-sleeve polyester ones. There is, however, something in theory to suggest that Hong Kong, with its free-trade regime, would be in a better position to compete in a market in which rapid shifts in production line respond to shifts in fashion than would a country where delays in obtaining import licenses for intermediate goods and raw materials would prevent quick shifts in response (see Morawetz, 1980).

6.2 LABOR MARKETS IN DEVELOPING COUNTRIES

Just as international economists initially started out by assuming that goods markets did not function very efficiently, and that protection would be essential if development was to proceed, labor economists in the 1950s and early 1960s assumed that labor markets were not functioning well and that government intervention would be required to correct market failure. Lewis's (1954) classic and insightful contribution was to argue that because there were large rural populations, labor was likely to be in highly elastic supply for non-rural activities for early stages of development. 'Highly elastic' was quickly interpreted to mean that this supply could be reallocated at zero price, or at least opportunity cost, and that labor could be regarded as virtually a free good from the viewpoint of resource allocation.

It took considerable research into rural labor markets before the alternative viewpoint prevailed – that there are many aspects of labor markets in rural areas in developing countries that are not well understood, but that, none the less, rural members of the labor force have positive marginal products (see Binswanger and Rosenzweig, 1984, Chap. 1) and opportunity costs. Whether the observed facts result from labor scarcity at peak periods with high marginal product (for example, see Hansen, 1969), and other parts of the year when it is substantially below the average, from informational frictions (which induce share-cropping, tenancy, and other institutional arrangements, giving rise to interrelated factor markets – see Bell and Srinivasan, 1985), or from other causes is not pertinent to the subject at hand here.

More generally, research has demonstrated that labor markets in developing countries functioned substantially better – in the sense of workers shifting occupations and locations in response to shifts in relative rewards – than had earlier been presumed.

Berry and Sabot, for example, reviewed the evidence available as of 1978. Their conclusion (Berry and Sabot, 1978, pp. 1230–1) is worth quoting at length:

> because the efficiency of unconstrained markets is an article of faith for some economists, while the pervasiveness of imperfections and their dire consequences are premises to which others give uncritical allegiance, it is necessary to exercise great caution in interpreting the available economic evidence. Nevertheless, certain key features ... appear to be firmly established.
>
> Our null hypothesis, that labour markets function at a comparatively high level of efficiency, is based on well-documented aspects of their macro dynamics. As development proceeds, time series and cross-country comparisons reveal changes in the occupational, industrial and spatial distribution of workers which are consistent with changes in the structure of production and economic growth. The success of labour markets in mobilizing workers for new growth-generating projects, and in other ways altering the distribution of labour services, does not, however, exclude the possibility that at any given time labour may be misallocated and a significant amount of productive potential be wasted. Furthermore, though microeconomic studies of migration and peasant agriculture have provided

conclusive evidence that workers respond to economic incentives to allocating their time, this is not in itself sufficient to confirm a high level of
labour market efficiency.

Our conclusion, that in most countries our null hypothesis is accepted,
rests primarily on the microeconomic evidence of observable causes of
misallocation . . . except where it is a genuine search phenomenon (a result
of inadequate information), it [open unemployment] is in most cases a
symptom of labour misallocation caused by the decisions of workers, more
and less educated alike, to forgo available low income employment opportunities and queue for the few high income positions available in a segmented labour market.

But, as the end of the quote implies, the proposition that labor markets
may function reasonably well in the absence of government intervention
does not imply that governments do not intervene. On the contrary, if
one observes the existence of a 'few high income positions available in a
segmented labor market', it is more likely the result of government
intervention than the consequence of inefficient private markets.

Government interventions affecting the conditions of employment
and structure of earnings are widespread in developing countries. They
include such phenomena as legislation directly governing both conditions of employment (including job security provisions) and fringe
benefits (including such diverse items as social insurance, housing and
training), the legal framework within which unions are able to bargain,
and conditions of employment within the public sector (which can be
very large in many developing countries).

Depending on the nature of the regulations and their enforceability
(and enforcement), the impact on labor markets can be varied. Employers may be reluctant to hire additional labor, for example, because
of their inability to lay off workers once on the payroll, thus tilting their
behavior toward selection of more capital-using techniques and production activities than might prevail in the absence of such enforced legislation. Minimum-wage legislation may reduce the incentive to hire
unskilled workers. And greater enforceability of this sort of regulation
in large industrial enterprises than in small-scale activities can and
usually does lead to segmented labor markets, with excess applications
for jobs as workers seek entry into the high-wage, heavily regulated
activities (or in public sector jobs).

Other forms of intervention may have quite different effects. In some
countries, policies have been put in place to use government-owned
parastatals to employ all university graduates who cannot otherwise find
satisfactory employment. While the motivation for this sort of policy
may have been political, the consequence for rates of return and wage
structures are significant: social rates of return may exceed private rates
of return for university education by large margins; private firms may

wait to observe performance and then 'bid away' the more able graduates, leaving others in the public sector (see Krueger, 1972, for an analysis of this phenomenon in Turkey).

Although too little is known about labor markets to be confident about any empirical generalization, a rough guess might be that regulations regarding social insurance and layoff provisions have been the most significant intervention in much of Latin America (see, for example, Corbo and Sánchez on the effects of removing these provisions in Chile); that minimum wages and conditions of employment in public sector enterprises have been effective in driving a sizeable wedge between the 'formal' and 'informal' sectors in Africa and the Middle East; and that regulations covering employers' obligations to provide housing, education and training, and other social services may have been more significant in South Asia.

These sorts of intervention led to the Harris and Todaro (1970) model of labor-market behavior in developing countries: workers earn a supply- and demand-determined wage in the rural areas of developing countries, and know that if they are fortunate enough to find employment in the 'formal' sector, they can earn an amount greater than the rural wage by some multiple, m, greater than one. They maximize expected incomes by migrating to urban areas in search of high-compensation jobs, as long as the higher earnings times the probability of finding employment exceeds the rural wage. The probability of finding employment, in turn, can be expressed in several ways (and the possibility of risk aversion can also be used to modify the analysis), of which the simplest is to regard it as equal to the fraction of the labor force who are employed.

There can be a number of outcomes, depending on the precise specification of the model. Open urban unemployment might occur if the basic relationships are as sketched above. An alternative might be that persons in the urban area are employed in an 'informal', presumably service or small-scale industry, sector while attempting to obtain high-wage jobs. In that event, there would be less open unemployment, but a significant compensation differential between those working in enterprises subject to the wage and employment regulations and those employed in the informal sector. There would also, of course, be observable differences in the behavior of profit-maximizing employers in the informal and formal sector.

For purposes of understanding the relationship between employment and trade, there are several important conclusions that arise from this. First, if earnings do not more or less appropriately reflect trade-offs and relative scarcity values of different types of labor, the observed distortion is more likely to be a consequence of government intervention than it is of inherent 'market failure'. Thus, in so far as one wants to analyze the consequence of distortions on the functioning of international trade, one can do so through modeling the various types of labor-market intervention sketched out above.

Second, while there is every reason to believe that developing countries are relatively well endowed with unskilled labor and, therefore, have a comparative advantage in the production of goods that use unskilled labor relatively intensively, it does not follow that governments must intervene to achieve an efficient trade pattern. Close inspection of models that generate an 'unlimited labor supply' suggests that the social opportunity cost (in terms of utility) of labor is likely to be close to the price at which workers are willing to migrate and to offer their services in the labor market.

Third, in so far as there is reason for concern with employment in developing countries, it arises either because the available income-earning opportunities generate very small income streams or because of Harris–Todaro-type unemployment. The latter has very different welfare implications from those that would arise if there were no alternative income stream: indeed, a key question is why some should have high-income jobs at the expense of others, and one policy that would reduce unemployment would be to lower wages in the high-wage sector. If concern is with the low incomes that are associated with existing employment opportunities (which is where the social and developmental issue surely lies), then the key policy question is how to shift the demand for labor upward. In the presence of rapid growth of the population and labor force, as is happening in many developing countries, the absence of a sufficiently rapid upward shift may indeed mean even lower earnings for the labor force in the future. It is primarily with regard to this question that the issue of the link between trade and employment is considered in the next section.

It should first be noted, however, that in the presence of Harris–Todaro conditions, it is at least possible that an upward shift in the demand for labor may result in greater unemployment. Suppose, for example, the 'stark' version of the model in which rural workers migrate whenever the expected wage, defined as equal to one minus the unemployment rate times the actual urban wage, equals or exceeds the rural wage. For given rural conditions, an upward shift in the demand for urban labor could conceivably induce the migration of enough rural workers so that both urban employment and urban unemployment increased. If such circumstances obtained, urban unemployment would most effectively be reduced by lowering the urban wage; second-best policy might well be to subsidize rural employment; if all else failed, downward shifts in the demand for labor might accomplish some reduction. In what follows, this possibility will be ignored, although the ramifications (via trade flows) of government-induced wage-setting – above levels that would prevail in the absence of intervention – will be considered.

6.3   TRADE AND EMPLOYMENT IN DEVELOPING COUNTRIES

The simple Heckscher–Ohlin model of international trade essentially posits that labor-abundant countries will have a comparative advantage in, and net exports of, labor-intensive goods. This would happen because a well-functioning factor market would ensure that lower wages in labor-abundant countries would render production costs for relatively labor-using commodities lower than in more capital-abundant countries.[4] Thus, it is a model based on the assumption that factor markets function reasonably well.

Conceptually, there are several ways in which trade policies and labor-market intervention could singly or through interactions affect the rate at which the demand for unskilled labor shifts upward. First, there is considerable empirical evidence that, in the long run, choice of trade policy significantly affects the rate of economic growth. Second, if there are systematic differences in choice of technique between import-competing and exportable industries, then alternative trade regimes can affect demand for labor shifting the composition of output. Third, the trade regime may affect the incentives of choice of particular techniques within given economic activities. Finally, regulations in the labor market may affect the quantity of labor demanded through a variety of channels, including especially their impact on the volume and composition of international trade under any particular trade regime.

In this section, these four distinct avenues of impact and interaction are addressed. The first covers the relationship between trade strategies and overall growth rates which are, after all, major determinants of the demand for labor. The second surveys the available evidence corroborating the basic Heckscher–Ohlin–Samuelson (HOS) model with respect to developing countries. The third covers the impact of trade regimes on the substitution of capital for labor. Finally, the fourth turns to the predictions that emanate from the HOS model if the link between labor abundance and low wages is broken because of Harris–Todaro or other mechanisms, and the empirical support for such predictions. This last question is the one about which there is least empirical evidence to date, and centers on the extent to which labor-market regulation may have choked off potential trade for developing countries.[5]

6.3.1   Alternative Trade Strategies and Growth

There is no need for in-depth analysis to recognize that if there are significant differences in overall rates of economic growth which arise because of differences in trade strategies, that in itself will very likely be the predominant effect of choice of trade strategy on the rate of growth of demand for labor. It would require some very peculiar shifts in the composition of output away from labor-using activities in order for this not to follow, and, in practice, some 50–60 per cent of output growth originates in domestic demand even in highly open, outer-oriented economies.[6]

However, there is little in standard trade theory that predicts any difference in growth rates between a highly restrictive trade regime and an open one, once the static losses associated with a restrictive trade regime have been incurred. One can point to a predicted higher ICOR under an inner-oriented trade regime, and suggest that, for a given investment rate, this would affect the observed growth rate, as noted earlier. Moreover, in so far as the rate of return on investment was higher under an outer-oriented trade regime, savings might rise; theory, however, suggests that for a labor-abundant country, the rate of return on capital might be higher under a restrictive trade regime, and, in any event if capital is internationally mobile, the rate of saving need not equal the rate of investment.

Empirically, however, the available evidence suggests that the impact on growth may be much stronger than consideration of these links alone would indicate. Several cross-country studies (including Balassa, 1978; Krueger, 1978; and Michaely, 1977) have all suggested a strong link: even for sub-Saharan Africa in the 1970s, Balassa found a strong positive effect on growth of less restrictive trade regimes. Direct contrasts of countries' performance with alternative strategies' all suggest very strong growth effects of alternative trade strategies, as does direct observation of differences in growth rates.

Comparison of observed ICORs also leads to the same conclusion: Balassa reports ICORs of 1.8 for Singapore, 2.1 in Korea, and 2.4 in Taiwan over the 1960–73 period as a whole, compared to 5.5 in Chile, 9.1 in Uruguay, and 5.7 in India. He also notes that the Brazilian ICOR fell from 3.8 in the 1960–6 period – a period of very high rates of protection to domestic industry – to 2.1 over the 1966–73 period, when the real exchange rate was realigned, protectionist barriers were sharply reduced, and exports grew rapidly.

Thus, there can be little question that there is generally more rapid overall growth when exports are growing more rapidly, and there is ample evidence (see Balassa, 1985, for a review) that exports grow more rapidly when regimes are more outer-oriented. However, if this were the only link between trade strategies and employment, it is not obvious that any separate analysis of trade as it affects employment would be required; the effect of more rapid growth of output on employment would be no different because the origin of more rapid growth was trade, than it would be if it were, for example, a set of macroeconomic policies more conducive to rational resource allocation.

6.3.2   Factor Intensity of Exports and Imports

The HOS model of trade posits a straightforward linkage between the degree of protection and factor proportions: the comparative advantage of a country with a relatively large endowment of unskilled labor will lie in exporting labor-intensive goods and importing relatively capital-intensive ones.[8] Indeed, it would be highly likely that some goods would not be produced domestically at all under free trade, if the proportions in which inputs were used were too different from the country's factor endowment. One would expect, under free trade, to observe a reasonably similar factor intensity of all goods produced domestically.

For very labor-abundant countries, protection could induce positive production levels of more capital-intensive goods that would not be produced at free trade. Hence, quite clearly, with protection it would be expected that, for labor-abundant countries, capital intensity of protected industries would be greater than that of exportables (and of import-competing industries that would be able to remain competitively in production at free trade). Hence, a decision to move from a more protected trade regime to a more open trade regime would imply a shifting commodity composition of output toward more labor-using activities, and this would shift the demand for labor outward.

Both of these hypotheses – a similarity of input proportions between non-protected import-competing and exportable industries, and a greater labor intensity of exportable than of protected import-competing industries – have been borne out by those empirical studies that have investigated the issue. In the National Bureau of Economic Research (NBER) project on Alternative Trade Strategies and Employment, the labor employed per unit of domestic value added (DVA) was greater in exportables than in import-competing industries in all countries but Chile (where intra-Latin American trade dominated); the ratio of labor inputs in exportables to import–competing industries was in excess of 2:1 for Brazil, Indonesia, and Thailand (see Krueger, 1983, p. 96). When labor inputs were disaggregated into the skilled components, the contrasts became even stronger, with exportables using more unskilled labor than protected import-competing industries for all countries for which the data were available (see Krueger, 1983, Table 6.1).

According to Carvalho and Haddad (1981), contrasts of the commodity composition of trade before and after Brazil's shift in trade strategy in the late 1960s showed a marked increase in labor intensity. They estimated the factor inputs per unit of output in exportable and import–competing industries for each year from 1967 to 1974, a period during which Brazil liberalized her trade regime substantially. These estimates were based on the assumption of fixed input–output coefficients for each activity, and thus ignored any substitution that may have taken place during this period. The shifting commodity mix of exports resulting from increased incentives to export is to have led to an increase in workers per unit of output from about 20–22 at the beginning of the period to 28–29 at the end, while the labor inputs per unit of output in import competing industries were unchanged (Carvalho and Haddad, 1981, p. 53). This would suggest that a one percentage point increase in the share of exports in GNP would result in an upward shift in the demand for labor of about one-third of a percentage point. Of course, in well-functioning labor markets, this entire shift would be offset by substitution of capital for labor and higher wages, but that does not diminish its importance. The effect would be to increase the wage rate for unskilled labor.

For Korea, the shift to an outer-oriented strategy also had a pronounced impact on the labor market. The labor intensity of Korea's exports rose markedly over the eight years following the shift to an outer-oriented trade strategy, 1960–8 (see Westphal and Kim, 1977). Non-farm employment is estimated to have risen from 2.15 million in 1960 to 4.63 million in 1970, during which time real wages rose by 74 per cent (see Krueger, 1987, Table 9). How much of this increase was attributable to the 'mix' effect reported in the Westphal–Kim numbers, and how much was the result of more rapid growth, remains an open question.

There is, thus, a reasonable amount of evidence that the orientation of the trade regime significantly affects the demand for labor; whether the 'mix' effect can result in a 25 per cent or 100 per cent increase in the number of employees firms wish to hire at a given wage remains, however, an open question.

6.3.3   Impact of the Trade Regime on Relative Factor Prices and Substitution between Factors

There are a number of mechanisms through which trade policy affects relative factor prices and the choice of technique within activities in developing countries. First and foremost, to the extent that trade strategy shifts the composition of output, it undoubtedly affects factor prices directly. In import-substitution regimes where new investment is directed into skilled-labor and capital-intensive activities, there is the standard trade-theoretic presumption that the relative prices and costs of these scarce factors of production would be driven up. This would imply, if uniform factor payments prevailed for all activities, that the mix of activities was more capital- and skill-intensive than it would be in the absence of protection, but all activities would substitute unskilled labor (whose relative wage would be lower) for scarce capital.[9]

Such a change in factor prices would thus affect the choice of input proportions for all activities, and would follow directly from the altered composition of output. Little further can be said beyond the previous discussion. There are, however, ways in which the trade regime can affect relative prices confronting producers differentially. Because many capital goods are imported, the most significant effect probably comes about through the impact of the trade regime on the relative price and availability of foreign exchange for the purchase of imported capital equipment.

This effect arises because protectionist trade regimes usually have two opposite impacts. On the one hand, because they discourage exports, there is excess demand for imports (at an overvalued exchange rate). Consequently, foreign exchange is allocated among competing claimants. Although governments typically accord 'priority' to capital-goods imports, not all applications for foreign exchange can be approved. The firms receiving approvals have access to imported capital goods at prices well below the opportunity cost of scarce foreign exchange, while other firms are unable to import legally or, if they can obtain imported capital goods, they do so at 'resale' prices. In either case, the end result is that there are two distinct groups of producers, one confronted for most practical purposes with relatively low prices for capital goods and another group confronted with much higher prices.[10]

The profitability of employing cheap goods increases still further if those with licenses can overinvoice their imports and sell the excess foreign exchange on the black market.

In many countries, the differential in capital costs arises between large-scale firms and smaller ones, although in some cases it can arise between public sector enterprises and private firms. For three countries included in the NBER project on Alternative Trade Strategies and Employment – Chile, Pakistan, and Tunisia – the cost of capital was estimated to have been reduced by more than 30 per cent by the trade regime,[11] at least for those producers with access to imports at the low prices.

The substitution that occurs in response to these changes in relative costs of employing different factors has by now been well documented. Behrman's (1982) estimates, covering 1,723 observations from 27 three-digit industries for 70 countries over the 1967–73 period provided strong support to earlier work, all of which found elasticities of substitution near unity. Behrman's (1982, p. 186) conclusion was that:

> my estimates provide strong support for an elasticity of substitution between capital and labor across industrial sectors and across countries near the Cobb–Douglas value of 1.0. This result is quite robust under the alternative specifications that I consider with a single caveat about the puzzling role of real per capita GNP.[12]

One other aspect of trade regimes and the impact on factor usage deserves note. Lipsey *et al.* (1982) examined the behavior of multinational firms, and their choice of location, product, and technique across countries. They found a systematic tendency of samples of both Swedish and American multinationals to have more fixed assets per worker in their home countries, and to locate more labor-intensive activities in low-wage countries. However, they found that the strongest substitution effect resulted from a shifting of factor proportions in response of relative factor prices (Lipsey *et al.*, 1982, pp. 252–3). This raises interesting questions as to the extent to which the trade regime, or domestic wage legislation, induces substitution of labor in one country for that in another. As will be discussed further below, one of the interesting and difficult-to-research questions is the extent to which the effects of wage restrictions may be felt through the failure of activities to locate, or develop, in countries with highly restrictive policies.

6.3.4   The Impact of Labor-Market Distortions on Trade

Thus far, attention has focused on the effect of the trade regime on factor markets and employment. Yet, there is another question which may be even more important, on which considerably less empirical research has been done. It focuses upon the impact of labor-market regulations and restrictions on the potential for employment under a given trade regime. In its baldest form, the hypothesis would be that labor-market interventions can and have choked off export growth, even under trade regimes that are not highly restrictionist.

To a point, theory is fairly clear. Brecher, Helpman, Jones, Magee and others have developed models of trade under the assumption that a factor-market distortion prevails.[13] It might be a legislated or union-imposed real wage rate throughout the economy at a level higher than was consistent with full employment; it might be such a wage restriction (or its equivalent in terms of job security and fringe benefits) applicable to the 'formal' sector.

In the theoretical literature, it has been demonstrated that, in the presence of these sorts of rigidities, almost anything can happen. In particular, the 'wrong' good, i.e. the good that would be imported under an efficient allocation of resources, might be exported; the commodity that would be 'labor-intensive' when identical factor prices confronted producers in both sectors could be 'capital-intensive' if a sufficiently higher wage prevailed than in the rest of the economy; the 'right commodity' might be exported but with the 'wrong' factor proportions, and there might be open unemployment.

There are also important links between the nominal exchange rate and the real wage. It can be argued that, in some countries, a depreciation of the nominal exchange rate is effective precisely because it lowers the real wage, at least in terms of traded goods. Turning that proposition around, an overvalued exchange rate in a labor-abundant country may make the real wage sufficiently high to reduce or wipe out comparative advantage in labor-intensive industries, and devaluation may in effect be an instrument for lowering the real wage. Even further complexities are introduced if wages are indexed in terms of domestic currency in highly open economies.[14]

From all of this, it is a plausible hypothesis that rapid growth in demand for unskilled labor will occur when the labor market is permitted to function fairly freely in the context of a reasonably open trade regime and a realistic exchange rate. For, if nominal wages were not artificially pegged at an unrealistic level, the prevailing nominal exchange rate would presumably then be reflected in the demand for labor. The converse hypothesis would then also follow: in economies where wages are, through whatever mechanism, held at levels above those that are consistent with their factor endowments, exports would be smaller in absolute value and as a share of GNP than they would be in the context of a well-functioning labor market.

Evidence already cited provides some tentative support for these hypotheses: the Lipsey *et al.* (1982) analysis suggested that multinationals tend, in part, to choose location based on labor costs; and there does not appear to be any instance of rapid growth in a country with an outer-oriented trade regime and labor-market interventions which effectively maintains wages at high levels.

But, relative to the possible quantitative importance of this effect, surprisingly little research has been done. Some of the reasons why are obvious: an investigator would have carefully to sort out those real wage increases that were endogenous to a growth process (such as, presumably, those in Korea) from those that were imposed upon an economy through regulation; simple examination of legislation and regulations does not suffice to indicate effective intervention, as minimum-wage legislation may be set below the prevailing market rate and/or not enforced; in addition, one would have to estimate deviations from 'natural' trade levels, which clearly differ for a variety of reasons including natural-resource endowment; and any test would presumably have to be carried out across countries. Furthermore, there appear to be no reliable indicators of real wage levels for unskilled workers on a comparable basis among developing countries.

None the less, the hypothesis that labor-market interventions that drive up the real wage may have their largest effect through their impact on export performance is one that is appealing and deserves a great deal more attention than it has so far received. For exporting is a highly visible activity. While it is conceivable that middlemen might export merchandise after purchasing goods produced in the informal sector (not subject to regulations resulting in high labor costs), this does not seem likely. The demands of the international market for uniformity, large-scale shipments, and timely delivery (see Morawetz 1980) all imply that the scope for substantial growth of exports based on informal sector production is probably highly limited.

If this is so, regulations raising labor costs to the formal sector would discourage exports even in the presence of a low-wage informal sector. Yet this proposition has not been examined empirically in any systematic way, despite its potential importance.

Reasons for the failure to do so are obvious: a meaningful measure of the labor-costs distortion and a measure of the 'deviation of exports' from what they would have been in the absence of the distortion are both needed. Neither measure is one for which the appropriate analytical construct has an obvious empirical measure.

Yet the potential effects of labor-market interventions are significant enough to warrant any effort, no matter how bold, to assess the quantitative significance of the phenomenon. The following discussion reports on the author's effort to tab at least a preliminary (if heroic) cut at the issue, in the hope that it might stimulate others to devise better tests.

A first problem is how to measure the wage distortion. There are obvious difficulties of across-country measures, yet natural within-country measures (such as the ratio of urban and rural per capita incomes or of average wages in industry relative to those in services) that are influenced by a host of variables other than distortions, and in any event, data are not readily available.

An alternative method, and one used here is to hypothesize that the shadow price of unskilled labor of the sort potentially employed in industries producing labor-intensive importables is positively and reasonably closely correlated with a country's per capita income, and that significant deviations of that wage rate relative to per capita income in a formal sector activity are reflections of labor-market interventions.

Tourist services, such as luxury hotels and restaurants, are usually visible enough to be in the covered sector, and they typically can attract international capital and management, and are reasonably intensive in the employment of unskilled labor.

Differences in the costs of these services across countries ought, therefore, to reflect primarily differences in labor costs, although other factors (such as site value in large cities) surely enter in.

A good measure of the cost of the tourist services is available in the United Nations per diem allowance in US dollars in capital cities. The advantage of that measure is its availability. There is a presumption that the per diem allowance reflects to some extent the cost of hotel services, restaurants, and taxis, all of which are presumed to be in some measure home goods and to be somewhat labor-intensive. Its major advantage as an indicator is that it is estimated across countries with a similar methodology and that it is changed frequently in response to changing conditions. To be sure, one could always argue that the costs of providing intercontinental hotel services in a very low-income country are likely to be high because of high transport costs or the remoteness of the country, and that cannot be ruled out. None the less, one could expect it to reflect to a large extent changes in the realism of the exchange rate, an important component of the real wage for tradable goods.

Taking the UN per diem in dollars relative to estimated per capita income in dollars was therefore used as a proxy for the distortion of the real wage; I shall refer to this variable as the 'wage proxy'. A higher ratio is presumed to reflect a real wage higher than would be warranted under competitive conditions.

The remaining question is the relevant variable to use for a country's exports relative to their 'natural' level. Here again, specification of a full-scale model of the determinants of the share of exports in trade was far beyond the scope of this chapter: the variable used, in fact, was exports per capita. The regression thus estimated was

$$X/P = a + b(UN/y) \tag{6.1}$$

where X is dollar value of exports, P population, UN the dollar per diem, and y per capita income. Data were gathered for 33 countries. Estimates were made for 1968, 1973, 1978, and 1983. The results are reported in Table 6.1. Astonishingly, all coefficients are signficant at the 95 per cent level and have the expected sign.[15]

As can be seen, the coefficient on the wage proxy was surprisingly stable over all four years. The implied elasticity of exports with respect to the wage proxy was close to -0.5 in all estimates. If the proxy accurately reflected real wage movements relative to per capita GNP and if the relationship between the real wage and real income in an efficient development process were truly linear, this elasticity would imply that a 1 per cent increase in the real wage (in the formal sector) relative to GNP would result in a reduction of exports of 0.5 per cent. Given the

Table 6.1 Estimated relationship between exports and real wages

	1968	1973	1978	1983
a	308.25	282.64	319.29	365.97
	(5.69)	(5.85)	(5.99)	(6.13)
b	−1,261.67	−1,106.84	−1,201.13	−1,577.63
	(−2.89)	(−2.60)	(−2.63)	(−3.20)
Implied elasticity				
at mean	−0.543	−0.498	−0.422	−0.591
R^2	0.20	0.17	0.17	0.24

Note: Countries included are Argentina; Bolivia; Brazil; Chile; Colombia; Congo; Costa Rica; Ecuador; Egypt; Guatemala; India; Indonesia; Jamaica; Japan; Kenya; Korea; Mauritius; Mexico; Nigeria; Pakistan; Paraguay; Peru; Philippines; Senegal; Sri Lanka; Thailand; Tunisia; Turkey; United States; Uruguay; Venezuela; Yugoslavia; and Zambia.

tenuous nature of the numbers, it would require too great a stretch of credulity to attempt to complete the specification of how such a reduction would feed through to employment (would resources be shifted to import-competing industries or would the growth of the urban sector be lower and hence more persons remain in rural areas? what would be the effect of a reduced export growth rate on overall growth?). None the less, the estimates are consistent with the hypothesis that the effects of labor-market interventions on employment may originate in significant part from their effects on a country's ability to compete in export markets.

Given the weaknesses of the data, little weight should be placed on the order of magnitude implied by these estimates. On the other hand, the same qualifications make the fact that the estimates appear to reveal a strong relationship all the more astonishing. The conclusion should not be that there is a strong and well-understood link, but that it is conceivable that labor-market interventions may have far greater costs than are revealed in a closed economy framework and that research on this relationship is urgently needed.

6.4   AGENDA FOR RESEARCH

The research agenda is large and challenging. Questions range from the effects of trade restrictions on industry structure and competition to the 'normal' levels of wages as functions of per capita income levels and other variables. Even such topics as differences in the industrial concentration, the size distribution of firms (and changes over time), and the characteristics of the split (if any) between the formal and informal sectors under open and restrictive trade regimes have hardly been touched.

However, if one were to attempt to identify priorities, an effort to ascertain empirical regularities in relations between urban and rural per capita incomes, between rural per capita incomes and unskilled wages, and other key variables would be very high on the list. This would be a first step, at least, toward estimating the effects of government regulations on wages. They would provide at least some presumptive evidence against which one might attempt to identify countries where these regulations have been effective in altering real wage levels.

There is no way that the underlying question can be definitively answered, but alternative approaches should all prove useful. What is surprising is the degree of our ignorance surrounding wage and labor-market issues in a comparative context. Knowledge, even of orders of magnitude, would help narrow the range of uncertainty. What empirical regularities are there between the evolution of real wages and that of per capita income? What meaningful indicators are there, if any, of the extent to which policy interventions affect the real wage? Can ratios of urban to rural incomes, or of average manufacturing wage to per capita income, be meaningfully used? Any data on these issues, across countries, would reduce our ignorance, but they would over time require considerable refinement: to what extent are there differences in experience, education, skill, and other variables between the labor forces in different countries, and especially those entering the urban labor force and seeking essentially unskilled employment in manufacturing? To what extent do social insurance regulations, provisions preventing the discharge of workers, and so on, affect the real cost of labor as perceived by employers? And, above all, to what extent do any of these phenomena affect the real wage relative to that prevailing in a well-functioning labor market?

A second line of research would focus on the effects of effective labor-market regulation. In part, this might build on the first, but there are undoubtedly useful pieces of information that might be assembled independently. A major difficulty is that, as is always the case with empirical work on international trade, theory predicts that the effect of intervention may well be to prevent the emergence or growth of particular lines of activity. It is exceptionally difficult to estimate what is not there. Nevertheless, there are enough steps in the linkage between labor-market intervention and employment levels that one would expect that research could improve understanding of these links one by one.

If, as trade theory and empirical evidence suggest, the exportation of labor-intensive products is a substitute for the movement of factors of production internationally, trade should be a major mechanism for permitting a rapid expansion of employment, and ultimately, real wages. To the extent that government regulation of the labor market then precludes the full exploitation of the opportunities trade might offer for employment growth, the costs would be significantly higher than a closed-economy model would suggest. And yet, to date, there is little if any research that guides us at all with regard to possible orders of magnitude. Surely, historical experience with shifts in trade regime, the behavior of multinationals, comparative analysis across countries, and/or other techniques can provide a better indication of possible orders of magnitude of these effects than we now have.

The third area for research centers upon the effects of differences in trade orientation on domestic economic variables. As indicated in the second section, there is reason to believe that competitive pressures are more likely to be felt in an outer-oriented trade regime than in a highly protectionist one. To what extent are there differences in industry structure between countries with outer-oriented trade regimes and those with protectionist ones? What differences are there in industry behavior, depending on structure? The question is, of course, of general interest and relates to a variety of areas in addition to the trade–employment linkage. Broader issues cover such phenomena as productivity growth (and the reasons for the sharp differences in growth rates under alternative regimes), differentials and reasons for them. Even with regard to the trade and employment issue, however, questions arise concerning the extent to which protected producers base their decisions to employ unskilled labor, skilled labor, and capital on different factors than do producers expecting to compete in international markets. The degree to which unions can effectively influence the wage might also be expected to differ significantly under alternative trade regimes. Indeed, the environment under the two regimes is so different that one would expect significant differences in behavior in a wide variety of ways. Yet, at the microeconomic level, these questions have barely been touched upon.

An honest summary will convince most of the urgency of the need for further research: given the present state of knowledge, it is equally plausible that labor-market restrictions are a major cause of the failure of exports to grow even under inner-oriented regimes, or that they are only negligibly effective in affecting trade patterns, regardless of the nature of the trade regime. Theory suggests that there is some degree of restriction of labor markets sufficient to reduce significantly the potential for trade. However, whether labor markets in developing countries ever are restricted to a degree sufficient to impede trade potential is an open question.

NOTES

1. To be sure, it was widely recognized that there would be considerable demand for imports in the development process. It was assumed that this demand could be met out of earnings from primary commodity exports (which, to be sure, would grow slowly) and capital inflows. Increases in demand would then largely be satisfied by import substitution.

2. There are also those who believe that the success was the outcome of a broad set of policy changes, and that the rapid growth of exports, like that of other key variables, was the result of policy changes other than the trade orientation. While it is certainly true that an outer-oriented trade strategy alone was not responsible for the entire increment in the growth rate which resulted, it is hard to see how the shift in trade orientation could not have been a significant, and probably necessary, contributory factor.

3. To be sure, resale is legal in some regimes, and is a common practice in some cases even where it is not legal. Even then, of course, the seller of the imports will charge the premium-inclusive price. Further, ability to deal with officials in obtaining licenses, etc., is at least as important a determinant of costs as is any other managerial ability with respect to cost minimization. Low-cost operation under protection and an import-licensing regime which confers quasi-monopoly positions probably requires a very different set of skills than managing to compete on the international market when bureaucratic red tape regarding operations is minimal.

4. I ignore the possibility of factor-price equalization; in the Heckscher–Ohlin–Samuelson (HOS) model, at free trade, either countries specialize in producing a range of goods which are 'near' to their endowments or there is factor-price equalization across countries. Even in that instance, the 'net factor export' embodied in the country's trade pattern would be related to the factor endowment.

5. A question that is not addressed here is the role that human capital plays in labor markets and how the HOS model may be amended to take into account that 'third' factor of production. Alternative treatments that have been attempted in the literature include Kenen (1965), in which investible resources are allocated between 'raw land' and 'raw labor' to increase their productivity, and three-factor models of trade, such as that of Jones (1971). See also Krueger (1977) for a discussion. Casual empiricism suggests that countries with high per capita incomes typically have more physical and more human capital per person than do countries with lower per capita incomes. For that reason, there is a strong presumption for developing countries that comparative advantage would lie in production of goods with a relatively high share of unskilled labor; for trade among developed countries, the question of relative abundance of physical and human capital might be more important.

6. See Kim and Roemer (1979) for estimates for Korea. They estimate that, even during the years of rapid export expansion from 1963 to 1973, domestic demand expansion accounted for about 54.7 per cent of total output growth, compared to 43.7 per cent of exports.

7. See Banerji and Riedel (1980) contrasting India and Taiwan. Shifts toward labor-intensive activities contributed to industrial employment growth of 10 per cent annually in Taiwan while shifts toward more capital-intensive activities led to slower employment growth of 3 per cent in India, despite

more rapid productivity growth in Taiwan. See also Fields (1984), Krueger (1987), and Myint (1985).

8. The factor intensity of different commodities is defined by positing the cost-minimizing factor usage that would occur at a particular set of prices of factor inputs, and then ranking commodities from more to less usage in terms of the ratios of inputs so derived. It is then assumed that the ranking would be the same for all possible sets of factor-input prices. Although there was a time when trade theorists worried about the possibility of 'factor-intensity reversal', subsequent work has indicated that it is not a significant empirical phenomenon. See Leamer (1980) for a discussion of this set of issues.

9. Using detailed Colombian earnings data, T. Paul Schultz (1982) analyzed the impact of protection on earnings of workers and employers in Colombia. He concluded that a large portion of effective protection went to providing quasi-rents to both employers and workers in protected industries, with a 10 per cent increase in effective protection raising workers' wages in those industries by about 3 per cent, compared to comparable workers in non-protected industries and employers' wages by an even larger proportion (Schultz, 1982, p. 98). Schultz regarded these effects as largely income-distributional, implying that much of the effect of protection is to build in quasi-rents which then accounted for a significant portion of observed wage differentials for workers of comparable education and experience. To the extent that the quasi-rent effect of trade regimes is important, that would suggest that the income distribution becomes more unequal under an inward-looking strategy, but that effect would not influence the demand for labor per se.

10. The differential in relative factor prices confronting different producers is increased still further when one group is subject to various labor-market regulations of the type discussed in Section 6.2, while another group is able to avoid observing them and also ineligible for easy access to import licenses. Credit rationing, and access to credit, may still further increase the differential. Here, focus is only on the impact to the trade regime on relative factor prices.

11. See Krueger (1983, Table 7.1). For Pakistan, Guisinger (1981) estimated that the rental cost of capital equipment for those with access to government privileges was about one-fourth what it would have been in a unified market. This included the implicit subsidy on import licenses, credit rationing, and tax incentives to investors.

12. See also the study by Corbo and Meller (1981) which was based on detailed Chilean data. They estimated translog production functions but found that the Cobb–Douglas specification was 'a satisfactory representation of technology' in a surprisingly high proportion of cases (p. 209).

13. Because the HOS model of trade assumes only two factors of production, it is the wage–rental ratio that affects factor substitution and product mix in the standard trade theoretic model. The ratio changes in the same way, regardless of whether the real wage rate rises (through labor-market intervention or for other reasons), or whether the real rental cost of capital falls (for example, through the implicit subsidization of capital goods imports discussed previously). In many developing countries, labor-market regulations drive up the real wage at the same time as credit rationing at artificially low interest rates, overvaluation of the currency with low

nominal tariffs on capital goods imports, and the tax treatment of investment all serve to lower the real cost of employing capital. Since all of
these effects work in the same direction, the term 'factor-market distortion'
is often used more or less interchangeably with terms connoting the maintenance of an artificially high real wage; for purposes of analyzing the
impact of labor-market interventions on trade expansion, however, it is
only the labor-market regulations that would appear to matter.

14. For an analysis of one highly open economy with full wage indexation, see
Garnaut and Baxter (1984).

15. Several other variants were estimated using the same basic data, including
rates of change of exports and wages, and manufactured exports, rather
than total exports. The results were not significant, often of the inappropriate sign, and the coefficients varied widely between the five-year
intervals.

REFERENCES

Baer, Werner and Michel Herve (1966). 'Employment and Industrialization in
Developing Countries', *Quarterly Journal of Economics*, vol. 80, no. 1,
pp. 88–107.

Balassa, Bela (1978). 'Export Incentives and Export Performance in Developing
Countries: A Comparative Analysis', *Weltwirtschaftliches Archiv*, vol. 1,
pp. 24–61.

Balassa, Bela (1985). 'Outward Orientation', Development Research Department discussion paper no. 148, World Bank, July.

Banerji, R. and James Riedel (1980). 'Industrial Employment Expansion under
Alternative Trade Strategies: the Case of India and Taiwan: 1950–70',
Journal of Development Economics, vol. 7, pp. 567–77.

Behrman, J.R. (1982). 'Country and Sectoral Variations in Manufacturing
Elasticities of Substitution Between Capital and Labor' In A.O. Krueger
(ed.), *Trade and Employment in Developing Countries*. Chicago: Chicago
University Press, vol. 2, pp. 159–92.

Bell, Clive and T.N. Srinivasan (1985). 'Agricultural Credit Market in Punjab:
Segmentation, Rationing, and Spillover', Development Research Department Working Paper no. 7, World Bank, June.

Berry, A. and R.H. Sabot (1978). 'Labour Market Performance in Developing
Countries: A Survey', *World Development*, vol. 6, pp. 1199–1242.

Bhagwati, Jagdish (1978). *Foreign Trade Regimes and Economic Development:
Anatomy and Consequences of Exchange Control Regimes*. Cambridge,
Mass.: Ballinger Press for the National Bureau of Economic Research.

Binswanger, Hans P. and Rosenzweig, Mark R. (1984). *Contractual Arrangements, Employment, and Wages in Rural Labor Markets in Asia*. New Haven,
CT: Yale University Press.

Brecher, Richard M. (1974). 'Minimum Wage Rates and the pure Theory of
International Trade'. *Quarterly Journal of Economics*, vol. 8, pp. 96–116.

Carvalho, Jose L. and Claudio Haddad (1981). 'Foreign Trade Strategies and
Employment in Brazil' in A.O. Krueger *et al.* (eds), *Trade and Employment
in Developing Countries*, vol. 1. Chicago: University of Chicago Press.

Corbo, V. and P. Meller (1981). 'Alternative Trade Strategies and Employment

Implications: Chile' in A.O. Krueger *et al.* (eds), *Trade and Employment in Developing Countries*, Vol. 2. Chicago: Chicago University Press, pp. 83–134.

Corbo, Vittorio and José Miguel Sánchez (1985). 'Adjustments by Industrial Firms in Chile during 1974–82' in Vittorio Corbo and Jaime de Melo (eds), *Scrambling for Survival: How Firms Adjusted to the Recent Reforms in Argentina, Chile and Uruguay*. Washington, DC: World Bank Staff Working Paper no. 764.

Díaz-Alejandro, Carlos (1976). *Foreign Trade Regimes and Economic Development: Colombia*. New York: Columbia University Press, for the National Bureau of Economic Research.

Fields, Gary S. (1984). 'Employment, Income Distribution and Economic Growth in Seven Small Open Economies', *Economic Journal*, vol 94, pp. 74–83.

Garnaut, Ross and Paul Baxter (1984). *Exchange Rate and Macro-economic Policy in Independent Papua New Guinea*. Canberra: Australian National University.

Guisinger, Stephen (1981). 'Trade Policies and Employment: The Case of Pakistan' in A.O. Krueger *et al.* (eds), *Trade and Employment in Developing Countries*. Chicago: Chicago University Press.

Hansen, Bent (1969). 'Employment and Wages in Rural Egypt', *American Economic Review*, vol. 59.

Harris, John R. and Michael Todaro (1970). 'Migration, Unemployment and Development: A Two-Sector Analysis', *American Economic Review*, vol. 60.

Helpman, Elhanan (1977). 'Nontraded Goods and Macroeconomic Policy under a Fixed Exchange Rate', *Quarterly Journal of Economics*, vol. 91, pp. 469–80.

Jones, Ronald W. (1971). 'A Three-Factor Model in Theory, Trade, and History' in Jagdish Bhagwati *et al.* (eds), *Trade, Balance of Payments, and Growth*. Amsterdam: North-Holland.

Kenen, Peter B. (1965). 'Nature, Capital and Trade', *Journal of Political Economy*, vol. 73, pp. 437–60.

Kim, Kwang Suk and Michael Roemer (1979). *Growth and Structural Transformation, Studies in the Modernization of the Republic of Korea, 1945–75*. Cambridge, MA: Harvard University Press.

Krueger, Anne O. (1972). 'Rates of Return to Turkish Higher Education', *Journal of Human Resources*, Autumn.

Krueger, Anne O. (1977). *Growth, Distortions, and Patterns of Trade among Many Countries*. Princeton, NJ: Princeton Studies in International Finance no. 40 (see also Chapter 2 of this volume).

Krueger, Anne O. (1978). *Foreign Trade Regimes and Economic Development: Liberalization Attempts and Consequences*. Cambridge, MA: Ballinger, for the National Bureau of Economic Research.

Krueger, Anne O. (1983). *Trade and Employment in Developing Countries: Synthesis and Conclusions*. Chicago: University of Chicago Press.

Krueger, Anne O. (1984). 'Trade Policies in Developing Countries' in Ronald W. Jones and Peter B. Kenen (eds), *Handbook of International Economics*. Amsterdam: North-Holland.

Krueger, Anne O. (1987). 'The Importance of Economic Policy in Development: Contrasts between Korea and Turkey' in Henry Kierzkowski (ed.), *Protection and Competition in International Trade*, Oxford: Basil Blackwell.

Leamer, E.E. (1980). 'The Leontief Paradox, Reconsidered', *Journal of Political Economy*, June.

Lewis, W. Arthur, (1954). 'Economic Development with Unlimited Supplies of Labour', *Manchester School*, May.

Lipsey, Robert E., Irving B. Kravis and Romualdo A. Roldan (1982). 'Do Multinational Firms Adapt Factor Proportions to Relative Factor Prices?' in Anne O. Krueger (ed.), *Trade and Employment in Developing Countries. vol. 2. Factor Supply and Substitution*. Chicago: University of Chicago Press, for the National Bureau of Economic Research, pp. 215–55.

Magee, Stephen P. (1976). *International Trade and Distortions in Factor Markets*. New York: Marcel Dekker.

Michaely, Michael (1977). 'Exports and Growth: An Empirical Investigation', *Journal of Development Economics*, vol. 4, pp. 49–53.

Morawetz, David (1974). 'Employment Implications of Industrialization in Developing Countries: A Survey', *Economic Journal*, September, pp. 491–542.

Morawetz, David (1980). *Why the Emperor's New Clothes Are Not Made in Colombia*. Washington, DC: World Bank Staff Working Paper no. 368.

Myint, Hla (1985). 'The Neoclassical Resurgence in Development Economics: Its Strength and Limitation', World Bank.

Prebisch, Raúl (1964). *Towards a New Trade Policy for Development*. New York: United Nations.

Schultz, T. Paul (1982). 'Effective Protection and the Distribution of Personal Income in Colombia' in Anne O. Krueger (ed.), *Trade and Employment in Developing Countries, Vol. 2. Factor Supply and Substitution*. Chicago: University of Chicago Press, for the National Bureau of Economic Research, pp. 83–148.

Spraos, J. (1980). 'The Statistical Debate on the Net Barrier Terms of Trade between Primary Commodities and Manufactures', *Economic Journal*.

Squire, Lyn (1981). *Employment Policy in Developing Countries: A Survey of Issues and Evidence*. Oxford: Oxford University Press.

Westphal, L.E. and Kwang Suk Kim (1977). *Industrial Policy and Development in Korea*. Washington, DC: World Bank Staff Working Paper no. 263.

7 · THE POLITICAL ECONOMY OF THE RENT-SEEKING SOCIETY

In many market-oriented economies, government restrictions upon economic activity are a pervasive fact of life. These restrictions give rise to rents of a variety of forms, and people often compete for the rents. Sometimes, such competition is perfectly legal. In other instances, rent-seeking takes other forms, such as bribery, corruption, smuggling, and black markets.

It is the purpose of this chapter to show some of the ways in which rent-seeking is competitive, and to develop a simple model of competitive rent-seeking for the important case when rents originate from quantitative restrictions upon international trade. In such a case (1) competitive rent-seeking leads to the operation of the economy inside its transformation curve; (2) the welfare loss associated with quantitative restrictions is unequivocally greater than the loss from the tariff equivalent of those quantitative restrictions; and (3) competitive rent-seeking results in a divergence between the private and social costs of certain activities. Although the analysis is general, the model has particular applicability for developing countries, where government interventions are frequently all-embracing.

Section 7.1 is concerned with the competitive nature of rent-seeking and the quantitative importance of rents for two countries, India and Turkey. In Section 7.2, a formal model of rent-seeking under quantitative restrictions on trade is developed and the propositions indicated above are established. Section 7.3 outlines some other forms of rent-seeking and suggests some implications of the analysis.

First printed in 1974. I am indebted to James M. Henderson for invaluable advice and discussion on successive drafts. Jagdish Bhagwati and John C. Hause made helpful comments on earlier drafts of this paper.

7.1   COMPETITIVE RENT-SEEKING

7.1.1   Means of Competition

When quantitative restrictions are imposed upon and effectively constrain imports, an import license is a valuable commodity. It is well known that under some circumstances, one can estimate the tariff equivalents of a set of quantitative restrictions and analyze the effects of those restrictions in the same manner as one would the tariff equivalents. In other circumstances, the resource-allocational effects of import licensing will vary, depending upon who receives the license.[1]

It has always been recognized that there are *some* costs associated with licensing: paperwork, the time spent by entrepreneurs in obtaining their licenses, the cost of the administrative apparatus necessary to issue licenses, and so on. Here, the argument is carried one step further: in many circumstances resources are devoted to competing for those licenses.

The consequences of that rent-seeking are examined below. First, however, it will be argued that rent-seeking activities are often competitive and resources are devoted to competing for rents. It is difficult, if not impossible, to find empirically observable measures of the degree to which rent-seeking is competitive. Instead, some mechanisms under which rent-seeking is almost certain to be competitive are examined. Then other cases are considered in which it is less obvious, but perhaps equally plausible, that competition results.

Consider first the results of an import-licensing mechanism when licenses for imports of intermediate goods are allocated in proportion to firms' capacities. That system is frequently used, and has been analyzed for the Indian case by Bhagwati and Desai (1970). When licenses are allocated in proportion to firms' capacities, investment in additional physical plant confers upon the investor a higher expected receipt of import licenses. Even with initial excess capacity (due to quantitative restrictions upon imports of intermediate goods), a rational entrepreneur may still expand his plant if the expected gains from the additional import licenses he will receive, divided by the cost of the investment, equal the returns on investment in other activities.[2] This behavior could be perfectly rational even if, for all entrepreneurs, the total number of import licenses will remained fixed. In fact, if imports are held constant as domestic income grows, one would expect the domestic value of a constant quantity of imports to increase over time, and hence installed capacity would increase while output remained constant. By investing in additional capacity, entrepreneurs devote resources to compete for import licenses.

A second sort of licensing mechanism frequently found in developing countries is used for imports of consumer goods. There, licenses are allocated pro rata to the applications for those licenses from importers/ wholesalers. Entry is generally free into importing/wholesaling, and firms usually have U-shaped cost curves. The result is a larger than optimal number of firms, operating on the downward-sloping portion of their cost curves, yet earning a 'normal' rate of return. Each importer/ wholesaler receives fewer imports than he would buy at existing prices in the absence of licensing, but realizes a sufficient return on those licenses he does receive to make it profitable to stay in business. In this case, competition for rents occurs through entry into the industry with smaller than optimally sized firms, and resources are used in that the same volume of imports could be efficiently distributed with fewer inputs if firms were of optimal size.

A third sort of licensing mechanism is less systematic in that government officials decide on license allocations. Competition occurs to some extent through both mechanisms already mentioned as businessmen base their decisions on expected values. But, in addition, competition can also occur through allocating resources to influencing the probability, or expected size, of license allocatioins. Some means of influencing the expected allocation – trips to the capital city, locating the firm in the capital, and so on – are straightforward. Others, including bribery, hiring relatives of officials or employing the officials themselves upon retirement, are less so. In the former case, competition occurs through choice of location, expenditure of resources upon travel, and so on. In the latter case, government officials themselves receive part of the rents.

Bribery has often been treated as a transfer payment. However, there is competition for government jobs and it is reasonable to believe that expected total remuneration is the relevant decision variable for persons deciding upon careers. Generally, entry into government service requires above average educational attainments. The human-capital literature provides evidence that choices as to how much to invest in human capital are strongly influenced by rates of return upon the investment. For a given level of educational attainment, one would expect the rate of return to be approximately equated among various lines of endeavor. Thus, if there appear to be high official-plus-unofficial incomes accruing to government officials and higher education is a prerequisite for seeking a government job, more individuals will invest in higher education. It is not necessary that government officials earn the same total income as other college graduates. All that is necessary is that there is an excess supply of persons seeking government employment, or that highly educated persons make sustained efforts to enter government services. Competition takes place through attaining the appropriate credentials for entry into government service and through accepting unemployment while making efforts to obtain appointments. Efforts to influence those in charge of making appointments, of course, just carry the argument one step further back.

To argue that competition for entry into government service is, in part, a competition for rents does not imply that all government servants accept bribes nor that they would leave government service in their absence. Successful competitors for government jobs might experience large windfall gains even at their official salaries. However, if the possibility of those gains induces others to expend time, energy, and resources

Table 7.1 Estimates of value of rents, India, 1964

Source of rent	Amount of rent (Rs million)
Public investment	365
Imports	10,271
Controlled commodities	3,000
Credit rationing	407
Railways	602
Total	14,645

Sources:
1) Public investment: Santhanam Committee (1964, pp. 11–12), placed the loss in public investment at *at least* 5 per cent of investment. That figure was multiplied by the average annual public investment in the *Third Five Year Plan* (Government of India, 1961)

2) Imports: Santhanam Committee (1964, p. 18) stated that import licenses were worth 100 to 500 per cent of their face value. Seventy-five per cent of the value of 1964 imports was used here as a conservative estimate.

3) Controlled commodities: These commodities include steel, cement, coal, passenger cars, scooters, food, and other price- and/or distribution-controlled commodities, as well as foreign exchange used for illegal imports and other unrecorded transactions. The figure is the lower bound estimate given by Monteiro (1966, p. 60). Monteiro puts the upper bound estimate at Rs 30,000 billion, although he rejects the figure on the (dubious) ground that notes in circulation are less than that sum.

4) Credit rationing: The bank rate in 1964 was 6 per cent; Rs 20.3 billion of loans were outstanding. It is assumed that *at least* an 8 per cent interest rate would have been required to clear the market, and that 3 per cent of bank loans outstanding would be equivalent to the present value of new loans at 5 per cent. Data source: Reserve Bank of India (1967–8, Tables 534 and 554).

5) Railways: Monteiro (1966, p. 45) cites commissions of 20 per cent on railway purchases, and extra-official fees of Rs 0.15 per wagon and Rs 1.4 per 100 maunds loaded. These figures were multiplied by the 1964 traffic volume; 203 million tons of revenue-paying traffic originated in that year. Third Plan expenditure on railroads was Rs 13,260 million. There were 350,000 railroad goods wagons in 1964–5. If a wagon was loaded once a week, there were 17,500,000 wagons of freight. At Rs 0.15 per load, this would be Rs 2.6 million; 100 maunds equals 8,228 pounds so at 1.4 Rs per 100 maunds, Rs 69 million changed hands; if one-fifth of railroad expenditures were made in 1964–5, Rs 2,652 million was spent in 1964; at 20 per cent, this would be Rs 530 million, for a total of Rs 602 million.

in seeking entry into government services, the activity is competitive for present purposes.

In all these license-allocation cases, there are means, legal and illegal, for competing for rents. If individuals choose their activities on the basis of expected returns, rates of return on alternative activities will be equated and, in that sense, markets will be competitive.[3] In most cases, people do not perceive themselves to be rent-seekers and, generally speaking, individuals and firms do not specialize in rent seeking. Rather, rent-seeking is one part of an economic activity, such as distribution or production, and part of the firm's resources are devoted to the activity (including, of course, the hiring of expediters). The fact that rent-seeking and other economic activities are not generally conducted by separate economic entities provides the motivation for the form of the model developed below.

7.1.2   Are Rents Quantitatively Important?

Granted that rent-seeking may be highly competitive, the question remains whether rents are important. Data from two countries, India and Turkey, suggest that they are. Gunnar Myrdal (1968, p. 943) believes India may 'on the balance, be judged to have somewhat less corruption than any other country in South Asia'. None the less, it is generally believed that 'corruption' has been increasing, and that much of the blame lies with the proliferation of economic controls following independence (Santhanam Committee 1964, pp. 7–8).

Table 7.1 presents crude estimates, based on fairly conservative assumptions, of the value of rents of all sorts in 1964. One important source of rents - investment licensing - is not included for lack of any valid basis on which to estimate its value. Many smaller controls are also excluded. None the less, it is apparent from Table 7.1 that import licenses provided the largest source of rents. The total value of rents of Rs 14.6 billion contrasts with Indian national income of Rs 201 billion in 1964. At 7.3 per cent of national income, rents must be judged large relative to India's problems in attempting to raise her savings rate.

For Turkey, excellent detailed estimates of the value of import licenses in 1968 are available.[4] Data on the c.i.f. prices of individual imports, their landed cost (c.i.f. price plus all duties, taxes, and landing charges), and wholesale prices were collected for a sizeable sample of commodities representing about 10 per cent of total imports in 1968. The c.i.f. value of imports in the sample was TL 547 million and the landed cost of the imports was TL 1,443 million. The value at the wholesale level of these same imports was TL 3,568 million. Of course, wholesalers incur some handling, storage, and transport costs. The question, therefore, is the amount that can be attributed to normal wholesaling costs. If one assumes that a 50 per cent mark-up would be adequate, then the value of import licenses was TL 1,404 million, or almost three times the c.i.f. value of imports. Imports in 1968 were recorded (c.i.f.) as 6 per cent of national income. On the basis of Aker's data, this would imply that rents from import licenses in Turkey in 1968 were about 15 per cent of GNP.

Both the Indian and the Turkish estimates are necessarily somewhat rough. But they clearly indicate that the value of import licenses to the recipients was sizeable. Since means were available of competing for the licenses, it would be surprising if competition did not occur for prizes that large. We turn, therefore, to an examination of the consequences of competitive rent-seeking.

7.2 THE EFFECTS OF COMPETITIVE RENT-SEEKING

The major proposition of this chapter is that competitive rent-seeking for import licenses entails a welfare cost in addition to the welfare cost that would be incurred if the same level of imports were achieved through tariffs. The effects of tariffs upon production, trade, and welfare are well known, and attention is focused here upon the additional cost of competitive rent-seeking. A simple model is used to develop the argument. Initially, free trade is assumed. Then, a tariff or equivalent import restriction is introduced. Finally, an equal import restriction with competitive rent seeking is examined.

7.2.1 The Basic Model

Two commodities are consumed by the country under investigation: food and consumption goods. Food is produced domestically and exported. Consumption goods are imported. Distribution is a productive activity whereby food is purchased from the agricultural sector, exported, and the proceeds are used to import consumption goods which are sold in the domestic market. Labor is assumed to be the only domestic factor of production.[5] It is assumed that the country under consideration is small and cannot affect its international terms of trade. Physical units are selected so that the fixed international prices of both goods are unity.

The agricultural production function is

$$A = A(L_A) \quad A' > 0, A'' < 0 \tag{7.1}$$

where A is the output of food and L_A is the quantity of labor employed in agriculture. The sign of the second derivative reflects a diminishing marginal physical product of labor in agriculture, due, presumably, to fixity in the supply of land.

The level of distribution output, D, is defined to equal the level of consumption-goods imports, M:

$$D = M \tag{7.2}$$

One unit of distributive services entails exchanging one unit of imports for food with the agricultural sector at the domestic terms of trade, and exporting the food in exchange for imports at the international terms of trade. Constant returns to scale are assumed for the distribution activity; one unit of distribution requires k units of labor. Total labor employed in distribution, L_D, is

$$L_D = kD \tag{7.3}$$

A distribution charge of p_D per unit is added to the international price of imports:

$$p_M = 1 + p_D \tag{7.4}$$

where p_M is the domestic price of imports. The domestic price of food is assumed to equal its unit international price.[6]

Society's demand for imports depends upon the domestic price of imports and total income generated in agriculture.[7]

$$M = M(p_M, A) \tag{7.5}$$

where $\partial M/\partial p_M < 0$ and $\partial M/\partial A > 0$. Demand decreases with increases in the price of imports, and increases with increases in agricultural output (income). Equation (7.5) is derived from micro utility maximization with the assumption that farmers, distributors, and rent-seekers all have the same consumption behavior. Domestic food consumption, F, is simply the quantity not exported:

$$F = A - M \tag{7.6}$$

Since the fixed international terms of trade equal unity, food exports equal consumption goods imports.

Finally, it is assumed that the economy under consideration has a fixed labor supply, $\bar{L}$:

$$\bar{L} = L_A + L_D + L_R \tag{7.7}$$

where L_R is the quantity of labor engaged in rent-seeking.

7.2.2 Free Trade

Under free trade, there is free entry into both agriculture and distribution and competition equates the wage in the two activities:

$$A' = p_D/k \tag{7.8}$$

Equations (7.1) to (7.8) constitute the free-trade system. These eight equations contain the eight variables A, M, D, F, L_A, L_D, p_M, and p_D. Since there is no rent-seeking under free trade, $L_R \equiv 0$.

It is easily established that free trade is optimal in the sense that the domestic price ratio under free trade equals the marginal rate of transformation between food consumption and imports. The consumption possibility locus is obtained by substituting equations (7.1) and (7.7) into equation (7.6):

$$F = A(\bar{L} - kM) - M$$

The locus has a marginal rate of transformation greater than one:

$$\frac{-dF}{dM} = kA' + 1 > 1 \tag{7.9}$$

which reflects the positive distribution cost of substituting imports for food consumption. The locus is concave:

$$\frac{d^2 F}{dM^2} = k^2 A'' < 0$$

since $A'' < 0$, which follows from diminishing returns in food production. Substituting equation (7.8) into equation (7.9),

$$\frac{-dF}{dM} = 1 + p_D$$

which establishes the aforementioned equality.

A free-trade solution is depicted in Figure 7.1. Domestic food consumption and import consumption are measured along OF and OM, respectively. The consumption possibility locus is $\hat{F}\hat{M}$. At the point $\hat{F}$ no imports are consumed and hence there is no distribution. If distribution were costless, society could choose its consumption point from the line $\hat{F}A$. However, to consume one unit of import requires exchanging one unit of food *and* withdrawing k workers from agriculture to provide the requisite distributive services. With diminishing marginal product of labor in agriculture, the cost of additional imports in terms of foregone food production rises. Thus, the price of distribution, and hence the domestic price of imports, increases in moving northwest from $\hat{F}$. The consumption point $\hat{M}$ has OB food exchanged for $O\hat{M}$ of imports. The distance $\hat{F}B$ is the agricultural output forgone to distribute $O\hat{M}$ imports.

If society's preferences are given by the indifference curve ii, point C is optimal. The price of distribution is reflected in the difference between the slope of $\hat{F}A$ and the slope of DD at C. At the point C, OG

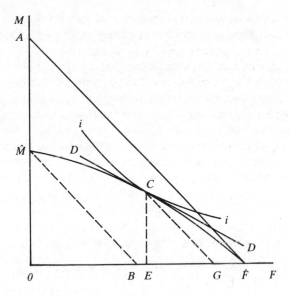

Figure 7.1 Free trade

food would be produced, with EG (= EC) exported, and the rest domestically consumed.

7.2.3 A Tariff or an Import Restriction Without Rent-Seeking

Consider now a case in which there is a restriction upon the quantity of imports

$$M = \bar{M} \tag{7.10}$$

where $\bar{M}$ is less than the import quantity that would be realized under free trade. Since entry into distribution is now limited, the competitive wage equality (7.8) will no longer hold. The relevant system contains equations (7.1) to (7.7) and (7.10). The variables are the same as in the free-trade case and again $L_R \equiv 0$. The system may be solved sequentially: given equation (7.10), D follows from equation (7.2), L_D from (7.3), L_A from (7.7), A from (7.1), F from (7.6), p_M from (7.5), and p_D from (7.4). Since equations (7.1), (7.6), and (7.7) remain intact, the solution for this case is also on the consumption possibility locus.

It is useful to establish the directions of change for the variables following a switch from free trade to import restriction. The reduced import level will reduce the labor employed in distribution and increase the labor force in agriculture. Diminishing returns will reduce the agricultural wage. The domestic price of imports, the distributive margin, and the wage of distributors will increase. Distributors will earn a rent in the sense that their wage will exceed the wage of those engaged in agriculture.

In the absence of rent-seeking, a tariff and a quantitative restriction are equivalent[8] aside from the resultant income distribution. Under a quantitative restriction the distributive wage is higher than the agricultural. If instead there were an equivalent tariff with redistribution of the proceeds, the marginal product of labor in agriculture would be unchanged, but agricultural workers would benefit by the amount of tariff proceeds redistributed to them whereas traders' income would be lower. Since the allocation of labor under a tariff and quantitative restriction without rent-seeking is the same and domestic prices are the same, the only difference between the two situations lies in income distribution.

The solution under a quantitative restriction is illustrated in Figure 7.2, where $\hat{F}\hat{M}$ is again the consumption possibility locus and C the free-trade solution. With a quantitative restriction on imports in the amount $O\overline{M}$, the domestic prices of imports, and hence of distribution, rise from free trade to import restriction. Food output (OJ) and domestic consumption of food increase, and exports decline to HJ ($= OM$). The indifference curve $i'i'$ lies below ii (and the point C), and the welfare loss may be described by the consumption and production-cost measure given by Johnson (1960).

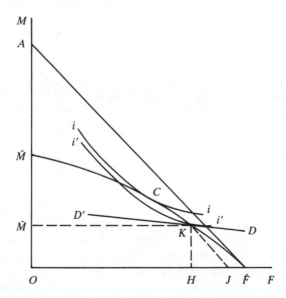

Figure 7.2 Import restriction without rent-seeking

The wage rate in distribution unequivocally rises for a movement from free trade to a quantitative restriction. The total income of distributors will increase, decrease, or remain unchanged depending upon whether the proportionate increase in p_D is greater than, less than, or equal to the absolute value of the proportionate decrease of imports. For the moment, let p_D, p_M, and M represent free-trade solution values, and let p_D^*, p_M^*, and $\overline{M}$ represent import-restriction solution values. The total arc elasticity of demand for imports for the interval under consideration, η, is

$$\eta = \frac{-(\overline{M} - M)}{\overline{M} + M} \cdot \frac{p_M^* + p_M}{p_M^* - p_M} \tag{7.11}$$

Total expenditures on imports will increase, decrease, or remain unchanged as η is less than one, greater than one, or equal to one. The total income of distributors will increase if

$$p_D^*\overline{M} > p_D M$$

Multiplying both sides of this inequality by $(p_M^* + p_M)/(p_M^* - p_M)$, substituting equation (7.11), and using (7.4),

$$1 + 2/(p_D^* + p_D) > \eta \tag{7.12}$$

Hence, distributors' total income can increase even if the demand for imports is price-elastic.[9] The smaller is the free-trade distributive markup, the more likely it is that the distributors' total income will increase with a curtailment of imports. The reason is that an increase in the domestic price of imports results in a proportionately greater increase in the price of distribution.

7.2.4 An Import Restriction with Competitive Rent-Seeking

In the import-restriction model just presented, the wage in distribution p_D/k exceeds the wage in agriculture A'. Under this circumstance, it would be surprising if people did not endeavor to enter distribution in response to its higher return. Resources can be devoted to rent-seeking in all the ways indicated in Section 7.1.1. This rent-seeking activity can be specified in a number of different ways. A simple and intuitively plausible specification is that people will seek distributive rents until the average wage in distribution and rent-seeking equals the agricultural wage:[10]

$$A' = \frac{p_D\overline{M}}{L_D + L_R} \tag{7.13}$$

One can regard all distributors and rent-seekers as being partially engaged in each activity or one can think of rent-seekers as entering in the expectation of receiving import licenses. In the latter case, the final solution classifies the successful seekers in L_D and the unsuccessful ones in L_R. Equation (7.13) implies risk neutrality in this circumstance.

The model for import restriction with rent-seeking contains the same equations, (7.1) to (7.7) and (7.10), and the same variables as the model for import restrictions without rent-seeking. In addition, the new model contains equation (7.13) and the introduction of L_R as a variable. The essential factor of rent-seeking is that L_R becomes positive.

Let us start with a solution for an import restriction without rent-seeking and ask what happens to the values of the variables when rent-seeking is introduced. By assumption $M = \bar{M}$ is unchanged, so that L_D is unchanged. Therefore, $dL_A = -dL_R$, because the labor that enters rent-seeking can only come from agriculture. Substituting into the total differential of equation (7.1) and using (7.6),

$$dF = dA = -A'dL_R < 0 \qquad (7.14)$$

Agricultural production and food consumption are reduced by the introduction of rent-seeking. Since the import level remains unchanged, rent-seeking entails a welfare loss beyond that for an import restriction without rent-seeking. The concavity of the agricultural production function results in a food loss that is less than proportional to decrements in L_A. Differentiating equation (7.5) totally,

$$0 = M_1 dp_M + M_2 dA \qquad (7.15)$$

where M_1 and M_2 are the partial derivatives of equation (7.5) with respect to p_M and A, respectively. Solving equation (7.15) for dp_M, and substituting equations (7.4) and (7.14),

$$dp_D = dp_M = \frac{M_2}{M_1} A'dL_R < 0 \qquad (7.16)$$

since $M_1 < 0$ and $M_2 > 0$. The domestic cost of imports will be lower under rent-seeking competition. This follows from the decrease in the consumption of food relative to imports.

The results of equations (7.14 and 7.16) are not dependent upon the particular form of the equilibrium of the labor market. They hold for any specification of competitive rent-seeking. Equation (7.13) serves to determine particular values for L_R and other variables of the system. The mere existence of competitive rent-seeking is enough to determine the directions of change of the variables.

The above results are sufficient to indicate that, for any given level of import restrictions, competition among rent-seekers is clearly inferior to the tariff equivalent of the restrictions, in that there could be more food consumed with no fewer imports under the latter case than the former. To the extent that rent-seeking is competitive, the welfare cost of import restrictions is equal to the welfare cost of the tariff equivalent *plus the additional cost of rent-seeking activities*. Measurement of that excess cost is considered below.

The tariff-equivalent and rent-seeking equilibria are contrasted in Figure 7.3. Equilibrium under rent-seeking will be at some point such as L, with the same consumption of imports, but smaller production and consumption of food than occurs under a tariff. The points K and C are the tariff-equivalent and free-trade equilibria, respectively. The line $D'D'$ corresponds to the domestic price of imports in Figure 7.2, and the steeper line $D''D''$ corresponds to the lower domestic price of imports under competitive rent seeking.

So far, it has been shown that for any given level of import restriction, a tariff is Pareto-superior to competitive rent-seeking, and the properties of rent-seeking equilibrium have been contrasted with those of the tariff-equivalent case in the absence of competition for the rents. A natural question is whether anything can be said about the properties of rent-seeking equilibrium in contrast to those of a free-trade equilibrium, which is, after all, the optimal solution. It has been seen that the number of persons engaged in distribution declines from free trade to import restriction without rent-seeking, and increases as one goes from that situation to competition for import licenses. Likewise, agricultural

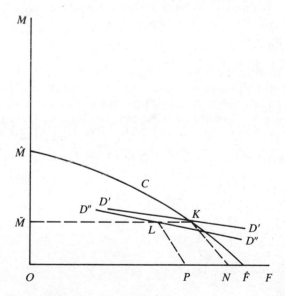

Figure 7.3   Rent-seeking import restriction

output increases between free trade and the tariff-equivalent case, and declines between that and rent-seeking. The question is whether any unambiguous signs can be placed on the direction of these changes between free trade and rent-seeking and, in particular, whether it is possible that society might produce and consume less of both goods under rent-seeking than under free trade.

The answer is that if inequality (7.12) is satisfied, the absolute number of persons ($L_D + L_R$) in distribution will increase going from a free-trade to a rent-seeking equilibrium. If import demand is more elastic, the number of persons in distribution will decline. Contrasted with a free-trade equilibrium, there would be less agricultural output *and* fewer imports when inequality (7.12) holds. If, with import restriction, the income from distribution $p_D^* \overline{M}$ is greater than distributors' income at free trade, more persons will be employed in distribution-cum-rent-seeking with import restriction than are employed under free trade.

7.2.5   Measuring the Welfare Loss from Rent-Seeking

A tariff has both production and consumption costs, and it has already been shown that rent-seeking entails costs in addition to those of a tariff. Many forms of competition for rents, however, are by their nature difficult to observe and quantify and one might therefore question the empirical content of the result so far obtained.

Fortunately, there is a way to estimate the production cost of rent-seeking. That cost, in fact, is equal to the value of the rents. This can be shown as follows. The rent per import license, r, is

$$r = p_D - kA' \tag{7.17}$$

This follows because the labor required to distribute one unit of imports is k, which could be used in agriculture with a return A'. Note that at free trade r equals zero. A distributor could efficiently distribute an import and earn his opportunity cost in agriculture with zero rent. The total value of rents, R, with competitive rent-seeking is thus the rent per unit of imports times the amount imported.

$$R = r\overline{M} = (p_D - kA')\overline{M} \tag{7.18}$$

Using equations (7.3) and (7.13),

$$R = \left(p_D - \frac{kp_D\overline{M}}{L_D + L_R}\right)\overline{M} \tag{7.19}$$

$$= p_D\left(1 - \frac{L_D}{L_D + L_R}\right)\overline{M}$$

$$= \frac{p_D\overline{M}L_R}{L_D + L_R}$$

Thus the total value of rents reflects the agricultural wage (A') times the number of rent-seekers.

The value of rents reflects the value (at current prices) of the domestic factors of production which could be extracted from the economy with no change in the final goods and services available for society's utilization. Thus, if the value of rents is known, it indicates the volume of resources that could be transferred out of distribution and into other activities, with no loss of distributive services from an initial position of rent-seeking activity. The estimates of rents in India and Turkey, therefore, may be interpreted as the deadweight loss from quantitative restrictions in addition to the welfare cost of their associated tariff equivalents if one believes that there is competition for the rents.

The value of the rents overstates the increase in food output and consumption that could be attained with a tariff to the extent that the marginal product of labor in agriculture is diminishing, since the equilibrium wage will rise between the tariff and the competitive rent-seeking situation. In the case of a constant marginal product of labor in alternative uses, the value of rents will exactly measure forgone output.

7.2.6   The Implications of Rent-Seeking for Trade Theory

Recognition of the fact of rent-seeking alters a variety of conclusions normally obtained in the trade literature and examination of such cases is well beyond the scope of this chapter. A few immediately derivable results are worth brief mention, however.

First, an import prohibition might be preferable to a non-prohibitive quota if there is competition for licenses under the quota. This follows immediately from the fact that a prohibition would release resources from rent-seeking and the excess cost of domestic production might be less than the value of the rents. Second, one could not, in general, rank the tariff-equivalents of two (or more) quotas, since the value of rents is a function of both the amount of rent per unit (the tariff equivalent) and the volume of imports of each item.[11] Third, it has generally been accepted that the more inelastic domestic demand the less is likely to be the welfare cost of a given tariff. For the quota-cum-rents case, the opposite is true: the more price inelastic is demand, the greater will be the value of rents and the greater, therefore, the deadweight loss associated with rent-seeking. Fourth, it is usually believed that competition among importers will result in a better allocation of resources than will a monopoly. If rent-seeking is a possibility, however, creating a monopoly position for one importer will generally result in a higher real income if not in a preferable income distribution for society. Finally, devaluation under quantitative restrictions may have important allocation effects because it diminishes the value of import licenses, and hence the amount of rent-seeking activity, in addition to its effects upon exports.

7.3   CONCLUSIONS AND IMPLICATIONS

In this chapter, focus has been on the effects of competition for import licenses under a quantitative restriction of imports. Empirical evidence suggests that the value of rents associated with import licenses can be relatively large, and it has been shown that the welfare cost of quantitative restrictions equals that of their tariff equivalents plus the value of the rents.

While import licenses constitute a large and visible rent resulting from government intervention, the phenomenon of rent-seeking is far more general. Fair trade laws result in firms of less than optimal size. Minimum-wage legislation generates equilibrium levels of unemployment above the optimum with associated deadweight losses, as shown by Harris and Todaro (1970) and Todaro (1969). Ceilings on interest rates and consequent credit rationing lead to competition for loans and deposits and/or high-cost banking operations. Regulating taxi fares affects the average waiting time for a taxi and the percentage of time taxis are idle, but probably not their owners' incomes, unless taxis are also licensed. Capital gains tax treatment results in overbuilding of apartments and uneconomic oil exploration. And so on.

Each of these and other interventions lead people to compete for the rents although the competitors often do not perceive themselves as such. In each case there is a deadweight loss associated with that competition over and above the traditional triangle. In general, prevention of that loss can be achieved only by restricting entry into the activity for which a rent has been created.

That, in turn, has political implications. First, even if they *can* limit competition for the rents, governments which consider they must impose restrictions are caught on the horns of a dilemma: if they do restrict entry, they are clearly 'showing favoritism' to one group in society and are choosing an unequal distribution of income. If, instead, competition for the rents is allowed (or cannot be prevented), income distribution may be less unequal and certainly there will be less appearance of favoring special groups, although the economic costs associated with quantitative restrictions will be higher.

Second, the existence of rent-seeking surely affects people's perception of the economic system. If income distribution is viewed as the outcome of a lottery where wealthy individuals are successful (or lucky) rent-seekers, whereas the poor are those precluded from or unsuccessful in rent-seeking, the market mechanism is bound to be suspect. In the United States, rightly or wrongly, societal consensus has been that high incomes reflect – at least to some degree – high social product. As such, the high American per capita income is seen as a result of a relatively free market mechanism and an unequal distribution is tolerated as a by-product. If, instead, it is believed that few businesses would survive without exerting 'influence', even if only to bribe government officials to do what they ought in any event to do, it is difficult to associate pecuniary rewards with social product. The perception of the price system as a mechanism rewarding the rich and well-connected may also be important in influencing political decisions about economic policy. If the market mechanism is suspect, the inevitable temptation is to resort to greater and greater intervention, thereby increasing the amount of economic activity devoted to rent-seeking. As such, a political 'vicious circle' may develop. People perceive that the market mechanism does not function in a way compatible with socially approved goals because of competitive rent-seeking. A political consensus therefore emerges to intervene further in the market, rent-seeking increases, and further intervention results. While it is beyond the competence of an economist to evaluate the political impact of rent-seeking, the suspicion of the market mechanism so frequently voiced in some developing countries may result from it.

Finally, all market economies have some rent-generating restrictions. One can conceive of a continuum between a system of no restrictions and a perfectly restricted system. With no restrictions, entrepreneurs would seek to achieve windfall gains by adopting new technology, anticipating market shifts correctly, and so on. With perfect restrictions, regulations would be so all-pervasive that rent-seeking would be the only route to gain. In such a system, entrepreneurs would devote all their time and resources to capturing windfall rents. While neither of these extreme types could ever exist, one can perhaps ask whether there might be some point along the continuum beyond which the market fails to perform its allocative function to any satisfactory degree. It will remain for further work to formalize these conjectures and to test their significance. It is hoped, however, that enough has been said to stimulate interest and research on the subject.

NOTES

1. This phenomenon is explored in detail in Bhagwati and Krueger (1973).
2. Note that: (1) one would expect to find greater excess capacity in those industries where rents are higher; and (2) within an industry, more efficient

firms will have greater excess capacity than less efficient firms, since the return on a given amount of investment will be higher with greater efficiency.

3. It may be objected that illegal means of competition may be sufficiently distasteful that perfect competition will not result. Three comments are called for. First, it requires only that enough people at the margin do not incur disutility from engaging in these activities. Second, most lines of economic activity in many countries cannot be entered without some rent-seeking activity. Third, risks of detection (especially when bribery is expected) and the value judgments associated with illegal activities differ from society to society. See Wraith and Simpkins (1963).

4. I am indebted to Ahmet Aker of Robert College who kindly made his data available to me. Details and a description of the data can be found in Krueger, 1974.

5. Labor could be regarded as a composite domestic factor of production. Extensions to two or more factors would complicate the analysis, but would not alter its basic results.

6. These assumptions establish a domestic numéraire. The real analysis would be unaffected by proportional changes in the domestic prices.

7. Food and imports are consumed. But, by choice of food as the numéraire (see equation (7.6)) and the assumed constancy of international prices, agricultural output serves as a measure of income.

8. The change in the price of the import from the free-trade solution is the tariff equivalent of the quantitative restriction described here.

9. Proof of equation (7.12) uses the step that $p_D^* \bar{M} > p_D M$ implies $(p_D^* - p_D)/(p_D^* \div p_D) > -(\bar{M} - M)/(\bar{M} \div M)$. Note that in the continuous case, equation (7.12) reduces to $1 + 1/p_D > \eta$.

10. As an alternative, the distributive production function (7.3) can be altered to treat all persons competing for import licenses as distributors so that L_D also encompasses L_R and $A' = P_D \bar{M}/L_D$. Another alternative is to introduce a rent-seeking activity distinct from distribution with a wage determined from total rents $(p_D - A'k)\bar{M}/L_R$, and require that this wage equal the wages in distribution and agriculture. These specifications give results equivalent to those that follow from equation (7.13).

11. I am indebted to Bhagwati for pointing out this implication.

REFERENCES

Bhagwati, J. and P. Desai (1970). *Planning for Industrialization: A Study of India's Trade and Industrial Policies since 1950*, Oxford University Press for OECD, London.

Bhagwati, J. and A. Krueger (1973). 'Exchange Control, Liberalization, and Economic Development', *American Economic Review*, May 1973, pp. 419–27.

Government of India, Planning Commission (1961). *Third Five Year Plan*, New Delhi.

Harris, J.R. and M.P. Todaro (1970). 'Migration, Unemployment, and Development: A Two-Sector Analysis', *American Economic Review*, vol. 60, pp. 126–42.

Johnson, H.G. (1960). 'The Cost of Protection and the Scientific Tariff', *Journal of Political Economy*, vol. 68, pp. 327–45.

Krueger, A. (1974). *Foreign Trade Regimes and Economic Development: Turkey*. New York: Columbia University Press.

Monteiro, J.B. (1966). *Corruption*. Bombay.

Myrdal, G. (1968). *Asian Drama*, Vol. III. New York: Twentieth Century Fund.

Reserve Bank of India (1967–8). *Report on Currency and Finance*.

Santhanam Committee (1964) *Report on the Committee on Prevention of Corruption*. New Delhi: Government of India, Ministry of Home Affairs.

Todaro, M.P. (1969). 'A Model of Labor Migration and Urban Employment in Less Developed Countries', *American Economic Review*, vol. 59, pp. 138–48.

Wraith, R. and E. Simpkins (1963). *Corruption in Developing Countries*. London: Allen & Unwin.

PART IV

POLICY PROBLEMS

8 · INTERACTIONS BETWEEN INFLATION AND TRADE-REGIME OBJECTIVES IN STABILIZATION PROGRAMS

Examination of the relationship between macroeconomic growth and the trade objectives of stabilization programs is an exceptionally difficult assignment. Three separate bodies of relevant literature – relating to trade regimes, to inflation and its causes and consequences, and to the determinants of economic growth – are pertinent to the analysis, and each has numerous points of contention. This in itself makes the assignment challenging. In addition, the kinds of problem that arise with inflation, trade and payments regimes, and development strategies in general are sufficiently different between countries so that no single model is appropriate for all of them.

To make the task manageable, a very elementary framework is used to analyze the relationship between the trade regime and monetary-macro aggregates. Within this framework, it is readily seen that in principle the interaction between different types of inflation and the trade regimes can be minimal. The costs of altering either the anticipated rate of inflation or the nature of the trade regime, and the effects of those states and changes on economic growth, are then briefly set forth. This chapter then examines the more prevalent case in which the authorities' efforts to contain inflation are reflected in a trade regime and real exchange rate different than would be chosen in the absence of the inflationary pressures, and traces the interaction between inflation and the trade regime. With that background, the next section presents a classification of the types of stabilization program and analyzes the kinds of policy issue that arise in each category and their relationship to economic development. Finally, the main trade-offs that arise in deciding on the components of a stabilization program are examined.

First printed in 1981.

8.1   THE PRICE LEVEL/EXCHANGE RATE/TRADE
REGIME RELATIONSHIP

Depending on the question at hand, the appropriate model for analyzing any one of the three topics discussed here can be quite different. Determination of the price level is a macromonetary phenomenon, although in the short term cost-push and microeconomic phenomena (such as a good harvest) can enter into its determination. In an open economy with full convertibility and no quantitative restrictions upon international transactions, the exchange rate is likely to be a monetary phenomenon as well. If, however, quantitative restrictions apply to a large number of international transactions, the exchange rate will also be an important variable in affecting two significant relative prices: that between home goods and tradable goods, and that between the domestic prices of exportables and of import-competing goods. Finally, the trade regime itself consists of the policies and instruments used by a country to achieve two targets: first, the relationship between domestic prices of import-competing and exportable goods; second, the balance in transactions between residents and foreigners.

In principle, appropriate use of policy instruments can achieve total separation of the causes and consequences of the rate of price-level increase from any impact upon the trade regime. Such a circumstance is seldom found in the real world (although as will be argued, the sliding-peg regime can provide a fairly close approximation to it), but it is useful to establish the basic relationships. Within that context, analysis of alternative trade regimes, and their causes and consequences for economic growth, can be carried out.

Table 8.1 provides a schematic representation of the three markets and their relationship to trade regimes. The basic proposition underlying the analysis is that for any price level, an exchange rate corresponds that will leave the real variables in the system unaltered. This is nothing other than an application of the dichotomy to the international arena; if all demand and supply functions are homogeneous of degree zero in prices and money income, then it follows that for any rate of increase in the money supply, there is a corresponding (and equal) proportionate appreciation or depreciation of the currency that will leave all excess demand functions in the system unaltered by the change.[1]

The three markets involved are traded goods, home goods, and the money market.[2] Under a flexible exchange rate regime, all three markets clear with individuals free to carry out their desired transactions at prevailing prices. The traded goods market clears with the exchange rate (price of foreign exchange), E, equating the foreign prices of the

Table 8.1 Characterization of alternative market interactions

Item	Flexible exchange rate	Payments deficit	Exchange control
Traded goods market	clears $p_x^d = Ep_x^*$ $p_m^d = E(1+t)p_m^*$	deficit $p_x^d = Ep_x^*$ $p_m^d = E(1+t)p_m^*$	clears $p_x^d = Ep_x^*$ $p_m^d > E(1+t)p_m^*$
Money market	clears $m^d = m^s$	surplus $m^d < m^s$	clears $m^d = m^s$
Home goods	clears at $p_h/E = (p_h/E)_0$	clears at $p_h/E > (p_h/E)_0$	clears at $p_h/E \gtrless (p_h/E)_0$

home country's importable and exportable (p_m^d and p_x^d) with foreign prices of the same goods, denoted with an asterisk. The term $(1 + t)$ is included in the import-price relation to indicate that flexible exchange rates are compatible with any tariff structure and level of desired protection for import-competing industries, a point developed later. Under flexible exchange rates, the money market naturally clears, as does the market for home goods. For later reference, the market clearing price for home goods is denoted under flexible exchange rates as $(p_h/E)_0$. This notation is useful in that the home goods market always clears. What differentiates different regimes is the relative price of home goods (and therefore their relative importance in domestic production): a higher market-clearing price for home goods corresponds to greater domestic production and, of course, consumption of those goods.[3]

Under a flexible-rate regime, any change in the anticipated rate of inflation is reflected in a shift in the excess demand function for foreign exchange. Abstracting from short-term phenomena (such as J-curve responses of exports and imports to the changed short-run price of tradable goods relative to home goods), the market for tradable goods will be unaffected in real terms. Thus, if inflation were perfectly anticipated, the time path of the exchange rate and the domestic price level would coincide in such a way that the relative price of tradable and home goods remained stable.

To be sure, inflation is never smooth and perfectly anticipated. Under fixed exchange rates, the real exchange rate is affected, as is explained below. For present purposes, however, the central point is that there is a way in which the payments regime can be fairly well insulated from the effects of inflation, permitting or ensuring that the real exchange rate is not influenced by changes in the domestic price level.[4] For purposes of analysis, it is useful first to proceed to discuss the costs of inflation and the costs of alternative trade regimes on the assumption that inflation does not affect the real rate of exchange and that the real exchange rate does not affect the rate of inflation.

8.1.1   Growth under Alternative Trade Regimes

In the context of developing countries' economies, the key link between the trade regime and economic growth is the way in which the trade regime is employed in relation to the domestic growth pattern. Economic theory tells us that new resources should be allocated among tradable-goods industries in such a way that at the margin resources devoted to saving a dollar of foreign exchange should be the same as the marginal resources devoted to earning a dollar of foreign exchange. However, there is also a need on the part of developing countries to provide infant-industry support to many of these activities. Such support can be of several kinds, but prominent among the techniques used in many developing countries has been the trade regime, which has been employed to protect domestic producers against competition from imports. Such a policy, import substitution (IS), has generally resulted implicitly or explicitly in discouragement of exports. The alternative means of encouraging growth of tradable goods industries consists of providing incentives primarily for production, in which case it usually results that a large fraction of incremental output is exported. Very often, encouragement is given to exports directly.

For a variety of reasons, most countries seem to have industrialization and trade policies that result in a significant bias toward either export promotion (EP) or IS. The extent of bias is defined as the degree to which the ratio of the domestic prices of importables to exportables diverges from their international price ratio. Thus, using the terminology of Table 8.1 and assuming the appropriate aggregation across commodity categories has been performed, bias, B, can be defined as

$$B = \frac{p_m^d}{p_x^d} \bigg/ \frac{p_m^*}{p_x^*}. \tag{8.1}$$

The greater the divergence of B from unity in either direction, the more biased the regime; Bs that are greater than unity represent a bias toward IS, while those less than unity represent biases toward EP.

Without detailing the reasons, IS regimes tend to become increasingly biased toward IS over time as export earnings fail to grow as rapidly as demand for imports, as the exchange rate tends to be set at unrealistic levels, as the incremental value of output per unit of investment decreases with small sizes of domestic markets, and as opportunities for further IS diminish rapidly. Also, IS regimes often tend increasingly toward quantitative restrictions upon imports and fairly detailed quantitative controls over domestic economic activity. All of these phenomena seem to result in a fairly unsatisfactory rate of economic growth for the countries undertaking the policies. A simplistic summary of experience with IS for most developing countries would be that after opportunities for 'easy' IS were exhausted, growth rates have tended to slow significantly, either secularly or in a stop-go pattern as foreign exchange availability has determined the rate at which the economy could grow. For present purposes, one of the self-reinforcing phenomena with IS is that the implicit discouragement of export growth tends to increase the apparent 'shortage' of foreign exchange.

The built-in tendency for IS to decelerate as it continues may be the most important long-run growth cost of IS regimes, but there are also other costs that should be noted briefly. Chief among these is that IS regimes tend to promote a fairly indiscriminate pattern of industrial development. High-cost, inefficient industries develop alongside lower-cost, potentially efficient ones. Even where the domestic market for the product is sufficiently large to permit efficient-size plants to be established, low-cost firms have difficulty expanding at a rate much faster than the rate of growth of domestic demand. Low-cost and high-cost firms therefore tend to expend *pari passu*, in part because the disincentive to export is so great that few firms can profitably do so, and in part because controls tend to set up quasi-monopoly positions for individual firms that ensure maintenance of market share: allocation of rights to import scarce intermediate goods and raw materials very often rigidify individual firms' market shares. Not all of these costs of an IS regime are inevitable, because alternative means of fostering IS can have significantly different results. None the less, the evidence strongly suggests significant tendencies in this direction.

Export promotion policies can also be carried out in a variety of ways, and some are superior to others. The reader should bear in mind that the definition of bias indicates the extent to which an EP strategy is followed. All countries have 'export promotion' strategies, but in many cases those strategies are really only a means of offsetting some of the disincentives built into the system by IS policies, as IS industries receive stronger incentives still. In those cases, exports often consist of 'excess capacity' output of IS industries and do not necessarily represent industries with long-term comparative advantages.

The reasons that countries which have genuinely biased their regimes toward export promotion have tended to experience more satisfactory growth rates can be summed up as the counterpart of the IS problems: stop-go patterns do not seem to emerge due to foreign exchange bottlenecks; efficient low-cost firms can expand very rapidly well beyond the limits of the domestic market; and domestic monopoly positions do not spring up as firms are forced to compete for their customers abroad and heed quality control and specifications. In addition, despite bias toward

EP, the extent of the bias cannot grow too high. Countries adopting IS with the domestic price of importables twice or more the international price are frequently noted; countries with EP with a bias of more than 25 or 30 per cent toward exports are rare.

From this brief glimpse of the factors differentiating growth patterns under EP and IS,[5] it is evident that the choice of strategy adopted can significantly affect economic growth rates. But, in the presence of a fairly convertible exchange rate permitted to move with changes in the rate of inflation, it is not evident that the rate of inflation need be a factor in the choice of trade strategy; the two are, or can be, independent.

8.1.2   Inflation and Growth

There is presently in economics a revival of interest in the costs of inflation and little time need be spent on those costs here. As inflation accelerates, transactions costs rise and individuals seek stores of value to replace money in that function. These can be costly activities, as potentially productive resources (such as those producing gold and real estate) are diverted to providing a store of value, resulting in little increase in society's real product. In addition, to the extent that countries have geared their spending and taxing policies to stable prices, the costs of the distortions introduced by the tax system may be quite large. Finally, in cases where there is credit rationing and borrowers pay negative real rates of interest, as has occurred in many developing countries, significant resource misallocation can arise on that account.

These costs may be highly significant, and it is not intended to minimize their importance. There is little hard evidence, however, that the rate of inflation itself affects the rate of growth via these channels. Given the structure of production in most developing countries, it is likely that the biggest impact of inflation on growth in developing countries has arisen when the underlying premise of this section has been violated: the erosion of the real exchange rate with significant results for a country's trade and payments position and the nature of its trade regime. These costs must be analyzed to evaluate the impact of stabilization programs upon economic growth.

8.1.3   Altering the Trade Regime

If bias toward IS were provided only by tariffs or export subsidies, alteration of the trade regime could be accomplished by altering the tariff or subsidy rates. However, as already stated, IS policies are often carried out through quantitative restrictions (QRs), and alteration of the bias of the regime entails shifting from reliance upon QRs to reliance upon prices and may indeed involve replacing the bias imparted by QRs with a similar bias imparted by tariffs.

One of the difficulties of altering trade regimes is that the extent of bias is frequently not known. Especially when QRs are important, it turns out that a move from QRs to tariffs alters the bias of the regime much more than intended by the authorities; they are simply unaware of the protective equivalent of the quotas.[6]

Regardless of the way in which bias toward IS is reduced,[7] resource reallocation will follow. Should the profitability of existing industries be reduced (for example, if there is an increase in the value of import licenses issued) without any offsetting stimulus to other industries, a reduction in the level of economic activity is the likely outcome. This is especially the case if expansion of the industries whose relative profitability has increased will require investments to expand capacity, while output can contract immediately in IS industries. Entrepreneurs without experience in exporting activities may be very reluctant to base large-scale investments on the expectation that they can profitably sell in international markets. On the one hand, they may be inexperienced in those markets and be unaware of the opportunities facing them; on the other hand, they may be well aware of those opportunities but fear that the altered bias of the trade regime (with a more favorable real exchange rate) may not last, thereby rendering investment unprofitable.

These considerations pinpoint two aspects of any adjustment process that involves a shift in the bias of the regime. There is likely to be something of a disparity between the rate at which existing industries cut back production and the rate at which potentially new industries increase output;[8] however, the role of expectations is crucial in determining how significant and long-lived the disparity is. If entrepreneurs are convinced that the change in incentives is permanent, the disparity may not last long. If, conversely, there are significant doubts about the ability of the authorities to maintain the new relative price structure, output of industries encouraged by the former bias of the regime may contract while there are few moves made to start increasing output along new lines. It is this latter case in which the growth costs of a shift in the trade regime can be potentially substantial.

It seems evident, therefore, that an attempt to alter the bias of a trade regime should be accompanied by some stimulus to activity in the newly profitable industries, and perhaps also some increase in the general level of aggregate demand to offset whatever decline will come about in the adversely affected industries. The severity of the downward pressure on the level of economic activity depends upon a number of factors, including the degree to whch bias is being altered, the height of the protective barriers being reduced, the degree of uncertainty as to the permanence of the altered incentive structure, and the length of time the incentive structure has been in place. Even in the absence of inflationary pressures or other objectives, a policy shift with regard to trade strategies is likely, therefore, to entail some short-term costs in terms of the rate of economic growth. If the shift is successful, however, the short-term loss may be earning a relatively high rate of return in the form of improved resource allocation and more rapid growth in future periods. A major question, of course, is how the costs of such a shift may be minimized and, simultaneously, the extent to which policies can be introduced to offset part or all of the short-term losses. It seems best, however, to consider that question in the context of a total stabilization policy package.

8.1.4   Costs of Reducing the Inflation Rate

Little needs to be said here about the difficulties involved in reducing the rate of inflation in developing countries. There have been a few notable instances of successful, and fairly painless, sharp drops in the rate of inflation, but they are the exception rather than the rule. Israel in the mid-1950s, Turkey in 1958–9, and South Korea in the late 1950s and early 1960s were able successfully to bring about a reduction in their inflation rates of two-thirds or more. In those instances, there was little retardation in the rate of economic growth.[9]

A more prevalent pattern appears to be one in which 'stabilization' programs are adopted, and some deceleration of inflation occurs. That deceleration, however, is accompanied by recession. In some instances, such as Brazil in the mid-1960s, the costs of stabilization in the form of below-capacity output were borne for several years, until the inflation rate had been significantly reduced. Even more frequently, however, recession and its effects have put such pressure on the political authorities that the stabilization attempt has been abandoned. The Chilean experience of the 1950s and 1960s seems to have been characterized by this sort of stabilization (see Behrman, 1976, for a full account). The cost of reduced inflation was recession, and resumption of economic growth occurred only after the stabilization effort was abandoned; with resumed growth, the rate of inflation (and the bias toward import substitution) once again increased.

For later reference, there is one aspect of attempts to reduce inflation that should be noted. There is one type of deflationary policy that can simultaneously help alter the bias of the regime and reduce the inflation rate: increasing the flow of imports. To the extent that financing can be found to achieve such an increase, purchasing power is absorbed while the implicit or explicit bias toward import substitution is substantially reduced. This feature is of special significance in considering stabilization policies and ways in which measures can be taken to improve the likelihood of their success and reduce their short-term costs.

8.2   INTERACTIONS BETWEEN INFLATION AND THE TRADE REGIME

As already mentioned, determinants of the rate of inflation and of the bias of the trade regime are, in principle, largely separate. One of the policy measures that can be taken to reduce the distortion and growth costs of inflation is a sliding-peg exchange-rate regime. To be sure, the optimal real exchange rate, which is itself a function of the desired bias in trade strategy and other variables, will not under all circumstances remain the same. As Carlos Díaz-Alejandro (1976) has noted, with the fluctuations that Colombia has faced in the price of coffee, there is probably no exchange rate that was not an equilibrium rate at one time or another. None the less, while alterations in the real exchange rate may prove desirable in response to altered prices for the country's exports on the world market or for other reasons (including a desire to shift the bias of the trade regime), there is little likelihood that rates of inflation will reflect only those changes.

Thus, if a country with a fixed exchange rate found that its price level was beginning to increase more rapidly than that of its trading partners, the best policy, in the absence of willingness to allow freely fluctuating exchange rates, would most likely be some form of indexation (sliding peg) of the exchange rate. Various formulas are possible; for example, the exchange rate can be set relative to a major trading partner in conformity with the differential between the country's and the trading partner's inflation rates, or a weighted average of the rates of inflation adjusted for exchange-rate changes of several major trading partners can be deducted from the country's own rate of inflation. In different circumstances, the number of countries it is desirable to include in the calculus can differ, but in all cases adjustment must be made at fairly short time intervals. Under any of these formulas, changes in the rate of inflation will not have a significant impact upon the nature of the trade regime. Such an indexation works best when inflation rates are fairly stable or declining; there is some tendency toward balance-of-payments deficit when inflation generated by excess demand is accelerating over into the foreign exchange market. None the less, contrasted with the maintenance of a fixed nominal rate of exchange under inflation, a sliding-peg policy is vastly preferred.

The difficulty, and one which results in the important interaction between trade regimes and inflation, arises in countries that fail to adopt such a strategy. In those cases, inflation tends to increase the purchasing power of domestic currency when spent abroad relative to its value when spent at home. As a consequence, domestic nationals tend to increase their purchases abroad and reduce their sales abroad. In the absence of capital controls, they also try to exchange domestic assets denominated in domestic currency units for foreign assets denominated in foreign currency units.

In those instances, countries have three choices: to incur open balance-of-payments deficits; to alter the price paid and received for foreign exchange *de facto* or *de jure*; or to impose QRs upon international transactions. In practice, the response is usually to adopt some price measures, such as surcharges upon imports and subsidies for minor exports, to impose some QRs, and to permit a deficit in the balance of payments to emerge, financed by running down foreign exchange reserves or borrowing from abroad. Indeed, one characteristic of many inflation-prone countries attempting to maintain a fixed exchange rate is the proliferation of fairly detailed, *ad hoc* measures designed to curb excess demand for foreign exchange side by side with the continued need to borrow from abroad to finance deficits that emerge despite measures taken. This welter of detailed and fairly specific measures itself has economic costs and can be one motive for a stabilization operation – 'tidying up' the regime.

For purposes of analysis, however, it is convenient to set aside the use of price measures and mixed responses. If sufficient price measures were undertaken on an across-the-board basis to remedy the underlying tendency toward excess demand for foreign exchange, such measures would amount to a sliding-peg exchange-rate policy. It is the absence of sufficient pricing measures that forces countries experiencing inflation at fixed exchange rates to adopt alternative measures.

The alternatives consist of incurring open balance-of-payments deficits, which are financed by running down reserves or borrowing from abroad, or of imposing QRs. Each of these measures has costs and affects the nature of any subsequent stabilization program. For purposes of analysis, it is useful to analyze each type of response separately, although, as already indicated, the two are often found in combination.

Table 8.1 is again useful as a frame of reference. It will be recalled that the sliding-peg (if pegged at the appropriate level) or flexible-exchange-rate case was one where each market cleared and participants were free to carry out desired transactions at the prevailing prices. Incurring an open payments deficit is equivalent to permitting an excess supply of money in the home market to spill over into realized excess demand for goods and services from abroad (which is reflected in the payments deficit). By contrast, exchange control is a case in which individuals are not permitted to carry out their desired transactions; the domestic price of importables exceeds the foreign price-cum-tariff, and the money market consequently clears. The precise mix of these two policies in use is a critical factor in determining the effects of policies that are undertaken in a stabilization program.

8.2.1 Payments Deficit

The key characteristics of a response to excess demand by permitting a payments deficit are two: there is an excess supply of money; on the other hand, the relative price of home goods is 'too high', as aggregate consumption is above sustainable levels, consumption of home goods increases, and the failure of the price of tradables to rise induces production to shift toward home goods.

The excess supply of money is in part a reflection of the fact that the fixed exchange rate acts as a suppressant to the inflation that would otherwise result from aggregate demand pressures. In the case of a sliding-peg exchange-rate policy, the entire inflationary stimulus is passed through both the home-goods and the traded-goods sector: both prices increase nominally and there is no relative price change. In the case of a fixed exchange rate, home goods' prices rise (although not by as much as they would under a sliding peg because consumers are permitted to substitute traded goods for home goods in their consumption bundle while producers shift production away from traded and toward home goods), but traded goods' prices are stable. The payments deficit can be thought of as a reflection of that part of the inflationary pressure that was not reflected in price increases.

A straightforward way of viewing the problem of a country experiencing inflation and a payments deficit at a fixed exchange rate is to recognize that the inflation rate is held below that which would otherwise be realized as long as the exchange rate can be maintained, both because the price of tradable goods does not rise and because the increase in the price of home goods is less than it would otherwise be. Under those circumstances, devaluation is inflationary; it permits the inflationary impulse to be passed on to the domestic market. Devaluation would therefore accomplish little if a country could continue indefinitely to finance its payments deficits.[10]

The fact is, however, that countries cannot indefinitely run down reserves or borrow from abroad for purposes of financing their deficits. Just as an individual consumer can live well beyond his means by running up credit card charges, borrowing from a bank, and depreciating consumer durables, so too can a country live beyond its means. In both cases, the situation is not sustainable.

It is for this reason that analysis of the costs, in terms of growth prospects, of measures taken to eliminate an unsustainable deficit is extremely difficult. In a sense, the economy incurring a deficit and then reducing its expenditures relative to its income is on a non-optimal path; its early level of expenditures and outlay is too high, at the cost of a later reduction in that level. For purposes of analysis, the best that can be done is to pose the question in the following way: given an economy that has incurred an unsustainable deficit, what is the lowest-cost way of altering its expenditure–income relationship to reattain a sustainable future expansion path? Consideration of this question is deferred until later in this chapter. At this point, the line of analysis sketched out here applies to any country's attempt to reduce the size of its payments deficit, actual or prospective. In many instances, stabilization programs have objectives pertaining both to reducing the size of the prospective deficit and to liberalizing the trade regime. Before analysis of those programs can be carried out, it is necessary to examine the differences between the goals and the problems implicit in the two alternatives.

8.2.2　Liberalizing the Trade Regime

As mentioned, inflation at a fixed exchange rate cannot long be sustained without incurring a payments deficit. That is unsustainable, and the alternative is alteration of the exchange rate or imposition of QRs once access to further foreign credits becomes limited, as it eventually must. The key characteristic of using QRs to keep foreign exchange payments in line with receipts, as shown in Table 8.1, is that the money market is permitted to clear while the domestic price of importables rises above the imported price (inclusive of landing costs, tariffs, and surcharges). Thus, whereas an open payments deficit is characterized by the inappropriate relative price of tradable to non-tradable goods (for any chosen tariff structure), the quantitative restrictions equilibrium is characterized by a greater bias of the trade and payments regime toward import-competing activities domestically than would be chosen simply on the basis of the industrialization strategy. Whether home goods' relative prices are likely to be higher or lower than in the flexible exchange rate alternative is not clear-cut; depending on the nature of the structure of production and the degree of substitution between exportables, importables, and home goods in both consumption and production, that relationship can go either way.

The difference between the price that prevails for an import in the home market if individuals were allowed to import all they wished at the prevailing price and the price that would prevail in the presence of QRs upon imports is referred to as the *premium* on an import license. The fact that there are premiums on import licenses is usually sufficient evidence to indicate that QRs are binding. Under those circumstances, the bias of the trade and payments regime toward IS is almost always greater than intended, and resource allocation costs can mount well above those associated with the tariff-generated protection.[11]

Thus, although either an open payments deficit or the tightening of QRs can result from inflationary pressure at a fixed exchange rate, the symptoms and resource-allocation effects of the two alternative responses are quite different. The realized rate of inflation for a given monetary stimulus will be greater under a QR response than under a deficit response; the degree of bias of the regime will be greater under the QR response than under the deficit response; and the home goods sector will likely expand more under the deficit response than under the QR response.[12] When stabilization programs are adopted, therefore, crucial considerations include the mix of the two policies chosen and how severely restrictive[13] the QRs have become or how sizeable the deficits are.

When the response to potential deficits has been the imposition of QRs, increasing the price of foreign exchange will operate rather differently than it will in the case of open deficit. Suppose, for example, that an open deficit has been incurred. Raising the price of foreign exchange while holding tariffs constant will, in the absence of quantitative restrictions, raise the price of tradable goods relative to the price of nontradables. For a small country with no monopoly power in trade, the relative price of exportables and import-competing goods will remain unaltered; the bias of the regime is unaffected, although production of both import-competing and exportable goods becomes more profitable relative to the profitability of producing home goods.[14] If, instead, QRs are in effect prior to the increase in the price of foreign exchange, part of the increase in price will go to absorbing the premiums on import licenses (thereby perhaps reducing the variance in effective exchange rates across commodity categories). If, as is usually the case, export subsidies are much smaller than premiums on import licenses, a far higher fraction of the increased price of foreign exchange will be reflected in the domestic price of exportables than it will be in the domestic price of import-competing goods. At the limit, in cases where the size of the devaluation is less than the size of the pre-existing premium on import licenses, there is no reason to expect the domestic price of importables to rise following a devaluation.[15]

Several points should be noted. First, as a consequence of premium absorption, the increase in the price level following a devaluation in the context of pre-existing QRs should be considerably smaller than the recorded price increase following a deficit-reducing devaluation. In a sense, this is the counterpart to the statement that a given inflationary stimulus will result in a larger rate of inflation under QRs than it will under an open deficit given a fixed exchange rate; the devaluation has more work to do correcting the relative prices of exportables and import-competing goods and less work to do in adjusting the price level. Second, in the absence of other policy moves, any devaluation is still likely to result in a reduction of the restrictiveness of whatever quantitative restrictions are in effect. That is, for given quantitative amounts of permitted imports, devaluation automatically liberalizes a given trade regime, unless other measures are taken to offset the increase in the price of foreign exchange.[16] Third, because devaluation absorbs premiums upon imports, it automatically alters the bias of the regime and thereby induces the resource reallocation mechanisms discussed earlier.

Finally, there is the question of the macroeconomic impact of a pure 'liberalizing' devaluation. Unlike the open deficit case, where expenditures clearly have to be cut relative to income, the liberalizing devaluation has no such imperative, except in so far as it was underlying the erosion of the real exchange rate which led to the necessity to impose QRs in the first place. In principle, therefore, if a QR regime were the result of past inflationary pressures which had subsided, leaving the exchange rate overvalued by a stationary amount, no deflationary stimulus or reduction in the level of aggregate demand would be necessary. Indeed, in the pure QR case, it can even be argued that the absorption of the premium by the exchange-rate increase, combined with the benefits from resource allocation resulting from the change in the bias of the regime, might well result in a mild deflationary pressure on the economy (Sohmen, 1958). Quantitatively, however, it is not evident that this deflationary pressure is likely to be significant.

8.3 STABILIZATION PROGRAMS AND LONG-TERM DEVELOPMENT

As the foregoing has indicated, there is no one action that can be described as a 'stabilization program'. The policies undertaken and their effects vary, depending on the underlying situation and the goals of the policy-makers.

It has already been indicated that the task of reducing the rate of inflation is an exceptionally difficult one. Almost inevitably there is a short-term reduction in the rate of growth of output, and, in many cases, recession. In these circumstances, deflationary policies are sometimes reversed so that few, if any, benefits are realized. Likewise, the resource reallocation that must accompany a successful effort to liberalize the trade regime and alter its bias away from import substitution cannot be achieved without inevitable adjustments of resources within the economy.

For these reasons, there are bound to be short-term adjustment costs of any stabilization program, whatever the nature of the policy package and regardless of the degree to which it is successful. There are, of course, ways to reduce those costs, but it is doubtful whether stabilization can be accomplished in the presence of unwillingness or political inability to withstand some short-term disallocations. The first and most important conclusion that can be drawn, therefore, is that it is senseless to incur the costs of adjustment only to reverse policies before they have had any chance to affect resource allocation and growth. Yet, the evidence is that a significant number of stabilization programs have foundered precisely because the authorities have been unwilling or unable politically to survive political pressure during the adjustment period.[17]

A second conclusion, which follows readily from the first, is that the reallocations will take longer and be more difficult, the greater are expectations that the realigned structure of relative prices and incentives will not continue. If it is expected that the devaluation and liberalization will be short-lived, businessmen and consumers are likely to stockpile foreign goods in anticipation of possible future reimposition of QRs. In doing so, they increase the current account deficit and therefore the foreign exchange outflow required to sustain the liberalization program through the adjustment period. In the context of a situation in which foreign exchange has earlier been in excess demand because of the trade regime, increases in imports and current account deficits may stimulate further speculation against the exchange rate, in turn tending to force the reimposition of controls. In addition, expectations of reversal discourage resource reallocation, thus blunting the increase in exports that might otherwise be experienced.

One objective of policy should be to ensure that a stabilization program, once undertaken, can be sustained long enough to provide an opportunity for its results to be felt. This in turn suggests that a desirable feature of any stabilization program is that it should be designed in such a way as to suggest to economic agents that it will succeed; expectations are likely to be self-fulfilling. This conclusion has numerous implications for policy, especially for the evaluation of the optimal lending strategy for donors in connection with stabilization programs.

For the longer term, the effects of stabilization on the rate of growth are a function of the objectives of the program (and especially the extent to which the bias of the regime is shifted away from undue emphasis upon is) and the degree to which they are accomplished. If stabilization policies are undertaken in the first place because existing policies are unsustainable, it is difficult to talk about the growth effects of a particular package except in the context of the alternative stabilization packages; continuation of the status quo ante is infeasible. It is for this reason that one can regard the biggest growth cost of stabilization programs as lying in their failure. When a program does not succeed, it is generally inevitable that another program, with the same sort of short-term costs, will have to be adopted in the future. To the extent that every failure of such a program intensifies expectations of the failure of the next one, an unsuccessful stabilization program may itself have growth costs, not only in the current slowdown in economic activity which by definition has no payoff, but also in the heightened cost of achieving the same objectives at any future date, when memories of past failures result in skeptical expectations about the likelihood of success.

The Colombian experience of the late 1950s and early 1960s is perhaps an excellent example. After unsuccessful devaluation attempts in 1956, 1959, 1961, and 1966, the authorities successfully began altering the bias of the related policies in 1967. Carlos Díaz-Alejandro (1976, pp. 237ff.) concluded that one of the major impacts on Colombian growth was that the consequent growth of foreign exchange earnings from increasing exports meant that the stop-go cycle of fiscal and monetary policy surrounding stabilization efforts finally stopped, which in turn permitted a more rapid rate of growth of the entire economy.

It therefore seems appropriate to attempt to categorize stabilization programs in terms first of their primary objectives, then of the pre-existing situation, and finally the policy measures taken.

8.3.1 Objectives

Despite the fact that almost all stabilization programs by definition have some bearing on both inflation and balance-of-payments objectives, the relative importance of the two objectives can differ. In some instances, stabilization programs are geared primarily toward reducing excess aggregate demand, with balance-of-payments targets secondary.[18] In other instances, the infeasibility of continuing to incur indebtedness or of further tightening QRs makes the primary target an alteration in the trade regime.[19]

One fundamental lesson that seems to emerge from examination of the cases in which devaluation did not succeed in relaxing the foreign exchange constraint is that it does not make sense to tie the success of the measures aimed at the foreign trade sector to success in reducing the rate of inflation. It appears that it is significantly easier to alter the real exchange rate and to increase the rate-of-growth earnings than it is to reduce the rate of inflation permanently. This is perhaps the strongest argument that can be made on behalf of a sliding-peg policy; it permits the success of the trade component of a stabilization program independently of whether the rate of inflation drops or not. In light of the already-stated result that one of the significant costs of inflation lies in the distortions introduced by a fixed exchange rate, it is difficult to understand countries that attempt to alter their trade and payments regimes and inflation rates by adopting a new, fixed exchange rate. If the rate of inflation does drop, a sliding peg will not significantly alter the exchange rate, and both objectives of the program will be met; if, however, inflation is not successfully controlled, both objectives of the package are bound to fail if a new fixed exchange rate is set.

Because controlling inflation is inherently the more difficult objective in most circumstances and because those primarily concerned with bringing the rate of inflation down are likely to object to a sliding peg as being more inflationary than a new fixed exchange rate, it seems to be the case that stabilization programs motivated more by a desire to alter the trade and payments regime have a somewhat greater probability of partial or total success than do programs aimed primarily at the rate of inflation.

To be sure, neither change – alteration of the trade regime or changing the inflationary nature of the economy – is likely to be easy, for reasons already mentioned. None the less, there are degrees of difficulty, and controlling inflation does seem much the more difficult of the two objectives.

8.3.2 Pre-existing Conditions

A number of circumstances in the pre-existing situation also have a bearing on the probable outcome of the stabilization package. Among the most important are 'chance' elements, the set of macroeconomic influences currently operating on the economy, the extent to which the trade regime has been characterized by QRs or by open deficit, and the magnitude of foreign short-term indebtedness.

Two chance factors should be noted. First, favorable harvests can significantly increase the probability that a stabilization program will prove successful. This is because good harvests tend to keep the domestic prices of foodstuffs relatively low, thereby exerting downward pressure on the overall price index, and also because bumper crops tend to increase quantities available for export, thus increasing foreign exchange earning. The latter results either in increased foreign exchange reserves, and thus conviction that the altered incentives will continue, or in an enhanced flow of imports, which in turn permits a relatively greater degree of bias toward exportables than would otherwise be possible. The other event that can positively affect the outcome of a stabilization program is favorable movements in the terms of trade. Such an outcome has the same sort of impact as the increased export earnings that can be attained with a good harvest, although the impact is less favorable on the inflation rate, and appropriate policies must be followed to prevent increased prices of key exports from resulting in large increases in domestic money supply and purchasing power. There have been instances of stabilization programs which, on the historical record, appear to have had a good chance of success, but have foundered on unfavorable movements in the terms of trade. The Brazilian devaluation and stabilization effort of 1957 appears to have been one such case; the volume of exports increased almost 50 per cent over the ensuing twenty-four months, but export earnings rose hardly at all (Fishlow, 1975).

There are several macro influences. First, there is the nature of the monetary and fiscal policies in effect in the six to twelve months prior to the stabilization effort. When those have been highly expansionary, the difficulties entailed in successfully carrying out stabilization are likely to be much greater than when monetary and fiscal stimuli have been moderate. Indeed, it can even be contended that in the presence of highly expansionary monetary and fiscal policy over the preceding year, a country would be better off to postpone (if possible) altering the trade regime (especially if a sliding peg is not a realistic alternative) until monetary and fiscal magnitudes have been brought under control.

Second, there is the extent to which price controls have prevented excess demand pressures from being realized. When those factors have been of importance, it is usually necessary to remove those price ceilings at the time the stabilization package is inaugurated. As prices must rise from their formerly controlled levels, any cost-push responses within the economy will be triggered by those increases as well as the increase in the price of tradable goods, thereby making the task of reducing the rate of inflation more difficult. None the less, when price controls have been operative before stabilization, their removal can be an essential part of the stabilization package. When those controls are over public sector products, they may have been a significant factor in contributing to the public sector deficit and thus to increases in the money supply. Such was the case in Turkey in the late 1950s, when public sector enterprises were required to maintain prices well below costs of production. Deficits, financed by central bank credits, were a chief source of inflationary pressure. Raising the prices of public sector enterprise outputs resulted in a once-and-for-all increase in the price level by 20 per cent, but simultaneously eliminated the further extension of central bank credits. The consequence was that after several years of inflation recorded at 25 per cent or more annually (despite the price controls which had suppressed it), prices actually fell in the two years following the increase in public sector enterprise prices.

Finally, there is the pre-existing situation with respect to the trade regime and the balance of payments. For reasons outlined above, it makes a significant difference if the stabilization program is aimed primarily at reducing or correcting an existing or prospective open deficit, or whether instead it is intended to liberalize the trade and payments regime and to reduce or eliminate quantitative restrictions as a means of keeping foreign exchange receipts in line with payments. In addition, the degree to which debt-servicing difficulties are being experienced and imports have been curtailed prior to the stabilization program is also significant in influencing the nature of the package and the probable effect of any given set of policy changes.

In general, if imports have been sharply curtailed in the months or years prior to stabilization, the prospects are that an increased import flow can significantly affect real output, even in the short term.[20] If, however, imports are running at high levels, a stabilization program that curtails imports will probably be necessary. Import curtailment is in itself inflationary and may also impair domestic production levels if imports of intermediate and capital goods are used more or less in fixed proportions in domestic production.

The extent to which debt-servicing commitments exist prior to the stabilization package and the ways in which rescheduling is needed and handled within it are also important. The existence of debt-servicing obligations that cannot be met reflects the fact that the country has lived beyond its means in the past. The fact that stabilization packages are often postponed until debt-servicing obligations force governments into negotiations with consortia of creditors is also a reflection of governments' unwillingness to take the short-term costs of stabilization.

The difficulties that can arise as a result of bargaining over debt rescheduling can be important, both politically and psychologically, in affecting a stabilization program. Pressing debt-service obligations can induce governments to accept conditions from consortia of creditors as a prerequisite for debt rescheduling. In some instances, this may enable politicians to take measures they would not otherwise be able to take politically. In other cases, politicians may not accept the necessity for those measures, in which case they may carry them out only belatedly and begrudgingly. In that case, prospects for the longer-term success of the stabilization program are small; the objectives are really those of the creditors and not those of the debtor country.[21] When debt-service rescheduling becomes critical, however, donors as well as debtors are caught. Failure to impose some conditions upon borrowers at that time will force them to lend more later in the absence of policy measures and if a government is unresponsive, creditors will eventually use the country's prospective default as a means of correcting the situation.

8.3.3   Policies

As already stated, there is no single set of policies that constitutes a 'stabilization program'. Programs can range from fairly minor adjustments of exchange rates and macroeconomic policies with only limited objectives to attempts to correct high rates of inflation and severely restrictive QRs. In terms of their effects on economic growth, the successful stabilization programs are those that succeed in one or more of the following: (1) significantly altering the bias of the trade and payments regime away from IS; (2) moving the economy away from reliance upon QRs and toward pricing measures; or (3) permitting a movement away from stop-go cycles of growth resulting from a foreign exchange 'bottleneck'.

Here, we discuss the policies that can constitute part of such a program. First, there are the already-mentioned monetary and fiscal policies. These often entail a reduction in the extension of credit within the economy, ceilings upon levels of government expenditures, and measures to increase tax collections. In addition, they may involve the removal of price ceilings and other measures that may have contributed to government deficits and increases in the money supply. Reichmann and Stillson (1978, p. 297) have tabulated the 'financial programs' implemented as part of stabilization programs for the seventy-nine instances in which higher credit tranches were utilized during the 1963–72 period. These cases involve both developed and developing countries but are none the less instructive. Their classification of cases is reproduced in Table 8.2. In their terminology, 'no deceleration' refers to cases where credit expansion was to be permitted to continue at its current rate. As can be seen, the single largest group of countries resorting to higher credit tranches in IMF standbys were categorized as having 'overly expansionary demand policies', and their rate of credit expansion was to be reduced as part of their stabilization programs. There were, however, thirteen cases in which the objective was to modify the exchange system, and deceleration of credit expansion was not called for. In some of these cases, the authorities had begun instituting restrictive credit policies prior to the standby agreement, so no further deceleration was warranted.

Table 8.2 Financial programs as a component of stabilization programs, seventy-nine countries, 1963–72

Main purpose	Credit policy to be implemented	
	Deceleration	No deceleration
Correction of overly expansionary demand policies	26	–
Modification of exchange system and correction of overly expansionary demand policies	4	–
Modification of exchange system	7	13
Other (of which)	3	26
Anti-recessionary program	(–)	(5)
Cope with temporary shortfall in exports	(–)	(11)
Total	40	39

Source: Reichmann and Stillson (1978, p. 297).

In some developing countries, notably Korea, a significant component of the altered growth structure of the economy originated from interest-rate reforms undertaken in conjunction with the reform of the exchange system. In Korea, inflation had made the real interest rate significantly negative, and interest-rate reforms raised the nominal rate of interest from 5 to 8 to 25 to 30 per cent (with an inflation rate of about 20 per cent). Although other factors also contributed, the Korean savings rate rose dramatically after the interest-rate reforms, and this factor contributed to the large jump in the growth rate achieved subsequently.

With the exception of the interest rate reforms, however, most macroeconomic policies adopted as part of a stabilization program do not directly affect the three variables listed above as being significant for growth prospects. Rather, they constitute part of the background setting for alterations in the trade and payments regime; their chief significance is in determining whether the chosen nominal fixed exchange rate can remain realistic in real terms for a significant time.

The trade and exchange rate components of stabilization programs are even more varied than their macromonetary counterparts. The kinds of policy adopted can be loosely categorized under four main headings: exchange-rate changes; liberalizing the import regime; altering the bias of the regime; and debt rescheduling.

Exchange-rate changes have been discussed. As indicated, a part of the change in the nominal exchange rate is often absorbed by the removal of export subsidies, import surcharges, and other partial measures taken prior to devaluation; and it is 'net', and not gross, devaluation that affects individuals' decisions. To be sure, there is probably some improvement in incentives resulting even from this tidying up, as the replacement of surcharges and subsidies with the exchange rate usually results in greater uniformity of incentives and effective exchange rates across transaction categories than exists prior to the change.

The preceding analysis also demonstrated that the impact of a net devaluation can be quite different depending on whether the pre-existing situation was one of a QR-achieved balance in payments or of an open deficit. In the former case, alteration of the exchange rate automatically results in some liberalization of the regime and, in so far as export subsidies were not as large as import premiums, a reduction in the bias toward import substitution. In an open-deficit prior situation, devaluation is more likely to result in an equiproportionate rise in the domestic prices of tradables, and the chief relative price effect is the relative price of tradables in terms of home goods.

Liberalizing the import regime can come about not only through exchange-rate changes when import premiums on licenses are absorbed, but also through alterations in the control mechanism itself.[22] Many stabilization programs have been accompanied by a revision of the licensing system, often with the introduction of a group of 'priority' or 'liberalized' imports for which licensing procedures are streamlined if not abandoned. Several techniques for achieving liberalization have been used. In some countries, a shift from a 'positive' list (only items listed are permitted to be imported) to a 'negative' list (all items not listed may be freely imported) has resulted in significant liberalization. In other countries, removal of 'guarantee deposit' requirements, under which would-be importers deposit amounts equal to some multiple of their import license with the central bank pending receipt of the import, can represent a sizeable liberalization. In Chile, for example, the authorities have imposed guarantee deposit requirements of 10,000 per cent in periods of severe foreign exchange shortfalls prior to devaluation, and removal of those requirements has *de facto* permitted a resumption of imports.[23] Even moving from monthly to quarterly or semi-annual import programs can result in liberalization of the regime, as can measures such as permitting the resale of import licenses and removing restrictions on currency areas in which licenses are utilized.

Alteration of the bias of the regime comes about through the exchange-rate change itself (in so far as it is net), with absorption of premiums on import licenses as the regime is liberalized and also through policies designed to encourage exports directly. Especially important can be assurances to exporters that the newly achieved real exchange rate for exports and other incentives for exports will continue. In some instances, this has been accomplished in part by the removal of domestic taxes on export production. In Brazil, for example, removal of state and federal taxes on exports made selling domestically and selling abroad at two-thirds the price approximately equally profitable (Carvalho and Haddad, 1981).

Finally, there is the matter of debt rescheduling and borrowing to finance an increased flow of imports. Debt rescheduling is often a prerequisite for any degree of liberalization of the regime and continued economic growth, because by the time of the stabilization program, the country's existing debt-service and repayment obligations are so large that the alternatives are default or an import bill so small that domestic economic activity will have to be severely curtailed. In addition to rescheduling, creditors and especially aid donors have often extended additional credits to the country at the time of stabilization to permit an immediate increase in the import flow before export earnings and other foreign exchange receipts respond to the altered incentives provided by devaluation and its accompanying measures.

8.4   TRADE-OFFS IN STABILIZATION PROGRAMS

Enough has been said already to pinpoint the chief areas of trade-off in deciding upon the nature of a stabilization program. Essentially, there are three crucial and interrelated areas where significant trade-offs exist. The first is between the short term and the long term. The second is between gradual but continuing small changes and large changes. The third is between more foreign borrowing and greater deflationary pressure as part of the stabilization program.

8.4.1   Short-Term versus Long-Term Trade-Offs

If one were to pinpoint the most significant trade-off in stabilization programs, it is clearly the trade-off between short-term costs and longer-term benefits. For reasons already spelled out, stabilization programs almost inevitably entail some short-term costs as a necessary price for achieving longer-term benefits. Especially when the changes that must be brought about involve both the rate of inflation and the bias of the trade regime, short-term adjustment is inevitable. Two or three additional percentage points per year of growth of GNP can be achieved by countries successfully altering their trade bias and payments regime. For those countries, the short-term costs, which are probably of the order of one or two percentage points of GNP for a year or eighteen months, are greatly exceeded by the discounted value of higher GNP at later dates.[24]

The difficulty, of course, is that politicians must inevitably face the short term before reaching the long term. The myopic nature of the political process is well understood. Thus one can well imagine some situations in which alteration of the bias of the regime might well yield a social rate of return in excess of 15 per cent on the short-term costs yet be rejected by the political process.

The fact that the politics of stabilization are difficult makes matters worse. Not only are politicians likely to use higher rates of discount than may be warranted, but the fact that they may be unwilling to withstand the pressures that arise during the transition period raises the possible costs of embarking on a stabilization program. Although the benefits to be achieved by a successful stabilization program that involve moving away from import substitution are not likely to be affected, the fact that politicians may decide to abort a stabilization program before its benefits begin to be realized raises potential costs. A donor, considering whether to push for a stabilization program and shift of trade-orientation, must weigh the possibility that the program may be aborted (which will raise costs for the next attempt) as well as weigh the costs of a successful program against the potential benefits. In large part, such a judgment is of necessity political, but that makes the calculus no less necessary.

8.4.2 Gradualism versus Shock

The fact that there are likely to be short-term costs associated with any change makes the case for some degree of gradualism: it may diminish the costs of adjustment. However, the fact that there are likely to be built-in resistances to change (especially among successful IS establishments) and that entrepreneurs must perceive changes in incentives makes a powerful case for a fairly rapid shift in relative prices and in the trade and payments regime.

Here again, the trade-off is much like that between the short term and the long term. There is no doubt that a gradual shift in signals is the more desirable policy if such gradualism does not affect the chances of success of the policy package. If, however, gradualism provides more of an opportunity for failure (as it almost surely does) than a once-and-for-all reversal of signals, then the case for a sharp once-and-for-all shift in policies is stronger.

As with the short-term/long-term trade-off, there are differences among countries in the likelihood that gradual alteration of the regime can be sustained. However, there is undoubtedly some critical minimum initial shift that is essential in order for businessmen and others to perceive that the regime is really altered, and it is probably a mistake to accept too gradual an approach. Indeed, there is not a great deal of evidence available as to the different costs of larger once-and-for-all changes and smaller ones spread out over a longer period of time. None the less, in view of the political difficulties that are likely to arise if there is a long period during which adjustment is taking place with few visible signs of success, there is a presumption in favor of a once-and-for-all sharp adjustment.

8.4.3 Foreign Borrowing versus Recession

To achieve a given degree of liberalization of imports (and consequent alteration of bias of the regime), either the level of imports must be increased or income must be reduced in such a way that the demand for imports shifts downward. Thus, liberalization can be achieved either by increasing the size of the flow of imports or by domestic recession. If, as is usually the case,[25] an increased flow of imports can be financed during the initial stabilization period only by foreign credits, an immediate question arises: under what conditions is a country justified in borrowing from abroad in the present (to finance increased domestic consumption) rather than accepting a reduction in the level of economic activity?

Again, an answer to the question is partly related to the probability of success of the stabilization program. If the country will, in any event, revert to exchange controls and a strong bias toward import substitution within a short period, it seems to make little sense to borrow currently and to mortgage the future for that purpose. However, to start out with the view that the program is likely to fail also is not acceptable.

Assuming that a program is started, therefore, it seems worthwhile to borrow from abroad to sustain the increased flow of imports. This can be seen in several ways. Suppose a country has a marginal propensity to import (with respect to income) of m. Then, for every dollar borrowed from abroad, domestic income can be greater than it otherwise could be (for the same degree of liberalization) by $1/m$. Unless the marginal propensity to import is extremely high, this would suggest that borrowing from abroad may have a very high social marginal productivity in terms of the additional level of domestic income it will permit.

Another way to view the importance of foreign credits during the stabilization period is to recall that increased flows of imports simultaneously liberalize the regime faster than would otherwise be possible (except with recession) *and* are deflationary in that they absorb excess aggregate demand. Contrasted with the alternatives of cutting back on the level of economic activity or of less liberalization, financing larger import flows appears to be superior, as long as the stabilization program appears to have a good chance of success.

8.5   IMPLICATIONS FOR DONOR COUNTRIES

The implications for aid-givers are several. First and most important, aid to support a sustained flow of imports at the time of a stabilization program may, if all goes well, have a very high marginal product *if* an objective of the stabilization program is to alter the bias of the trade and payments regime. Such aid can be used not only to finance an enlarged flow of imports, but also to reassure potential speculators that the new policies are permanent. Aid that simply increases reserves can be extremely productive.

Second, despite the fact that a country *should* devalue, considerations pertaining to the domestic political situation are not irrelevant to the decision to undertake a stabilization package, especially decisions about its timing. Particularly since the failure of a given stabilization policy makes the next attempt more difficult, there is something to be said for waiting, if possible, for domestic political sentiment to support the package. While increasing demands for new loans may force aid donors' and creditors' hands, postponement of pressure to stabilize may be warranted when feasible. In this connection, other fortuitous circumstances may affect the outcome of the stabilization effort; especially if signs are for a below-average crop or for deteriorating terms of trade, postponement of pressures on the debtor country may be wise.

Finally, a successful stabilization program will have its significant growth impact through the resource reallocation and restructuring of the economy that can result. Those achievements, in turn, can occur only in so far as countries are able successfully to compete in world markets. On the one hand, that requires that the countries altering their regimes provide appropriate incentives and support for their enterprises attempting to export. On the other hand, it also requires that donors be willing to permit entry of exports from developing countries into their markets. In terms of the prospects for increased growth through alteration of the bias of the trade regime, the most significant determinant in the long term will be the growth of world markets. For developed countries, the creditors, as a group, maintaining free access to their markets for the products of developing countries may be the single most important policy they can undertake to ensure the success of stabilization programs with positive effects on the rate of economic growth.

NOTES

1. For economy of language, I am assuming throughout that the rest of the world is stationary and that there is no inflation or other change abroad. An alternative would be to phrase every statement in terms of maintaining a constant difference in the rates of price increase between the country under consideration and the rest of the world. In the context of economic growth, of course, real exchange rates may have to alter even in the absence of changes in the inflation rate.

2. In principle, there is also a bond market in the system. But in keeping with conventional macroeconomics, I follow the time-honored tradition of assuming that if the money market clears or if all three other markets taken together clear, then the bond market must clear. In practice, among countries with convertible currencies, it can and has been argued that the excess supply of money is more likely reflected in an excess demand for bonds than in the goods market. For present purposes, however, that set of questions is well away from our central concern.

3. At first sight, it seems paradoxical that a higher relative price of home goods is associated with greater production. The paradox is resolved if one considers the move from a 'full equilibrium' under flexible exchange rates to a new 'equilibrium' with the exchange rate held constant but with aggregate demand increased: an upward shift in the demand for home goods means the price of home goods must rise, *and* production of home goods increases. Production of traded goods falls while consumption rises, thereby generating a payments deficit in the new 'equilibrium'. Increased demand for home goods, in turn, usually arises because of excessive money creation or fiscal policy.

4. This is not to state that the real exchange rate should remain unaltered under all circumstances; the proposition is that the underlying determinants of the real exchange rate that will clear the market for traded goods are probably independent of the determinants of the rate of inflation and changes in the rate.

5. For a fuller discussion of these issues, see Krueger (1978, esp. chaps 11 and 12).

6. There are at least two historical instances which are well documented and where the authorities were apparently surprised by the pre-existing level of protection prevailing. See Michaely (1975) and Baldwin (1975).

7. The analysis is similar, although not entirely symmetric, for increasing bias toward IS. The reason for the difference is that entrepreneurs can be expected to be more familiar with the domestic market when IS strategies are adopted or intensified than they can be for moving toward EP. The reason for couching the discussion in terms of a move toward EP is that most stabilization efforts entail a reduction, or an attempted reduction, in the extend of bias toward IS.

8. If the existing bias of the regime has been relatively short-lived at the time of the policy shift, it is possible that excess capacity might exist in EP lines to pick up the slack from reduced IS activities. That outcome is less likely the longer IS policies have been in place. A more frequent pattern is that IS industries find that they can cover marginal costs in exporting out of existing capacity once incentives change. The commodity composition of exports in the year or two after shifting strategies, therefore, may bear little relation to the longer-run mix of exports.

9. All three reverted to relatively high inflation rates in the mid-1970s and encountered much more difficulty in reducing their inflation rates than they had earlier experienced.

10. It is important to recognize that foreign lending and aid, motivated by prospects of a reasonable rate of return or undertaken for development purposes, can sustain a current account deficit and contribute, as long as the deficit lasts, to development objectives. In those cases, the current account deficit is offset by 'autonomous' capital inflows. Deficits, as used in the text, refer to payments imbalances in which the desired transactions by

individuals result in an excess demand for foreign exchange which must be met by the authorities by running down their reserves or seeking foreign financing which they would not seek simply for long-run developmental objectives. While the distinction is conceptually clear, there are often significant difficulties in practice of identifying particular types of transaction as being 'autonomous' and others as being 'accommodating'. In practice, however, few worry about the 'deficit' of Korea, as the financing is motivated by long-term commercial prospects, while it is straightforward to identify countries whose borrowing needs originate from their efforts to sustain an infeasible exchange rate. As at 1981, Turkey represents a classic case of a country attempting to maintain an unrealistic exchange rate, borrowing for that purpose in excess of the amount she would otherwise borrow. It should be noted, however, that in an alternative economic context, Turkish net capital inflows might be much larger than they currently are. The reason, of course, is that commercial lending and investing have virtually ground to a halt as expectations of an exchange-rate alteration lead potential creditors with commercial motivations to delay their activities.

11. There are exceptions, of course. Notable among them is the Korean case. The Koreans appear to have maintained QRs on imports of luxury consumer goods which were not domestically produced. Interestingly, licenses to import those goods were awarded to exporters, thereby linking QRs (which were not intended as a balance-of-payments measure in the first place) to profitability of exporting.

12. This is because the higher price of import-competing goods under QRs is likely to pull some resources out of the home-goods sector.

13. A regime is said to be more restrictive the larger the aggregate value of premiums expressed as a percentage of the landed cost of the import bill.

14. This statement assumes that raising the price of foreign exchange is not accompanied by a sufficient increase in aggregate demand so that the domestic price level increases still further. Obviously, a devaluation of x per cent, followed by an increase in the domestic price level of ax, with $a >$ 1, will lead to a decline in the relative price of tradable goods and should intensify either the restrictiveness of the regime or the size of the deficit.

15. The empirical results from the Foreign Trade Regimes and Economic Development project tended to confirm the results. See Krueger (1978, chap. 8) and the individual studies, especially Díaz-Alejandro (1976) and Behrman (1976), for analysis of this phenomenon.

16. If, for example, surcharges on imports and export subsidies are removed simultaneously with the devaluation, the changes in the effective exchange rates perceived by producers and consumers will be considerably smaller than the size of the devaluation. It is useful to refer to 'net devaluation' as being the change in the price of foreign exchange once account is taken of the removal of export subsidies, import surcharges, and the like.

17. The difficulties are very real. Cooper (1971) documented these problems neatly. A sizeable proportion of finance ministers at the time of devaluation have lost their jobs within eighteen months. There is also no doubt that luck is an element. As Cooper showed, perhaps the best indicator of the likelihood of success is the quality of the harvest: a good harvest provides a buffer which makes the reallocation vastly easier. Of the twenty-two devaluations in the NBER project on Foreign Trade Regimes and Economic Development, in fifteen cases the inflation in the ensuing two

years was larger proportionately than was the initial devaluation. See Krueger (1978, pp. 82–3 and Table 5.3).
18. Many Latin American programs, especially those of Chile and Argentina, seem to have been geared primarily toward inflation.
19. Turkey and India are examples of this type.
20. This clearly happened in Turkey following the 1958 devaluation.
21. For an analysis of the political implications of donor behavior with respect to one devaluation, see Bhagwati and Srinivasan (1975, chap. 10). Díaz-Alejandro (1976) reports that, prior to undertaking its own liberalization program in 1967, the Colombian president even went on television to state that he would not abide by the wishes of Colombia's creditors!
22. Liberalizing the regime cannot be carried very far without increasing the flow of imports. In the short run, that can usually be achieved only when financed by foreign credits, which are discussed in 8.4.3.
23. Removal or reduction of guarantee deposit requirements can have a significant effect on the money supply. For this reason, it sometimes makes sense to provide for their gradual removal, rather than to abandon them at the time of devaluation.
24. See Krueger (1978, chap. 11) for the statistical evidence on this point for a pooled time-series cross-section of devaluations in the NBER project countries. See also Balassa (1978).
25. In some instances, expectations of an exchange-rate alteration induce exporters to withhold their goods and importers to stock up. Reverse flows after devaluation can then finance increased imports. While that can happen, it is difficult to rely on it.

REFERENCES

Balassa, B. (1978). 'Exports and Economic Growth: Some Further Evidence', *Journal of Development Economics*, vol. 5, no. 2, pp. 181–9.
Baldwin, R. (1975). *Foreign Trade Regimes and Economic Development: Philippines*. New York: Columbia University Press, for the National Bureau of Economic Research.
Behrman, J.R. (1976). *Foreign Trade Regimes and Economic Development: Chile*. New York: Columbia University Press, for the National Bureau of Economic Research.
Bhagwati, J. and T.N. Srinivasan (1975). *Foreign Trade Regimes and Economic Development: India*. New York: Columbia University Press, for the National Bureau of Economic Research.
Carvalho, J. and C. Haddad (1981). 'Brazil' in A.O. Krueger, H.B. Lary, T. Monson and N. Akrasanee (eds), *Trade and Employment in Developing Countries, 1: Individual Studies*. Chicago: University of Chicago Press, for the National Bureau of Economic Research.
Cooper, R. (1971). 'An Assessment of Currency Devaluation in Developing Countries' in G. Ranis (ed.), *Government and Economic Development*. New Haven, CT: Yale University Press.
Díaz-Alejandro, C. (1976). *Foreign Trade Regimes and Economic Development: Colombia*. New York: Columbia University Press, for the National Bureau of Economic Research.
Fishlow, A. (1975). 'Foreign Trade Regimes and Economic Development:

Brazil', paper presented to Bogotá Seminar, April.

Krueger, A.O. (1978). *Foreign Trade Regimes and Economic Development: Liberalization Attempts and Consequences*. Cambridge, MA: Ballinger, for the National Bureau of Economic Research.

Michaely, M. (1975). *Foreign Trade Regimes and Economic Development: Israel*. New York: Columbia University Press, for the National Bureau of Economic Research.

Reichmann, T. and R. Stillson (1978). 'Experience with Programs of Balance of Payments Adjustment: Stand-by Arrangements in the Higher Credit Tranches, 1963–72', *IMF Staff Papers*, vol. 25, p. 297.

Sohmen, E. (1958). 'The Effects of Devaluation on the Price Level', *Quarterly Journal of Economics*, May.

9 · PROBLEMS OF LIBERALIZATION

The experience of the past three decades has convinced almost all analysts that systems of direct controls and attempts to 'thwart the market' are inefficient, if not ineffective, instruments to achieve virtually any objective of policy. The enormous success of Europe and Japan in expanding output and raising living standards during the post-war era has clearly been related to sustained liberalization of trade and capital flows. Among the developing countries progress has varied markedly, but notably the most successful developing countries have generally maintained liberalized trade and payments regimes, which in turn have been made feasible only by relatively liberal domestic economic policies.

Still, despite the clear evidence on the subject, a large number of developing countries remain caught in a stifling web of controls over economic activity. In many cases, there is general agreement that the controls no longer serve the purposes for which they were imposed, even if they once did. Many countries have had periods in which efforts were made to alter the regime and reduce or eliminate direct controls on one or more aspects of economic activity. Those efforts have sometimes met with failure, and have made others reluctant to attempt removal of controls. The question is why that should be so: what are the problems of liberalization? Why, given the evidence that the benefits are so great, is it so difficult to accomplish? Why are politicians (and often the entire community of informed citizens) so reluctant, if not downright unwilling, to liberalize their economies?

A simple answer might, of course, be that politicians are misinformed and, for one reason or another, oblivious to the benefits attainable by liberalization. While there are undoubtedly instances where this is so (or where vested political interests have enough stake in the existing system to render its maintenance rational from the viewpoint of those in power), that set of circumstances is disregarded here. Instead, our focus

---

First printed in 1984.

is on the difficulties that arise in the process of attempting to liberalize the system, and reasons – both political and economic – why a prime minister, even if convinced of the long-term benefits of liberalization, might be reluctant to attempt it; or attempting it, might fail to achieve his objectives.

At the outset, it is necessary to define what is meant by 'liberaliza-tion'. A narrow definition would be that a market is liberalized if there are no quantitative restrictions attempting to control either buyers or sellers – from which it would follow that liberalization is the act of removing quantitative controls. The difficulty with this definition is that there are a variety of economic policies that can have the effect of reducing the restrictiveness of quantitative controls, such as releasing more foreign exchange to permit imports under a licensing regime. Since a more 'restrictive' set of controls is presumably one in which market participants would pay more to carry out the transactions that are not permitted, liberalization of controls, to be consistent, must imply a greater reduction in the scarcity value attached to restrictions. Hence for purposes of this chapter, liberalization is defined as any policy action that reduces the restrictiveness of controls – it may be their complete removal, or the replacement of a restrictive set of controls with a less restrictive one. Under this definition, it should be noted, an action such as devaluation in the context of an import-licensing regime 'liberalizes' that regime.

A second initial question has to do with the range of markets to be analyzed. Of course, there are direct controls in almost every country – rent controls in New York City, underpricing of telephone and electrical services in many developing countries, and pricing of urban transport almost universally, to name just a few. While their removal can result in difficulties of the sort discussed here, it proves convenient to focus on a narrower set of markets, but a set that is interrelated and frequently subject to controls in developing countries. This includes the foreign exchange market (for both current and capital-account transactions), the financial market, the labor market, and the market for agricultural commodities. Controls on these markets have related to one another in ways that have had important macroeconomic effects, and have been a focal point of many liberalization efforts.[1]

As a starting point, it is convenient to sketch the conditions that pre-vail, or have prevailed, in many developing countries in which direct controls have been used. Thereafter, we will turn our attention to the macroeconomic and microeconomic issues of liberalization. This will set the stage for consideration of the issues of timing and sequencing of liberalization efforts, which seem to be the focus of most unresolved questions.

Finally, we provide some conjectures as to factors increasing the likelihood of successful liberalization attempts.

9.1   THE PROTOTYPICAL ILLIBERAL ECONOMY

In many ways that are not well understood, there seems to be a logic to the evolution of direct controls on prices and quantities over time. Once intervention has occurred, e.g. in the foreign exchange market, the responses by private agents to the initial intervention often elicit modifications, and usually intensifications, of the control system. To illustrate, an initial move to import-licensing generally reduces incentives to export, evokes cries of 'unfair' from many who attempt to persuade the authorities that the system should be altered to take into account their particular circumstances, and provides incentives to evade the regime via smuggling, under- or overinvoicing, or engaging in black market transactions. All of these responses tend to induce the authorities to restrict imports even further, to modify and usually to complicate the allocation rules for those imports, and also to increase surveillance. These actions in turn are likely to evoke from agents a further response to the altered incentives. As the profitability of evading or avoiding regulations increases, the discrepancy between private and social profitability widens with mounting consequences over time.

Because of these 'dynamic' tendencies, the typical economy in which liberalization is contemplated and would yield high returns is not one in which a single market is regulated; rather, it is usually an economy in which a variety of markets is subject to controls of varying degrees of severity and enforcement. Often these controls are accompanied by macroeconomic difficulties that may or may not stem from the same underlying factors.

Because multiple markets are subject to intervention, the very concept of liberalization itself can mean different things in different contexts, and an attempt to sort out liberalization problems conceptually must start with identification of the types of controls initially in effect, and must recognize the interaction between them. As a starting point, it is useful to consider the interaction between macroeconomic imbalances and intervention in individual markets.

9.1.1   Inflation and Controls

Economists have long recognized that a perfectly anticipated inflation might have relatively low economic costs, largely because markets would adjust to inflationary expectations so that the real interest rate and other relative prices would not differ significantly from those that would obtain in the absence of inflation. In reality, however, price increases and altered inflation rates usually result from an effort on the part of the government to gain control over resources without offsetting tax increases. Sometimes this effort to obtain resources is part of planned increases in public-investment programs, although sometimes it is the immediate counterpart to direct controls (as, for example, when food prices to consumers are maintained below market levels through rationing while farmers are paid higher prices).

Either way, once inflation starts, the usual response of governments is to attempt direct controls to offset some of its apparent effects. Maintaining a fixed nominal exchange rate, with reluctant adjustments that lag significantly behind inflation, is one of the most frequent responses. In many cases, governments have kept constant the prices of public-sector services, including utilities, transport, and outputs of public enterprises, in an effort to 'control inflation'. In the presence of an underlying inflationary process, of course, the budget deficit induced by financial losses from those actitivies tends further to intensify inflationary pressures, while simultaneously increasing the degree of distortion in the economy due to regulated prices. In some instances, governments have also attempted to impose price controls over private-sector economic activity. There have also been efforts to index wages and, even more frequently, to regulate nominal interest rates.

These markets – especially foreign exchange, credit, and labor – play key roles in the allocation of resources throughout the economy. When they are controlled, costs can be very high, and their liberalization is essential for markedly improved economic performance. Usually, however, liberalization measures are combined with policies aimed at least in part at reducing the rate of inflation, rather than at freeing the individual markets while permitting inflationary pressures to continue. Thus, it proves impossible to analyze direct controls and efforts to eliminate them without taking into account the macroeconomic setting in which those efforts are undertaken. While some countries have experienced inflation without direct controls, and a few countries (most notably India) have resorted to direct controls in the absence of inflation, the majority of direct controls either have been imposed in an effort to reduce inflation rates or have intensified their restrictiveness because of domestic inflation (as with a fixed nominal exchange rate).

Hence, there are strong and important interactions between the macroeconomic processes – the government budget and the determination of the money supply and domestic credit – and control conditions in individual markets. Moreover, when the nominal rate of interest and/or the exchange rate is fixed, reduction in the rate of inflation automatically permits some degree of liberalization, in the sense that the relevant price deviates less from the level that would obtain with prices that appropriately reflect opportunity cost than it would at a higher inflation rate.

9.1.2 Balance-of-Payments Difficulties

In principle, a country experiencing internal inflation would live within its budget constraint either by permitting its exchange rate to float (although there are interesting questions as to why domestic residents should continue to hold domestic money) or by strictly rationing available foreign exchange by one system or another. The latter technique would, of course, entail the distortion costs associated with disparities between the domestic marginal rate of transformation in production and the marginal rate of transformation through trade. However, either system would permit continuation of domestic inflationary policies without necessarily triggering balance-of-payment difficulties.

In practice, however, few governments that have experienced inflation have fully adopted either policy. Indeed, the same political and economic factors that lead to domestic inflation usually lead to balance-of-payments deficits. Even when exchange controls and import-licensing systems are in place, the nominal exchange rate is often adjusted too little and too late, and excess demand for goods is satisfied partially by imports financed by running down reserves or borrowing from abroad.

Often, the build-up of debt permits the continuation of trade and payments imbalances, and hence of expansionary macroeconomic policies, for a period of time. However, as debt and debt-service obligations increase while foreign exchange earnings stagnate or decline, lenders are increasingly reluctant to extend additional credit. Debt-servicing difficulties, or the inability to borrow sufficiently to finance existing import orders, are frequently the condition that triggers policy changes.

Serious debt-servicing obligations in themselves confound any process of adjustment. This is in part because such obligations must be met, and in part because the level of expenditure must be cut by at least the amount to which borrowing was previously excessive. However, difficulties are intensified largely because foreign debt has political connotations that make the perceived 'foreign intervention' troublesome, and the 'debt-crisis' atmosphere is probably not conducive to systematic preparation of a liberalization plan and its political acceptance.

While a few genuine liberalizations have taken place where existing foreign debt or inability to sustain previous borrowing levels was neither a trigger nor a serious problem (e.g. South Korea in the early 1960s), such liberalizations have been the exception rather than the rule. And, as international financial markets have become increasingly integrated in recent years, debt-servicing difficulties have, if anything, assumed increasing importance as both an impetus to policy reform and as an additional problem to be resolved if those reforms are to be successful.

This complication is especially important in countries where earlier there had been substantial reliance on quantitative restrictions to restrain import levels. For in those cases, a necessary condition for liberalization is that the domestic price of importables must be permitted to fall relative to the domestic price of exportables, for when imports have been so restrained, both imports and exports are below the levels and shares of GNP that would prevail in the absence of the distortion. What is required, therefore, is an expansion of both imports and exports. The least inflationary means of achieving this would be to combine an increase in the nominal exchange rate with simultaneous import liberalization. This would bring down the domestic price of importables while raising that of exportables, which would in turn minimize inflationary consequences of liberalization. However, when import levels have been sustained by borrowing and when further credit is not possible, it becomes necessary to curtail imports. Such further curtailment is consistent with liberalization only if either the level of economic activity declines to shift import demand downward, or the nominal exchange rate is adjusted upward by a substantially larger amount than would be the case with an increased import flow.

The former choice – domestic recession – is politically painful and economically wasteful (economic activity would have to shift downward by the amount that imports must decline *times* the inverse of the marginal propensity to import). Especially if there are lags prior to an export response to increased incentives, the size of the required shift may be significantly greater than would be consistent with liberalization in the long run. The latter alternative – a larger devaluation – could in principle permit the removal of import-licensing mechanisms and the simultaneous adjustment of the demand and supply of foreign exchange. However, the larger size of the required devaluation would in itself give rise to a larger once-and-for-all jump in the price level, which would in turn contribute to the momentum of inflation and reduce the likelihood that the desired degree of real devaluation could be achieved.

While the observant skeptic may wonder whether a floating exchange rate might attain the desired result, it must be noted that such a solution would be consistent with liberalization only if the financial markets were also simultaneously liberalized and the rate of interest were permitted to be market-determined. For in the presence of controlled (and usually negative real) interest rates, full liberalization of the exchange regime for both current and capital account and a floating exchange rate would surely result in capital outflows and rapid depreciation of the currency in excess of the rate of inflation.

And, while full liberalization is clearly desirable, few governments (and perhaps even their economic advisers) are willing to take the complete plunge into full liberalization of financial and exchange markets simultaneously. There is insufficient experience with the 'cold shower' approach to liberalization to provide confidence that its short-term costs can be contained within reasonable bounds. Indeed, if there were legitimate doubts in the early 1970s about the feasibility and desirability of complete instantaneous liberalization, the experiences of Argentina, Chile, and Uruguay have provided further support for the skeptics. Whether those experiences should be so interpreted is a topic deferred until later. At this juncture, the important point is that in the context of an initial debt-servicing crisis, attention is usually focused on the foreign exchange market; and the unpleasant choice, in the absence of additional lending from abroad, lies between greater inflationary pressures to restore equilibrium or domestic unemployment and deflation. Obviously, this highlights one of the important contributions international lending can make to a country when its leaders are genuinely committed to a full liberalization: it can permit higher levels of imports than would otherwise be feasible to bring about a quick adjustment of relative prices. Not only does this reduce the economic and political strains associated with liberalization, it also reduces business's uncertainty as to the likelihood that liberalization will persist.

9.1.3   Microeconomic Aspects of Liberalization

As has been seen, the same reluctance to maintain government expenditures in line with receipts that generates inflationary pressures in the first place also often results in government controls that – superficially at least – are intended to reduce the observed inflationary consequences. In many instances, these controls themselves introduce further macroeconomic distortions into the economy (as, for example, when price controls on output of public enterprises further fuel the government deficit), but they also distort important markets in the economy.

Inflationary pressures are not the only reason for sectoral distortions, however. Important markets are controlled for other motives as well: unwillingness to pass on increased energy prices; desires to 'keep food prices down'; maintenance of below-market-clearing rates of interest to 'encourage capital formation in key sectors' or for other reasons; investment-licensing to 'guide new investments into socially desirable channels'; and the raising of the real wage in the controlled part of the economy above its level elsewhere to 'protect the worker'.

These controls not only have significant economic costs in themselves, they also interact with other distortions. High labor costs combine with import restrictions to encourage development of very capital-intensive, import-competing activities. Exchange-rate overvaluation discourages the production of agricultural exports, and domestic controls on food prices further depress agricultural incomes, which in turn further stimulate out-migration to the cities. Moreover, some controls (such as domestic marketing boards for agricultural commodities) sever the link between domestic prices and international ones, thereby insulating the market in question from any automatic impact in the event of an exchange-rate change or other policy shift.

There are interesting and important questions concerning the pay-off from various types of liberalization – in the presence of controlled markets elsewhere in the economy – to which economists do not as yet have satisfactory answers. What is clear is that the same liberalization measures may have very different impacts depending on the circumstances in other markets in the economy in question, and that an analysis of the effects of liberalization, one market at a time, may yield misleading results.

9.2   DIFFICULTIES OF LIBERALIZATION

One of the major difficulties with liberalization is that it is usually undertaken in the midst of an exceedingly difficult situation, and often in a crisis atmosphere. Moreover, the fact that the prevailing distortions have induced uneconomic activities or techniques of production implies that a successful liberalization will necessarily penalize some of those who had earlier responded apppropriately to the existing incentive structure.

These difficulties are in and of themselves serious enough. In practice, they are often confounded by the simultaneous effort to restore some degree of macroeconomic equilibrium and, in greater or lesser degree, to liberalize some key markets. That is, efforts to bring the government budget under control and to reduce the rate of inflation are often intertwined with policies designed to liberalize imports, to restore producers' incentives in agriculture and energy, and to eliminate price controls and licensing mechanisms.

In most developed countries, moreover, inflationary pressures usually have been permitted to be passed through into price increases; hence few direct controls have accompanied the inflationary process. As a consequence, anti-inflationary policies in developed countries have generally been undertaken under circumstances in which distortions in key markets are substantially smaller than those in some developing countries. Even for developed countries, however, efforts to reduce inflationary pressures have been at best partially successful and have required fairly determined political resolve for considerable intervals of time.

In developing countries in which inflation has been a substantial problem and direct controls have been an initial policy response, anti-inflationary programs are even more complex and fraught with difficulty than in developed countries because of the existence of so many controlled markets. A major difficulty with many liberalization efforts, and especially those focused on the trade sector of the economy, has been the presumption that an anti-inflationary program, simultaneously embarked upon, would succeed.[2]

It seems clear that, in practice, efforts to liberalize the trade sectors of developing countries have foundered more often upon the failure of the accompanying anti-inflationary program than on any other single factor. Space limitations preclude a full analysis of the difficulties of combining an anti-inflation program with efforts to liberalize other key markets. Only two fairly obvious points need to be made. First, there are ways in which the dependence of trade liberalization on curbing inflation can be at least reduced. Most notably, a crawling peg, rather than a higher fixed nominal exchange rate, can assure some degree of independence in the two reform efforts. Second, liberalization is more likely to be achieved by anti-inflationary programs designed to assure that governments will not resort to direct controls than by programs aimed at attaining the lowest recorded rate of price increase over the short term. For example, to remove controls on prices of essential government services will reduce the inflation rate more effectively in the long run than to set an initially realistic nominal price that will quickly erode again unless inflation is contained. Paradoxically, anti-inflationary programs structured to succeed only if the inflation rate declines are less likely to bring down the rate of inflation than are programs designed to liberalize markets regardless of whether or not the anti-inflationary policies succeed.

With those comments as background, let us set aside the difficult questions surrounding inflation control – and for that matter the issue of whether there can be sustained liberalization against the background of rising inflation rates – and focus henceforth on actual liberalization of markets. Two general questions need to be addressed: (1) what reforms, undertaken individually, are likely to be welfare-improving even in the presence of other controlled markets; and (2) which are the more important markets to liberalize when one starts from a situation with multiple controls and distortions? Thereafter, our focus is directed on each of the important markets, and the most frequently encountered problems of liberalization in each market are discussed in turn. The difficult questions surrounding the timing and sequencing of reforms are deferred to Section 9.3.

9.2.1 Welfare-Improving Liberalizations of Individual Markets

The generalized theory of the 'second best' tells us that whenever there are significant links between markets, it is in general impossible to ascertain the direction in which welfare will change as the result of a small reduction in the distortion operating in a single market. Yet in most countries in which liberalization efforts are contemplated, total liberalization is generally infeasible; reforms, if undertaken at all, will be undertaken in some markets before they are undertaken in others.

The question arises, therefore, when a particular market can be freed in reasonable confidence that the net effect will be welfare-improving. In attempting to answer this question we will ignore considerations such as the degree of rent-seeking and the greater incentive effects of competition that may result from liberalization, which tend to lead to the presumption that freeing up any market may yield welfare benefits. Moreover, the analysis must of necessity be empirical rather than theoretical. As such, it must be recognized that situations could arise that would deviate sufficiently from the usual case so that the presumptions set forth here would be invalid.

Let us look at each of the major markets subject to controls in turn. Consider, first, agriculture. Here, the available evidence seems to suggest that producers base their production decisions on relative prices within their sector. For countries that are exporters of food crops, consequently, anything that moves relative prices of agricultural commodities closer to their international levels is probably on net potentially welfare-improving. (I ignore here the important short-run welfare losses of low-income persons paying higher prices for food, on the grounds that superior measures can be found to yield the same real income transfer.) Thus, freeing producer prices in agriculture to permit them to rise will improve welfare even if the exchange rate is overvalued: the relative prices of alternative agricultural crops will reflect their opportunity costs in the international market *vis-à-vis* each other, while the price of agricultural commodities relative to other goods and services will move in the appropriate direction.

A more difficult question arises in countries in which comparative advantage lies in export crops. These countries would, under efficient resource allocation, import food. In that circumstance, the decontrol of domestic producer prices under import-licensing may raise food prices relative to export crops. In the presence of an overvalued nominal exchange rate, resources may be further pulled from export crops to food, possibly with negative welfare implications. Hence, there is probably some question as to whether liberalization of domestic prices of agricultural commodities is necessarily welfare-improving unless it is accompanied by moves toward a more realistic exchange rate.

Likewise, it would appear that welfare could always be improved by liberalizing the financial market and permitting the real interest rate to become positive. Exchange-rate overvaluation and artificially low nominal interest rates tend to work in the same direction: they encourage the introduction of overly capital-intensive activities. Consequently, there is a presumption that moving either the exchange rate or the interest rate in an appropriate direction is likely to improve welfare.

Similar considerations would appear to apply to the labor market: even in the presence of exchange-rate overvaluation, the move to a freer market should be welfare-improving. Indeed, to the extent that there is exchange-rate overvaluation, reduction in the real wage will increase the profitability of activities in which a labor-abundant country has a comparative advantage.

Finally, there is the exchange rate and the market for traded goods. A first question is whether the move from a licensing system to a uniform tariff, holding the total level of imports constant, is welfare-improving. In theory, anything could happen as a result of such a move: resources previously allocated to exportables could be pulled into import-competing activities previously subject to less-than-average protection, possibly resulting in a further loss in welfare. In practice, however, it seems likely that, provided exporters are permitted to purchase their intermediate goods and raw materials at international prices,[3] a uniform rate of tariff is to be potentially welfare-superior to import-licensing and associated dispersion of implicit tariff rates.

In addition, there is the question of the welfare effect of raising the nominal exchange rate in the presence of other controls. One can imagine a number of circumstances (e.g. the presence of domestic price controls) that would tend to reduce the impact of a change in the exchange rate, but it is difficult to imagine a situation in which increasing the nominal exchange rate would not be welfare-improving. Such a move necessarily reduces the bias of the trade regime toward import substitution. This follows because with import-licensing, the domestic price of exportables will increase. With the quantity of imports unaltered or increasing, the relative price of exportables must increase.

As we have already seen, this will move agricultural relative prices in the appropriate direction, and simultaneously offset in part any distortion in factor markets arising from lower than average duties on imported capital equipment.

Another question arises with respect to the exchange rate – namely, whether it is advisable to liberalize capital flows in the presence of a highly restrictive set of controls on domestic financial flows. While there are some types of partial liberalization that may be welfare-improving in the presence of distorted domestic capital markets (e.g. easing of the restrictions on the inflow of private capital), it seems reasonably clear that the total liberalization of capital flows is infeasible in the presence of a controlled domestic interest rate: capital outflow would immediately result. A related problem pertains to liberalization of capital flows in the presence of a highly restrictive regime covering current-account transactions. This is a difficult and important question, and one on which analysis to date has not shed very much light. There is no strong presumption: one could legitimately argue that, since exchange of assets is exchange of the capitalized values of income streams, income streams generated by distorted prices are probably the inappropriate ones at which to trade. It would then follow that capital-account liberalization should not be undertaken unless both current account and domestic financial transactions are already liberalized. Whether further analysis can shed additional light on this important question remains to be seen. It would appear, therefore, that with the possible exception of liberalization of agricultural prices in the context of overvaluation in a country with comparative advantage in tree crops, and a liberalization of capital-account transaction in the presence of domestic financial controls or current-account controls, there is a presumption that liberalization of any of the other markets typically subject to controls is likely to be welfare-improving.

9.2.2   Which are the Most Important Markets to Liberalize?

Whereas some theoretical presumptions permit inferences about the direction of welfare change resulting from liberalization of individual markets, it is much more difficult to provide a solid a priori basis for inferring the order of magnitude of costs associated with controls in different markets. Circumstances vary with both the nature of the controls in place and the structure of the domestic economy.

It might be, for example, that two countries had controls in both labor and capital markets. Country A might have had relatively little intervention in the labor market but high negative real rates of interest. Perhaps country B's labor legislation, by contrast, significantly raised the real cost of labor but its nominal interest rate was only slightly below that which would prevail in the absence of regulation. In some countries, controls may be relatively light in some markets and much more stringent in others, so that the welfare ranking would differ for that reason.

Differences in economic structure may also matter. For example, it is probably a reasonable conjecture that controls on producer prices in agriculture are more detrimental to welfare in some poor African countries than are overvalued nominal exchange rates – although the combination of the two is certainly more harmful than either one alone would be. The same distortions in South Korea would very likely be ranked in the opposite order in terms of their welfare effects: given the level of development of the economy and the diminished relative importance of the agricultural sector, exchange-rate overvaluation might clearly be more costly.

All that can be done, therefore, is to venture some tentative hypotheses about circumstances under which different controls might be more or less detrimental. Starting with the foreign trade market, it is likely that controls are more costly the smaller the size of the domestic market and the higher the per capita income of the country (because a larger fraction of economic activity is affected by the relative price of tradables with economic growth). Certainly, for the countries now considered middle-income, it would appear that controls over foreign trade and overvalued exchange rates have been a major, if not the biggest single, source of distortion.

By much the same reasoning, controls over producer prices in agriculture have probably been more costly the lower the country's per capita income (because of the higher share of GNP originating in agriculture), the more the country's comparative advantage within agriculture lies in export crops, and the greater its overall comparative advantage in agriculture.

This leaves the labor and financial markets. Here, there is less evidence on which to base a judgment. There can be little doubt that subsidization of capital goods, either explicit or implicit, can become increasingly costly over time, as the South Korean and Israeli experiences have amply demonstrated. That this distortion is probably the major source of difficulty is a reasonable conjecture in both of these economies. The interesting questions, however, center more on the interaction between labor- and capital-market distortions, on the one hand, and trade and exchange liberalization, on the other.

In particular, a question of some importance is the extent to which the benefits of liberalization of the trade regime can be realized in the presence of highly restrictive wage legislation or of controlled financial and capital markets. It is of some interest that the highly successful Far Eastern exporters had relatively free labor markets as well as liberalized trade regimes, while regulation of financial markets and interest rates persisted. There is no instance that I know of, however, where a country's trade liberalization has been highly successful in the context of highly restrictive and enforced regulations surrounding the labor market.

9.2.3　Problems of Liberalizing Individual Markets

It now seems fitting to examine the issues associated with liberalization in each of the key markets that affect overall resource allocation – the foreign exchange market, the labor market, the financial (and implicitly capital) market, and sectoral markets (most notably the agricultural market).

With regard, first, to foreign exchange, three issues are of particular importance. One – the interrelationship between anti-inflationary programs and the liberalization of the trade regime – has already been discussed. It bears repeating that more efforts at liberalizing the trade regime have foundered because a new nominal exchange rate was pegged and inflation did not abate than for all other reasons combined. The second issue pertains to the elimination of quantitative restrictions, while the third relates to the difficulties surrounding the transition process.

Obviously, if it were possible to move to a completely open trade regime, questions concerning the dismantling of quantitative restrictions would arise only in connection with the pace of the program, a subject treated below. In most instances, however, the range of policy choices acceptable to politicians does not include an immediate move to free trade, but may include alterations of the existing machinery of controls. In some instances, quantitative restrictions have lost most if not all of their force through administrative devices, including the transference of items to a liberalized list for which licensing is not required, or abolishing licensing requirements altogether. (These actions were taken by Turkey in the devaluations of 1970 and the liberalization of 1980–1, respectively.) In other instances, administrative changes have significantly reduced the restrictiveness of the regime. These can include such measures as reducing the number of approvals required for a license, changing the import regulations from a negative list (in which all items not enumerated may not be imported), or simply granting licenses more readily to all comers. Finally, in a few instances, a country has dismantled quantitative restrictions with the intent of liberalizing but maintaining the degree of protection afforded to domestic producers. Two such cases were Israel and the Philippines.[4]

This latter attempt, while seemingly the most rational from an economist's viewpoint, is apparently the most difficult. While once-and-for-all administrative changes may have very different effects on the degree to which protection is reduced in different industries, experience suggests that reduction in protection afforded through quantitative restrictions in that way is feasible. By contrast, laborious efforts to replace quantitative restrictions with tariffs provide ample time for political pressures to be brought to bear; efforts of tribunals to find 'fair' criteria for determining protection levels and then to apply them seem destined inevitably to slow down the entire process, if not to render it entirely ineffective.

One other troublesome aspect of import liberalization should be noted: in some countries, raw material and intermediate-goods imports have been liberalized first, on the plausible assumption that all producers will be better able to compete when confronted with international prices for their inputs. While this argument is impeccable as far as producers of exportables are concerned, it is flawed for import-competing producers: if protection on inputs is reduced or removed before protection on output, effective protection to domestic producers in fact increases in the process of liberalization. This consideration brings clearly into focus the distinction between moving toward free trade and liberalizing the trade regime.

When it comes to the labor market, much less is known, and systematic study of liberalizations and how they have come about is urgently needed. One has the general impression that most successful liberalizations appear to have come about not by the removal or reduction of existing wage levels but rather by a failure to adjust wage levels fully with future inflation. Carvalho and Haddad, for example, have demonstrated how the Brazilian minimum wage gradually became ineffective as ever-higher percentages of the labor force were paid wage rates in excess of the minimum.[5]

Financial-market liberalization has been the focal point of considerable analysis,[6] although most of it was undertaken on the assumption that capital was relatively immobile internationally. This may have been an acceptable assumption in the 1960s, but with the greater willingness of developed countries' private financial institutions to lend to developing countries in the 1970s, a host of new issues has arisen, and there seems to be a large number of poorly understood problems. In the 1960s, some countries, notably Brazil and South Korea, seem to have been able partly to liberalize their financial markets without great difficulty. In more recent years, several efforts at financial liberalization have encountered financial difficulties of major magnitude: Argentina, Chile, and Turkey appear to be recent examples. Whether difficulties arose because of liberalization in the financial sector and the resulting competition between banks, or whether instead there was interaction between the liberalization of financial markets and that of the foreign exchange market, is a question requiring further analysis.

With regard, finally, to sectoral markets, the issues appear to be more political than economic. Whereas there are questions about the response of the banking sector to deregulation, the speed of response of the trade sector, and so on, there are fewer questions regarding economic behavior where sectoral markets are concerned. Instead, however, the difficulties become increasingly political, as questions of income distribution come to the fore. Resistance to reforms in the pricing of food, urban transport, energy, and other publicly provided goods and services is encountered largely because of consumer, rather than producer, interests.

9.3   TIMING AND SEQUENCING OF REFORMS

Our discussion up to this point has focused largely on what is known about liberalization and its problems. There remain two major issues on which much less is known, but that may be important if the probability of successful transition to a more liberalized economy is to be increased. These relate to the appropriate sequencing and timing of reforms.

The issue can best be posed by positing a set of initial conditions and then raising a series of interrelated questions. Take the case of an economy subject to exchange control, import-licensing, a negative real interest rate with credit rationing, indexed real wages with resulting open unemployment, and suppression of producer prices in agriculture. Assume further that the objective is to remove all of these distortions to the system, with a minimum present value of expected costs of the transition. A preliminary question is whether total and simultaneous removal of all controls is cost-minimizing. Unless the answer to that question is affirmative, questions arise as to the speed at which controls should be dismantled (the timing issue) and the chronological order (sequence) in which individual markets should be decontrolled.[7] A final question is whether, if a single distortion will remain in the system (e.g. domestic inflation due to a large government budget deficit), total and simultaneous removal of all other distortions is optimal.

The issues of sequencing and timing arise only if one believes that simultaneous and immediate removal of all controls is neither optimal nor feasible. There are some grounds for believing that the rapid removal of all controls may be the least painful way of proceeding: new signals in place will prevent resource misallocation in response to altered signals before the transition is complete; instantaneous adjustment may prevent political opposition to the move from diluting it; and, since there is considerable evidence that uncertainty about the likelihood that policy initiatives can be sustained causes delays in the responses to altered policy signals, an immediate transformation of the economic environment may reduce uncertainty. If these considerations are over-riding, the issues of timing and sequencing do not arise except in a second-best context.

There are those, however, who believe that total and instantaneous dismantling of all controls may be non-optimal. The difficulties associated with opening up capital-account transactions before the current account has been liberalized have already been discussed. A plausible argument can be made that optimal dismantling of controls might start with current-account transactions, agricultural pricing, and the domestic labor and capital markets, leaving capital-account transactions initially subject to controls. These controls would be removed (gradually? suddenly?) in a second stage of the liberalization once domestic resources had responded to altered policy signals.

Assuming that one could demonstrate that capital-account liberalization should be delayed, I know of no theory or set of conditions to provide any presumption as to the length of delay, nor for that matter whether the capital-account liberalization should then be gradual or instantaneous.

While the capital account would appear to be the best candidate for delayed liberalization, others have argued for gradual liberalization of current-account transactions or of domestic financial markets. The basis for the argument is largely judgmental, however, and it is difficult to present a systematic case. Clearly, further analysis of the liberalization efforts of the 1970s, especially in cases where domestic and international capital markets were important, is called for.

9.4   CONCLUSION

The major problem with liberalization, as with so many other economic policy problems, is that politicians, government officials, and the informed public can readily foresee those interests that are likely to be damaged in the short run by any liberalization effort; they cannot as readily see the economic activities that were harmed, and hence did not prosper, because of regulations. Moreover, even some who would in the long run benefit by liberalization (such as the Korean businessmen who became exporters in the 1960s but were entrepreneurs in import-substitution industries in the 1950s) perceive the short-run harm that it would cause their interests and fail to recognize the new opportunities that would arise in the longer run.

That difficulty is political, and it pervades discussions of almost all changes in economic policy. But especially in the case of developing countries, the political resistance to liberalization is intensified by the enormous magnitude of the changes called for. It is almost unthinkable to citizens who have lived with exchange control, poor-quality domestic products, and domestic inflation that their country's economy could behave far differently under a liberalized regime.

Add to this the genuine difficulties of transition – the necessary dislocations, the period of uncertainty that is likely to obtain until new signals have been maintained for a while, and the macroeconomic difficulties that in themselves present overriding problems – and it is small wonder that liberalizations are difficult to undertake and carry out. While it is clear that further research can increase our understanding of ways in which the costs of transition can be reduced, it also seems likely that determined leadership in individual countries is necessary if successful liberalization efforts are to be undertaken.

NOTES

1. In the 1970s, the energy market was subject to controls very similar to those of agriculture in many countries. Most of the analysis of agriculture that follows also applies to energy.
2. See Cline and Weintraub, (1981) for a series of analyses of these issues in individual countries. See also Krueger in that volume for further analysis of the interrelationship between inflation and liberalization.
3. This qualification is made because most licensing systems implicitly or otherwise permit imports of intermediate goods and raw materials at lower-than-average rates of duty. To increase duties on these goods without permitting exporters to purchase at international prices would lower effective protection rates – presumably already negative – to them.
4. For a description of these efforts, see Baldwin (1975) and Michaely, (1975).
5. See Carvalho and Haddad, (1981).
6. See McKinnon, (1973) for an analysis of the importance of developing financial markets.
7. There is another reason why instantaneous abandonment of the entire control regime might be infeasible: when liberalization starts from a situation in which there is a large government deficit, it inherently requires time to reduce government spending and to raise taxes. In that circumstance, one might question whether total decontrol of all other markets should precede macroeconomic stabilization. I have not seen any analyses of this circumstance; hence I subsume it under other reasons for objecting to instantaneous decontrol.

REFERENCES

Baldwin, Robert E. (1975). *Foreign Trade Regimes and Economic Development: The Philippines*. New York: Columbia University Press, Chapter 3.

Carvalho, Jose and Claudio Haddad (1981). 'Foreign Trade Strategies and Employment in Brazil' in Anne O. Krueger, Hal B. Lary, Terry Monson and Narongchai Akraasanee (eds), *Trade and Employment in Developing Countries*, vol 1: Individual Studies, Chicago: University of Chicago Press.

Cline, William R. and Sidney Weintraub (1981) (eds), *Economic Stabilization in Developing Countries*. Washington DC: Brookings Institution.

Krueger, Anne O. (1981). 'Interactions Between Inflation and Trade Regime Objectives in Stabilization Programs', refer Carvalho and Haddad (1981).

McKinnon, Ronald (1973). *Money and Capital in Economic Development*. Washington DC: Brookings Institution.

Michaely, Michael (1975). *Future Trade Regimes and Economic Development: Israel*. New York: Columbia University Press, Chapter 2.

10 · SOME ECONOMIC COSTS OF EXCHANGE CONTROL: THE TURKISH CASE

One of the most persistent and difficult problems confronting the Turkish government since the mid-1950s has been a deficit in the balance of payments. The Turkish lira, despite the devaluation of 1958, is over-valued (at TL9 = US $1). In order to keep its international obligations within the limits imposed by foreign exchange availability, the Turkish government has adopted a variety of measures to restrict imports and capital outflows and to encourage exports and capital inflows. Major emphasis has been placed on import restriction rather than on export promotion.

In the early 1960s, the Turkish government become increasingly concerned with accelerating economic growth. Its foreign-exchange problem came to be viewed primarily in relation to development planning, since Turkey was dependent on imports of many capital and intermediate goods. Exchange control was used as an instrument of development planning, and development planning in turn was geared, at least in part, to alleviating the foreign-exchange problem. As a consequence, the exchange control system was important, not only in affecting current economic activity, but also in influencing Turkish economic growth.

This chapter is concerned with the evaluation of the economic costs of the Turkish exchange control system. The empirical work is based upon primary data gathered in 1965 for a relatively small sample of Turkish manufacturing firms. The Turkish manufacturing sector accounts for about 13 per cent of the country's Gross Domestic Product and 8 per cent of its exports. A large fraction of Turkish manufacturing activity

First printed in 1966. The research for this paper was undertaken for the Agency for International Development. I am indebted to the many individuals in the agency who were very helpful in their comments and in enabling me to obtain the basic data. The views expressed in this chapter, however, are my own and do not necessarily reflect those of the agency. Professors James M. Henderson and Harry G. Johnson made many constructive suggestions on an earlier draft of the manuscript.

consists of processing Turkish raw materials[1] and producing light consumer goods for the home market. However, the first Turkish Development Plan[2] placed emphasis on manufacturing, and especially import
substitution, as the means of accelerating economic growth. The stated
targets in the period of the first plan were a 7 per cent annual rate of
growth in income and an 11.5 per cent rate of growth for manufacturing
(Government of Turkey, 1962, p. 124). The emphasis given to import-
substitution projects in the investment program is shown in Table 10.1.
Investments in chemicals, machinery, steel,[3] and domestic assembly of
imported components in transport equipment are all primarily for the
purpose of import substitution. Paper investment was for the production
of kraft paper, which had previously been imported. Similarly, rubber-
products investment was intended to foster domestic production of tires,
also formerly imported.

Part of the impetus to import substitution originated in the foreign-
exchange shortage. A major regulatory tool used to encourage import-
substitution projects is a prohibition upon imports once domestic
productive capacity is established. The economic costs of this system
are the subject of this chapter. Before presenting the data, a brief
sketch of the effects of exchange control systems is required.

10.1 THE EFFECTS OF OVERVALUATION
AND EXCHANGE CONTROL

An exchange control regime is one wherein an *ex ante* balance-of-
payments deficit is eliminated through foreign-exchange rationing. In
Figure 10.1, this situation is represented with the price of foreign exchange set at p°, below its equilibrium level, and the foreign exchange
earned, Od, rationed. If a foreign-exchange auction were held, licenses
to buy abroad would sell domestically at the price Oa per unit. Domestic
import-competing activities would implicitly be subsidized by ab per
unit, while domestic export production would implicitly be taxed bc per
unit. Regardless of the system for allocating foreign exchange, any exchange control system will tend to encourage some import-substitution
activities. So long as there is rationing of foreign exchange, the system
will result in the expenditure of more domestic resources per unit of
foreign exchange saved through import substitution than per unit of
foreign exchange earned through exporting.

In Turkey and most other countries using exchange control, import
licensing is accompanied by a series of tariffs (and import prohibitions),
and licenses are allocated by the government differentially to various
applicants. If the equilibrium exchange rate were known, each system

Table 10.1 Turkish investment allocation and production targets, 1963–7

Sector	1962 Value added as a percentage of all manufacture	1963–7 investment as a percentage of all investment in manufacturing	1967 target production as a percentage of 1962 production
Food, beverages, and tobacco	34.2	10.3	150
Textiles and clothing	31.4	9.0	140
Wood and cork products	0.2	1.0	277
Paper	1.1	5.5	144
Rubber	1.3	2.5	433
Chemicals	5.4	27.1	209
Non-metallic products	3.6	3.0	146
Basic metal industry	9.2	21.1	169
Metallic products	7.2	2.4	143
Machinery	2.3	10.6	610
Electrical machinery	0.9	2.4	275
Transport equipment	1.4	4.1	551
Other industry (including plastic)	1.8	1.0	338

Source: Government of Turkey (1962, pp. 183–6).

could be represented as a series of percentage deviations in domestic prices from world prices (calculated at the equilibrium exchange rate). Once these tariff equivalents were known, the economic cost of the system could be calculated.

Economic cost, throughout this chapter, will be defined as the international value of goods and services that could be produced and extracted from the economy through resource reallocation and trade, while leaving final consumption of all goods and services unchanged. This concept is identical to Johnson's (1960) definition of production cost, and understates the welfare loss attributable to a system, since it ignores the possibility of substitution in consumption.

Johnson's measure of production cost is:

$$P = \sum_i k_i e_i x_i, \tag{10.1}$$

where x_i is the quantity produced of ith tariff-protected good, with units so chosen that domestic prices equal unity; k_i is the non-rent portion of the excess of domestic over foreign price; and e_i is the percentage effective tariff[4] protection. In this equation, P measures the value of goods that could be produced and extracted from the economy through efficient resource allocation, since the non-rent portion of the excess of domestic over foreign price is assumed to reflect the opportunity cost of factors utilized in the protected industries per unit of output.

The empirical problem in estimating P in an exchange control system is that the equilibrium exchange rate is not known. Either the equilibrium

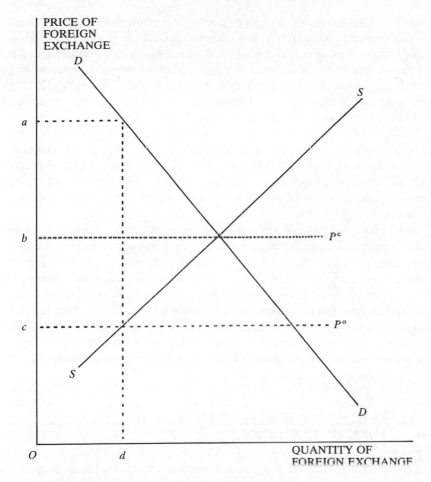

Figure 10.1   Demand and supply of foreign exchange

exchange rate must be estimated, or an alternative procedure developed. The latter course is followed here. The measure used, R, resource cost, of a set of domestic prices differing from world prices is similar to the notion of production cost, except that the unit of measure is the minimum (domestic) cost activity that could produce the same international value of output. R is defined as:

$$R = \sum_i (k_i p_i - c) x_i, \tag{10.2}$$

where x_i is the physical quantity produced in the ith activity, with units so chosen that one unit of output represents one unit of value added on the international market. The p_is are domestic value added in the various value-adding industries in units of domestic currency, and k_i, as before, is the non-rent portion of value added domestically in the ith activity. The critical term is c, which is defined as the minimum cost per unit (in domestic currency, with normal profit and no rent) of producing the same international value of output as was actually produced. If, for example, there were two constant-cost activities, one of which required TL50 of Turkish resources and the other TL20 per dollar of value added internationally, the resource cost of producing one hundred units of the first as compared with the second would be TL3,000, since producing the first would cost TL5,000 of resources to produce $100 of goods valued at international prices, whereas the same $100 worth would have been obtained by producing the second at a cost of TL2,000 of domestic resources.

The empirical tasks of estimation are, therefore, to ensure that costs are reasonably constant within the relevant range, to adjust for any elements of rent in the domestic prices, and to make any data adjustments necessary to ensure that factor prices correctly reflect resource costs. Section 10.2 outlines the manner in which these steps were taken and presents estimates of the resource costs of the system. Section 10.3 presents some pertinent data relevant to the effects of the Turkish trade regime on incentives, and examines the foreign-exchange saving argument for these activities. Section 10.4 summarizes the results and presents some tentative conclusions.

10.2 THE DOMESTIC-RESOURCE COST OF FOREIGN EXCHANGE

10.2.1 The Sample

Turkish trade policy involves a variety of regulatory instruments.[5] Import-licensing, tariffs, surcharges, guaranty deposits, and the prohibition of importation of certain goods are all utilized.[6] The combined aggregate effects of these instruments would be estimable if reliable data were available on a broad basis for international and domestic prices and inter-industry relations. Such data are not available. Hence, the current analysis is based upon specially gathered price and cost data for individual manufacturing firms and industries.[7] Information on prices and costs was gathered from various sources for over sixty firms. Two criteria were used for initial selection: availability of data, and representativeness of either a recent import-substitution project or an industry believed to have export potential. The data-availability criterion was the limiting one. Of the many sources of data (loans from an institution requiring accurate cost and price data, feasibility studies, interviews with individual firms, and industry studies), few had complete information on capital cost (including the foreign-exchange component) and the cost breakdown of inputs purchased from other firms. In practice, therefore, much of the information gathered was used either to obtain estimates of the cost of purchased inputs or to verify information from other sources.

Data were rejected if they (a) could not be verified (at least with respect to prices and current costs) from at least two sources, or (b) were not believed to be sufficiently accurate, a judgment decision. Altogether, price and cost data for ten industries survived these tests. Six produce import-competing goods, and four either currently export or formerly exported some part of their outputs. Since the question under consideration is the degree to which Turkish trade policies affect resource allocation and growth, it was decided to err in the direction of understating the cost of import substitution and overstating the cost of potential export activities. For import-substitution firms, current costs were rejected in favor of the firms' estimates of what their costs will be when full-capacity operations have been achieved for several years.[8] In all cases, the unit whose costs were estimated is a plant or set of plants for which it was judged that costs could not be materially reduced by adding to capacity within the plants.

Most of the cases considered here are reputed in Turkey to represent outstanding examples of import substitution and are cited as justification for the import-substitution policy.[9] Most have received loans from sources generally considered to be highly conservative in their loan policies.

All these factors considered together suggest that the sample, while small, will yield an estimate of the maximum 'benefit', however defined, of the import-substitution schemes. Since the cost estimates are based on full-capacity projections for new plants, none of these projects can be considered infant industries. Further, since the projects jointly constitute a small fraction of Turkish manufacturing activity, there is every reason to believe that similar plants could be built, and hence that average unit cost at full capacity is representative of marginal cost of additional output if new plants were built. The assumption that costs are constant within the relevant range therefore seems warranted.

Fewer data manipulations were necessary for the export firms. The major consideration in choice of firms was assurance that a product could be sold abroad in fairly large quantities (relative to the prevailing volume of output) without affecting price. This test was met by all four potential export firms. Only one did in fact export in 1965, and the amount exported was considerably less than the quantity ordered abroad. In the case of the other three firms, export markets were known; in one case, the foreign price did not cover out-of-pocket costs; in the other two, it was anticipated that with new additions to capacity some exports would occur until about 1970, when domestic demand was expected to absorb all output.

Table 10.2 presents data on foreign and domestic prices of the goods produced by firms in the sample.[10] The price differentials of the products listed are not significantly different from others where less complete information was available. In Table 10.2, column 1 gives the Turkish sale prices ex-factory[11] of Turkish firms producing the commodity in question.[12] Column 2 indicates the landed price of imports with all customs charges paid. In cases where the landed price is below the Turkish sale price, the price quoted is that which prevailed when importation was allowed. The prices in column 2, therefore, are the current or past cost of imports, whereas the prices in column 1 are the present or projected prices of the domestically produced goods. For most import-substitution industries,[13] the fact that the good may no longer be imported implies that, if cost projections prove too low for a good, its domestic price can be increased.

Column 3 presents the import price c.i.f. of import-substitution goods,[14] and the f.o.b. price of potential export goods. Column 4 gives the nominal tariff rate inclusive of all surcharges, stamp taxes, and the like.[15]

In cases where a good cannot be imported, the tariff is the percentage by which the domestic sale price exceeds the c.i.f. price of imports. For export goods, no such calculation is made, although exports are sold abroad at prices substantially below domestic sale prices.

Column 5 presents the effective tariff rates on imported commodities. Despite the presence of duties on raw materials and intermediate goods, the effective tariff rates are above the nominal rates in all cases except electric motors. As column 5 indicates, the degree of protection afforded domestic industry is generally fairly substantial. However, Turkish producers often must pay a higher price for some of their purchased inputs domestically than they would if they could purchase the good abroad, even if they had to pay a sizeable duty. Although every effort was made to estimate the cost differential on inputs, in practice it proved impossible to make adjustments on minor purchased inputs. The effective tariffs may therefore overstate the degree of protection given to a specific firm, since it may purchase some inputs from a high-cost domestic producer,[16] and the allowance for this may be inadequate.

10.2.2   Domestic-Resource Costs

After the adjustments described above were made, computation of the domestic-resource costs of each output required only an adequate

Table 10.2 Prices, tariffs, and effective tariffs (in dollars)

Commodity	Sale price of domestic production ex-factory (1)	Imported price with duties (2)	Foreign price f.o.b. exports, c.i.f. imports (3)	Nominal tariff (percentage of c.i.f. price) (4)	Effective Tariff* (percentage of c.i.f. price) (5)
Potential export:					
Windowglass[†]	287.70	....	227.70‡	....	....
Cast-iron radiators	8.89	....	5.89‡	....	....
Nylon	4.44	....	2.74‡	....	....
Canned tomato paste	.285	....	.19‡	....	....
Import substitution:					
Refrigeration units §	70.00	68.00	43.10	62	80
Electric motors §	22.00	20.00	12.85	71	66
Ammonium nitrate fertilizer	46.00‖	46.00	38.40	71	186
Superphosphate fertilizer	32.51	32.51	25.50	27	925
Truck tires #	130.52	96.01	56.48	131	170
Kraft paper	n.a.	256.50	150.00	77	n.a.
Plastic	722.00	780.00	385.00	102	916
Electric cables	1,092.00	n.a.	600.00	82	147

* Effective tariffs were computed according to the formula given in n. 4.
† Glassware products are also produced by this firm.
‡ Represents price at which goods are exported.
§ Refrigeration units and small electric motors were to be produced by the same firm.
‖ Production is subsidized. Costs per ton are estimated at $105.21.
Passenger tires also are produced by this firm.
Source: Mimeographed data are available on request.

concept of cost. The major questions concern the treatment of taxes, duties, interest, and differential profit rates. Also, it is of some interest to enquire how sensitive the estimates are to a change in the wage capital–rental ratio. Table 10.3 presents estimates of the domestic-resource costs (in Turkish liras) of $1.00 of international value added under alternative interpretations with regard to the appropriate measure of economic cost. International value added was derived by subtracting the c.i.f. price of direct and indirect imported inputs[17] from the c.i.f. price of the imported final product.[18]

The columns of Table 10.3 indicate alternative measures of domestic-resource cost. Column 1 was derived by taking the Turkish sale price ex-factory of the product, subtracting the c.i.f. value of imported direct and indirect inputs per unit of output, and dividing that estimate of cost by the estimate of international value added.

The remaining columns adjust the measure of domestic-resource cost. In column 2, all duties paid by firms on imported inputs are subtracted from the domestic cost of column 1. Column 3 was derived by subtracting all other tax payments from the estimate in column 2. Column 4 adjusts for any rent in the profitability of the good in Turkey by recomputing

Table 10.3 Domestic cost of $1.00 of foreign exchange (TL required to produce $1.00 of net output)

Activity	(1)*	(2)	(3)	(4)	(5)	(6)
Export industries:						
Glassware	11.2	10.2	9.0	7.5	7.7	7.9
Windowglass	12.0	10.8	9.5	8.9	9.8	10.4
Radiators	14.0	14.0	12.6	10.8	11.4	14.0
Nylon	12.1	10.5	– †	9.9	9.8	11.0
Tomato canning	14.5	13.3	– †	15.1	14.0	13.4
Import-substitution industries:						
Cooling units	24.7	19.5	18.4	18.2	19.9	21.4
Electric motors	20.5	18.0	17.2	18.9	24.2	31.9
Fertilizer:						
Sodium phosphate‡	98.1	91.8	91.8	n.a.	n.a.	n.a.
Ammonium nitrate‡	63.6	58.1	58.1	n.a.	n.a.	n.a.
Truck tires	97.9	78.0	– †	66.7	74.5	81.4
Passenger tires	102.5	88.2	– †	55.5	70.3	79.2
Kraft paper	20.1§	– §	19.3§	26.6	25.0	31.9
Plastic	292.5	139.5	– †	68.5	60.1	66.1
Electric cables	49.2	27.8	– †	23.7	34.9	46.0

* See text for explanation.
† No breakdown given. Only income before tax estimates available.
‡ No data on fixed capital were available. The calculations made here are based on cost data. The operation is heavily subsidized by the government of Turkey.
§ Cost data only. No income estimate available.

what the price of the output would have been with a 20 per cent return on fixed capital investment (net of duties). Since, in principle, there is no reason why there should be a difference between debt and equity financing, column 5 represents the resource cost when it is assumed that debt capital also yields a 20 per cent rate of return. This was done by omitting actual interest costs from the unit cost as estimated in column 4 and then adding an interest charge equal to a 20 per cent rate of return on debt capital when all capacity is utilized.

These calculations are open to the objection that market prices may not reflect resource costs. In particular, it is widely held that in less developed countries the price of labor is higher, and the yield on capital lower, than would be the case with optimal resource allocation. In order to test the sensitivity of the results to this possibility, the domestic-resource cost given in column 5 was recalculated on the assumption that the 'shadow price' of labor is 25 per cent below its market price, while the shadow rate of return on capital is 30 per cent. The results are given in column 6.

While one may debate which measure is the 'best' indicator of resource cost, the discrepancies among projects are so great relative to the differences in concept that it would require some very bizarre adjustments to the data to change the conclusions reached here. The lowest cost import-substitution scheme (motors) has, at a minimum, a cost of TL18 per dollar, while the most costly potential export industry (tomato paste)[19] has a maximum resource cost of TL15.1 per dollar. Depending on whether or not one believes that market prices reflect 'shadow prices', either column 5 or column 6 is probably the best estimate. It is of some interest that the rank ordering of costs is identical under the two concepts except for cast-iron radiators and tomato paste, which interchange fourth and fifth positions.

The aggregate resource cost to Turkey at a point in time and in terms of economic growth can hardly be estimated from the data presented above. Calculations with regard to the sample are, however, indicative of orders of magnitude, especially when it is recalled that the cost estimates were designed to understate the cost of prevailing trade policies.

If TL10 million of Turkish resources were allocated evenly among the import-substitution schemes in the sample, the increment to Turkish output at international prices would be $292,140.[20] On average, it would require TL34.2 of domestic resources to increase net output by $1.00. If the same resources were allocated evenly among the potential export industries, the increment to Turkish output would be $986,000, requiring TL10.1 on average to increase the international value of output by $1.00. If that output were exported, Turkey could pay for 3.4 times as many import goods as she could produce with the same resources.

The economic costs of exchange control for the sample may be calculated as follows. Assume that column 5 of Table 10.3 represents the resource cost of $1.00 of output in the various activities. If all the firms in the sample produced at full capacity, they would hire TL509,161,000 of resources to produce goods with an international value of $27,280,900. If these same resources were used in glassworks and textile plants at the constant costs of the firms in the sample, the same international value of output could be obtained for TL253,105,500. To state the same result another way, the TL509 million of resources could produce goods, under these assumptions, worth $53,200,000 on the international market. While such numbers appear small, $27 million is equivalent to more than 10 per cent of Turkey's largest deficit on goods and services account in the 1960s and more than one-third of the 1964 deficit. Alternatively, the $27 million would enable a 10 per cent increase in *total* manufacturing investment or, if foreign exchange really is the only factor limiting investments, a 30 per cent increase. Even if the only resource misallocation in the entire economy occurred among the nine firms, the orders of magnitude are large.

There is no reason to believe, however, that the firms included in the sample represent greater resource misallocation than occurs in the rest of Turkish manufacturing. If the sample is representative, the international value of Turkish manufacturing output per unit of new investment could almost double. The growth-*rate* costs of choosing import substitution probably outweigh the resource costs estimated above. By definition, the growth rate of any sector of the economy is the percentage growth of capital stock times the incremental output-per-unit-of-capital ratio. If the latter can be doubled, the growth rate will double. If a part of additional income results in a faster rate of capital accumulation, the growth-rate effects of resource reallocation will be even greater. While it certainly cannot be claimed that the data presented above provide conclusive evidence that doubling of the rate of growth of manufacturing output could result from trade liberalization in Turkey, it appears reasonably certain that the effects of liberalization on both the level of output and its growth rate would be substantial.

10.3   RELATIONSHIP OF RESOURCE COSTS TO INCENTIVES AND FOREIGN-EXCHANGE SAVING

10.3.1   Incentives

In a free-trade economy with an equilibrium exchange rate and no protection, most of the import-substituting firms examined above would be contracting and the export firms expanding. With exchange control, however, incentives are somewhat different. Although the government of Turkey has undertaken production of import-competing goods in the State Economic Enterprises, the data presented in Table 10.3 originated from private firms, many of them including some foreign participation. The motive for their investments was expected profit. Since the incentives given by the system determine the directions into which new entrepreneurial activity flows, the contrast between the incentives that would occur under free trade and actual incentives is important in estimating the degree to which exchange control affects the growth and composition of Turkish manufacturing. Column 1 of Table 10.4 presents the actual rate of return, either realized or anticipated, for those firms on which fixed-investment data were available. In cases where two products are produced in the same plant, the rate of return is for the total investment. The wide dispersion in actual rates of return is a result of several factors. One major factor is the difference between the actual and the optimal percentage of capacity operation. On the import-substitution side, there is clearly an element of rent accruing to some firms as a result of their protection from the world market.

The remaining columns of Table 10.4 present the rates of return that would be realized with free trade and no duties, with full-capacity operations at alternative exchange rates. The most profitable firms with free trade would be those with the lowest domestic-resource cost at any exchange rate. By contrast, the two most profitable firms in actuality are import-substituting producers who would, with free trade, lose money

Table 10.4 Hypothetical rates of return on investment under alternative exchange rates (percentage of fixed investment)

Firm	Actual rate of return	Rate of return* at world prices with free trade and exchange rate of		
		TL9 = $1	TL18 = $1	TL27 = $1
Potential export:				
Glassworks	31.2	29.9	83.8	115.5
Radiators	50.8	− 1.8	71.0	108.6
Nylon (textiles)	36.0	38.4	63.7	74.0
Tomato paste	− 5.2	−37.1	69.2	126.3
Import substitution:				
Refrigeration motors	6.4	−43.3	− 1.8	31.0
Tires	98.6	−76.3	−26.8	− 10.4
Paper	n.a.	−30.2	− 3.5	8.2
Plastic	87.9	−58.9	−34.0	− 19.8
Electric cables	23.6	− 5.9	6.7	12.8

* All hypothetical rates of return are calculated before taxes on the basis of full-capacity operations.

at any exchange rate up to TL27 = $1, and have the highest domestic-resource cost.

It is noteworthy that only the glassworks firm, which does export (at a lower price than it sells domestically), and the textile firm, which plans to export at a price below its domestic sale price, could do as well at the present exchange rate of TL9 per dollar under free trade as they do with the prevailing trade policies. Moreover, they would be the most profitable lines of activity. They are not, however, the most profitable firms

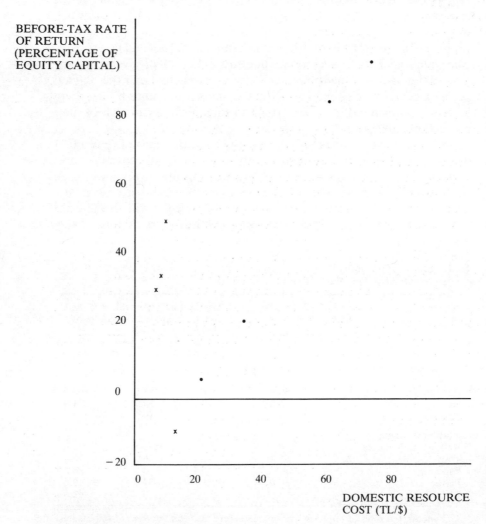

Figure 10.2　Relationship between domestic resource costs and rates of return

under the prevailing trade regime. Two other firms, the radiator manu-
facturer and the tomato canner, could compete profitably in the international market at a TL18 = $1 exchange rate.

The relationship between actual rates of return and the domestic-
resource cost per dollar of net output is plotted in Figure 10.2. The
resource-cost figures are taken from column 5 of Table 10.3, since
elements of rent associated with the trade regime and any other ab-
normal factors in actual profitability are netted out. In Figure 10.3, the

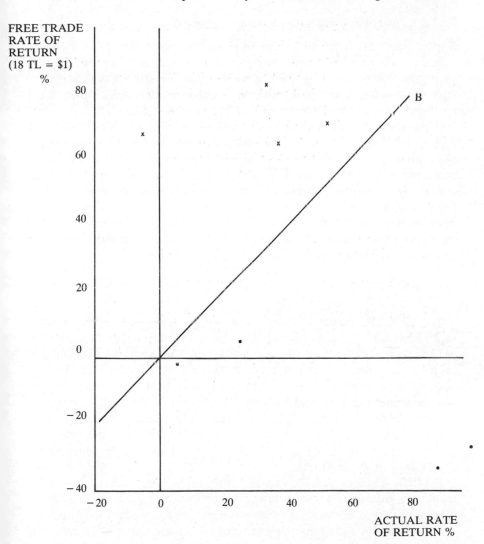

Figure 10.3 Actual and free trade rates of return

acutal rate of return on fixed investments is plotted against that which would occur at free trade with an exchange rate of TL18 = \$1. In both figures, crosses indicate the positions of the potential export firms. In Figure 10.3, the line B indicates equality of the actual and free-trade rates of return. The greater the vertical distance below the B line, the greater is the advantage enjoyed by the industry from Turkish trade policies.

10.3.2 The Foreign-Exchange Saving Argument

Import-substitution schemes have been advocated in Turkey and elsewhere on the grounds that they are 'foreign-exchange saving'. In order to justify foreign-exchange saving as the sole investment criterion, it must be shown that domestic resources are free goods. Such a viewpoint has been set forth in the 'two-gap' theory of development.[21]

If domestic resources were truly free goods, the only limitation on investment would be the available supply of foreign exchange, and the appropriate criterion for choice among investments would be the foreign-exchange rate of return per unit of foreign exchange invested.

For any given project, the foreign-exchange saving per year can be calculated as the difference between what the trade balance would have been without the investment (given the same internal consumption of each good) and what the trade balance will be with the investment. The rate of return on foreign exchange, r_{FE}, is defined by

$$r_{FE} = \frac{dX - dM}{I_{FE}},$$

where dX is the change in export earnings per year as a result of the investment, dM the change in imports, and I_{FE} the foreign exchange cost of the investment. If 'foreign-exchange savings' for import-substitution projects are defined as the difference between what imports would have been without the project and what they are with the project, the level of final consumption with and without the project is implicitly assumed constant. In order to treat all schemes alike, it must therefore be assumed that the entire output of a potential export industry is foreign-exchange saving, since without the project, the output domestically consumed would have to be imported.

On these assumptions, the rate of return on foreign-exchange investments was calculated for each firm. The results, as a percentage of the foreign-exchange component of investment, are shown in Table 10.5.

It is evident that the import-substitution schemes cannot be defended as improving the trade balance more than investment in potential export industries. On the contrary, the rate of foreign-exchange saving on

Table 10.5 Rate of return on foreign-exchange investments (percentage)

Firm	
Potential export:	
Glassware	321.4
Radiators	224.1
Nylon	97.3
Tomato paste	290.1
Import substitution:	
Refrigerators and motors	105.4
Tires	25.0
Paper	29.6
Plastics	31.1
Electric cables	13.2

three of the four potential export industries is considerably in excess of 100 per cent, whereas only one import-substitution project examined achieved above a 100 per cent return per year on foreign exchange.[22]

Even if domestic resources were free goods, it would not follow that import substitution is justified. More fundamental, however, is the fact that overvaluation of the exchange rate results in a foreign-exchange 'gap'. The activities that would expand at free trade are the same ones as those yielding the highest rate of return in foreign exchange. It is difficult to see how domestic resources can be considered free goods with rates of return such as these attainable within the economy.

10.4 SOME CONCLUSIONS

There is little doubt that Turkish trade policies remove virtually all incentive for the potential export firms studied. Manufacturing firms with export potential find the home market considerably more profitable than exporting. In general, their attitude as reflected in interviews was that they 'meet domestic needs' and then sell abroad to the extent that they have additional productive capacity and can sell above the variable cost of production.

For countries with significant overvaluation, this 'dual pricing' system may explain the failure of non-traditional exports to grow. To the extent that the foreign market is secondary to the home market, economic growth will generate increasing domestic demand for the output of potential export industries. With a sheltered domestic market, and little profitability in expanding capacity for export production, it is difficult to see how manufacturing exports can experience major growth. To the extent that the behavior of firms in the Turkish sample is representative, it may very well be the case that economic growth will aggravate balance-of-payments problems as much by reducing exports as by increasing imports.[23]

While this situation prevails in potential export industries, new and privately profitable import-substitution plants are being built. The returns on investment in these plants are substantial. Each new import-substitution firm which could not compete at free trade and an appropriate exchange rate adds another interest opposed to any change in the present trade policy. The more such firms there are, the greater will be the capital losses associated with trade liberalization policies, and the larger the group in opposition. Meanwhile, few (if any) producers in the manufacturing sector identify their interests with those of a liberalized trade regime, partly because of the dual pricing system and overvaluation, and also because, given the prevailing price and incentive structure, few firms look to the export market as their major source of income.

The calculations of economic costs of the Turkish trade regime suggest that twice as much output, in value terms, could be obtained from new resources with a liberalized trade regime and an equilibrium exchange rate. While these results were obtained from a small sample, the order of magnitude is sufficiently large to suggest that more attention needs to be paid to the effects of less-developed countries' policies on their level of income, and on their success in accelerating their growth rate.

NOTES

1. Turkey is well endowed with both agricultural and mineral resources. Her exports consist mainly of primary commodities, and six commodity classifications account for two-thirds of Turkish exports: tobacco, cotton, fresh fruit, dried fruit, hazelnuts, and copper. Only in tobacco and hazelnuts is Turkey's share of any country's imports of these commodities greater than 2 per cent.
2. Government of Turkey (1962). Prior to this time, the government did not have any formal planning mechanism, although the government participated extensively in economic activity.
3. As of 1962, the basic metal industry consisted primarily of copper (an export commodity) processing and some pig-iron production. The major investment in this sector was in the Eregli Iron and Steel Works. No attempt has been made to gather cost data in this sector, since many individuals believe the infant-industry argument applies. The price of iron and steel products in Turkey has risen to two to three times its former (protected) level on those goods produced by Eregli.
4. The effective tariff rate is defined as

$$c_i = \frac{t_i - \sum_j a_{ij}t_j}{V_i},$$

where t_i is the nominal tariff on the ith commodity, a_{ij} is the fraction of sales prices of i of the jth input per unit of output (at world prices), and V_i is the fraction of the world sale price, which is value added by the country.

5. For a description of Turkish trade policies, see Department of Commerce (1964). Although goods classifications and rates are frequently changed, the basic tools of regulation remain the same.

6. The dominant tool of import regulation is the semi-annual 'Import Program'. This decree enumerates those categories of goods that are eligible for import, and divides them into goods that are subject to explicit quota limits and those for which licenses will be issued without specific quantitative ceilings. A major part of increasing restrictionism in Turkey has taken the form of transferring goods from the 'liberalized list' to the quota list and removing goods entirely from the eligible list. Generally speaking, when import-competing production is undertaken domestically, the goods are removed from the list of eligible imports.

7. There are several effects of the regulatory system of which no account is taken in the analysis that follows. Among them are the uncertainty of all firms as to their foreign-exchange allocation beyond the current period, the lack of competition within Turkish industry (since the foreign-exchange allocation generally determines market share), and heavy inventory costs attributable to the requirement that all imports for the six-month period be purchased in one order. It is impossible to estimate the costs of these factors, though they may be substantial.

8. In practice, few Turkish firms operate at full capacity. The reasons for this are several. Since they have sheltered markets, they set price to maximize profits and produce the quantity ordered at that price. Also, many firms cannot produce at full capacity due to a shortage of imported inputs. Both of these factors are at least partly the result of the exchange control system, and no account has been taken of these costs. Also, no provision is made in the cost estimates that follow for the write-off of losses (or smaller returns) accruing in the early years of the project.

9. The possible exception is the fertilizer industry. Although fertilizer investment is a substantial portion of the chemical sector's allocation, there is heavy subsidization of fertilizer production by the government.

10. Mimeographed copies of the cost breakdowns for the individual firms are available on request.

11. A 12–30 per cent production tax is levied on output. The prices quoted are those received by the firm.

12. Although kraft paper is now being produced in Turkey and will no longer be imported, no data on the present sale price are available. The cost data used here were drawn from a feasibility study undertaken in 1964 by a foreign firm considering investing in the project. The feasibility study indicated that domestic production in the best location would be unprofitable at the international price plus the 77 per cent tariff. When private firms did not undertake investments on paper, the government did.

13. The exception is fertilizer where domestic production is sold far below cost, and imports continue.

14. Many individuals believe that the quality of Turkish production is below that of imported goods. To the extent that is true, the price differentials are understated. The manager of the one firm that did export in 1965 pointed out in conversation that the firm sells its quality product abroad and its seconds domestically, but receives a higher price for the latter.

15. The Turkish structure of import duties contains a basic rate and a large number of additional taxes. The total tax bill is used in Table 10.2, col. 4. Total taxes on imports range from an average 20 per cent on raw materials to 50 per cent on intermediate goods and 80–120 per cent on finished goods.

16. The Turkish import regulation system tends to encourage vertical integration. For the activities covered by the sample, the lowest percentage of Turkish value added by the firm was 39 (tomato canning and kraft paper). Six activities had in excess of 75 per cent of domestic value added originating in the firm. Because major purchased inputs were identified, the resulting error must be rather small.

17. Indirect imported inputs include depreciation of foreign equipment and the import content of inputs purchased from other firms. In some cases, estimates had to be made for some of these items. All interest cost was treated as a domestic input, which overstates the domestic value added, since there is considerable borrowing abroad. Turkish depreciation laws require a fairly long life of plant and equipment. There was no basis for believing that the depreciation rates used were unrealistically high.

18. For export goods, the f.o.b. price of the final product less the c.i.f. price of inputs was used to estimate international value added. This tends to bias further the estimates in favor of import substitution.

19. Tomato paste used to be exported, and orders are still received. Managers in several firms in the industry, in addition to the one for which data are presented, stated that the unit cost at which they could purchase tomatoes and tinplate exceeds the price at which they can sell abroad. Because the infant-industry argument may be valid for steel production, no investigation of costs was undertaken. It might be the case that costs of canning Turkish agricultural products would decline even more than the estimates in Table 10.2 suggest if Turkish processors had access to the world market.

20. The calculation is based on the use of column 5 of Table 10.3.

21. See McKinnon (1964); Chenery and Strout (1965). It is of interest that Chenery and Strout identify Turkey as one of the countries for which the foreign-exchange constraint is the 'growth-limiting' factor.

22. It should be observed that an import-substitution scheme can result in negative foreign-exchange saving. There are three ways in which this can occur: (1) inefficient use of imported inputs; (2) when the c.i.f. price of the inputs exceeds that of the final product; and (3) when a portion of the profits of the industry accrue to foreigners, and the domestic industry is protected.

23. In late 1964, the government of Turkey recognized the competitive difficulties of Turkish producers and inaugurated rebates to manufacturing exporters for any direct tax payments they might incur. A 10 per cent across-the-board rebate is allowed, with higher rates attainable through negotiations with the government. Exports in 1965 were above the level anticipated, but at the time of writing, no breakdown by commodity was available to the author to test the significance of this change. The exporters in the sample were all aware of the rebates and included them in their calculation of export profitability.

REFERENCES

Chenery, Hollis B. and Alan M. Strout (1965). 'Foreign Assistance and Economic Development', AID Discussion Paper no. 7 (revised).

Department of Commerce (1964). *Overseas Business Reports*, OBR 64–52. Washington, DC: US Government Printing Office.

Government of Turkey, State Planning Office (1962). *First Five Year Development Plan, 1963–67*. Ankara.

Johnson, Harry G. (1960). 'Protection and the Scientific Tariff', *Journal of Political Economy*, vol. 68, no. 3.

McKinnon, R. (1964). 'Foreign Exchange Constraints in Economic Development and Efficient Resource Allocation', *Economic Journal*, vol. 34.

11 · AN EMPIRICAL TEST OF THE INFANT-INDUSTRY ARGUMENT

Anne O. Krueger and Baran Tuncer

Since the Second World War, many developing countries have provided high levels of protection for newly established industries. These policies have generally been followed on the grounds that new industries are 'infants', and that dynamic factors will come into play to ensure later economic efficiency.[1]

At a theoretical level, the infant-industry exception to the proposition that free trade is optimal has always been noted.[2] Skeptics have centered their misgivings on two grounds: (1) they have questioned whether protection through the trade regime would achieve the goals of infant-industry protection;[3] and (2) they have pinpointed the combination of 'dynamic factors' and 'externalities' that would have to arise to justify infant-industry intervention and questioned the empirical likelihood of such circumstances.

Interestingly, the debate has been entirely theoretical. There has been virtually no systematic examination of the empirical relevance of the infant-industry argument. This is remarkable in light of the importance of the question, and the fact that thirty years' evidence or more has accumulated in a number of countries. Even if there are conditions under which dynamic factors and externalities in an infant industry might

First printed in 1982. We wish to thank the National Science Foundation for research support, grant no. SOC77–25776. We are also grateful to the Turkish Industrial Development Bank for its assistance in the project. We have benefited greatly from the comments and suggestions of W.M. Corden and James M. Henderson. Ebbe Yndgaard, Claus Vastrup, Martin Paldam, and other members of the faculty at Aarhus University provided helpful comments and suggestions at an early stage of the research, as did colleagues at Bogazici University, including especially Maxwell Fry. Members of the Trade and Development Workshops at the University of Chicago made many useful comments on an earlier draft of this chapter. Zafar Ahmed, Roger Johnson, Inci Mubarek, Lale Tezel, and Paitoon Wiboonchutikula provided research assistance at various stages of the project.

warrant intervention, that does not prove that those conditions are in fact met. In the last analysis, defense of infant industry protection must rest on empirical grounds: do the long-run benefits justify the short-run costs of starting up an initially high-cost infant?

It is the purpose of this chapter to develop a test of whether infant-industry criteria are satisfied, and then to apply the test to one developing country, Turkey. Section 11.1 sets forth the infant-industry argument and necessary conditions for there to be a valid case for intervention. Section 11.2 then examines the various ways in which the necessary dynamic externalities might manifest themselves. This immediately suggests a simple empirical test. Section 11.3 then presents results of the test for Turkey. Section 11.4 contains some concluding observations and suggestions for further work. The data and details of procedures for estimation are given on page 232.

11.1   THE INFANT-INDUSTRY ARGUMENT

It is simplest to state the infant-industry case in naive form, and then to consider the conditions under which it would be valid. The basic argument, crudely put, is that:

(a)   some newly established activities are initially high-cost relative to established foreign enterprises and it requires time for them to become competitive;

(b)   it does not pay any individual entrepreneur to enter an infant industry at free trade prices; but

(c)   the industry, if developed, would be economic enough to permit a reasonable rate of return on the initial losses; and therefore

(d)   the industry requires a *temporary* period of protection or assistance during which its costs will fall enough to permit it to survive international competition without assistance.

The first proposition is essentially that costs of a new activity may initially be high. Reasons put forth as to why they might be high include learning by doing and the possibility that there are 'linkages' between industries, as set forth by Hirschman (1958). In the latter case, in the early stages of development the absence of complementary activities or small size of the industrial sector of an economy might constitute a reason why all industrial activities would initially be high-cost.

The reasons why there might be learning by doing are numerous. Workers might require a period of training. There might be an initial shake-down period as the activity became operational. Management itself might gain in experience. These possibilities have been neatly encapsulated by Arrow (1962) in the notion that output per unit of input might increase as cumulative output within a given line of activity (the plant? the firm? the industry? the entire industrial sector?) increased.[4] Regardless of which reason is put forth, an essential feature of the infant-industry notion is that a new activity will initially be high-cost, but that unit costs will decline over time.

The second proposition is that, while costs will decline, they will do so in a way that individuals initially starting the activity will not reap the full rewards. Otherwise, there would be no case for protection: if start-up costs are high but the activity is economic, it would pay an individual entrepreneur to incur those costs in order to reap later benefits. For there to be a case for intervention, there must be positive externalities from the development of an infant activity which accrue to individuals other than those undertaking the activity initially. Thus, the presence of externalities is necessary in order to show that private activity will not generate the optimal development of infant industries in a market-oriented economy. Whether the externalities are at the individual industry level, or rather at the level of the entire industrial sector, is an open question, discussed further in Section 11.2. Clearly, whatever infant-industry assistance is provided should be provided to the industry, group of industries, or sector generating the externalities at a relatively uniform rate. Different levels of protection to different activities would be warranted only if the sector containing the more-protected activity were expected to experience greater cost reductions than the less-protected sector.[5]

The third proposition asserts that the losses associated with an initial period of high costs must be recovered (with interest) at a later date, although not by the individual entrepreneur starting up the activity. In essence, the costs of production of those benefiting by the development of the activity must fall enough to repay the initial losses and to provide a reasonable rate of return on those losses (since resources could otherwise have been allocated to unprotected activities with incremental international value added).

The fourth proposition is really a logical consequence of the first three. All analysts have been willing to concede that if the first three propositions were valid, some form of assistance (and intervention with a laissez-faire outcome) to the externality-generating activity is warranted. However, protection would never be first best (contrasted with a production subsidy), and might not even achieve its intended purposes, as argued by Baldwin (1969).

For the present, the important aspect of the infant-industry case seems summarizable in the proposition that, in order for it to be empirically valid, a necessary (but not sufficient) condition is that costs in (temporarily) assisted or protected industries should have fallen over time more rapidly than costs in non-protected or less-protected industries. This interpretation coincides with the case where it is assumed that prices in the rest of the world are given, and do not change over time due to differential rates of technical change in the rest of the world.[6] If there were also technical change in the corresponding industries abroad, the infant-industry case would need to be reformulated to state that intervention would be warranted only if unit costs were expected to decline more rapidly in the infant industry than in the mature industry abroad (with the same qualifications as above regarding externalities and recovery of the initial investment with interest). For the purposes of this chapter, it is assumed that world prices are given, so that a decline in costs in one industry at a more rapid rate than in another constitutes more of an infant-industry case.

11.2 A SIMPLE EMPIRICAL TEST

There are two ways in which one industry's costs per unit of output (or value added) can change relative to another's: either its share-weighted inputs per unit of output must fall more (or rise less) than the other's, or the relative price of the factor it uses relatively intensively in production must fall.

This can readily be seen as follows. Define the total cost, C_i, of the ith industry as

$$C_i = \sum_j W_j V_{ji} \tag{11.1}$$

where W_j is the reward to the jth factor of production and V_{ji} is the quantity of the jth factor employed in the ith industry.

Clearly, the change in i's costs is

$$dC_i = \sum_i dW_j V_{ji} + \sum_j dV_{ji} W_j \tag{11.2}$$

and the change in cost per unit of output is

$$d\left(\frac{C_i}{X_i}\right) = \sum_j \frac{dW_j}{W_j} \frac{W_j V_{ji}}{C_i} \frac{C_i}{X_i} + \sum_j \frac{dV_{ji}}{V_{ji}} \frac{W_j V_{ji}}{C_i} \frac{C_i}{X_i} - \frac{dX_i}{X_i} \frac{C_i}{X_i}. \tag{11.3}$$

Denoting the share of the jth factor in total costs in industry i by a_{ij}, equation (11.3) can be rewritten:

$$d\frac{[C_i/X_i]}{C_i/X_i} = \sum_j a_{ij} \frac{dW_j}{W_j} + \sum_j a_{ij} \frac{dV_{ji}}{V_{ji}} - \frac{dX_i}{X_i}, \tag{11.4}$$

Thus, the proportionate change in costs per unit of output in the ith industry represents the share-weighted sum of changes in input prices plus the share-weighted sum of factor inputs less the rate of change of output. Let $\dot{C}_i$ represent the proportionate rate of change in costs per unit of output. Contrasting changes in costs between the ith and the kth industry yields

$$
\dot{C}_i - \dot{C}_k = \sum_j (a_{ij} - a_{kj}) \frac{\mathrm{d}W_j}{W_j} + \left[\sum_j a_{ij} \frac{\mathrm{d}V_{ji}}{V_{ji}} - \frac{\mathrm{d}X_i}{X_i} \right]
$$
$$
- \left[\sum_j a_{kj} \frac{\mathrm{d}V_{jk}}{V_{jk}} - \frac{\mathrm{d}X_k}{X_k} \right]
\tag{11.5}
$$

The first term on the right-hand side of equation (11.5) represents the change in relative costs due to changing relative input prices. Clearly, that relative input prices may change in the process of growth is not grounds for infant-industry protection.[7] If there is to be a dynamic cost reduction, it must be reflected in a difference between the two bracketed terms on the right-hand side.

We are thus led to the straightforward proposition that if there are dynamic factors warranting intervention, they will be reflected in a difference in the two right-hand terms of equation (11.5). Define, now,

$$
\frac{\mathrm{d}A_i}{A_i} = \frac{\mathrm{d}X_i}{X_i} - \sum_j a_{ij} \frac{\mathrm{d}V_{ji}}{V_{ji}}.\text{[8]}
\tag{11.6}
$$

Substituting equation (11.6) into (11.5), and dropping the first term as irrelevant for infant-industry purposes,

$$
\dot{C}_i - \dot{C}_k = \frac{\mathrm{d}A_k}{A_k} - \frac{\mathrm{d}A_i}{A_i}.
\tag{11.7}
$$

In order for infant-industry considerations to have warranted intervention in favor of industry i, costs per unit of output must have fallen more in i than in k. Equation (11.7) shows that a necessary condition for this to occur is that inputs per unit of output decrease more rapidly in industry i than in industry k. As formulated, this unit cost reduction could come about because of technical change, the overcoming of indivisibilities, the realization of scale economies, or for genuine infant-industry reasons.

This, then, is the empirical test. Should industry i have been protected on infant-industry grounds and its costs have fallen relative to k, it will be judged that there were some dynamic factors in industry i that *may* have warranted intervention (although there is no presumption whatsoever that intervention was optimal). Passing the test is a necessary condition for there to have been an infant industry. It is not sufficient to prove that infant industry protection was warranted because: (a) the industry might have developed anyway; (b) the rewards may all have gone to the entrepreneurs in the industry; (c) the reduction in costs might have come about for reasons other than externalities; or (d) the reduction in costs was not sufficient to provide an adequate rate of return on earlier losses. It might not have been optimal because an alternative intervention instrument or a lower level of protection might have achieved the same or better results with lower costs.

If, however, costs in industry i did not fall relative to industry k, clearly protection was not warranted.[9] It is in this sense that a contrast of rates of growth of output per unit of input between more- and less-protected industries constitutes a test for the empirical validity of the infant industry argument.

Before proceeding to the empirical results, two questions remain. A first question is the time period over which infant-industry considerations might warrant intervention. The second pertains to the range of activities over which the test should be carried out.

The first is the simpler question, since all that is required is a period sufficiently long so that, if cost reductions were not incurred, it could reasonably be concluded that the costs of protection would not in all likelihood be recovered. Since the Turkish data pertain to a period of thirteen years (and longer), we note simply that with a real rate of return of 10 per cent,[10] the present value of cost savings ten years hence is less than 40 per cent of the anticipated amount. It seems doubtful whether protection for a period of more than ten years, with no beginning of a reduction in costs, could conceivably come under the heading of justified infant-industry protection.

The second question is the more difficult. It will be recalled that the infant-industry argument presumes *both* dynamic factors *and* externalities. The test described above is straightforward in evaluating for the presence of dynamic factors, but does not indicate to which units it might apply. Since protection is granted at different rates to different industries, it seems natural to suppose that the relevant i and k to contrast would be different industries subject to different levels of protection. Having done so, a higher dA/A would be required for a more-protected industry than for a less-protected one to satisfy the infant-industry test. Most proponents of the infant-industry argument seem to adopt this notion that the benefits are external to the firm but internal to the industry. This would appear to imply that rates of growth of output per unit of input should be higher for the industry than for new firms (or new investments of existing firms). It is also possible, however, that externalities spread across new entrants, and do not affect more traditional firms within industries. In that event, one would expect output per unit of input to grow more rapidly in newly established firms or activities than in pre-existing ones.

Both of these possible relationships imply that the relevant unit for externalities to be recaptured is somewhere within a given, protected, industry. While this seems the most plausible infant-industry interpretation (and the one used here), some might argue that the benefits of new industries are spread across the entire industrial sector, and are not centered in the protected industries themselves. One might be skeptical of the argument, on the grounds that it is hard to see why different levels of temporary protection should be accorded to different industries unless their own costs would fall differentially. But if the relevant source of externalities is the entire industrial sector, the industrial sector as a whole should be observed to have experienced a relatively high rate of growth of output per unit of input in contrast to the rest of the economy (in contrast to mature industrial economies). Comparison of output per unit of input across countries is inherently difficult, but can provide a partial check on the plausibility of this possibility.

11.3 RESULTS

As already mentioned, Turkey has provided protection, on infant-industry grounds, to a variety of new industries. Protection has been largely automatic because the authorities have generally prohibited imports of any good once domestic production has begun.[11] Rates of effective protection have been fairly high, and estimates must be based upon direct price comparisons rather than upon tariff schedules. The best available estimates are given in Table 11.1.

The details of data sources and procedures for estimating output per unit of input are given in the list on page 232. Here, only three points need to be noted. First, there are two sets of estimates available: one from a sample of 92 firms and the other for two-digit manufacturing industries in the private sector of the Turkish economy. Second, the main thrust of import-substitution activity (on infant-industry grounds) in Turkey was during the early and mid-1960s. The two-digit industry data cover the period 1963–76, while data for individual firms cover at least that period when the firms were already in existence but shorter periods in some instances when the firms started operation in the late 1960s. Finally, since much of the import-substitution process consists of replacing imported inputs with domestic materials, estimates were generated for three separate inputs: labor, capital, and material inputs.[12]

Table 11.1 gives the main findings. The list on page 232 gives sources and procedures and the underlying data on rates of growth of outputs and inputs from which these estimates were derived.

Table 11.1   Effective rates of protection and rates of growth of output per unit of input

Industry	ERP$_1$	ERP$_2$	DRC	Rate of Growth of Output/Input	
				Firm Sample	Industry
Food products	13	n.a.	18	0.25	0.16
Fur and leather products	14	−24	−15	n.a.	−1.17
Wood and cork products	16	58	−13	−3.34	−0.55
Furniture and fixtures	16	n.a.	n.a.	n.a.	−0.56
Non-metallic mineral products	23	−27	1	1.61	0.72
Textiles	42	−23	12	0.72	0.84
Apparel and footwear	42	47	n.a.	5.24	4.10
Metal products	57	140	682	−0.05	1.61
Chemicals	60	200	21	−0.04	0.46
Electrical machinery	63	113	36	5.76	1.41
Paper and products	72	105	97	n.a.	1.55
Rubber products	77	NIVA	279	n.a.	4.27
Basic metals	80	113	14	2.21	−0.93
Non-electric machinery	142	132	36	n.a.	0.62
Petroleum refining	n.a.	236	n.a.	n.a.	−8.80
Transport equipment	209	134	131	n.a.	0.94
All manufacturing				1.91	1.84

Source: ERP$_1$: Özfirat estimates given in Krueger (1974, Table IX.2); ERP$_2$: Baysan estimates given in Baysan (1974, Table 1, p. 126). DRC: Krueger (1974, Table VIII.1). *Notes:* 1) Beverages and Tobacco are not reported here due to lack of a measure of effective protection; both are traditional. Estimated rates of growth of output per unit of input are 4.31 per cent annually for Beverages and 5.97 per cent for Tobacco. 2) All rates of growth are continuous natural rates. NIVA denotes negative international value-added.

The first three columns of Table 11.1 give three different estimates of sectoral protection all pertaining to the late 1960s. The first are based on sectoral averages computed by the State Planning Organization for 1968. Sectors are listed in order of increasing protection based on these estimates. The second are based on input-output tariff data adjusted for the estimated additional protection accorded by import quotas and pro-hibitions. The third are domestic resource-cost estimates taken from a sample of firms. While the last are most closely based on price com-parisons, they suffer from the drawback that levels of protection vary so much within each sector that sampling error is probably fairly large.[13] This variability stems partly from the fact that an import-licensing regime inherently provides varying levels of protection to the same industry at different points in time. Even more important is the consideration that there are import-substitution industries within 'traditional' sectors (such as synthetic textiles), and 'traditional' activities within import-substitution sectors (such as copper-processing within basic metals). Thus, the variability reflects the underlying reality that levels of protec-tion differ widely even within particular industries.[14]

Despite the wide variability, the three sets of estimates together provide a fairly good indication of the height of protection in the mid- to late 1960s, and its differential across industries. Essentially, the first seven are all regarded as traditional industries within Turkey; the last nine are regarded as the import-substitution sectors.[15] The latter are those that were encouraged in the early 1960s, and were the focus of Turkey's import-substitution polices on infant-industry grounds. The positive rates of protection for the traditional sectors probably did little more than offset currency overvaluation in the late 1960s; the Turkish lira was devalued by 66 per cent in 1970.

The last two columns in Table 11.1 give estimated rates of growth of output per unit of input. The firm-sample column gives estimated rates for the sample of firms. As can be seen, there were some industries for which no firm data were available. In some instances (such as petroleum refining) this was because the activity is undertaken primarily by one large firm; in other instances, there were simply no firms in the sample data. Rates for the industry cover the years 1963–76, the period for which State Institute of Statistics data are available.

As can be seen, there is no systematic tendency for more-protected firms or industries to have had higher growth of output per unit of input than less-protected firms or industries. Two industries – apparel and footwear and rubber products – appear to have experienced relatively rapid growth of output per unit of input. Apparel and footwear is a traditional industry in Turkey, and its medium rate of effective protection reflects currency overvaluation and the negative protection to textiles, rather than positive nominal protection directed toward apparel and footwear. Rubber products is a sector with a sizeable traditional component and import-substitution activities consisting primarily of tire production. This latter activity was extremely high cost, as reflected both in Tercan Baysan's estimate that international value added was negative and in a very high DRC estimate. No firms producing rubber products were in the sample, so only a sectoral rate is available.

There is likewise no apparent tendency for the new activities, as reflected by the firm data, to have experienced rates of growth of output per unit of input systematically higher or lower than the industry to which they belonged. Thus, the externality argument does not seem borne out by the data: if anything, sample firms experienced a slightly higher rate of growth of output per unit of input than their corresponding industries, but surely the difference is well within the margin of error of the calculations.

Finally, there is the question as to whether externalities could have been realized elsewhere in the manufacturing sector. Here, the only way of judging is to evaluate the estimated rate of growth of output per unit of input in the manufacturing sector as a whole. That, in turn, involves a comparison of the rate realized in Turkey with that in other countries. Because data are not entirely comparable, and because the estimates are residuals and therefore subject to fairly wide margins of error, such comparisons are necessarily extremely hazardous. Typical estimates are 3–4 per cent for developed and other developing countries.[16] Despite problems of comparability, it hardly seems plausible that differences in measurement account for the lower figure in Turkey.

To see just how low the estimated rates of growth of output per unit of input are, consider the following. Suppose a firm initially experienced a 50 per cent cost disadvantage (i.e. required 50 per cent effective protection). Output per unit of input would have to grow 4 per cent annually more rapidly than in other industries in order for it to be able to survive without protection ten years hence.[17] This, however, would provide no return on the initial loss. It is thus an underestimate of the differential in growth of output per unit of input that would be necessary to warrant protection of the infant industry.

For the Turkish case, when all manufacturing was experiencing increased output per unit of input at a rate of 1.8 per cent annually, this would imply that industries experiencing 50 per cent protection should increase output per unit of input at a rate of at least 5.8 per cent annually. More concretely, consider rubber products, the 'best' Turkish case. If the *low* estimate of the ERP for rubber products is accepted, the output per unit of input would have to grow at 7.34 per cent annually in order for their costs to fall enough for them to become competitive in ten years. At their existing rate of growth of output per unit of input, it would require twenty-three years for them to become competitive.[18] Even that calculation takes the low estimate of the rate of protection, allows for no return on the investment over the twenty-three-year interval, and is for the two-digit industry with the highest estimated rate of growth of output per unit of input. Obviously, for 'infant' industries such as paper where outputs per unit of input grew at less than the average rate of all manufacturing, there can never be a 'catch-up' as long as existing relative rates are maintained.

11.4 CONCLUSIONS

This chapter has attempted two things: to develop an empirical test for the validity of the infant-industry argument; and to use that test on Turkish data. The test is simple and straightforward: input per unit of output must fall more rapidly in more protected industries if there is to be any rationale for infant-industry protection. In the Turkish case, there was no such tendency over the period covered.

The fact that protected Turkish industries did not experience rapid increases in output per unit of input is sufficient to prove that protection was not warranted. It does not, however, prove that there was no infant industries. It might be that the trade regime itself provided the wrong incentives. It is at least possible that, under an alternative incentive structure, output per unit of input might have grown more rapidly in some, or possibly even all, Turkish industries.[19] What can be concluded is that, at least in the Turkish case, protection did not elicit the sort of growth in output per unit of input on which infant-industry proponents base their claim for protection.

11.5 DATA SOURCES

The major thrust of import substitution into new industries occurred in the early and mid-1960s. For the period 1963–76, there are industry-level data available with which to estimate inputs and outputs. A Census of Manufacturers and Annual Survey of Industries provides detailed data on number of employees, wage bill, value of purchased inputs, value of output, investment made by firms, and number of firms for private activities within each industrial sector employing ten or more employees. These data, combined with estimates of capital stock provided by the State Planning Organization and appropriate price deflators[20] form a data set from which it is possible to infer the behavior of inputs and outputs for two-digit manufacturing industries in the private sector in Turkey.[21] Since much of the import-substitution process consists of replacing imported inputs with domestic materials, three inputs were separately estimated: labor, capital, and material inputs.

A second set of data is at the firm, rather than industry, level. It covers those firms which received loans from the Turkish Industrial Development Bank. For them, data were available on a variety of their attributes (size, date of inception, precise composition of output, etc.) and also for annual investments, annual labor force and wage bill, annual purchases of raw materials and intermediate goods and inventory changes, sales, profits, depreciation, and so on. Altogether, there are ninety-one firms for which data were available on a reliable basis for a period of more than five years.[22] Most new investments of these firms were undertaken in response to incentives provided by the trade regime, although some were in more traditional industries. Since there was credit rationing in Turkey, there is some presumption that borrowers from the Industrial Development Bank were firms of above-average quality, according to the criteria used by the Bank for its lending.

On the basis of these data, it was possible to compute an estimated

Table 11.2 Underlying growth rates of output and input for private-sector industries and sample firms (per cent per annum)

	Industries' 1963–76 growth rate of:			Sample firm growth rate of:		
	Labor	Capital	Real output	Labor	Capital	Real output
Food products	4.6	14.2	7.7	7.5	13.3	9.5
Beverages	18.0	14.2	22.5	–	–	–
Tobacco	–3.3	–.3	5.7	–	–	–
Textiles	4.6	13.3	11.0	6.2	14.1	10.2
Apparel and footwear	23.3	13.3	28.3	1.9	8.0	6.8
Wood and cork products	10.0	14.2	12.6	9.1	27.9	15.8
Furniture and fixtures	4.7	14.2	6.6	–	–	–
Paper and products	16.7	26.0	23.7	–	–	–
Chemicals	8.4	15.4	15.1	4.2	12.4	12.0
Rubber products	5.1	13.3	16.8	–	–	–
Fur and leather products	7.8	17.0	8.6	–	–	–
Petroleum and coal products	28.1	60.5	33.7	–	–	–
Non-metallic minerals	8.0	16.7	15.3	5.0	7.4	7.4
Basic metals	18.1	25.3	21.5	7.6	14.9	15.8
Metal products	7.8	13.1	11.8	9.0	17.1	13.3
Non-electrical machinery	15.2	17.6	17.9	–	–	–
Electrical machinery	12.5	20.1	19.8	–	–	–
Transport equipment	22.7	30.5	30.1	–	–	–

Note: All rates of growth are continuous natural rates, computed by running a logarithmic regression of each variable on time.

capital stock for each firm using perpetual inventory techniques. Doing so was judged better than using balance-sheet estimates (which were also available) since the latter made no allowance for price-level changes in their capital stock in the context of a relatively high rate of inflation. Depreciation rates were estimated from American engineering data found in Park (1973),[23] and then scaled to equal the State Planning Organization's estimate of the average rate for all manufacturing. Investment deflators available from the State Planning Organization were first employed to convert nominal investment into constant-price estimates of additions to capital stock. Investment in a given year was treated as becoming effective capital only at the beginning of the following year.[24] Period $t - 1$'s capital stock was depreciated, and then real investment in $t - 1$ was added to obtain capital stock in period t.

In addition, data from the firms could be directly used for the number of workers. Purchased inputs, adjusted for inventory changes, were deflated to yield an estimate of material inputs. Finally, for some firms a physical indicator of homogeneous output (for example, tons of cement)

Table 11.3 Computation of possible changes in relative costs due to changes in relative factor prices

Industry	Wage share of value added	Rate of cost change
Food products	.264	−0.4
Beverages	.101	−2.0
Tobacco	.183	−1.3
Textiles	.368	0.3
Apparel and footwear	.521	1.7
Wood and cork products	.485	1.4
Furniture and fixtures	.381	1.5
Paper and products	.372	.4
Chemicals	.319	−.1
Rubber products	.274	−.5
Fur and leather products	.484	1.4
Petroleum and coal	.016	−2.8
Non-metallic minerals	.326	−0.0
Basic metals	.201	−1.2
Metal products	.384	0.5
Non-electric machinery	.320	−0.1
Electrical machinery	.332	0.0
Transport equipment	.562	3.7
All manufacturing	.245	0.0

Notes: Real wages are estimated to have risen at a continuous rate of 6 per cent from 1963 to 1976, based on average weekly earnings covered under social insurance. The median share of labor was 33 per cent. Relative cost changes were computed be weighting these rates of change by each industry's actual (1968) shares. For the median industry's costs to have remained constant, capital costs would have had to decline at a continuous rate of 2.95 per cent.

was available and used to indicate output. For others, it proved preferable to take deflated sales adjusted for inventory change as the measure of output.

Thus, for both firms and industries, data were available on materials inputs, outputs, labor inputs, and capital stock inputs, along with the shares of the respective factors in the value of output. For purposes of estimating changes in input per unit of output, the *average* share (over the life of the firm and for the entire 1963–76 period for two-digit industries) of labor, material, and capital was used. This procedure was judged superior to employing a Divisia index because of the volatility of shares from year to year.[25]

Table 11.2 provides the estimates of rates of growth of labor and capital inputs and outputs. All rates are computed for the period 1963–76 at the industry level. For firms, rates were computed over the period for which data were available, and a minimum of five years. In some instances, firm data span a period of twenty years, but some newer import-substitution activities did not start until the late 1960s; data on these firms are also included in the estimates.

Table 11.3 gives data on the wage share in each two-digit industry and computes the maximal rate of change in relative costs that could have been associated with the very steep increase in real wages that occurred in Turkey during the period. The real wage increase was the result of labor legislation and did not reflect underlying labor-market conditions: urban unemployment was rising rapidly during most of the period.

NOTES

1   The 'infant-industry argument' is also the basis on which developing countries are excepted from some provisions of the GATT.
2. See Samuelson (1958, chap. 8), for a discussion of the history of thought with regard to the optimality of free trade. The optimum tariff argument is irrelevant to the concerns of this chapter and therefore not considered here.
3. See Baldwin (1969) for an excellent statement of the reasons why, even in the presence of infant-industry considerations, tariff protection might fail to correct the assumed market imperfection.
4. See Baldwin (1969) as to other mechanisms by which externalities have been said to affect the profitability of start-up of new activities.
5. It might be contended that a more-protected sector would generate greater externalities accruing to other activities. The unresolved question in that case is why protection should be temporary. If it were not temporary, infant-industry considerations do not apply.
6. It might be anticipated that the world price of a particular commodity would rise over time (for reasons other than technical change), and therefore a presently uneconomic industry might become economic. This would

not constitute a case for infant industry protection, however, because: (a) it is not clear that because the price in the future will rise, activity now is economic; and (b) there is no reason for intervention since those undertaking the activity now will benefit from the higher future price.

7. As a practical matter, changes in relative factor prices do not seem to be a major source of relative cost changes. Turkey had a very large change in relative factor prices due to government intervention in the labor market, and yet the changes in costs that these could have induced seem relatively small. See Table 11.3 for the calculations. It has also been suggested that commercial policies themselves might induce changes in relative factor prices and that this is a dynamic factor that should be considered. However, if commercial policies *caused* changes in relative factor prices, they would clearly increase costs in protected industries and thus tend to weaken whatever dynamic case there was for intervention.

8. The dA/A is nothing other than the conventional formula for total factor-productivity growth, which is the rate of growth of output less the share-weighted rate of growth of inputs per unit of output. For present purposes, however, the assumptions necessary to justify use of dA/A as a measure are far weaker than those necessary for a total factor-productivity growth interpretation.

9. This does not prove that there might not have been an infant-industry case. It is conceivable that incentives other than those created by the forms of protection actually used might have induced entrepreneurs to engage in cost-reducing activities. See Krueger and Tuncer (1981) for an analysis of the effects of the trade regime on incentives in Turkey.

10. Most observers would put the real rate of return in Turkey at a number substantially higher than this.

11. One would anticipate that, in the absence of expected monopoly power from entering a given line of activity first, the automatic protection mechanism would provide an incentive for the more economic among the import-competing industries to be developed first.

12. No data were available with which to estimate changes in skills of the labor force.

13. See Krueger (1974), where the variance in the estimated sectoral means was also calculated.

14. While data in nominal terms are available for three- and four-digit industries, no appropriate price deflators or detailed estimates of effective protection rates are available.

15. The import-substitution industries generally experienced more rapid growth of output. See Table 11.2.

16. Chen (1977) estimated rates of manufacturing total factor productivity growth of 2.29, 3.47, 3.50, and 3.75 per cent for Hong Kong, South Korea, Taiwan and Singapore, respectively, for the 1960s. Estimated rates for developed countries include 3.5 per cent for Norway (Ringstad, 1971), 3.66 for Japan (Nishimizu and Hulten, 1978), 3.75 for Italy (Conti and Filosa, 1979), and 2.9 per cent for the United States (Kendrick, 1976). In some of these cases, quality adjustments have been made to estimated inputs. Using unadjusted data would raise those estimates, making the contrast with Turkey even sharper.

17. This number is found by solving $I_t = I_0(1 - r)^t$ for r when $I_t = 0.667$, $I_0 = 1$, and $t = 10$.

18. This calculation is based on the assumption that output per unit of input in

rubber products continues to grow at 4.27 per cent annually while in the entire manufacturing sector it continues to grow at 1.84 per cent annually.

19. See Krueger and Tuncer (1981) for an attempt to trace the links between the growth of output per unit of input and the ebbs and flows of the trade regime.

20. Wholesale price indices were available for outputs of each two-digit industry. These data were then used, in conjunction with the Turkish input–output tables, to obtain a weighted input price for each sector's purchases. The same price deflators were used for two-digit industries and for the firm data.

21. In Krueger and Tuncer (1981) the behavior of the private and public sectors is analyzed and contrasted, and a fuller description of the data is given.

22. Interviews were held with more than a quarter of the firms, which provided a check on the reliability of the data, and also provided additional information on characteristics of firms and their management.

23. It is an interesting question whether one should a priori expect depreciation rates to be lower or higher in Turkey than in the United States. On one hand, cheaper labor should encourage more maintenance and thus a longer economic life. On the other hand, poor and irregular materials quality, irregular supplies of electric power, and workers with less experience in the care of equipment might tend to the opposite result.

24. For some older firms, data were not available from inception. In those cases, initial balance sheet data were converted to an estimate of real capital stock based on knowledge of the firm's history and starting date.

25. Initial estimates, based on Divisia indices, yielded occasionally bizarre results. For example, for firms or industries suffering losses, the capital share was negative, and firms with heavy investment were calculated to have increased output per unit of input!

REFERENCES

Arrow, Kenneth J. (1962). 'The Economic Implications of Learning by Doing'. *Review of Economic Studies*, vol. 29, pp. 155–73.

Baldwin, Robert E. (1969). 'The Case Against Infant-Industry Tariff Protection', *Journal of Political Economy*, vol. 77, pp. 295–305.

Baysan, Tercan (1974). 'Economic Implications of Turkey's Entry into the Common Market', unpublished doctoral dissertation, University of Minnesota.

Chen, Edward K.Y. (1977). 'Factor Inputs, Total Factor Productivity and Economic Growth: The Asian Case', *Developing Economies*, vol. 15, 3 June, pp. 121–43.

Conti, Vittorio and Filosa, Renato, (1979). 'A Disaggregate Analysis of Accumulation, Productivity, and Labor Costs in the Manufacturing Industry', in *Economic Papers, 2*. Rome: Bank of Italy Research Department, June.

Hirschman, Albert O. (1958). *The Strategy of Economic Development*. New Haven, CT: Yale University Press.

Kendrick, John W. (1976). 'Productivity Trends and Prospects' in *U.S. Economic Growth from 1976 to 1986*. Washington, DC: Joint Economic Committee of Congress, 1 October.

Krueger, Anne O. (1974). *Foreign Trade Regimes and Economic Development: Turkey*. New York: Columbia University Press.

Krueger, Anne O. and Tuncer, Baran (1981). 'Growth of Factor Productivity in Turkish Manufacturing Industries', unpublished paper.

Nishimizu, Mieko and Hulten, Charles R. (1978). 'The Sources of Japanese Economic Growth: 1955–71', *Review of Economics and Statistics*, vol. 60, pp. 351–61.

Park, W.R. (1973). *Cost Engineering Analysis*. New York: John Wiley and Sons.

Ringstad, V. (1971). *Estimating Production Functions and Technical Changes from Microdata*. Oslo: Statistisk Sentralbyrå.

Samuelson, Paul A. (1958). *Foundations of Economic Analysis*. Cambridge, MA: Harvard University Press.

12 · THE IMPORTANCE OF ECONOMIC POLICY IN DEVELOPMENT: CONTRASTS BETWEEN KOREA AND TURKEY

In the early years of thinking about development, the majority of policy-makers and development economists were skeptical – to put it mildly – about the importance of the traditional 'neo-classical' analysis and policy prescriptions. In no field was this more true than international trade, where doubts were expressed about the rate at which developing countries could expand their exports (elasticity pessimism), the probable future of terms of trade for primary commodities and the ability of developing countries to experience satisfactory industrial growth in the absence of high walls of protection surrounding their infant industries.

Three phenomena proved that much of that skepticism was ill-founded. First, empirical evidence failed to support elasticity pessimism with regard to the terms of trade. Second, analytical developments revealed difficulties with a protectionist strategy even beyond those that had earlier been pointed out by advocates of free trade. Third, experience in developing countries that adopted protectionist strategies proved less satisfactory than had been anticipated, while those developing countries that adopted more outer-oriented trade strategies had performance that usually exceeded expectations.

Of the analytical developments that were important, development of the concept of effective protection was certainly key. In demonstrating that the same nominal tariff rate might imply very different rates of protection to value added for producers of different specific items, the concept served to underscore the infeasibility of a 'rational' protective structure: the only uniform effective tariff was a uniform nominal tariff, which, in turn, implied a zero rate of protection or uniform nominal tariffs and export subsidies once it was recognized that tariffs did not affect the prices of exportables.

First printed in 1987. I am indebted to Bela Balassa, Vittorio Corbo, Kemal Dervis, Kwang Suk Kim, Chong Nam, Julio Nogues, Sarath Rajapatirana and Rusdu Saracoglu for helpful comments on an earlier draft of this chapter.

Max Corden's seminal work on effective protection was a key element in the gradual shift in thinking about trade policy in relation to development. His emphasis, in both his teaching and his research, on the importance of trade policy, and his contributions to trade-policy discussions, helped focus attention on the importance of these issues, and influenced both his colleagues and a generation of students. His careful, straightforward, analytical approach did much to clarify the issues and to speed the time when policies might shift.

Although good theory can inform policy decisions, it cannot by itself yield guidance as to the quantitative importance of those decisions. Moreover, most policies are implemented in an environment where myriad other changes are occurring simultaneously, and it is often difficult for the analyst, based on the experience of a single country, to infer the quantitative importance of a particular change. Hence, a variety of other methods of attempting to assess the quantitative importance of policy shifts are needed, none of which, in and of itself, can prove conclusive but which, through the weight of cumulative evidence, can permit firmer judgments to form.

One such method involves a comparison of countries with different policy regimes. An interesting pair is Turkey and Korea, the subject of this chapter. Both started out, in the 1950s, with a legacy of highly restrictive trade policies and severe macroeconomic imbalances. Turkey maintained a broadly restrictionist trade strategy until 1980, whereas Korea shifted in the early 1960s. While all countries have unique circumstances that make any comparison subject to numerous qualifications, the similarities and differences between these two countries make an interesting case study that demonstrates the importance of trade policy, and therefore of Corden's contributions, in the development process. An essay on the contrasts between Turkish and Korean experience therefore seems an appropriate tribute to him.

Out of this contrast, the lesson that 'policies matter' emerges clearly. Any observer of developing countries in the 1950s would have concluded that, in almost all regards, Turkey had the more favorable development prospects. The Korean reforms of the early 1960s, however, led to a fundamental transformation of the economy. Although Turkey also undertook some necessary changes in policy in the late 1950s, the reforms centered only on immediate correction of macroeconomic imbalances, and did not encompass any overhaul of the incentive structure.

Section 12.1 provides background information on the economic structures and other circumstances of the two countries in the early 1950s. Section 12.2 then traces the evolution of economic policy over the 1960–85 period in the two countries, and Section 12.3 contrasts the economic performance of the two countries.

12.1   INITIAL SIMILARITIES AND DIFFERENCES

12.1.1   Pre-1953 Heritage

Comparison of any two countries, especially countries with widely disparate cultural and geopolitical backgrounds, is always hazardous. And, in some fundamental regards, the Turkish and Korean backgrounds are very different.

Although the Turks were always a distinct group, Turkey was the seat of the Ottoman Empire until the First World War, and emerged thereafter as an independent Turkish nation under the leadership of Atatürk (see Lewis, 1968). Disassociation from the Ottoman rule brought with it (1) the declaration that Turkey was a secular state, (2) the introduction of Latin alphabet, and (3) a conscious effort to 'modernize' and adopt political, legal and economic systems much more akin to those of Europe than to those associated with the Ottoman legacy. None the less, the vast majority of Turks are Muslim and cultural ties to the Middle East remain. One might even venture the generalization that Turkey was and is caught between Europe and the Middle East and confronts a challenge to find her own unique identity between those two large and dissimilar regions.

In the 1920s and 1930s, many of the institutions that would be important in the post-war years were established. For present purposes, concern must be limited to noting those developments that significantly affected growth in the post-1950 period. After an initial period of relatively laissez-faire policies in the 1920s and very low overall growth, the government rejected the philosophy and shifted to a policy of 'Etatism' in the 1930s. Although 'Etatism' as enunciated contained a large number of elements with important implications for policy (such as the view that there were no distinct economic interests and hence no recognition of any role or rights for particular groups such as unions or industrialists), the chief and lasting legacy was the establishment of a number of State Economic Enterprises (SEEs) which produced and marketed a variety of agricultural, mineral and manufactured commodities. Many of these SEEs produced manufactured goods that had previously been imported. High tariffs were established to protect the new enterprises. By the end of the 1940s, it is estimated that more than half of Turkish industrial production originated in SEEs. They produced, and continue to produce, a variety of import-substitute commodities, ranging from textiles, clothing and footwear to petroleum products, paper, fertilizer and steel. In most activities there is also private production.

The 1920s and 1930s also witnessed a rapid expansion of Turkish schools, and an increase of educational attainments in Turkey. Even so, in 1950 about half of the male population over 14 years of age was illiterate.

Korea, by contrast, had a long history as a distinct nation prior to the twentieth century, but was occupied as a Japanese colony in 1910. Korea is situated between the two geographic giants of East Asia – China and Japan – just as Turkey is situated between Europe and the Middle East. Although there is a Confucian tradition in common with the country's Asian neighbors, Koreans have been a distinct ethnic group and nation for many centuries. They have tended to be somewhat inward-looking throughout their history, except when invaded or occupied by one of the two large Asian powers.

During the 1920s and 1930s, considerable manufacturing activity developed in Korea under Japanese occupation, although much of it was in the North and was owned by Japanese who also constituted a very high proportion (probably 80 per cent) of the technical manpower. Under the Japanese, little emphasis was placed on educating Korean children, and such education as did occur was provided in the Japanese language; use of Korean and teaching of Korean language and culture were forbidden.

During the Second World War Turkey was not an active combatant, but was still largely cut off from international markets. Inflation rose sharply, reaching peak rates of 92 and 74 per cent in 1942 and 1943 respectively (Hale, 1981, p. 69). Economic activity was stagnant owing in large part to the cut-off from international trade. As of 1946 Turkey was the poorest country in Europe, with the lowest per capita income and the highest rate of inflation. It is estimated that real GNP in Turkey grew at an average annual rate of about 2 per cent over the decade 1938–48.

Whereas the Second World War was a period of very slow growth for Turkey, it was a period of economic decline for Korea as the Japanese directed their efforts to the war. In 1945 the Japanese left, and the country was partitioned along the 38th parallel: the South and North got approximately equal land (and arable land) areas, but the South got 17 million people, contrasted with the North's 8.8 million. The result was that there were only 1309 square meters of arable land per capita in the South – the highest density of population in the world at that time. The Americans occupied what is now South Korea.

The North had been the source of most electric power and minerals, and a very high proportion of manufactured output of metal and chemical products, while the South had been predominant in textiles, processed foods and machinery. The economic disruption after the war and partition, therefore, was probably as great, if not greater, than that of some of the countries in which fighting had occurred. For example, it is estimated that, by 1948, production of textiles was only about 18 per cent of what it had been in 1939; machinery production stood at 40 per cent of its 1939 level, and overall manufacturing production was about 14 per cent of its 1939 level (Frank *et al.*, 1975, p. 26). The real economic dislocations were accompanied by hyperinflation; the Seoul retail price index of 1949 was 123 times what it had been in June 1945.

Thus, Korea's wartime legacy was vastly worse than Turkey's, although both countries had immediate reconstruction problems and low incomes. Both countries were recipients of sizeable amounts of foreign aid from the United States, starting in the immediate post-war years. But that is almost the only similarity, and even there, Korea received proportionately much more aid than Turkey. The events of the decade after the war ended in 1953 made the contrast much stronger, with everything apparently favoring Turkey's rapid growth and hindering Korea's.

For Turkey, US aid under the Point Four Program and then the Marshall Plan was directed largely toward the development of infrastructure and agriculture. The government established very high support prices for agricultural commodities, and, in addition, a sizeable proportion of aid was allocated for the importation of tractors, and for the conversion of pastureland and forests in the Anatolean plateau into wheat-growing areas. Wheat production boomed at a time when world prices were high and European demand was rising rapidly. By the early 1950s, Turkey was the largest exporter of wheat in the world, exporting a net of 600,000 metric tons in 1953 and 950,000 metric tons in 1954 (Krueger, 1974, p. 43) while simultaneously building up domestic stocks.[1] The price supports translated rapidly into heavy budgetary costs, which were a major cause of inflationary pressure in the mid-1950s, but until 1953 these were offset by Marshall Plan aid and export earnings at favorable terms of trade. It is estimated that Turkish real GNP at 1961 prices rose 15 per cent in 1951, 8.5 per cent in 1952 and 11.2 per cent in 1953 – exceptionally rapid growth by any standard.

The Korean economy's evolution over the 1946–53 period falls into two parts. As already mentioned, aid receipts were channeled toward reconstruction efforts and attempts to mitigate the dislocations of partition. The US military occupation carried out a successful land-reform program (see Mitchell, 1952, for an account), and in addition assisted with educational reforms that provided virtually universal primary education. Thus, although Korea's stock of manpower and new entrants to the labor force in the late 1940s were probably less well educated than the Turkish labor force, the educational reforms of the late 1940s laid a basis for rapid increases in educational attainments in later years.

Spurred by reconstruction activities and an inflow of aid, Korean output grew significantly until June 1950, although it probably did not reattain the levels of the late 1930s. Per capita income figures are not available, but an unweighted index of production (Frank *et al.*, 1975, p. 9), with 1946 = 100, stood at 171 in 1948 and 149 in 1949 (although items that probably had large weight in the index, such as rice, wheat and barley, were up only 20 per cent over their 1946 levels, while items such as nails and chinaware had increased 4 and 8.5 times, respectively).

However, whatever gains in output had been achieved by early 1950 were again lost with the outbreak of the Korean war, which lasted until mid-1953. During those years, the excess demand generated by wartime expenditures and by the demands of United Nations troops (including Turkish) intensified inflationary pressures. Meanwhile, the initial invasion of large parts of South Korea by the North was repulsed by UN troops, only to be followed by reinvasion, which was in turn followed by a final repulsion. The fighting destroyed much of the infrastructure that had been rebuilt in the late 1940s. When the war ended in 1953, the South Korean economy was once again severely dislocated.

12.1.2   Political and Geopolitical Situations

It would take this chapter too far afield to sketch in any degree of depth the domestic and international political situations of the two countries over the decades after 1953. But a few brief observations are necessary.

First, the perceived threat from the North led to a degree of cohesion in the South Korean body politic that might otherwise have been absent. There was a powerful imperative for economic development that arose not only because of low living standards but also because of rivalry with the North. This phenomenon may have permitted the government to pursue economic goals more singlemindedly than would otherwise have been the case, but it also had its costs: the large defense budget was one such cost. Second, because of these same concerns, Korean foreign policy was firmly based on alliance with the United States. The large aid inflows of the 1950s, and the continued US military presence, were consequences. Third, because of memories of the colonial era, Korea did not even have formal relations with Japan until 1965, when a formal treaty was signed, and Japan agreed to extend what were in effect reparations. At least until 1965, proximity to a rapidly growing Japan was not a significant plus to Korea's growth, and the Japanese share of Korean trade fell up to 1965.

Although Turkish proximity to the Soviet Union is not the same as the Korean partition, Turkey's strategic location none the less also determined her international policy stance. Turkey has been a member of NATO and has supported the largest army of any European NATO country, receiving military as well as economic aid from the United

States and Western European countries. In terms of both trade and aid, the United States and Western Europe were the dominant economies. Because of proximity as well as a commonality of religion and heritage, there were also strong links to the Middle East.

As to domestic politics, Turkish elections in 1950 brought Adnan Menderes to the prime ministership, and turned the Republican Peoples' Party (RPP), the recipient of the Atatürk heritage, out of office. This ended the era of single-party rule in Turkey. Atatürk, who had been a general, had left a strong legacy to the military, which regarded itself as the guardian of the nation and of Atatürk's tradition. Menderes was re-elected to office during the 1950s in an environment that was regarded as increasingly oppressive, and by the late 1950s there were charges of a rigged election. In 1960 the military intervened, and sponsored the writing of a new constitution which took effect in 1961, when elections were held and a civilian government was returned to office (with the RPP winning the 1961 election, and the Justice Party, the successor to the Menderes heritage, winning election in 1965). The military inter-vened once again in 1971, but again there followed a return to civilian government and democracy under the 1961 constitution. Starting in the mid-1970s, however, there were several years of increasing violence and a deteriorating economy, with excessive and unsustainable borrowing. The government seemed unable to resolve either the economic or the political issues, in part because neither of the two major parties could attain a majority in Parliament and had to enter into a coalition with one of several minority parties. In early 1980 the military once more inter-vened. This time a new constitution was written, partly with the intention of reducing the influence of the smaller parties, but also with a view to preventing a recurrence of some of the apparent excesses of the 1970s. When elections were held in 1983, the civilian government under Prime Minister Turgut Özal was operating with somewhat more limited powers than had earlier elected regimes.

Thus, throughout the post-war period the Turkish military was a major presence in the country's political life. However, for the majority of time the government was democratically elected under a constitution.

The Republic of Korea was founded in 1948; Seungman Rhee became president and remained in that office until 1960. The Rhee regime was aptly characterized as follows: 'Despite the existence of certain trappings of democracy, the Rhee regime was indubitably an authoritarian govern-ment' (Mason *et al.*, 1980, p. 44).

In 1960 a student revolution, with widespread support from other groups, led to Rhee's resignation. A one-year interim government (clearly democratically elected) was unable to maintain law and order, and was overthrown after about a year by a military coup. General Park

Chung Hee became chairman of a military council which revised the constitution to permit more centralized government in the expectation that centralization would prevent the apparent excesses of the earlier government; elections were held in late 1963. Although the opposition received 53 per cent of the votes, it was badly fragmented and Park was elected president, with his party controlling 110 of 175 seats in the National Assembly. In subsequent elections Park was returned to office, first with a 'landslide victory' in 1967 (Mason *et al.*, 1980, p. 51), which effectively endorsed the economic success of the regime, but then with smaller fractions of the total vote and more charges of voter irregularities. But the major turning point of the political process came after the 1971 presidential election, in which Park was elected for a third term. In 1972 the government, apparently alarmed by the reduced margin of victory of popular support, abruptly abolished the existing constitution and introduced a new one in which the procedure for electing the president was converted to an indirect one, thus paving the way for President Park's indefinite stay in power.

Park was assassinated in October 1979, after which there followed an interim period of about a year before General Chun Doo-Hwan became president. His government, which has ruled to the date of writing, announced that he would serve only one term as president, and held elections for the Assembly in February 1985, which were intended to lead up to an indirect national election in 1988 for determination of President Chun's successor.

Even during the period when President Park's office had clearly been won in a free and open election, all observers would agree the government and power in Korea were highly centralized. And, for periods including the late 1950s and from the late 1970s to the present, the government has been arguably authoritarian. Its basis of support, however, has been the challenge from the North and its ability to deliver a strong economic performance. Indeed, Mason *et al.* (1980, p. 56) concluded that: 'As long as the possibility of aggression seemed real to a majority of the population, and as long as continued growth assured increased real incomes to both rural and urban communities, the legitimacy of the Park Government in Korea was widely accepted'.

12.1.3 Structure of the Two Economies, mid-1950s

By the mid-1950s the Korean war was over and the reconstruction effort begun, while the initial period of rapid growth in Turkey had ended and the underlying macroeconomic imbalances were becoming increasingly evident. It is thus useful to contrast the economic structures of the two countries at that time as a starting point for later analysis.

Tables 12.1, 12.2 and 12.3 give an idea of some key magnitudes. The population sizes of the two countries were very similar, each in excess of 20 million (see Table 12.1). Korea was by far the poorer country: by UN estimates, the only Asian countries with lower per capita incomes in those years were India and Burma. Turkey's estimated per capita income of $210 was considerably higher than Korea's, although well below that of the richer Latin American countries and lower than any other European country covered by the UN estimates at that time. Thus, although both countries were poor, Korean living standards were probably among the lowest in the world, while Turkey was probably at the lower end of the spectrum of 'middle-income' developing countries.

Table 12.2 gives some idea of the structure of production in both countries in the mid-1950s. As can be seen, both were predominantly agricultural: in Turkey 74 per cent of the population lived in rural areas, and agricultural output accounted for 41.9 per cent of national income. Despite these similarities, there was and is an important difference: Turkey is relatively land-abundant, and Korea is land-scarce. Turkey is favored with a variety of climatic conditions, including: (1) the Mediterranean coast, where cotton, citrus, tree crops (especially olive trees) and fresh fruit and vegetable vie for rich land; (2) the Anatolean plateau, colder and with somewhat poorer soil, which probably has a comparative advantage in livestock and, to a lesser extent, wheat and other grains; and (3) the Black Sea region, where tobacco and hazelnuts are major

Table 12.1 Comparative data on the Korean and Turkish economies, 1952–4

	Population (million)	NNP ($ million)	Per capita income ($)
Korea	21.38	1500	70
Turkey	22.46	4717	210

Source: United Nations, *Per Capita National Product of Fifty-Five Countries: 1952–54*, Statistical Series L, no. 4, New York, 1957.

Table 12.2 Structure of output, Korea and Turkey, 1955 (per cent)

	Agriculture	Manufacturing	Construction	Other
Korea	44.8	11.2	3.0	41.0
Turkey	41.9	14.2*	5.8	38.1

* Includes all industry.
Sources: Korea: Bank of Korea, *National Income Statistics Yearbook, 1953–1967*, Seoul, 1968; Turkey: State Planning Organization, *First Five Year Plan, 1963–1967*, Ankara, 1964, p. 13.

crops. Turkey's resources are so large that one would expect her to be a net exporter of agricultural commodities throughout the development process: one foreign visitor aptly suggested that 'Turkey should be the California of Europe'. In addition to land, the country has large deposits of chrome, copper, coal, iron ore and a variety of other minerals. However, there is very little oil, and the country imports its entire supply.

By contrast, Korea had the smallest amount of arable land per capita (and not necessarily good-quality land) of any country in the world in the 1950s. Although the country was a net exporter of rice to Japan in the 1930s, that export reflected the realities of colonial administration; once land reform was undertaken, Korea became a net importer of grains. Korean policy toward agriculture in the 1960s was one of relative neglect; in the 1970s policy shifted toward protection for domestic food production, largely on income distribution grounds. Korea is lacking in almost all mineral resources – minerals and oil are major import items.

Table 12.3 gives data on the structure of expenditures in the two countries in 1955. As can be seen, both had imports considerably in excess of exports; in Turkey's case, foreign aid and other capital flows represented 2–3 per cent of GNP in the 1950s. In the Korean case, however, domestic savings were very small, as foreign aid accounted for about 8 per cent of GNP, or four-fifths of 1955 investment.[2]

Table 12.4 presents data on the composition of exports and imports

Table 12.3 Structure of expenditures, Korea and Turkey, 1955 (percentage of GNP)

	Consumption	Investment	Government consumption	Exports	Imports
Korea	86.4	12.3	8.7	1.6	9.8
Turkey	74.0	14.0	15.0	4.3	6.6

Source: Krueger (1974, p. 12); Bank of Korea, *National Income Statistics Yearbook, 1953–1967*, Seoul, 1968, p. 10.

Table 12.4 Composition of exports, Korea and Turkey, 1955*

	Total exports ($ m)	Agricultural exports	Mineral exports (% of total exports)	Manufactured exports
Korea	17.6	23.4	51.6	25.0
Turkey†	305.0	75.3	15.7	9.0

Sources: Korea: Hong (1976, Tables A.11 and A.12); Turkey: Krueger (1974, p. 182).
* The commodity classification may not be identical for the two countries.
† Turkish data are for 1956.

in the two countries. As can be seen, Turkey's exports were about 17 times larger in total value than were Korea's. Turkey's exports were predominantly agricultural, with cotton and tobacco the two leading agricultural export commodities. Even so, her exports of minerals (primarily chrome and copper) were three times as large as Korea's *total* exports. Other exports, which in Table 12.4 are recorded as manufactures, constituted no more than 9 per cent of total exports. By contrast Korea's exports were so small that a percentage composition table almost does not make sense. However, what exports there were were primarily minerals, with some forestry products and some agricultural and fishery products (especially marine products) constituting the balance.

One final aspect of trade structure deserves at least brief mention: that is, the geographic pattern of trade. Table 12.5 gives data on the share of trading partners in Korean and Turkish exports and imports. As can be seen, the United States is important for both countries, but much more so for Korea. Reflecting their respective geographies, however, Japan was relatively more important for Korea (although the Japanese share of Korean exports fell by all least half over the subsequent decade) and Europe for Turkey. The large 'other' category for Turkey reflects the importance of bilateral trading arrangements (especially with Council of Mutual Economic Assistance (CMEA) countries) in Turkey's exports in the mid-1950s.

In sum, there were remarkable similarities between the two countries. They were of approximately equal size in terms of population. Both were heavily agricultural and had low per capita incomes, although Korea's was considerably lower than Turkey's. Both had sizeable military expenditure burdens and were recipients of military and economic aid. Both countries had periods of authoritarian rule and periods where the government was legitimized by relatively free elections, although on average the Korean government was considerably more centralized and authoritarian than the Turkish.

Table 12.5 Geographic distribution of exports and imports, 1955 (per cent)

	Korea		Turkey	
	Exports	Imports	Exports	Imports
United States	41.9	34.9	15.5	22.4
Japan	39.1	14.7	0.3	0.7
EC	0.7	19.7	43.1	38.1
Other Europe	–	2.1	5.3	5.8
Middle East	–	–	5.8	6.7
Other	18.3	28.6	30.0	26.3

Source: United Nations, *Yearbook of International Trade Statistics*, 1955.

There were also significant differences. Turkey had by far the more generous resource endowment, both in terms of land per man in agriculture and in terms of other natural resources. And Turkey had the period from 1946 onward in which policies could focus on growth and efforts to raise living standards. Korea, by contrast, had been much more devastated by the political aftermath – partition, the departure of the Japanese, and the Korean war – and was, in the mid-1950s, much less far ahead of the immediate post-war situation than was Turkey.

12.2   ECONOMIC POLICY REGIMES

Turkey's economic performance until 1955 was regarded as one of the most promising of any developing country, while Korea remained a war-devastated country. Over the following five years, both countries pursued rather similar economic policies, each with relatively unsatisfactory results. Those policies are the subject of Section 12.2.1. In the late 1950s each country embarked upon some needed policy reforms, although the centerpiece of the reform packages and the scope and extent of reforms differed vastly. These reform packages are the subject of Section 12.2.2. In each case, the reform packages set the pattern for the economic policies that were pursued throughout the 1960s, which are discussed in Section 12.2.3. Section 12.2.4 then covers the reactions to the oil-price increase of 1973, while Section 12.3 traces economic performance in each country.

12.2.1   Policies in the late 1950s

Turkish economic policy in the late 1950s was shaped by the difficulties that arose out of the unsustainable and expansionary fiscal and monetary policies that had been pursued in the early 1950s; Korean economic policy was formulated in response to the exigencies of post-war reconstruction against the backdrop of heavy aid dependence. Interestingly, despite the difference in origins, the resulting policies and problems were remarkably similar. The difficulties in each instance manifested themselves in the balance of payments.

As already seen, Korea was heavily dependent on US aid and receipts from US military outlays to cover the import bill. Americans in effect borrowed Korean currency to purchase local goods and services and to provide US troops with domestic currency for local expenditures. At a later date, negotiations were then held covering the exchange rate at which the loan would be repaid in dollars. Inflation was rapid during the war period, when prices as reflected in the cost of living index rose at rates of 167, 402, 126 and 53 per cent in the years 1950–3, respectively.[3]

Despite that, the Korean authorities attempted to keep the nominal exchange rate constant in the expectation of higher dollar receipts for won loans. By the time the war ended, the exchange rate was thus already heavily overvalued. Frank *et al.* (1975, p. 32) estimate that, in 1965 constant won per US dollar, the official exchange rate (which had fluctuated between 180 and 250 in 1949) was only 55.6 won per dollar in August 1953 when the Korean war ended. Despite periodic devaluations, the real rate fluctuated between 55.7 and 154.8 in the years before 1960, and did not reattain the 1949 level until the end of 1960. Thereafter, it was always well in excess of 200 1965 constant won per dollar.

In response to the pressures that arose on the balance of payments, the authorities took a number of measures. First, there were multiple exchange rates, with as many as eight different rates for different classes of transaction in the late 1950s. Second, there was extensive exchange control, including licensing of all imports, which were not permitted unless they were on a list of 'eligible' commodities. Finally, tariffs and surcharges were imposed on those commodities that were imported in an effort to contain excess demand. There were numerous changes in regulations, and the overall exchange regime was chaotic. Despite occasional efforts to provide some relief and incentives to exporters, the discrimination against exports and in favor of the domestic market was enormous. Among the consequences, there was considerable import substitution in consumer goods industries; in addition, corruption increased among those trying to obtain imports, which was a significant factor in the downfall of President Rhee. Needless to say, exports lagged badly as a consequence: even in 1960, Korean exports were only $33 million compared with $40 million in 1953, representing about 2.4 per cent of GNP.[4]

Underlying the erosion of the real exchange rate, of course, was macroeconomic imbalance. Although annual inflation rates did not again reach 100 per cent after 1953, the consumer price index rose more than 20 per cent every year until 1958, and as much as 66 per cent in 1955. At that time, these rates were among the highest in the world.

The origins of inflation lay in the government budget deficit and its financing. As a percentage of GNP, the budget deficit rose from 1.9 per cent in 1953 to a peak of 7.6 per cent in 1955 and remained at about that level until 1958. Once economic policy reforms began, it fell sharply. Budget deficits were financed largely through credit creation, as financial markets were almost non-existent because of regulation. Nominal interest rates were controlled at very low levels throughout the period, and were negative in real terms until 1958 (see Kim and Roemer, 1979, p. 73).

The growth rate in Korea was lacklustre until 1960, despite the opportunities present in a reconstruction era for rapid growth. In 1960 real GNP is estimated to have been 589 billion won, compared with 422 billion won in 1953 – an increase of 39 per cent, or an average annual rate of less than 5 per cent (Bank of Korea, *National Income Statistics Yearbook*, 1953/57, p. 16). Investment remained at about 10 per cent of national income, and foreign aid continued to finance the bulk of investment.

For Turkey, the origins of the macroeconomic difficulties lay in a decision to maintain an exchange rate of TL2.8 per dollar in 1946. This rate was manifestly unrealistic, given the Turkish inflation during the Second World War. But the boom in wheat exports, the ability to run down reserves that had earlier been accumulated and the availability of Point Four and Marshall Plan aid permitted maintenance of this rate for an extended period of time. When commodity prices fell sharply in 1953, the government reacted by imposing quantitative restrictions on imports – no importer was to receive permission to import more than a specified percentage of his preceding year's imports. From this point onward, excess demand for foreign exchange increased as inflation persisted, but was contained through a complex set of regulations.[5] The trade and payments regime became an extremely complex amalgam of multiple exchange rates with surcharges of different levels for different categories of imports, and export premiums for specified exports, import-licensing, tariffs, bilateral trading arrangements and export-price checks (see Krueger, 1974, chap. 2, for a description).

There was little conscious 'industrialization' policy in Turkey during the 1950s, but the foreign trade regime provided a highly protected domestic market to any domestic supplier of import-competing goods. The SEEs and private industry both increased their output fairly rapidly until 1956. Almost all of it was in consumer goods, just as in the Korean case. After 1956 the inability to obtain raw materials, intermediate goods and spare parts severely constrained the output of Turkish industry.

Even without inflation, foreign exchange difficulties would have been acute, but there were inflationary pressures arising out of the budgetary deficits incurred as a result of agricultural price supports and large public expenditures on infrastructure. The budgetary deficits were aggravated by the government's effort to suppress inflation by holding down the prices at which SEEs could sell their output. The consequence was large losses by these enterprises, which were financed by central bank credits, which further fueled inflation.

Price controls led to significant discrepancies between official prices and market prices, so that inflation exceeded, and probably substantially so, the rate recorded in official price indices. Even those indices, however, record rates in excess of 20 per cent for the years 1955–7.

12.2.2   Economic Reforms of the late 1950s and early 1960s

In both Korea and Turkey, the economic policy stance of the mid-1950s was unsustainable without a significant change in some key parameters. For Korea, export earnings were stagnant, and growth could proceed only if that situation would change or if foreign aid could be expected to grow indefinitely. The United States had informed the government of her intention to reduce aid, which made prospects in the absence of policy change even bleaker. Moreover, the government budget was sufficiently imbalanced that the prospect would probably have been for an accelerating rate of inflation even if aid levels had been sustained in the absence of measures to adjust expenditures relative to income. Whereas for the Koreans it was recognition of the infeasibility of maintaining growth over the long run which prompted policy reform, for the Turks reforms were forced upon them by the imperatives of a balance-of-payments crisis.

Stated another way, in Turkey the option of changing the underlying parameters of economic policy with respect to protection was not considered. The role of SEEs in the economy and the need for control of economic activity were unquestioned, and there does not appear to have been any significant group within Turkey advocating a significant shift in policies of control and regulation. A deep-seated suspicion of private economic activity and belief in the need for detailed regulation and control pervaded Turkish society. While there was opposition to the changes in Korea with dominant businessmen dependent on the restrictive trade regime and controls for their profits, the change in government in 1960 seems to have led to the formation of a consensus on the need for growth-oriented policies and an export orientation. Once begun, President Park's commitment to growth, and the highly visible success of the new policies, assured the maintenance of the strategy.

In the Turkish case, imports were financed by borrowing from abroad, on ever-worsening terms, until finally even suppliers' credits were unavailable to would-be importers. By the summer of 1958, harvests were left in the fields in the absence of gasoline to power the tractors and trucks to bring produce to the ports and markets, and many activities were running at far below capacity because of import shortages. Indeed, the situation could be described as having been critical for at least a year before that time, but the Menderes government resisted policy reforms until it became apparent that there would be no alternative.

The major Turkish policy reforms were carried out under the aegis of an IMF stabilization program in the summer of 1958. The centerpiece was a major realignment of the exchange rate (from TL2.8 per dollar to TL9 per dollar, although the change was implemented through surcharges on imports and subsidies on exports until it was legitimized in the summer of 1960). Other measures included credit and budgetary ceilings, an attempt to rationalize the import regime and a rescheduling of the debt. In addition, Turkey received a sizeable credit to permit a resumed flow of imports. The intent of the government, if there was an intention other than to satisfy international creditors enough to be eligible for resumed lending and foreign aid, was to remedy the short-term macroeconomic imbalances.

Even the rationalization of the import regime took the form of instituting three semi-annual 'import programs': one program listed goods eligible for importation without quantitative restrictions (mostly raw materials and intermediate goods used in production where there was no domestic source of supply); another program listed quotas for imports of other commodities; yet a third listed commodities that were eligible for importation only under bilateral trading arrangements. Commodities not listed on any of these were not legally importable.

The inauguration of regular import programs, and especially a liberalized list, represented a significant improvement over the chaotic conditions that had prevailed when importers, even with valid licenses, had to queue at the central bank for six and even eight months in order to obtain a foreign exchange permit. None the less, the new system permitted the government to liberalize or restrict the trade regime in accordance with the dictates of foreign exchange availability and/or desires to protect domestic industry: shifting of commodities to the quota list, or removing them from any list, automatically heightened restrictions. And during the 1960s shifts of this sort were a major means by which domestic import substitution was encouraged. The import programs remained the basic instrument of protection for domestic industry throughout the following two decades. Once domestic production of an item had begun, imports of the import-competing good were placed on the 'Quota List'; when production was deemed 'adequate' to supply the domestic market, the item was removed entirely from the import lists, which meant that it could not legally be imported.

The Korean reforms started in 1957–8 with a first effort at macroeconomic stabilization and the introduction of some export incentives. Thereafter, the process of liberalization continued, and it continues to this day.[6] Cutbacks in expenditures permitted a sharp reduction in the rate of monetary expansion, and the rate of inflation plummeted from its 30–50 per cent range to virtually zero by 1959. In 1960 (after the student revolution), reforms of the trade and payments regime began. The initial effort was geared primarily at stimulating exports: the official exchange rate was adjusted (for the first time since 1955), and in addition tax rebates and a number of export subsidies were introduced to compensate for the bias against export activities that would otherwise have resulted from the tariff structure. After 1960, the real exchange rate for exporters was kept relatively constant.

Along with the increased incentives for exporting, the Korean government, through its policy pronouncements, assured exporters that those incentives would be maintained. Over the next several years these assurances were accompanied by a number of policy measures that gave them credibility. In the first place, the rates of export subsidies and tax incentives were adjusted periodically to ensure that exporters did not lose when inflation was not offset by exchange-rate changes. Second, procedures were developed so that exporters could import their needed raw materials and intermediate goods duty-free provided only that they re-exported these materials within a year; indeed, the provisions were sufficiently generous so that there was probably an element of subsidy in the scheme. Third, exporters were the only ones eligible to receive import licenses and were thus the recipients of whatever premiums there were on imports (primarily consumer luxury goods). Finally, exporters were extended highly preferential treatment in receiving credit. Because of interest-rate ceilings and credit rationing, the real interest rates applicable were negative, at least until 1965, and the value of credit was substantial.

Thus, the initial set of Korean reforms had two distinct parts: on the one hand, there was a major effort to realign monetary and fiscal policy in order to reduce the rate of inflation drastically; on the other hand, there was a huge shift in incentives away from import substitution and toward export promotion.

Turkey and Korea were similar in that (1) they both started with trade and payments regimes that were highly protective of import-substitution activities and discriminated against exports; (2) they had relatively high rates of inflation (as seen from the perspective of the 1950s and 1960s) and attempted to reduce excess demand; (3) new governments in 1960 were, if anything, more committed to the economic programs and reforms than had been their predecessors.

They differed in three respects. (1) The Turkish reforms were driven by the exigencies of a balance-of-payments and debt crisis, whereas the Korean reforms were motivated largely by a commitment to economic growth through an export-oriented strategy, given that aid flows could not be expected to sustain the sort of growth of imports that would be essential for satisfactory overall economic development. (2) There was no real intent on the part of the Turkish authorities to alter the underlying incentive structure of the economy with regard to exportables and import substitutes. As pronouncements in the First and Second Five-Year Plans amply demonstrate, it was intended to develop industry as a leading sector through import substitution. (3) The Korean government recognized the role of incentives and was essentially pragmatic in its efforts to stimulate economic performance, whereas the Turks remained highly suspicious of private economic activity and remained committed to a policy regime based on direct controls.

12.2.3   Policies during the 1960s

In both Korea and Turkey, policy during the 1960s and 1970s really evolved in response to the perceived needs originating from the basic strategy that had already been decided upon. In Turkey, perceived needs originated largely in foreign exchange difficulties; in Korea, perceived needs were actions that would support the export drive.

In Turkey the initial results of the 1958 reforms were highly successful. The stabilization was accompanied by receipt of new credit which financed a resumed flow of imports; partly for this reason, but also because there was a good harvest, the initial response to the stabilization program was a substantial increase in output, combined with a sharp reduction in the rate of inflation (after an initial, once-and-for-all, increase in prices of products of the SEEs). Perhaps because of that, the Menderes government began to exceed the credit and budget ceilings agreed upon with the IMF by late 1959, and signs of inflation reappeared. In May 1960 a military coup removed Menderes from office; interestingly, among the first actions of the new government was the reinstatement of the stabilization program.

Throughout the 1960s Turkish inflation remained moderate, averaging just under 5 per cent annually over the decade. Economic policy was articulated in the First and Second Five-Year Plans, which set industrialization as a major goal, to be achieved through import substitution. Aid in support of Turkey's development plans constituted 2–3 per cent of GNP during most of the 1960s. The real exchange rate for traditional exports in 1958 prices, which had reached TL7.69 per dollar after the devaluation, fell to TL6.82 per dollar in 1963 and to TL5.45 per dollar by 1969. For non-traditional exports, some subsidies were given to offset part of the disincentive inherent in an appreciating real exchange rate, but, the real rate in 1958 prices fell from TL9 per dollar in 1958 to TL7.18 in 1965 and to TL6.00 by 1969 (see Krueger, 1974, p. 187).

Exports responded to the significantly increased incentives which resulted from the more realistic exchange rate in the early 1960s. Turkish exports, which amounted to $396 million in 1953, had fallen to a low of $247 million in 1958: they rose by over $100 million in 1959, and reached a level of $458 million in 1965. While this did not represent exceptionally rapid growth, the availability of aid in addition to export earnings led to a fairly comfortable balance-of-payments position, and the major motive for the import programs in the first half of the 1960s was to protect domestic industry.

By the mid-1960s, however, the cumulative effect of inflation at rates of 5 per cent against the backdrop of stable international prices was beginning to take its toll, and growth of export earnings slowed down markedly. The government attempted to mitigate the situation by providing export incentives, in the form of subsidies, for non-traditional exports, and these grew somewhat more rapidly in the late 1960s. However, export earnings from the traditional sources of foreign exchange – agricultural and minerals – stagnated. Meanwhile, the import content of planned investment and output in import-substituting industries generally exceeded expectations, so that demand for foreign exchange was rising rapidly.

With only slow growth in availability and more rapid growth in demand, the import programs became increasingly restrictive in 1966, 1967 and 1968. None the less, foreign exchange difficulties increased, so that by 1969 even those who had received import licenses under an import program were waiting six to eight months before they received their foreign exchange allocation from the central bank. In this environment, incentives for producing domestic substitutes of almost anything were very great: no competing imports were permitted; those products dependent on imported raw materials or intermediate goods had virtual monopoly positions as their shares of these materials were determined by the import-licensing regime. As foreign exchange availability decreased, premiums on import licenses rose, and growth rates fell in the late 1960s.

A devaluation in 1970 was aimed at providing more incentives for exports. In the short run it did so, but the authorities were unable to sterilize the inflow of funds associated with the remittances of repatriated workers (who had earlier held their funds abroad) and with reverse capital flight. As a consequence, inflation accelerated rapidly. Thus, despite the fact that exports rose from $537 million in 1969 to $1,317 million in 1973, inflation as measured by wholesale prices rose from 5.6 per cent in 1970 to 19.8 per cent in 1973.

Whereas Turkish economic policy with regard to the relative incentives for exportable and import-competing production was driven largely by foreign-exchange availability, Korean economic policy in the 1960s and early 1970s was determined largely by the desire to maintain the momentum of the export drive. Once the export incentives were in place, they were generally altered in order to maintain their constancy in real terms: the real effective exchange rate for exports hardly changed from 1960 to 1968, although the exchange rate itself was pegged in the early 1960s and floated after 1964, and the fraction of the real rate that originated in export incentives (including tax rebates, export subsidies and subsidized credit) varied widely. Over time, there was a trend toward greater reliance on the exchange rate, and less on individual incentive schemes, than had earlier been the case. Over time, too, the real effective exchange rate began to be adjusted in response to the degree to which export performance was deemed to be flagging or unsustainably rapid.

In support of this general thrust, however, further reforms were undertaken in the 1960s. In 1961 a major overhaul of the protective system was undertaken, as quantitative restrictions were largely replaced by tariffs. In 1964, budgetary reform consolidated the government accounts and increased fiscal discipline, with the result that the inflation rate fell from about 30 per cent in 1963 and 1964 to 6 per cent in 1965 and remained under 20 per cent for the remainder of the 1960s; in the same year, financial reforms resulted in positive real interest rates to depositors for the first time in the post-war period and reduced the degree of subsidy in official lending rates. In 1967, imports were further liberalized, as the earlier positive list of imports was replaced by a negative list (one that specifically itemized those goods that could *not* be imported).

As mentioned earlier, US aid was phased out during the 1960s. Until 1966 Korean policy largely discouraged foreign investment and foreign borrowing. But with decreased aid flows, the government reversed its stance and began to encourage private capital inflows, initially in the form of bank lending. These inflows were carefully controlled, with the government deciding upon the aggregate amount of borrowing that would be permitted and reviewing individual applications for it. After 1970 somewhat greater encouragement was given also to direct foreign investment, although it has remained relatively small contrasted with borrowing.

In all of this effort, however, the export drive was central. Monthly joint meetings of government officials and businessmen were held, chaired by President Park, in which export performance, industry by industry, was reviewed. In cases where exports appeared to be lagging, inquiry was made as to the difficulties; in many instances officials were then directed to remove restrictions or otherwise facilitate performance. In the Korean system, government officials tried to keep low targets for their industries (because higher targets meant more work for them), and had every incentive to facilitate private economic activity – the opposite of the incentive system in many import-substitution regimes, including that of the Turkish.

No measure of the biases of the two regimes can capture the difference between them, largely because the commitment of the Korean government provided a degree of assurance to exporters that was probably more valuable than some of the incentives that are measurable. None the less, for the study on Foreign Trade Regimes and Economic Development (Krueger, 1974; Frank *et al.*, 1975), the bias of the Turkish and Korean regimes was estimated as of the early 1960s: for Korea, it was estimated that in 1966 the relative price of import-competing goods to exportables in the domestic market was 0.94 times that in the international; in Turkey in 1969, it was about 3.01 times as great.

Moreover, the variation in effective exchange rates and effective rates of protection was much greater in Korea than in Turkey. Table 12.6 gives some estimates. Although both means and variances are affected by the degree of disaggregation and the coverage of the estimates, the data in the table give an idea of the difference between the Turkish and Korean regime. In many sectors, the incentive for exporting in Korea

Table 12.6   Estimated incentive levels in Korea and Turkey, 1963

(a) Korea: effective subsidy rates (%)

	For export	For domestic industry	Average
Agriculture, forestry and fisheries	−9.4	21.7	21.3
Processed food	1.8	−19.6	−18.0
Beverages and tobacco	12.6	−20.8	−19.5
Mining and energy	2.7	4.5	4.1
Construction materials	4.4	−12.9	−12.1
Intermediate products I	26.0	−21.9	−15.7
Intermediate products II	11.6	13.1	13.0
Non-durable consumer goods	4.1	−15.7	−11.2
Consumer durables	1.5	23.6	19.5
Machinery	1.9	21.0	20.2
Transport equipment	−5.6	80.8	80.3

(b) Turkey domestic resource costs (TL per dollar)

	Mean	Variance		Mean	Variance
Food and beverages	14.11	46.06	Glass and ceramics	10.80	28.35
Textiles	13.48	43.77	Iron and steel	13.68	29.70
Forest products	10.44	n.a.	Iron and steel		
Leather products	10.24	n.a.	products	93.87	43,737.12
Paper products	23.69	67.40	Other metal		
Rubber products	45.59	890.49	products	14.17	22.89
Plastic products	37.05	843.90	Machinery and parts	21.81	139.31
Chemicals	14.56	16.92	Transport		
Cement	14.80	6.26	equipment	27.78	278.88

Sources: (a) Frank *et al.* (1975, Table 10.3). Subsidies were computed under the Corden treatment of home goods; (b) Krueger (1974, Table VIII-1).

was greater than the incentive for selling in the domestic market; the opposite was the case only when there were very few exports. Moreover, there was only one sector where the average rate of protection exceeded 80 per cent; the next highest was 20 per cent, and the range was from a negative 20 per cent to a positive 20 per cent. In Turkey, by contrast, almost all incentives were for production in the internal market; there was probably no sector in which the incentive to export even equalled the incentive to sell domestically. And, as between activities, the range of incentives varied tenfold, or by 1,000 per cent, with variances commensurately great.

There can be little doubt, based not only on the data in Table 12.6 but also on other evidence, that the Korean incentive structure was much more uniform across activities than was the Turkish, and that the average incentive to export was probably at least as great as that to produce for the domestic market. This contrasts sharply with Turkey's inner-oriented policies.

12.2.4   Response to the Oil Price Increase

As was mentioned in Section 12.1, neither Turkey nor Korea has any significant amount of oil. Consequently, the terms of trade of both countries were seriously affected by the oil price increase of 1973–4, although the prices of Turkey's primary commodity exports rose as a partial offset to the oil-price increase. Relative to 1972, Korea experienced a 23 per cent deterioration in her terms of trade by 1974 (based on export and import unit values) contrasted with Turkey's 20 per cent drop. Because trade was much more important in Korean GNP, the total impact on Korea was much greater than on Turkey.

The policy responses of the two countries were quite different. In part because reserves were high and the response to the 1970 devaluation was still improving the balance of payments, the Turkish government did virtually nothing in the short run. By comparison, the Korean reaction was immediate and sharp. In Turkey the nominal exchange rate was adjusted only with significant lags, despite the rapid inflation; in 1976 the nominal exchange rate was TL16.67 per dollar as compared with TL14.93 at the end of 1970, although the price level was almost triple its 1970 level. Even after adjusting for inflation in dollar prices, the real price of foreign goods had fallen 40 per cent relative to domestic output in the six-year period.

As inflation was seen to be a major policy problem, the domestic price of energy was restrained. No significant alterations were made in the key parameters confronting the private sector, and public expenditures and the tax structure were not altered. In the absence of any marked policy response to the oil-price increase, the initial impact was, therefore, a significant increase in the current-account deficit: after a current-account surplus of $660 million in 1973, there were deficits of $561 million, $1,648 million and $2,029 million in the ensuing three years.

The Korean policy response was substantially more complex. The nominal effective exchange rate for exports was increased from 310 won per dollar in 1970 to 398 in 1973 and 484 in 1975. This adjustment more than compensated for the differential between domestic and foreign inflation, so that the purchasing-power-parity, price-level-deflated effective exchange rate (PPD PLD EER) for exports was increased from 308 won per dollar in 1970 to 396 won at the end of 1973; even at the end of 1975 it still stood at 231 won per dollar, a higher real rate than had prevailed at any time in the 1960s (Hong, 1981, Table 8.6).[7] On the import side, the adjustment was even greater; the PPP PLD EER had been 260 in 1970, rose to 332 in 1973 but then fell back to 287 by 1975.

In addition to raising the real exchange rate, the domestic price of energy was adjusted promptly, with some adjustments in domestic tax rates undertaken to offset the impact on low-income groups. Also, systematic efforts were begun to find new sources of foreign exchange earnings, and the government actively encouraged Korean efforts to develop a market, especially in the Middle East, in construction activities.

Despite these adjustment measures, a large jump in the current-account deficit and a sharp increase in inflation were both triggered by the oil-price increase. However, the government was able to increase borrowing in the international private capital market to cover the current account deficit; with that, growth promptly resumed.

The Korean economy suffered a year of relatively slow growth in 1974, but then resumed rapid growth in 1975. Gaining confidence from the country's ability to withstand the oil-price increase, but recognizing that the increase would strengthen the need for earning and saving foreign exchange, policy-makers concluded that Korea was ready to enter the 'next stage' of development, and undertook measures to start development of 'heavy industries', including machine tools, shipbuilding and an array of other engineering industries.

For Turkey, the period 1976–9 was one of increasing short-term macroeconomic imbalance, as expansionary demand policies resulted in an acceleration of inflation, the balance-of-payments situation worsened, and the rate of growth diminished, so that per capita income began falling by 1978. Even without the oil-price increase of 1979, the Turkish government would have been unable to sustain its macroeconomic policy stance (including exchange-rate policies and the trade regimes as well as fiscal, monetary and domestic credit policies). There were simultaneously mounting political difficulties, as domestic violence increased, and the government was unable to come to grips with either the political or the economic problem.

In January 1980 the Turkish government announced a series of far-reaching reforms, starting with a massive devaluation and an announcement that henceforth there would be frequent adjustments in the exchange rate to keep pace with differentials between domestic and foreign inflation. In addition, prices of outputs of public sector enterprises were increased sufficiently to reduce their deficits and thus sharply cut the size of the public sector deficit.

This general stance of reform, begun under the Demirel government, was continued under the military government headed by General Evren which took power in September 1980. In 1983, however, after some abrupt bankruptcies in the financial markets following very high nominal and real interest rates, the leadership of economic policy was changed, and with it the fiscal-monetary stance was eased. With the election of late 1983, however, Prime Minister Özal, who had earlier led the reform effort, resumed the reform program. Quantitative restrictions on imports were virtually eliminated; efforts were made to rationalize, and perhaps even privatize, some of the SEEs; and a variety of moves to increase currency convertibility, liberalize the credit market and banking system and open up the economy were gradually undertaken.

In Korea, the strains placed upon the economy by the expansionary policies pursued to develop the heavy engineering and chemical industries were already becoming apparent in 1977 and 1978. The demand for some types of technically trained personnel rose so rapidly that real wages and salaries for skilled labor tripled within a three-year period and the wage differential between skilled and unskilled workers rose substantially. Furthermore, the investment and import costs of the new factories were extremely high. Partly for that reason, and partly for concern about the financial implications to domestic producers who were indebted in foreign currency, the won was not revalued to maintain purchasing-power parity with major competitors; and, with a few exceptions (most notably shipbuilding), the new enterprises tended to incur large losses and to operate at small fractions of their intended capacity. Difficulties were compounded by the oil-price increase of 1979, and then by the political uncertainties that followed the assassination of President Park Chung Hee. By late 1980 the economy was in severe macro-imbalance – real GNP growth in that year was – 6.4 per cent. The wholesale price index increased 40 per cent from December 1979 to December 1980, the current-account deficit jumped to 9 per cent of GNP, and the rate of gross investment was virtually zero for the last half of the year.

Policies were set in place to address these issues. These included an exchange-rate realignment, and also a concerted effort to restore macro-economic balance. Monetary growth, which had been 27 per cent in 1980, fell to 15 per cent in 1983 and 8 per cent in 1984; the fiscal deficit simultaneously fell to 1 per cent of GNP by 1983. The GNP growth rate returned to the 7 per cent range, the deficit on current account had been reduced to 1.7 per cent of GNP by 1984, and inflation was down to 2 per cent per annum.

Thus, both Korea and Turkey entered the early 1980s with economic problems resulting from past policies as well as the effects of world-wide recession and the 1979 oil-price increase. In the Korean case, the source of the difficulty was the attempted shift of the industrial base toward heavy chemical and engineering industries and the other policies, especially exchange rate, that had been adopted in support of that stance. In Turkey the problems essentially had their origins in the inner-oriented policies that had been pursued for several decades; the oil price increases and other events of the 1970s had exacerbated the underlying inefficiencies of the economy, but adjustments to these phenomena could not be undertaken independently of addressing the underlying issues.

12.3 CONTRASTS IN PERFORMANCE

Table 12.7 provides data on overall economic performance. As can be seen, real GNP in Korea increased sixfold between 1960 and 1984, whereas Turkish GNP rose at about half that rate. Turkish growth in the 1960s had been somewhat less rapid than Korea's, but the differences became much more pronounced in the 1970s, and especially the late 1970s.

The differential in per capita incomes rose even more sharply than that of GNP. Although both countries had rates of population growth of around 2.9 per cent in the late 1950s, the Turkish rate fell only to 2.5 per cent in the late 1960s and to 2.1 per cent in more recent years. By contrast, the Korean population growth rate had already fallen to around 2 per cent by 1970 and to 1.6 per cent by the late 1970s and early 1980s. Whereas Korea and Turkey each had populations of just over 20 million in the early 1950s, the Turkish population is estimated to have been 48.27 million in 1984, while Korea's was 40.58 million. It will be recalled that estimated per capita incomes (in 1955 prices) were $70 and $210 for Korea and Turkey, respectively, in the first half of the 1950s, a differential which increased during that decade. By 1983, however per capita incomes in 1983 dollars were estimated to be $1,240 for Turkey and

Table 12.7   Indicators of economic performance in Korea and Turkey, 1960–84

	Real GNP		Per capita income		Exports	
	Korea	Turkey	Korea	Turkey	Korea	Turkey
	(1960 = 100)		(1960 = 100)		($b)	
1961	105.6	102.0	102.6	99.4	0.041	0.347
1962	107.9	108.3	101.9	102.9	0.055	0.381
1963	117.7	118.8	108.1	110.2	0.087	0.368
1964	129.0	123.6	115.1	111.9	0.119	0.411
1965	136.5	127.5	119.0	111.8	0.175	0.464
1966	153.9	142.8	131.2	122.7	0.250	0.491
1967	164.1	148.8	134.5	125.3	0.320	0.522
1968	182.6	158.7	146.2	130.0	0.455	0.496
1969	207.7	167.3	162.7	133.7	0.622	0.537
1970	223.6	177.0	171.3	137.9	0.835	0.588
1971	243.1	194.9	182.7	148.1	1.068	0.677
1972	257.0	209.5	189.5	155.2	1.624	0.885
1973	293.4	220.8	212.5	159.5	3.225	1.317
1974	315.9	237.1	224.9	167.1	4.460	1.532
1975	337.8	255.9	236.5	175.6	5.081	1.401
1976	385.5	275.6	265.6	185.3	7.715	1.960
1977	434.5	294.9	294.8	194.3	10.047	1.753
1978	476.7	286.5	318.5	184.9	12.711	2.288
1979	507.7	293.9	321.0	185.8	15.055	2.261
1980	481.3	290.9	311.9	180.0	17.505	2.910
1981	511.1	302.8	326.0	181.8	21.254	4.703
1982	539.9	316.5	339.1	188.0	21.873	5.746
1983	592.2	327.2	365.7	190.0	24.445	5.728
1984	636.2	346.7	387.6	201.3	29.244	7.134

Source: International Monetary Fund, 'International Financial Statistics', *Yearbook*, 1985.

$2,010 for Korea: whereas Turkey's estimated per capita income was about three times Korea's in the early 1950s, it was only about 60 per cent of Korea's by the early 1980s. While international comparisons of living standards are always subject to difficulty, there is little question that Korea was the poorer country in the 1950s and the more affluent in the 1980s.

This fundamental transformation affected all sectors of the economy. As can be seen from Table 12.8, agricultural production as well as industrial production rose more rapidly in Korea than in Turkey, although manufacturing was unquestionably the leading growth sector. Interestingly, in both Korea and Turkey, agriculture's share in GNP fell sharply: from 36.5 to 13.9 per cent between 1960 and 1984 for Korea, and from 37.5 to 18.4 per cent over the same years for Turkey. But despite the sharper fall in Korea, agricultural production was almost 2.5

Table 12.8 Indices of agricultural and manufacturing production, 1960–84 (1960 = 100)

	Agricultural production		Industrial production	
	Korea	Turkey	Korea	Turkey
1961	110	102	105	105
1962	102	106	139	106
1963	112	110	158	122
1964	132	117	170	159
1965	134	110	180	176
1966	144	125	226	215
1967	136	127	292	238
1968	138	134	397	266
1969	158	134	479	298
1970	156	139	535	305
1971	160	149	623	337
1972	166	153	724	373
1973	170	142	982	434
1974	178	158	1268	468
1975	202	169	1515	506
1976	220	181	1997	556
1977	236	183	2405	601
1978	252	186	2976	616
1979	258	190	3335	584
1980	210	192	3271	554
1981	232	195	3709	599
1982	238	203	3882	628
1983	240	203	4500	662
1984	250	208	n.a.	n.a

Sources: World Bank EPD databank. For Korea, statistics from Bank of Korea, *National Income*, supplemented by IBRD Economic Report, various issues; for Turkey, data from State Planning Organization.

times as great in 1985 as in 1960, whereas in Turkey agricultural production rose a still respectable, but still substantially smaller, 62 per cent. For manufacturing, the structural shift was sharper in Korea; whereas 13.7 per cent of GNP originated in manufacturing in 1960, the 1984 figure was 29.2 per cent (with an estimated increase in manufacturing output of 1,255 per cent). In Turkey the manufacturing share increased from 11.6 to 23.0 per cent of GNP, for a total increase of 548 per cent. Thus, it was not that manufacturing growth led in one country while agricultural growth led in another; manufacturing rose more rapidly in both countries, but the dominant phenomenon was Korea's faster overall growth.

This faster growth implied, among other things, a much more rapid increase in real wages and urban employment in Korea than in Turkey.

Table 12.9 provides some estimates of the orders of magnitude of the increase. For Korea, real wages had been virtually stagnant in the late 1950s, and remained so in the early 1960s, although non-farm employment rose rapidly, from 2.15 million in 1960 to 3.14 million in 1965. After 1965 non-farm employment continued to grow at rates of almost 10 per cent annually, but real wages also began rising. By 1970 real wages had risen about 45 per cent over their 1960 level. Thereafter, as labor became scarcer, more of the increase in demand for labor was

Table 12.9 Real wages and employment, 1957–84

	Korea		Turkey	
	Real wages* 1970 = 100	Non-farm employment** (millions)	Real wages 1970 = 100	Non-agricultural employment[†] (millions)
1957	54.8	2.01	n.a.	n.a.
1958	61.3	1.95	n.a.	n.a.
1959	62.5	1.94	n.a.	n.a.
1960	57.3	2.15	72.2	n.a.
1961	60.5	2.55		
1962	60.8	2.58	77.6	2.90
1963	57.9	2.72	78.9	n.a.
1964	54.9	2.81	85.2	n.a.
1965	56.8	3.14	90.7	n.a.
1966	59.0	3.30	91.3	n.a.
1967	65.5	3.65	87.8	3.68
1968	72.8	4.00	90.4	3.68
1969	89.7	4.26	98.1	n.a.
1970	100.0	4.63	100.0	n.a.
1971	109.2	5.05	93.5	n.a.
1972	111.4	5.22	90.7	4.61
1973	119.5	5.51	98.3	4.82
1974	133.9	5.88	99.7	5.02
1975	133.5	6.23	103.4	5.20
1976	151.8	6.70	118.2	5.43
1977	175.8	7.28	125.2	5.63
1978	206.3	7.95	105.9	5.64
1979	226.4	8.31	95.1	5.72
1980	213.3	8.59	71.1	5.79
1981	206.0	8.89	65.7	n.a.
1982	225.8	9.61	63.0	n.a.
1983	245.1	10.20	66.6	n.a.
1984	259.1	10.51	68.1	n.a.

* *Source:* Kim and Roemer (1979) for 1957–75.
** *Source:* Kim and Park (1985, p. 13) for 1963–82.
[†] *Source: IBRD Policies & Prospects for Growth*, 1980, p. 145.
Real-wage data updated from Ugur Korum, 'Turkish Export Structure and Foreign Trading Companies in Outer Oriented Framework,' mimeo, October 1985.

reflected in a rising real wage – which more than doubled between 1970 and 1980 – while non-farm employment grew more slowly, although it almost doubled over the decade.

Data for Turkey are incomplete, but over the entire two decades after 1960, non-farm employment is estimated to have risen only from 2.8 million to about 5.7 million (compared to the rise from 2.1 million to 8.59 million in Korea), and real wages at most rose by about 60 per cent. Even then, real-wage increases had been caused in part by the political impasses and the power of unions in Turkey to obtain wage increases independently of conditions in the labor market; such increases as there were were at the expense of expanded employment. There is considerable evidence that much of the effort of employers in the late 1970s was to find ways to automate their factories and reduce their vulnerability to strikes and labor agitation. One of the unfortunate but probably essential parts of the Turkish reforms of the early 1980s was the decline in real wages that took place.

Rapid growth in Korea was reflected not only in rising real wages and employment opportunities, but also in rising real incomes for all segments of society. Indeed, except for the early 1960s, when the evidence is ambiguous, and the period of 'heavy industry emphasis' in the late 1970s, the evidence would suggest that the Korean income distribution, which was relatively egalitarian at the beginning of the period, became more so. By contrast, the available evidence would suggest that Turkish income distribution was more unequal in the 1950s, and became even more so with growth.[8]

The biggest contrast is in export performance of the two countries. Data are given in Table 12.7. In 1960 Korea's exports were on $33 million, compared to Turkey's exports of over $300 million. By 1984 Korea's exports were $29.2 billion, and Turkey's were $7.13 billion. In both cases, the composition of exports had changed; by 1984 almost 94 per cent of Korean exports were manufactures, whereas for Turkey the figure was 54 per cent. And, whereas export represented only 2.4 per cent of Korean GNP in 1960, they were 38.4 per cent of Korean GNP in 1984. By contrast, Turkish exports were about 4 per cent of GNP in 1960, 6 per cent of GNP in 1978 and 10 per cent of GNP in 1984. To be sure, the relative importance of imports to the domestic economy had also increased in the Korean case.

Of course, the expansion of manufactured exports in Korea was the main stimulus to industrial growth. Korean industrial production rose 45-fold over the 23 years after 1960; Turkish industrial production in 1983 was 6.6 times what it had been 23 years earlier. The data in Table 12.8 show vividly the difference in performance.

Along with Korea's export performance came creditworthiness and her ability to access international capital markets. As Table 12.10 shows, a major part of the structural transformation in Korea was the rapid rise in the domestic savings rate – from only 0.8 per cent of GNP in 1960 to well over 20 per cent in the late 1970s and around 20 per cent in the early 1980s. It will be recalled that real interest rates had been negative in the late 1950s; financial reforms in the mid-1960s assured savers of positive real returns on their savings, and the savings rate began rising dramatically.

Even so, it proved highly profitable to attract foreign capital, especially in the late 1960s and early 1970s. As can be seen from Table 12.10,

Table 12.10 Savings, investment, capital flows, and inflation, 1960–84 (as a percentage of GNP)

	Domestic gross savings		Gross investment		Capital inflow		Inflation rate	
	Korea	Turkey	Korea	Turkey	Korea	Turkey	Korea	Turkey
1960	0.8	13.7	10.9	16.1	8.6	0.5	10.7	5.3
1961	2.9	12.9	13.2	15.8	8.6	0.4	13.2	2.9
1962	3.3	11.6	12.8	15.3	10.7	2.0	9.4	5.7
1963	8.7	11.1	18.1	15.4	10.4	1.6	20.6	4.2
1964	8.7	13.6	14.0	15.3	6.9	1.6	34.6	4.4
1965	7.4	13.4	15.0	14.9	6.4	1.3	10.0	8.9
1966	11.8	15.8	21.6	17.6	8.4	1.1	8.9	4.4
1967	11.4	16.5	21.9	17.3	8.8	1.0	6.4	5.1
1968	15.1	16.0	25.9	18.0	11.2	1.4	8.1	3.4
1969	18.8	15.9	28.8	17.5	10.6	1.8	6.8	6.0
1970	17.3	16.8	26.8	19.5	9.3	2.3	9.2	5.6
1971	15.4	13.6	25.2	17.3	10.7	2.1	8.6	17.0
1972	15.7	16.4	21.7	20.1	5.2	4.3	13.8	18.4
1973	23.5	15.7	25.6	18.1	3.8	1.1	6.9	19.8
1974	20.5	14.4	31.0	20.7	12.4	0.6	42.1	29.7
1975	18.6	14.3	29.4	22.5	10.4	3.7	26.6	11.0
1976	23.1	17.7	25.5	24.7	2.4	6.3	12.1	16.0
1977	25.1	16.9	27.3	25.0	0.6	7.0	9.0	23.5
1978	26.4	14.6	31.1	18.5	3.3	4.0	11.6	50.1
1979	26.6	14.2	35.4	18.3	7.6	0.9	18.8	64.8
1980	19.9	13.5	31.5	21.4	10.2	3.5	38.9	107.9
1981	19.6	15.8	28.4	21.5	7.9	2.0	20.4	37.5
1982	21.5	16.9	26.2	20.3	4.8	2.2	4.7	25.8
1983	26.9	16.4	27.8	20.7	3.1	2.7	0.2	30.4
1984	30.1	11.0	30.0	20.1	3.5	2.4	0.7	51.6

Sources: Korean savings, investment and capital inflow: Kim and Park (1985, Table 2.7); Korean and Turkish prices: International Monetary Fund, *International Financial Statistics Yearbook*, 1985, pp. 100–1; Turkish gross domestic investment and savings: State Planning Organization, Turkey; capital inflow: International Monetary Fund, *International Financial Statistics Yearbook*, 1985, pp. 628–9.

Korea's capital inflows were much more important relative to GNP than were the Turkish – and Korea's were mostly private inflows, whereas much of Turkey's was official financing negotiated to cover balance-of-payments difficulties. For Korea, foreign capital augmented domestic savings by as much as 60 per cent in the late 1960s – permitting an investment rate well in excess of 25 per cent of GNP while domestic savings rates were still below 20 per cent. For Turkey, by contrast, capital flows have remained 2–3 per cent of GNP, and Turkish investment, which was initially a much higher proportion of GNP than Korean, has not exceeded 20 per cent.

It should be noted, however, that the difference in savings performance has been far smaller than the difference in growth rates – the greater difference has been the efficiency with which investment was allocated and employed.

There is also an interesting contrast on the macroeconomic front. As the last two columns of Table 12.10 show, until the 1970s Korea's inflation rate generally exceeded the Turkish. Both countries experienced accelerating inflation right after the 1973 and 1979 oil-price increases, although Turkey was in any event undergoing a period of accelerating inflation during the latter part of the 1970s. After 1980 it was a major objective of policy in both countries to bring inflation under control, although in the Turkish case this objective was combined with that of opening up the economy. As the figures in Table 12.10 show, Turkey continued to experience double-digit inflation rates, with rates of around 50 per cent in 1984 and 1985; by contrast, in Korea the rate of inflation is estimated to have fallen to less than 1 per cent annually in 1984 and 1985.

12.4   CONCLUSIONS AND POSTSCRIPT

There are too many factors at work influencing economic performance in any given country, or any pair of countries, for analysis to permit iron-clad conclusions. None the less, the contrast between Korea and Turkey is striking. By almost any measure, Turkey was the more affluent country in the 1950s, and was better positioned for economic development: her natural resources were far superior; her initial savings rate and level of per capita income was higher; and her record of growth during the 1950s appeared exceptionally good.

Korea in the 1950s was unable to grow rapidly despite the opportunities for above-average growth that usually arise in the aftermath of a war. Her savings rate was exceptionally low, her export performance was very bad. The country's per capita endowment of natural resources was also poor.

In so far as there are either economic advantages or economic disadvantages to a military alliance with the United States, both countries had them. And, in so far as proximity to a rapidly growing region of the world affects growth, Turkey and Korea had Europe and Japan, respectively.

Both countries in the 1950s were subject to macroeconomic imbalances and rates of inflation that were then regarded as very high by world standards. Both adopted reforms in the late 1950s and early 1960s. In the Korean reforms the trade regime was central, and shifting its orientation was the lasting achievement of the period. Inflation did decelerate, and shifts in the government budget and rising real interest rates encouraged domestic savings. These were significant shifts, but the centerpiece was the move toward an outer-oriented trade regime. Korean analysts suggest that there was a fair degree of unanimity in the view that Korea could no longer depend on aid and that there was no choice but to make the outer-orientation work. While US aid officials and others participated in the discussions and decisions (and may have been instrumental in convincing policy-makers that there was a feasible alternative), the decisions of the late 1950s appear from all accounts to have been Korean decisions.

By contrast, by mid-1958 the Turkish government recognized that the economic situation was unsustainable, but only in the sense that economic activity was severely disrupted because import flows had virtually ceased. Reforms were adopted only reluctantly, and only because there appeared to be no other way to reschedule debt and provide for a resumed flow of imports that were deemed essential to halt the decline in economic activity. While rationalization of the chaotic trade regime that had preceded the August 1958 program was clearly an objective of policy, there was no intention whatsoever to open up the economy, or to abandon the traditional suspicion of private economic activity. Partly because there was little faith in the efficiency of incentives, and partly because of the belief in direct controls, the aims were purely for macroeconomic balance. There was no intention to alter the balance of incentives between exportable and import-competing production. While Turkey was, during the 1960s, probably more successful in maintaining price stability than was Korea, the degree of protection accorded to domestic firms increased, and Turkey became, if anything, more inner-oriented with the passage of time.

If there are any central lessons from the contrast of Korea and Turkey, they are probably two. First, the prevailing economic structure of a country can never be taken as a given; it must be seen in light of the economic incentives that arise from the policy environment and condition people's behavior. Second, there is an important difference between 'liberalization' efforts where the sole intent is to remove some of the bias against exports that existed in the last phase of a balance-of-payments crisis, and a reform effort aimed at fundamentally altering the bias of the trade regime.

In this regard, it is important to note that significant mistakes were made by Korean policy-makers. It is not that economic policy in one country was 'right' and in the other 'wrong'. If there was a difference in policy formulation itself, it rather lay in the speed with which policy-makers recognized their mistakes and dealt with them. By the early 1980s, all members of the Korean economics community were agreed that the effort to promote heavy industry had been a mistake; there were incipient debt-servicing difficulties in 1969 and in later years. The problems were rapidly identified in each instance, and efforts were then made to ensure that the same mistakes would not be repeated. Likewise, Korean performance has not been without its drawbacks: import liberalization has proceeded only slowly and reluctantly, and financial liberalization is still far from completed.

Turkey's economic difficulties were clearly apparent to all observers in 1957, in 1969 and by 1976. Yet in each instance, the fact that the economy was inner-oriented permitted policy-makers to persist in 'patch-up' efforts rather than to address their fundamental problems. In one sense, the outer-orientation of the Korean trade regime must be given the fundamental credit for the more satisfactory Korean perform-ance compared with the Turkish. At a deeper level, however, it might be argued that it was the Korean policy-makers' willingness to confront their problems and to recognize difficulties early which, on the one hand, led to the decision for an outer-oriented trade strategy, and, on the other hand, led them to address perceived difficulties more quickly, and (perhaps more importantly) more fundamentally, than did the Turkish policy-makers.

Turkey's effort at a shift toward a more outward orientation began in the winter of 1980. Even then, quantitative restrictions were not re-moved, and the major shift was through the guarantee to maintain a more realistic exchange rate. Although those in authority clearly recog-nized the need for a fundamental change in economic policy, there were many influential Turks, in and out of government, who did not accept the changes.

None the less, the commitment to an outer-oriented regime has con-tinued to the time of writing. Against the background of world-wide recession, Turkey has liberalized quantitative restrictions substantially, and maintained real incentives for exporters. Export performance in consequence has been impressive, with exports, which stood at only $2.9 billion in 1980, rising to $7.1 billion in 1984. Performance has been impressive enough to persuade many Turks that the earlier suspicion of private economic activity may have been overdone.

While the commitment to an outer-oriented regime has been much less firm than was the Korean commitment two decades earlier, there has been enough success to provide some momentum for its continuation. Whether initial successes with the shift will have resulted in enough of a shift in Turkish thinking, or whether the next shift in political power will reverse the liberalization achieved so far, remains to be seen.

The centrality of trade policy in both Korea and Turkey is beyond dispute. The experience of these two countries vividly demonstrates the central importance of trade policy, and the importance of analyses of the sort pioneered by Max Corden, in affecting countries' economic well-being.

NOTES

1. It is doubtful if the conversion of land from forests and grazing land to wheat was economic in the long run; see Hirsch and Hirsch (1963).
2. It is unclear how military expenditures and military imports enter into the national income accounts in either country. Korea has continued, throughout the period of rapid development, to devote sizeable resources to military expenditures. However, Turkey, as a member of NATO, has also had a large military budget and has received military aid. It seems likely that the drain of resources into military expenditures in the two countries was fairly comparable, and that this constitutes a similarity, rather than a difference, between them.
3. Data from International Monetary Fund, *International Financial Statistics*, supplement to 1966/7 issues, Korea page.
4. This result was not unintended. The object of the Rhee government had been to maximize aid inflows, and 'balance-of-payments needs' were used as a lever in and negotiations; see Cole and Lyman (1971).
5. Despite the measures, a sizeable black market developed, and trade statistics of that period undoubtedly understate the actual value of trade.
6. Once the export drive was under way, exporters were permitted to import any item used in production for export duty-free. The percentage of imports subject to any quantitative restriction fell sharply in the early 1960s, but in 1967 still stood at 39.6 per cent, although these restrictions did not apply to exporters. The ratio fell gradually thereafter, reaching 15.2 per cent by 1984 (see Nam, 1985, Table 3).
7. All PPP PLD EER estimates are in constant 1965 won prices.
8. All estimates of income distribution are fraught with difficulty. For 1973 it is estimated that the bottom 20 per cent of the Turkish income distribution received 3.5 per cent of all income, while the top 20 per cent received 56.5 per cent. For Korea, the corresponding 1976 estimates are 5.7 and 45.3 per cent (see World Bank, *World Development Report*, 1985, Table 28).

REFERENCES

Cole, David C. and Princeton Lyman (1971). *Korean Development, The Interplay of Politics and Economics*. Cambridge, MA: Harvard University Press.

Frank, Charles R., Jr, Kwang Suk Kim and Larry E. Westphal (1975). *Foreign Trade Regimes and Economic Development: South Korea*. New York: Columbia University Press, for the National Bureau of Economic Research.

Hale, William (1981). *The Political and Economic Development of Modern Turkey*. New York: St Martin's Press.

Hirsch, Eva and Hirsch, Abraham (1963). 'Changes in agricultural output per capita of rural population in Turkey, 1927–60', *Economic Development and Cultural Change*, vol. 14, no. 4, pp. 440–57.

Hong, Wontack (1976). *Factor Supply and Factor Intensity of Trade in Korea*. Seoul: Korean Development Press.

Hong, Wontack (1981). 'Export promotion and employment growth in South Korea' In A.O. Krueger *et al.* (eds), *Trade and Employment in Developing Countries*. Chicago: University of Chicago Press.

Kim, Kwang Suk and Joon-Kyung Park (1985). *Source of Economic Growth in Korea:1963–1982*. Seoul: Korea Development Institute.

Kim, Kwang Suk and Roemer, Michael (1979). *Growth and Structural Transformation*. Cambridge, MA: Harvard University Press.

Krueger, Anne O. (1974). *Foreign Trade Regimes and Economic Development: Turkey*. New York: Columbia University Press, for the National Bureau of Economic Research.

Krueger, Anne O., Hal B. Lary, Terry Monson and Narongchai Akrasanee (eds) (1981). *Trade and Employment in Developing Countries, vol. 1: Individual Studies*. Chicago: University of Chicago Press.

Lewis, Bernard (1968). *The Emergence of Modern Turkey*. London: Oxford University Press.

Mason, Edward S., Mahn Je Kim, Dwight H. Perkins, Kwang Suk Kim and David C. Cole (1980). *The Economic and Social Modernization of the Republic of Korea*. Cambridge, MA: Harvard University Press.

Mitchell, Clyde (1952). *Land Reforms in Asia, A Case Study*, Washington, DC: National Planning Association, Pamphlet no. 78.

Nam, Chong Hyun (1985). 'Trade Policy and Economic Development in Korea', Discussion Paper no. 9, Korea University, Seoul.

PART V

THE INTERNATIONAL ENVIRONMENT FOR DEVELOPMENT

13 · THE ROLE OF THE WORLD BANK AS AN INTERNATIONAL INSTITUTION

The World Bank is the international organization whose primary function is to deal with the economic development needs of the developing countries. It discharges this responsibility through a variety of inter-related activities which center, at least proximately, on lending and extending credit to them.

The Bank is one of the twin institutions, along with the International Monetary Fund, which were founded at Bretton Woods. Although it is a United Nations affiliate, it and the Fund are both distinct from the United Nations in governance and largely independent in operation. According to its Articles of Agreement its objectives were to help finance reconstruction after the Second World War and to foster developmental efforts.

The Bank's mandate with respect to development is straightforward. Its purposes are:

> the encouragement of the development of productive facilities and resources in less developed countries; ... to promote private foreign investment by means of guarantees or participations in loans and other investments made by private investors; and when private capital is not available on reasonable terms, to supplement private investment by providing ... finance for pro-ductive purposes out of its own capital, funds raised by it and its other resources; ... to promote the long-range balanced growth of international trade ... by encouraging international investment for the development of the productive resources of members, thereby assisting in raising produc-tivity, the standard of living and conditions of labor in their territories (Articles of Agreement; Article 1, Sections i, ii, and iii).

First printed in 1983. I am deeply indebted to Helen Hughes and Larry Westphal for helpful comments and suggestions on a preliminary draft of this chapter, and to Allan Meltzer for helpful comments on the penultimate draft. Needless to say, none of them is responsible for the contents of this chapter and there are, indeed, occasional differences of viewpoint. This chapter was written before I joined the World Bank and in no way reflects official Bank positions.

The Bank's name aptly conveys the intent of its founders and its major *modus operandi*. It is an international development bank. It was thought that the world capital market was likely to be imperfect. The role of the Bank was envisioned as providing a correction to a distortion that would otherwise impede the efficient allocation of investible resources among countries.

The functioning of the Bank as an international institution has been the outcome of its mandate as reflected in the Articles of Agreement, the constraints to which it is subject in the Articles, the personality and philosophy of its president, the course of the international economy, and possibly the thinking of the economics profession about development economics.[1]

At the present time, the Bank can be regarded as having five inter-related roles: (1) it provides a resource transfer to developing countries; (2) it clearly influences policies for development; (3) it is an international development bank lending on a banking basis for economically viable projects; (4) it is a provider of technical assistance to developing countries; and, finally (5) it is a major supplier of information about developing countries to the private international capital market. These five roles and the way in which the Bank fills them have evolved over time.

Section 13.1 provides background on those aspects of the Bank's evolution necessary for an evaluation of its role as an international institution. Section 13.2 sets forth the rationale for the Bank as an international developmental institution and considers its role as provider of a public good – information. Section 13.3 sets forth and evaluates the Bank's macroeconomic role in the transfer of resources. Section 13.4 then covers the Bank's role in project-lending and technical assistance. Section 13.5 evaluates the Bank's role in affecting development policy. Section 13.6 summarizes the argument.

13.1   EVOLUTION OF THE BANK

In its early years, the Bank was almost exclusively concerned with loans for reconstruction purposes to now-developed countries. Development lending gradually became increasingly important and, until the mid-1960s, the Bank functioned both as a lender to developed countries for reconstruction purposes and as a source of funds to developing countries for growth. Since that time, all new loans have been destined for developing countries, and focus in this chapter is exclusively on the Bank's functioning as a developmental agency.

As a development bank, the International Bank for Reconstruction and Development has been constrained to lend on fairly 'hard' terms. This reflects the conception of the Bank as a mechanism for improving the functioning of the international capital market. Although the Bank never acted as a guarantor of loans as envisaged at Bretton Woods, it borrows in the capital markets of developed countries, using both its own equity (with a one-to-one ratio of debt to equity) and the guarantees of the governments of borrowing countries to provide a double cover for all Bank borrowing. It then lends to developing countries, using a mix of borrowed capital and its own equity, at interest rates sufficiently high to cover its borrowing and transactions costs. Although the use of its equity capital in this 'blend' of lending provides an element of 'aid' to borrowing countries, the Bank essentially functions as a development bank, facilitating the transfer of resources to 'sound' projects but lending at relatively 'hard' interest rates.

There were two immediate consequences of this banking approach. First, Bank lending financed individual projects, especially in the public-utility sector. To this date, the vast majority of the Bank's loans are made on an individual project basis: each loan is carefully researched ahead of time, and Bank personnel are often responsible for overseeing that the loan proceeds are used in ways intended under the loan. This project approach to Bank lending has had a number of important consequences over the years. In particular, it has led to difficulties in enabling the Bank to influence overall development policy in borrowing countries, a subject to which attention returns in Section 13.5. Analysis of the Bank's role as a project appraiser and lender is covered in Section 13.4.

A second consequence of hard-loan financing was the recognition that the 'concessional', or grant, component of Bank lending was relatively small. For very poor countries, the Bank could not provide the transfer of resources which the member countries deemed desirable. To change this, the International Development Association (IDA) was formed in 1960. It was intended to be the 'soft-loan' window of the Bank, specializing in project loans on low-interest terms to low-income countries. As of 1980, a per capita income of $625 was the indicative, or judgmental, cut-off point for eligibility for IDA credits. Countries with per capita incomes close to the cut-off point were recipients of a 'blend' of Bank loans and IDA credits. At the time of writing (winter 1982), Bank loans are extended at an interest rate of 11.6 per cent, with a ten- to fifteen-year maturity after a five-year grace period. When exchange risk is considered, it is not obvious that IBRD loans are cheaper than commercial borrowing. Their advantage to borrowing countries, however, is twofold: (1) maturities are longer than are commercially available; and (2) an IBRD borrower has, in a sense, a 'seal of approval' which may permit receipt of more favorable credit terms from private lenders. It is this approval function which constitutes the Bank's provision of a public good to the private-capital market IDA credits are subject to an annual service charge of 0.75 per cent with a maturity of forty to fifty years.

Although IDA is legally a separate institution, it has no distinct staff or physical location. It is standard practice to regard IDA as part of the World Bank[2] but also to distinguish between the various 'windows' from which the Bank lends. In effect, the Bank extends loans to borrowing countries, while IDA grants credits to its borrowers. The convention of regarding IDA as part of the World Bank will be followed in this chapter. Unless otherwise specified, the term 'World Bank' will refer to all activities carried out by the staff of the Bank, although IDA credits will be separately reported. As might be anticipated from the vastly different terms on which the two affiliates lend, the World Bank has had little trouble in raising resources for lending at hard interest rates and has had actively to seek creditworthy lending projects, while there has been an excess demand for IDA credits.

Since the Bank's focus shifted exclusively to the developing countries, several additional factors have strongly influenced its role and scope. In the early 1970s, the then largest single bilateral donor to developing countries, the United States, decided to channel substantially more of its development assistance through the World Bank and other multi-lateral institutions (primarily the regional development banks) than had earlier been the case. Until the 1970s, the World Bank was the origin of no more than 10–12 per cent of governmental transfers to developing countries for developmental purposes. As will be seen in Section 13.3, it now accounts for about one-quarter of all public resources transferred to developing countries.[3]

The Bank is thus the international institution given responsibility for facilitating both the multilateral transfer of resources to developing countries and their economic growth. It has both donors and borrowers represented among its executive directors. It suffers from many of the same bureaucratic constraints as do all international institutions. As already mentioned, however, voting rights of members are allocated in proportion to their subscriptions to the Bank's capital. Obviously, differences arise between donor and borrower countries. Because voting rights are proportional to subscriptions to the Bank's capital, the Bank has not been dominated by 'South' interests. The need to be responsive to those interests and still attract the support of developed countries has made the role of the president of the Bank pivotal to its evolution. The presidency of the Bank was transferred in July 1981 to A.W. Clausen from Robert S. McNamara, who had been president since 1968.

13.2   THE ROLE OF THE BANK IN THEORY

The ultimate rationale for the Bank is that it corrects an imperfection in the private-capital market by providing information on individual developing countries. This in turn provides credits for longer periods than are commercially available and extends credit to countries where private rates of return are substantially below social rates of return. In addition, there are economies of scope in performing these, and some related, operations in the same institution.

The information function is most readily understood in terms of its public-good nature. Although there are many investment projects in developing countries that may have high economic real rates of return, the realization of those rates of return and the ability of borrowers to repay international lenders generally depends crucially upon overall economic policies and situations in the individual developing countries.[4]

For developing countries, two kinds of information are required: short-term considerations relating to monetary, fiscal, and related policies and longer-run questions concerning growth prospects. The former set of considerations has historically been the domain of the International Monetary Fund, while the latter are within the purview of the Bank. Although there is obviously overlap between them, the determinants of growth rates, and therefore of real rates of return, on a number of activities are the crucial considerations for long-term financing. These considerations involve a number of situations quite different from those affecting short-term economic prospects. The capacity to assess the growth prospects and performance of individual developing countries (and to influence those prospects through its activities – see Section 13.5) is the Bank's major asset.

Information about policies and conditions in individual developing countries is costly to obtain. Generally, it requires a fairly intimate knowledge of conditions in each country and ongoing familiarity with the situation. Such information, once obtained, is relatively costless to disseminate to individual participants in the international capital market, and greater use of information by one market participant does not reduce the availability of the information to others. Individual lenders, in the absence of a low-cost source of information, would probably not find it worth their while to invest in obtaining it to evaluate individual loans.

It is difficult to imagine that international private-capital markets could have functioned on their present scale in the absence of the Bank's informational role in providing a 'seal of approval' for individual developing countries. The Bank has been important in improving the flow of information about development prospects and performance, debt-servicing obligations and capabilities of individual countries, and hence in permitting potential lenders to arrive at informed judgments.[5] A critical question, therefore, is how the Bank obtains information more efficiently than do alternative private institutions. The public-good nature of information which is costly to collect has already been mentioned. But there are additional considerations. Many of the factors influencing prospects for growth and therefore high rates of return are functions of government policies. Knowledge of those policies is therefore essential to provision of information. In a sense, the problem is one of incentive compatibility: a potential supplier of information must be able to obtain reliable information about government policies and other economic phenomena in individual countries. The Bank, by virtue of its nature as an international organization, and also be virtue of its being able to offer loans and credits, is well-placed to gain access to government officials to obtain the necessary information.

Obtaining information in part takes place automatically in the process of extending loans and credits. Indeed, much of the Bank's information about individual countries is acquired in the process of negotiating individual loans and credits. While it is conceivable that the Bank could function solely as an information source, it is doubtful whether the Bank could receive reliable information as readily as it now does at its present cost levels. For the Bank itself to lend and extend credit provides credibility to its assessments of individual situations which published reports by themselves lack. In addition, it is probably simpler to signal judgments by indicating who is creditworthy to be a recipient of Bank funds than to indicate who is not creditworthy.

Once it is granted that the Bank's basic informational function is best filled through its lending activities, it can readily be argued that there are economies of scope in its simultaneous participation in two other related activities: most notably, attempting to influence policies of individual developing countries and undertaking research on various aspects of economic development. It is well understood by economists that ill-advised economic policies have high economic costs and that high rates of return may be obtainable if some policies are altered. The Bank's influence in this regard is another by-product of its relationship to developing countries, which would not be possible in the absence of its role as a lender.

For middle-income countries, the Bank can perform its multiple functions through its lending operations. For low-income countries, however, extension of IDA credits has been the focal point of activity. The rationale for foreign aid entails considerations additional to those pertaining to Bank loans. A straightforward argument is that developed countries have a political interest in transferring resources to the poorer countries and that a multilateral approach minimizes costs and simultaneously permits the Bank to perform the informational function for all developing countries.

In a world with well-functioning international capital markets, the notion that there should be a transfer of resources over and above that which would occur through market forces is essentially equivalent to the assertion that the rate of return on investment in poor countries should, in equilibrium, be below that in richer countries. This is because the role of a resource transfer other than through private capital markets would presumably be to provide investible resources over and above those commercially available. Thus, if commercial sources would equalize the rate of return on investments in rich and poor countries, a 'gift' from the rich to the poor countries would either provide an additional income stream equal to the rate of return times the amount of the gift or it would have to drive the rate of return on investments in the poor country below those available in rich countries.[6]

Some defenders of aid would assert that there is an imperfection in the private-capital market at low levels of per capita income. The argument goes that high social, but low private, rates of return, or returns with sufficiently long payoff periods, characterize low-income countries. Hence, private markets cannot handle poor countries' financing needs even though the true social return justifies the investment. Investment in human capital, with its long gestation period and high specific risks, is perhaps the paramount example of such a phenomenon.

In reality, there is strong evidence to support the low rate of return in the very poorest countries. A neo-classical economist might be tempted, therefore, to argue that well being in the poorest countries could be improved if, instead of providing additional resources for investment in those countries at low rates of return, aid donors invested the funds in their own countries at higher rates of return and gave residents of low-per-capita-income countries a claim to the stream of income from those investments. There are three counterarguments to this proposition, even if the underlying premise, that rates of return are lower in developing countries, is correct. The first counterargument is that there is no mechanism by which governments in poor developing countries can transfer the incomes effectively to the poor people in that country (although that argument might be made about the returns on domestic investment undertaken with the proceeds of foreign aid). The second is that there is a political imperative for domestic investment and growth of productive capacity in poor countries; thus, motives for the extension of foreign aid are also essentially political. In effect, foreign aid can be regarded as payment of compensation by developed countries for the unwillingness to permit free international migration, which would be the sensible alternative if rates of return are truly low in the poor countries. The third is that there is a necessary period of investment at relatively low rates of return in infrastructure, human resources, and land in order to realize higher rates of return at a later data. Most development economists implicitly or explicitly subscribe to all three counterarguments or accept the view that social returns exceed private returns, especially at very low levels of income.

Even if rates of return are lower in poor countries than in rich ones, there is still a question as to what aid does when allocated within a country. Here, the issues are two: the fungibility of resources, and the 'additivity' of the resource transfer. Assume that there are n possible investments, each of equal size, say \$1, in a particular country, and that m of these would be undertaken if only domestic resources were available. Assume further that those m investments would be appropriately chosen and were the ones with the highest rates of return. Suppose, in that circumstance, a foreign-aid donor provides \$1 so that the $m + 1$th investment could be undertaken. A first question is whether there might not be some offset in terms of a reduction in domestic saving: after all, rational individuals will generally choose to increase both present and future consumption when receiving a windfall gain. While the transfer of resources presumably provides an increase in welfare regardless of whether it is allocated to consumption or to investment, the usual goal stated for foreign aid is to foster economic growth. To the extent that aid is judged by its impact on growth, the 'offset' factor inherent in reduced domestic saving makes \$1 of aid less than a \$1 increase in domestic capital stock.[7]

Even if one ignores the potential 'savings displacement' issue in evaluating the effect of resource transfers, there remains the issue that, regardless of which project aid resources finance, the net effect of aid will be to permit the $m + 1$th project to be undertaken. If a potential aid donor wishes to show very high rates of return accruing to his projects, the recipient government can in principle let the donor finance a project high on the list. If the recipient is then enabled to undertake the $m + 1$th project, using the rate of return observed on the donor's project will overstate the impact of aid.

To this point, discussion has proceeded on the assumption that the transfer of resources was quantitatively identifiable. Here, too, there are problems, although the issue is conceptually far more clear-cut than those already raised. Clearly a gift of \$1 is worth more than a loan of the same amount at commerical interest rates. Indeed, there is an interesting question as to whether a loan at a commercial rate of interest is a 'transfer of resources' (as contrasted with an efficient allocation of resources). In practice, most foreign aid consists of 'loans',[8] although the repayment may be on easy terms, as in the case of IDA. Ideally, one would like to identify 'development assistance' with the difference between the present value of loans under the Bank terms and the present value when evaluated at market rates of interest. That practice is rarely followed, and official measures of the transfer of resources to developing countries[9] typically add together private foreign investment, governmental grants, and governmental loans.

Figures given in Section 13.3 are based on official estimates. As such, they do not accord with an economist's definition of 'aid'. Interpretation of the macroeconomic estimates of the role of the World Bank should therefore be made with caution.

13.3   MACROECONOMIC ASPECTS

Tables 13.1 and 13.2 provide data on the role of the Bank in the transfer of resources to developing countries and the growth of Bank lending in the 1970s.

Table 13.1 presents data on the total transfer of resources to developing countries as recorded by the DAC, the official source of statistics on the subject. As can be seen, private capital flows (including direct private

Table 13.1 Transfer of resources to developing countries, 1970–2 average and 1980 (millions of current dollars)

Net Disbursements	1970–72 average	1980
I. Official development assistance	7,905	26,776
A. Bilateral development assistance	6,212	17,641
B. Contributions to multilateral institutions	1,693	9,135
1. Grants	755	4,137
2. Capital subscription payments	900	4,959
2.1. IBRD	45	141
2.2. IDA	619	3,101
2.3. Regional development banks	232	1,641
2.4. Other	5	76
II. Other official flows	1,543	5,280
A. Bilateral	1,231	5,386
B. Multilateral institutions	311	− 106
(of which IBRD)	(300)	(− 111)
III. Grants by private voluntary agencies	936	2,371
IV. Private flows at market prices	7,440	40,635
TOTAL RESOURCE FLOWS	17,823	75,061

Source: OECD, *Development Cooperation, 1981 Review*, Table A17.

investment) constituted more than half of what is officially regarded as the transfer of resources in 1980. This reflects the outcome of the availability of OPEC funds in the international money market and a continuing trend toward the greater importance of private capital markets and the diminished importance of official flows. Even of official flows, which were about $32 billion in 1980, $23 billion constituted one form or another of bilateral assistance. The total multilateral transfers of resources, including those which were effected through regional development banks, the International Monetary Fund, and other United Nations activities as well as the World Bank, were only about $9 billion.

. As can be seen from Table 13.1, the relative importance of multilateral institutions in the flow of new lending increased somewhat during the 1970s. Of official flows, 79 per cent were bilateral in 1970–2, and by 1980, 71 per cent were bilateral.

As of the end of 1979, it was estimated that total outstanding debt of developing countries was $414 billion. Of that total, $127 billion was bilateral official debt, $83 billion was debt to multilateral institutions, and $204 billion was debt to private creditors.[10] Of that debt, $180 billion had been incurred since 1976. If one takes into account the negative real rates of interest on debt incurred prior to that date, the 'true' transfer of resources in the late 1970s consisted of the new loans extended plus the erosion of the real value of debt and debt-service payments on indebtedness outstanding as of 1976.

Table 13.2 gives data specifically pertaining to the Bank and its operations. Bank loans rose from about $1.6 billion in 1970 to $8.9 billion in 1981, and IDA credits increased from about $600 million to $3.5 billion over the same period. Disbursements have always lagged far behind loan and credit approvals, however, so that a more accurate reflection of the Bank's macroeconomic impact may be seen in columns 3–7 of Table 13.2. Thus, credits and disbursements from the Bank rose from $1.3 billion to $4.8 billion over the period 1970–9. When viewed on a net basis (disbursements minus interest payments and repayments of principal), the Bank's total lending appears even smaller. Finally, when adjusted for the change in world prices, it would appear that net bank transfers have been approximately constant in real terms throughout the 1970s.[11]

Several comparisons may be helpful. All drawings on the IMF were $7 billion in 1976 and ranged between $1.8 billion and $3.8 billion in the years 1977 to 1980. Seen from another perspective, the total current account deficit of all non-oil developing countries was $70 billion in 1981 excluding official transfers, or $70 billion after official transfers.

For the reasons discussed in Section 13.2, all of these numbers provide at best rough guides to the magnitude of the impact of the Bank. None

Table 13.2   Bank loans and credits, 1970–81 ($ millions)

| | Approvals | | Disbursements | | | | |
| | Loans | Credits | Loans | Credits | Total | Net | Net at 1970 |
Year	(1)	(2)	(3)	(4)	(5)	(6)	prices (7)
1970	1,580	606	754	606	1,360	856	856
1971	1,921	584	915	235	1,150	572	538
1972	1,966	1,000	1,182	261	1,443	797	694
1973	2,051	1,357	1,180	493	1,643	915	642
1974	3,218	1,095	1,533	711	2,244	1,315	672
1975	4,320	1,576	1,995	1,026	3,021	1,864	876
1976	4,977	1,655	2,470	1,252	3,722	2,392	1,102
1977	5,759	1,308	2,636	1,298	3,934	2,317	981
1978	6,098	2,313	3,602	1,062	4,664	2,717	1,046
1979	6,989	3,022	3,602	1,222	4,824	2,877	926
1980	7,644	3,838	4,363	1,411	5,774		
1981	8,809	3,482	5,063	1,878	6,941		

Source: World Bank Annual Report, 1979 and 1981
Notes: Columns 1 and 2 represent loan approvals from the World Bank and credits approved by IDA, respectively. Columns 3 and 4 indicate disbursements from those approvals. Column 5 is the sum of columns 3 and 4. Column 6 is column 5 less total Bank income, which is intended to reflect net lending by the Bank. Column 7 is column 6 deflated by the International Monetary Fund's world index of export prices, and thus indicates the 'real' net transfer of resources.

the less, the numbers are sufficient to indicate that, in a macroeconomic sense, the transfer of resources to developing countries was not huge, as officially defined. Of that transfer, the official flows were swamped in importance by private capital flows. Of official flows, all multilateral transfers were far smaller than bilateral flows. While the World Bank was the leading multilateral source of funds, it was by no means the predominant influence on the macroeconomic size of resource transfers, except possibly in the sense that its provision of information was necessary for the flow of private capital.

13.4   PROJECT LENDING

It has already been indicated that most bank loans and IDA credits are 'project finance'. That is, they are loans and credits designed to finance specified investment activities, just as are bank loans. As mentioned in Section 13.1, the Bank early acquired considerable competence in public utility projects (including irrigation and rural electrification and transport), and much of its early lending was concentrated in that area. More

Table 13.3 Distribution of bank loans and credit by nature of activity (percentage of total lending)

Sector	1969–73	1974–78	1979	1980	1981
Agriculture and rural development	20	30	25	30	31
Development finance companies	10	9	6	7	9
Education	5	4	5	4	6
Energy	1	1	1	4	5
Industry	5	9	10	4	7
Non-project and structural adjustment	6	5	4	5	8
Population, health and nutrition	–	1	1	1	1
Transportation	25	17	19	13	9
Water supply and sewage	4	4	10	5	4
Other	5	4	5	4	8

Source: World Bank Annual Report, 1981

recently, projects have been funded for more diverse purposes, including utilities and transportation, but also for more unconventional areas such as education, population control, agricultural credit, livestock, and rural area development.

Table 13.3 gives an idea of the sectoral destination of Bank loans and IDA credits, based on data provided by the Bank. Most categories are self-explanatory. Development finance companies (DFCs) are local institutions designed to provide credit and foreign exchange (often on relatively favorable terms to worthwhile borrowers), generally to activities in the industrial sector. The Bank was apparently the 'inventor' of DFCs and has devoted considerable attention to working with development finance companies on techniques of project evaluation and on devising meaningful criteria for the granting of loans and *ex post* evaluation of financed projects. This may have been one of the more important forms of technical assistance provided by the Bank.

As can be seen, less than 10 per cent of Bank loans has been extended on a non-project basis. The 'structural adjustment' loans represent a recent effort of the Bank to tie its lending activities more closely to developing countries' domestic policies. The important issue of structural adjustment is deferred until Section 13.5, since it pertains to the overall impact of the Bank on the policies of borrowing governments.

In this section, three issues require discussion. First, the shift in the thrust of Bank lending during the 1970s marked a significant change in its philosophy and merits attention. Second, the available evidence with respect to the economic effects of project lending is discussed. Last, the allocation of bank resources among geographic regions and countries in different income groups is considered.

13.4.1   Reaching the Poorest of the Poor

As mentioned in Section 13.1, the Bank is required by its charter to 'lend only for productive purposes'. The mandate was initially interpreted to imply that each loan had to be revenue-generating and evaluated on that basis. Loans for electricity, railroads, and the like, where revenues would fund loan repayments, were accordingly given heavy emphasis, and loan conditions often focused upon public-utility pricing (probably with significant improvements in resource allocation). In the early 1970s, however, emphasis was shifted sharply. The shift was prominently announced in the 1973 'Nairobi speech' of the Bank president, Robert McNamara.[12]

McNamara announced that, henceforth, greater attention would be given to projects which 'directly reached the poorest of the poor'. While it can be argued that this constituted a sound economic balancing of the Bank's portfolio, the enunciation of the shift and subsequent pronouncements were less soundly based. In effect, McNamara's speech, and a considerable number of other documents coming from the World Bank, seemed to articulate the viewpoint that rapid growth of real GNP might not be compatible with increasing the well-being of the world's poor.[13]

The central operational idea was that Bank and IDA activities should be reoriented to projects which 'directly reached' the poor, especially the rural poor of the world. In some instances, the shift amounted to little more than relabeling of project loans, as in the case of irrigation and several rural electrification projects which had earlier been undertaken without the nomenclature. In other cases, however, the new emphasis did result in major new lending initiatives.

The emphasis was well articulated in the Bank's introduction to its activities in its 1981 *Annual Report* (p. 3):

> While the World Bank has traditionally financed all kinds of capital infrastructure such as roads and railways, telecommunications, and ports and power facilities, its present development strategy places a greatly increased emphasis on investments that can directly affect the well-being of the masses of poor people of developing countries by making them more productive and by integrating them as active partners in the development process. This strategy is increasingly evident in the agriculture and rural development projects that the Bank and IDA help finance. It is also evident in projects for education and family planning and nutrition, and in the Bank's concern for the urban poor, who benefit from projects designed to develop water and sewerage facilities, as well as 'core' low-cost housing, and to increase the productivity of small industries.

While there was increasing evidence that investments in human resources, including nutrition, health, sewage, clean water, and so on, had very high payoffs, the Bank's stated philosophy implied a different basis for reorienting its lending policies. In particular, there was strong implication that lending on strictly economic criteria was not compatible with this 'direct' approach and that, in some ways, current lending policies were not justifiable in cost-benefit terms.

It is thus possible, at least in principle, to agree with the shift in emphasis of Bank lending on the grounds that investments that increase the health, nutrition, and education of the poor have extremely high returns, but to question the coherence of the Bank's stated criteria for making the loans. In particular, there is an important question as to whether choosing projects with lower rates of return (and thereby presumably contributing to a lower overall growth rate) is in the short-run or long-run interest of the poor.[14] There is also the difficult question as to whether loans which 'directly reach' the poor are those most benefiting the poor. It is quite possible to make a strong case that the observed instances of increasing inequality with growth were the outcome of particular governmental policies that favored a small group of urban elite (including governmental bureaucrats, urban workers, the intellectuals, and the employers) and that changing those policies would have removed cases of inconsistency.

The Bank documents (and especially Chenery *et al.* 1974) have emphasized a policy of 'redistribution with growth', implying that it is possible to attain satisfactory rates of growth and improved conditions for the bottom 40 per cent of the income distribution. As will be seen below, the available evidence on rates of return on Bank projects tends to support the view that the shift in emphasis has not significantly lowered the rate of return on Bank projects. The rhetoric has probably been more questionable than the performance.

13.4.2   Project Evaluation

The Bank's directly observable activities are its lending and credit operations. While it may have a significant effect on the international economy through other channels (and particularly on the policies of borrowing countries), the operational outcome of Bank activities is the effect of its various loans.

Project evaluation is always difficult and never more so than in developing countries. It requires access to internal and unpublished Bank documents if an independent appraisal is to be made of the results of project lending. Hirschman (1967) attempted his own analysis of development projects but primarily to analyze the process of project lending and development. Mason and Asher (1973), in their monumental review of the first twenty-five years of the Bank, noted that the Bank had begun by emphasizing engineering and financial criteria in its project evaluation and had progressed considerably over the years to sound economic project evaluation. Their overall assessment (Mason and Asher 1973, pp. 257–8) was that:

It cannot be said that the Bank has been an outstanding leader in applying new techniques of project appraisal or analysis of development projects. It came rather slowly to the use of the discounted cash flow technique of calculating rates of return; and its methods of correcting for price distortions in the economies of its borrowers, at least until recently, have been neither systematic nor comprehensive. Whether the Bank's appraisers have taken possible 'side effects' of project development as fully into account as they should have is difficult to say.

Since 1974, the Bank has had an internal unit, the Operations Evaluation Department, which has been kept relatively independent of operating divisions and which is charged with *ex post* project evaluation. In practice, that unit makes its evaluations, which are little more than post-project audits, the moment the loan is entirely disbursed. None the less, the three published reports of the Operations Evaluation Department provide the only information available to outside scholars on which to form a judgment as to the efficiency of Bank loans. A summary of their findings was published in 1978, 1979, and 1980.[15]

The data presented in their public summary of their findings are not adequate to form an independent judgment as to the overall impact of Bank projects, but they do give some useful information. The 1980 report, for example, reviewed $2.8 billion worth of Bank loans and credits and about $10.2 billion of total investments.[16] Altogether 130 projects, most of which began in the 1970s, were evaluated. Their overall findings were that 1.6 per cent of the investments had had 'unsatisfactory or uncertain' outcomes; that 3.3 per cent of the total investments was 'marginally worthwhile'; and that 94 per cent of the total investments had 'achieved [its] major objectives'. There were 76 projects for which economic returns were estimated; it was stated that all but ten yielded economic rates of return of 10 per cent or more.

No information is available to indicate whether these estimated rates of return were adjusted to take into account indirect benefits and costs; whether corrections were made for inappropriate prices of inputs and outputs (which can be of great importance for projects in which government price ceilings, labor legislation, overvalued exchange rates, and credit rationing affect the observed financial rate of return); or whether adjustments were made to financial returns to take into account distributional weights, regional considerations, and so forth. Indeed, it seems to be a characteristic of the Bank, commented upon by many observers, that its operations are sufficiently internal that scrutiny by independent scholars is not possible.

From a reading of the *Annual Review of Project Performance Audit Results*, there appears to be a tendency to evaluate projects in light of the expectations for them when they were originally undertaken. That is, a project seems to be deemed successful if it achieved what it was intended to achieve. While the economic rate of return estimates cited above appear to be impressive, one wonders what an analysis of initial project selection, of ways in which chosen projects might have been redesigned, and critical analysis of projects with a view to asking how they might better have been carried out would have revealed. While the Bank's record is undoubtedly one of 'sound' project lending, there has been little communication of its experience that would permit academic analysts to scrutinize it or to learn from it.

In light of the shift in Bank emphasis to reach directly the poorest of the poor, the 1980 *Review*'s assessment is of particular interest. This was the first year when sufficient time had elapsed to have had projects completed which had started under the new emphasis on rural development. One of the emphases in the *Review* is upon the 'targets' that were to be reached by different loans. In summarizing results, the Operations Evaluation Department (*Annual Review*, 1980, pp. 16–17) reported that:

> Thirty-nine projects for which information is available were to reach about 612,000 families, or about 3.4 million people . . . The achievement exceeded the target: a total of 816,000 farm families comprising 4.5 million people are estimated to have benefitted . . . The projects oriented mainly towards small farmers had, on average, eight times more beneficiaries than those aimed at medium and larger farmers, but similar cost overruns, shorter delays in implementation, and almost similar rates of return.

This raises again the earlier question: if rates of return on small-farmer projects are similar to those on larger-farmer projects, why should a 'reorientation' be necessary in order to justify the projects?[17]

13.4.3 Distribution of Resources

Table 13.4 gives data on the destination of new commitments by per capita income of the recipient country. As would be expected, the low-income countries are recipients primarily of IDA credits. In 1979–81, they received 84 per cent of all new commitments of IDA resources and 35 per cent of new loan and credit commitments. Low-middle-income countries received 36 per cent of all Bank loans and 25 per cent of all new commitments of Bank resources. As can be seen, there has been

Table 13.4 Geographic destination of World Bank loans and IDA credits, selected years, 1968–81 (percentage of Bank of IDA commitments)

Country group	1969–73	1974–78	1979–81
Low-income countries			
Bank loans	9	15	13
IDA credits	78	84	84
Total	30	32	35
Low-middle-income countries			
Bank loans	13	20	21
IDA credits	12	14	16
Total	13	19	19
Middle-middle-income countries			
Bank loans	14	14	17
IDA credits	4	1	–
Total	11	11	12
Upper-middle-income countries			
Bank loans	38	35	36
IDA credits	5	1	–
Total	28	26	25
Upper-income countries			
Bank loans	27	16	14
IDA credits	–	–	–
Total	18	12	9

Source: World Bank Annual Report, 1981.
Note: Low-income countries are defined as those with per capita incomes up to $370 in 1981. Lower-middle-income countries are those with per capita incomes of between $371 and $680. Middle-middle-income countries are those with per capita incomes of between $681 and $1,170. Upper-middle-income countries are those with per capita incomes between $1,171 and $1,895. Upper-income countries are those with per capita incomes over $1,895.

some shift away from lending to higher-income countries toward more resources for low-income countries, although the constraint upon IDA resources has limited the extent of the shift.

As of 30 June, 1981, the Bank's biggest debtors (lumping together Bank loans and IDA credits) were India ($12.8 billion); Brazil ($6.2 billion); Mexico ($5.2 billion); Korea ($3.3 billion); Turkey ($3.3 billion); Columbia ($3.3 billion); Yugoslavia ($3.0 billion); and the Philippines ($3.0 billion). All except India are middle-income countries. They do not by any means represent the 'star performers' of the developing world in terms of growth rates and domestic economic policies. However, these eight countries accounted for $40 billion of the Bank's entire lending of $92 billion. To be sure, these debt figures reflect the cumulative history of the Bank and do not indicate the allocation of more recent loans, a topic to which attention turns in Section 13.5.

13.5   IMPACT ON DEVELOPING COUNTRIES' POLICIES

It is widely recognized that development is essentially an internal, domestic process. When domestic policies and circumstances are right,
additional resources yield a very high rate of return. When, however,
domestic policies are inimical to efficient resource allocation, the return
on additional investment is low.

Even if one were to impute a real rate of return of 10 per cent after
allowing for payment of interest charges on all past Bank and IDA loans
(that is, assuming that the total rate of return on the project is the
interest rate paid to the Bank plus 10 per cent), and inflate those past
loans to current dollars, the estimated total increase in developing countries' incomes due to Bank lending and credits would be less than $30
billion. On the other hand, developing countries' total GNP in 1979
(excluding China, which was not a Bank borrower until recently) was
approximately $1,697 billion.[18]

These assumptions are generous in attributing additional income to
the Bank's operations. They suggest that cumulative Bank lending and
credits would have represented an increase of 1.7 per cent in 1979 developing countries' average per capita (and total) income over the above
that which would have been experienced in the absence of the World
Bank (and no replacement of its lending and credits by either domestic
saving or other international capital flows). For poor countries, an additional 2 per cent is obviously significant and not to be dismissed lightly.
None the less, if the Bank is to have a major impact on developing
countries' economies, it clearly must be through the interaction of its
loans and credits and its influence on the domestic economic policies of
borrowing countries.[19]

Assessing the influences that affect policy-making is, under any circumstances, a difficult task. When it comes to evaluating the effects
which Bank economists and officials may have had on economic policies
in borrowing countries, there seems to be no way of reaching an informed
judgment. Obviously the situation may have differed from country to
country (in part as a function of the receptiveness of the local political
process to the policies of which the Bank approved).

There can be little doubt that the Bank has provided extremely useful
technical assistance and policy advice on a number of issues related to
individual loans. As mentioned earlier, many loans to public utilities
were conditional upon a reform of public-utility pricing. Bank expertise
in a number of areas of construction projects, project planning and
appraisal, and other aspects of investment management has undoubtedly
contributed significantly to policy formulation and execution at the
microeconomic and sectoral level.

If there are questions about the influence of the Bank on policies, they clearly relate to policy design: policies toward export promotion relative to import substitution; monetary and fiscal management; decisions to 'promote' heavy industry; pricing policies toward agriculture relative to industry; and so on. It seems clear that the early expectation was that Bank-lending projects would be organized to make a coherent whole and provide guidance with respect to macroeconomic management. This failed to materialize for a variety of reasons. First, Bank loans were on sufficiently 'hard' terms that there was little 'leverage'; indeed, the Bank found itself in a position of actively seeking projects rather than reluctantly dispensing a valuable good. Second, Bank loans were extended for long-run purposes. It is difficult to see how 'conditions' on macroeconomic policies, imposed in connection with those loans, could sensibly be enforced. Third, there was, and continues to be, a question as to the role of the Bank, relative to that of the International Monetary Fund, in affecting overall policy design.

Here, all that can be done is to indicate some of the considerations that enter into a balanced assessment of the Bank's impact. First, consideration must be given to the roles of the Bank and the Fund, respectively, in influencing developing countries' policies. Second, the constraints under which the Bank has operated must be noted. Third, the 'economic philosophy' of the Bank, as reflected in its publications, can be recorded. Fourth, the Bank's recent 'structural adjustment' program can be considered. Finally, the shifts in Bank lending over time in response to governments' policies can be considered.

Underlying this discussion are two premises which should be made explicit. The first is that, for maximum effect on borrowing countries' policies, the Bank would have most influence if it shifted (or were willing to shift) its allocation of loans among borrowers in response to the 'soundness' of their economic policies. Obviously, Bank economists and publications could, through their contribution to knowledge, affect borrowers' philosophies and attitudes toward policy alternatives. And, as is well known in the economics profession, the Bank has built up a highly competent professional economics staff, which continues to make major contributions to knowledge. It would require a subjective, insider's evaluation of the degree to which that competence has enlightened the policies the Bank has advocated in individual cases, and that task is beyond the scope of this chapter. For present purposes, the more important consideration is that, regardless of what the effect of Bank thinking on the 'atmosphere for policy' has been, it would clearly have even greater influence if the Bank reallocated its resources to alternative borrowers in response to the degree to which the borrowers' policies were compatible with development.[20]

The second assumption is that there is at least some body of knowledge as to what constitutes 'good policy' in developing countries. In the sense that economists, or others, 'know what is right', that assumption is mistaken. Fortunately, however, it is considerably easier to identify circumstances of 'bad policy'. There may be ample disagreement over optimal monetary, fiscal, and exchange-rate policy, but almost all observers agree that large fiscal deficits financed by expansion of the domestic money supply and accompanied by fixed exchange rates for sustained periods of time are a formula for slow growth, if not disaster. On an impressionistic basis, it seems a reasonable assumption that the Bank, and especially its economists, have recognized 'bad economic policy'. With those assumptions set forth, attention can now turn to individual considerations.

13.5.1 The Bank and the IMF

One of the dilemmas confronting the Bank in promoting development has been its role relative to that of the IMF in various discussions with governments facing economic difficulties. Partly because the Bank often did not have an active role in overall policy formation, there gradually developed a general view that the IMF effectively policed member countries' macroeconomic policies, while the Bank was the 'friend' of the developing countries. That this view was not precisely correct is reflected in the fact that the Bank often took leadership in 'consortia'. These consortia consisted of both bilateral donors and the Bank and the IMF. They would jointly negotiate with a country in difficulty, extending bilateral aid, Bank loans and credits, and IMF credits in return for a particular government's adopting certain monetary, fiscal, and other policies.

That the IMF was often identified as the villain of the piece was largely because IMF loans were frequently renewable; and policies countries were forced to adopt, including frequent devaluation and fiscal and monetary restraints, were generally perceived to be 'IMF policies'. Nevertheless, it is true that the IMF has had a much greater role in affecting policies in developing countries than has the Bank. While one can question whether certain Bank policies are developmental, and not germane to short-run stabilization measures, there are enough recorded instances of Bank lending to countries whose domestic economic policies were clearly non-optimal with respect to growth to indicate that the Bank has not made 'good' economic policy a precondition for receipt of its loans (see the discussion of Turkey in Section 13.5.3).

13.5.2 Lending Constraints

Several constraints have limited the Bank's scope for shifting its resources in response to countries' changes in policies. Most important has been the fact that virtually all lending has been on a project basis. That in itself makes sharp and dramatic shifts in flows of resources difficult, and probably uneconomic: there are serious questions as to whether it makes sense to halt a project in mid-stream. Even more to the point, projects must be prepared and evaluated, generally with considerable delays between first formulation and the start of implementation. That constraint sharply limits the amount of leverage the Bank has through accelerating or slowing down the disbursal of funds.

The second constraint is that the Bank is, after all, a membership institution. Its directors are representatives of borrowing, as well as donor, countries. As noted above, the fact that voting rights are proportionate to subscriptions has prevented the Bank from having a majority vote from borrowing countries (which has led on occasion to a call for changes in the Bank structure). While one can question how important this constraint has been, it cannot be totally overlooked in evaluating Bank performance, although the IMF has a very similar composition of its executive directors.

The third constraint is more a matter of philosophy. Even if government policies are non-optimal, is that a basis for deciding not to fund projects which appear demonstrably viable and promise high rates of return? Use of the leverage inherent in altering lending levels may penalize the poor of a country in the sense that failure to build an irrigation system or extend rural credit will yield lower incomes in rural areas than would otherwise be the case. It is problematic how much leverage 'should' be used in these cases.

13.5.3 Bank Economics

It has already been mentioned that the professional economics staff of the Bank is a highly competent group. Many of them have contributed significantly to our understanding of the development process. The Bank has devoted substantial resources to research on various aspects of economic development. Whether those resources have always been effectively allocated is a question that cannot be evaluated here.

But there is another question, and that pertains to the ways in which the Bank's economic research staff has been effectively utilized in Bank policies toward its borrowers. What is not evident from Bank publications, and thus cannot be adequately judged by an outsider, is the extent to which economists are used in the project evaluation, macroeconomic policy evaluation, and other areas of the Bank's operations.

Mason and Asher (1973), who had access to Bank documents and relied extensively upon interviews with Bank officials, based their conclusions on Bank analyses of the 1950s and 1960s. In the absence of more recent evidence, however, their conclusions are worth restating here. They reported (Mason and Asher, 1973, p. 447) that the Bank's lending policy

> reveals a heavy emphasis on indicators and policies relating to creditworthiness and, furthermore, to creditworthiness judged on a not very long-term basis. Indeed, so large has creditworthiness loomed in the Bank's calculations, it is doubtful whether, given a viable project in a country judged to be creditworthy by traditional standards, Bank lending policy looks beyond the project to any other development indicators or aspects of development policy.

Whether this remains the case in the 1980s is questionable. One's casual impression is that other policies may be examined, but they cannot be evaluated. There is also the consideration that creditworthiness may be the outcome of appropriate policies and, as such, may be a suitable criterion for lending. However, there surely are instances of creditworthiness coexisting with internal economic policies inimical to economic growth as, for example, among oil-exporting countries.

Mason and Asher (1973, p. 443) reported that the 'performance indicators' used in the evaluation of creditworthiness were the growth rates of per capita and total real income, domestic and public-sector savings rates, sectoral output and growth rates, sectoral and aggregate capital–output ratios (as measures of efficiency of resource use), and various measures of 'external viability'.

Mason and Asher analyzed four instances in which the Bank reported that lending had ceased due to doubts about a country's policies. Their conclusion (Mason and Asher, 1973, p. 449) was that creditworthiness was the dominant criterion, but that

> the principal cause of dissatisfaction was an inadequate savings-investment effort on the part of the borrowing country. And in all these cases there is some doubt whether the principal cause of Bank action was not inadequate project preparation and failure to provide necessary local expenditure financing for Bank projects rather than poor macroeconomic policy. In any case it seems reasonable to conclude that, given viable projects in a creditworthy country, the Bank's inquiry into overall performance is not apt to probe more deeply than to question whether public savings are adequate to meet the local expenditure costs of what are considered to be desirable infrastructure investments.

The Mason–Asher evaluation correctly reflects the perception of most observers of the World Bank and the IMF: the World Bank has generally lent for development purposes and only in extreme cases has it used or withheld its lending powers explicitly in response to perceived policy inadequacies. The IMF, by contrast, is the institution which is generally regarded as the 'policeman' of developing countries' policies.

Another way of examining the issue is to consider the behavior of Bank lending over time in a country where policies were clearly non-optimal and later altered. One such instance is Turkey which, in the late 1970s, was in serious economic difficulties. These difficulties arose for a variety of reasons, not the least of which was a rapid rate of inflation (itself in large part the outcome of a substantial deficit incurred by State Economic Enterprises whose output prices were kept artificially low by government decree) and the maintenance of a fixed exchange rate. It was apparent to most Turkish economists and foreign observers that the Turkish economy was in serious trouble, at least by 1977.

Turkish debt, and debt-servicing, was a serious problem throughout the latter half of the 1970s, and all donor governments and international institutions met as a consortium to deal jointly with the Turkish government. It was not until January 1980, however, that the Turkish government adopted a series of economic reforms of sufficient scope to have any hope of improving the long-run outlook for the Turkish economy. Yet, if one examines the disbursals of World Bank loans to Turkey, as reported by the IMF, one would not believe there had been any difficulty. Drawings on World Bank loans by Turkey, as reflected in Turkish balance-of-payments statistics, were $70 million in 1975, $100 million in 1976, $124 million in 1977, $132 million in 1978, and $136 million in 1979. It can be argued plausibly that some of the assistance was either politically warranted (regardless of its effect on economic policies) and that some may have been necessary simply in order to buy time until policy reforms were politically feasible in Turkey. Even granting these arguments, however, the extension of assistance in 1978 and 1979, when conditions were clearly chaotic and in desperate need of immediate reform, appeared unwise then and now. Morever, when reforms were undertaken in January of 1980, the additional assistance which the donor countries could raise for support of those reforms was substantially less than might have been economically justified.

The Bank itself has recognized that it needs to provide more support for countries undertaking programs of major economic reform. This was reflected in the Bank's decision to develop some 'structural adjustment assistance' lending programs. That decision is discussed in Section 13.5.4, and indicates that the Bank itself recognized the need to take a stronger stance in support of internal policy changes.

Before turning to structural adjustment assistance, there is one other source from which one can infer the Bank's 'economics'. That is the economic analyses of the Bank as reflected in their country reports. Here, the picture is somewhat uneven. Some country studies appear to reflect relatively sophisticated economic understanding of the policies of individual countries and their effects on economic growth. Others seem to be relatively less analytical and critical than circumstances seem to warrant to an outside observer. While it is not evident that the published studies reflect what Bank officials really are emphasizing in terms of policies, the blandness of some of the country studies gives one pause as to the degree to which policies have been critically evaluated.[21]

13.5.4 Structural Adjustment Lending

A large number of developing countries have adopted trade and industrialization policies that are generally 'inner-oriented'. Such policies are usually accompanied by the proliferation of a variety of direct domestic controls. There is considerable evidence that the economic costs of these policies mount over time and that growth rates tend to taper off dramatically. Levels of protection tend to increase, exchange rates are increasingly overvalued, import licensing becomes increasingly restrictive, and the observed incremental capital–output ratios and other indicators of inefficiency rise sharply.

The pay-off for a successful policy change toward a more liberal, free-trade stance is apparently great. A variety of policy changes is usually needed and often entails liberalizing large numbers of direct controls, thus moving toward greater reliance upon incentives and the international marketplace in the accumulation and allocation of resources.

Although the pay-off from a change in policies is very sizeable, the transition from 'inner-oriented', highly restrictive policies toward a more balanced set of incentives is extremely difficult. A large number of firms and industries built up behind walls of heavy protection results in high costs and will inevitably suffer. The owners, managers, and workers employed in those firms and industries are bound to use their political influence to resist change, while potential exporters do not themselves know which firms are involved. While a successful transition is usually accompanied by rapidly rising employment opportunities, existing industrial workers perceive first that their jobs and industries are threatened. Thus, the political forces failing to support, and perhaps opposing, a shift in policies are likely to be substantial. Even worse, the switch in incentives requires a period of transition during which export industries have appropriate incentives for expansion (which takes time), while the protective barriers against imports must be removed.

However, countries with a long history of inner-oriented policies have experienced sluggish export earnings. They do not have sufficient foreign-exchange reserves or commercial-borrowing opportunities to realize the demand for imports. Yet, unless they do so, expectations quickly form for a return to the highly restrictive regime, and speculation against the currency can thwart reform efforts. The response to increased incentives for exporting takes time, both because producers need to be convinced that the altered incentive structure is permanent and because expansion of productive capacity takes time, once they are convinced.

In the absence of sufficient foreign exchange to convince observers that a policy reform is permanent, the only way liberalization can occur is through a reduction in the level of economic activity to cut down import demand through the income effect. It has long been arguable whether the pay-off to making foreign exchange available to support genuine policy reforms is substantial and constitutes a valid case for foreign aid (see Krueger, 1981). This follows not only because of the direct economic pay-off to aid, but also because the reduced need for deflationary domestic policies sharply reduces the political opposition to the transition. Increasing imports at a time of policy change, rather than reducing income, substantially alleviates inflationary pressures that otherwise arise and thus enhances the likelihood that monetary reforms can succeed.

In response to the perceived need to make needed reforms less costly and politically less unattractive, the Bank has inaugurated a new lending facility for 'structural adjustment.' It is designed, according to the *World Bank Annual Report* (1980, p. 67), to

help supplement, with longer-term finance, the relatively short-term finance available from commercial banks and the resources available from the IMF in order that the current account deficits of many developing countries do not become so large as to jeopardize seriously the implementation of current investment programs and foreign-exchange producing programs.

This move, which only began in 1980, has to date been on too small a scale for a full analysis of its promise and likely effects. It is clearly a move away from the Bank's traditional reliance on project lending, although it its first two years of operation, the total allocation for structural-adjustment lending amounted to only $600 million and $800 million. And, since some earlier 'project' loans had an element of program support (as in the case of loans to finance industrial imports for India), there is a real question as to how much actual change there is.

As of the 1981 *Annual Report* of the Bank, recipient countries of structural adjustment loans were Guyana, Malawi, Mauritius, the Philippines, Senegal, and Turkey. The Bank report further indicated that total structural-adjustment lending was not expected in the future to absorb even 10 per cent of the Bank's overall lending effort (*Annual Report*, 1981, p. 70). This ceiling apparently reflects the Bank's belief that it is still constrained by its charter to concentrate on project lending.

While the move to structural-adjustment lending obviously opens an avenue through which the Bank could apply more leverage than it has in the past, an important question is whether the structural-adjustment facility so far developed will permit a major change toward more selectivity in lending based on evaluation of borrowing countries' policies. Two years' experience with structural-adjustment loans is not sufficient to permit an analysis of their ultimate role. It seems apparent that the institution of that facility represents a move in the right direction, especially for middle-income countries where the pay-off for 'getting the signals right' is substantial. There is also, however, a basis for believing that the Bank's operations may still be open to the allegation of being insufficiently discriminating among customers, and that the Bank is inadequately using, or even trying to use, its influence to affect member countries' policies.

13.6   SUMMARY AND CONCLUSIONS

The World Bank is obviously an important institution in the international economy and is the premier institution dealing with issues of economic development. Its activities encompass a variety of routes through which its influence is felt. In operational terms it is a bank, lending and extending credits to borrowing countries. These lending activities have obviously been 'sound' and yielded rates of return that most observers would agree are above the average for most governmentally-directed allocations of resources.

None the less, the magnitude of the Bank's lending and credits is sufficiently small that one must, on balance, judge that its impact has arisen primarily through other channels. Provision of information about developing countries' situations and prospects is clearly a major contribution to the international capital market. Other channels, such as the influence of Bank thinking and research on development issues in developing countries, is extremely difficult to estimate or evaluate (although no less important for that reason).

One would anticipate that there is a sizeable payoff for an international institution that can assist in the reform of inefficient economic policies in developing countries. To be sure, there are questions as to what appropriate policies might be, and there are also questions as to the extent to which politicians in individual developing countries are open to persuasion, regardless of the amount of leverage used. However, there are grounds for believing that the Bank (as well as individual donor governments in their bilateral activities) has used less 'leverage' than it perhaps might have used in affecting borrowing countries' domestic policies, leaving the International Monetary Fund the major influence in borrowing governments' policies. To be sure, the Bank has been constrained to lending for individual projects and cannot be faulted in that regard. While the Structural Adjustment Lending program of the Bank represents a step in the right direction, it is questionable whether that program will go far enough in increasing selectivity among recipients of foreign assistance. The program is too recent, however, to permit a full evaluation.

On balance, if one contemplates the alternative directions in which the World Bank might have moved in the past quarter-century, the conclusion must surely be that the Bank has been one of the more rational international institutions. The evidence is strong that it has used its limited resources productively, and improved the growth prospects of the developing countries. To conclude that it might improve its productivity is not a critique. Indeed, such a review may go to show that the international community is gradually acquiring a better understanding of the development process.

NOTES

1. Unlike the United Nations, member governments are represented among the executive directors of the Bank with voting rights in proportion to their subscriptions to the Bank's equity capital. The Bank is unusual in the degree to which the president influences policy. Although wishes of member governments, as reflected through the executive directors, clearly influence Bank operations, the influence is less than might initially be surmised.
2. The International Finance Corporation is also part of the World Bank group, although it does have a separate staff. It is much smaller, and its role is to provide equity capital to the private sector.
3. Given the Bank's relatively hard terms, it is questionable whether Bank loans should be regarded as a public transfer of resources. An offset to this consideration is the Bank's role in signaling creditworthiness to private lenders.
4. There are also important political considerations affecting the creditworthiness of different countries. Although the Bank does not and obviously cannot provide assessments of these risks, information as to underlying economic policies can contribute significantly to an assessment of those risks.
5. For that matter, there has been a great deal of learning about the determinants of developing countries' prospects and performance over the past three decades. The Bank has played a significant role in improving understanding of the development process.
6. Arnold Harberger (1974), in his assessment of the role of foreign aid, essentially adopts this approach. He estimates the increment in income that might have been expected in aid-receiving countries on the assumption that the average rate of return on investments was 10 per cent in real terms.
7. If saving increases with income, that portion of foreign aid that raised income levels would also increase domestic saving at subsequent dates.

Total saving at future dates might therefore anyway overtake the total saving that would accrue on the no-foreign-aid growth path.

8. Some countries' foreign-aid programs consist entirely of grants as a matter of principle. Australia, France, and Sweden follow that practice.

9. The World Bank makes an effort to estimate the grant component of loans outstanding to developing countries. See Section 13.3.

10. *World Bank Annual Report*, 1981, p. 133.

11. Since the index of world export prices includes the price of oil, the constancy of bank transfers refers to a borrower's ability to import goods and services. The altered terms of trade between importing and oil-exporting countries led to an additional transfer of resources away from oil-importing countries.

12. For analyses that center on the Bank's impact upon poverty, and especially rural poverty, see Ayers (1982) and Van de Laar (1980).

13. The best known of these is the volume by Chenery *et al.* (1974), although that volume was more careful than most statements to point out that growth with redistribution was possible.

14. The Bank does, of course, retain a cut-off estimated rate of return below which it will not lend on projects. To date, there has been no problem because there is not a backlog of projects awaiting funding with higher rates of return.

15. World Bank, *Annual Review of Project Performance Audit Results* (November 1978; November 1979; and November 1980).

16. Investments are financed partly by the Bank but primarily by local participants in a project.

17. The evidence available from agricultural economists strongly supports the view that small farmers allocate resources at least as efficiently as larger farmers. See, for example, Schultz (1964).

18. Developing countries' GNP was calculated by multiplying their population by their per capita income as estimated by the World Bank in the 1981 *World Development Report*. The estimate includes all low- and middle-income countries, except China, whose data are reported in the *World Development Report*. If one excludes middle-income, oil-exporting countries, the estimated total GNP is $1,321 billion, so that the substantive conclusion is unaltered without regard to whether oil-exporting, middle-income countries are included or excluded. As seen in Section 13.4, the majority of World Bank resources have been allocated toward the middle-income countries.

19. It can be argued that some countries are so poor that, regardless of the appropriateness of their economic policies, they require a period of sustained resource accumulation (human capital, infrastructure, and other) before they have any prospect for a satisfactory rate of economic growth. The case cannot be made iron-clad, nor can it be dismissed. Even admitting its validity, it would apply only to low-income countries and for a finite period of time. The arguments made in this section have considerably more force, at any event, for middle-income countries which have been major recipients of Bank loans. The issues discussed here can, therefore, be interpreted as applicable to Bank lending and credits to middle-income countries.

20. There is also a question as to whether the effect on thinking of the 'anti-poverty' orientation of the Bank was negative or positive. It can be argued that the Bank staff adequately recognized the imperative for increasing the

size of the pie in its 'redistribution with growth' work, but that the emphasis was sometimes seized by others who interpreted it as a mandate for emphasis on redistribution without regard to resource allocation and growth.

21. This author has, however, read some unpublished studies of particular countries' policies that have seemed to be astute analyses of domestic policies and their effects. In some of those instances, the reason for the failure of the studies to be published centered on the government's refusal to agree to it because of its critical nature. Considerations such as these render the forming of a judgment particularly difficult.

REFERENCES

Ayers, R.L. (1982). *Banking on the Poor: The World Bank's Anti-Poverty Work in Developing Countries*. Washington DC: Overseas Development Council.

Chenery, H. *et al.* (1974). *Redistribution With Growth*. London: Oxford University Press.

Harberger, A. (1974). 'Issues Concerning Capital Assistance to Less-Developed Countries' in David Wall (ed), *Chicago Essays in Economic Development*. Chicago: University of Chicago Press.

Hirschman, A.O. (1967). *Development Projects Observed*. Washington, DC: The Brookings Institution.

Krueger, A.O. (1981). 'Loans to Assist the Transition to Outer-Oriented Policies', *World Economy*, September, pp. 271–281.

Mason, E.S. and Asher, R.E. (1973). *The World Bank since Bretton Woods*. Washington, DC: The Brookings Institution.

Schultz, T.W. (1964). *Transforming Traditional Agriculture*. New Haven, CT: Yale University Press.

Van de Laar, A. (1980). *The World Bank and the Poor*. Boston: Martinus Nijhoff

14 · ASPECTS OF CAPITAL FLOWS BETWEEN DEVELOPING AND DEVELOPED COUNTRIES

After the Mexican problems of mid-1982, a large number of other developing countries found themselves in deep difficulty with respect to their debt-servicing obligations. Some of these countries were middle-income, Latin American countries with relatively high debt–service ratios; others were low-income African countries where debt–service ratios were low; some were oil importers and some oil exporters; some had a record of rapid growth while others had grown slowly, if at all. The fact that the countries affected seemed to have little in common other than their debt-servicing difficulties led most observers to focus upon the 'debt problem' as the phenomenon for analysis, although not all countries experienced debt-servicing difficulties and there had been earlier instances of these problems.

Explanations abounded: the world-wide recession had cut debtor countries' export earnings and thereby their ability to pay; the sharp increase in interest rates had made previously sustainable levels of debt unsustainable; countries had borrowed foolishly and were finally paying the penalty; there had been too great a shift from reliance on official capital flows to the private markets and especially to debt financing. Forecasts of future prospects likewise varied: some asserted that private banks had been so badly burned that they would not voluntarily resume lending, while others viewed the abrupt reduction in new lending as a temporary phenomenon likely to be reversed as soon as debt–service ratios attained more reasonable levels. As to developing countries'

First printed in 1987. In writing this chapter, I benefited greatly from reading papers by Harberger and Swoboda on the subject of international debt, and from the discussion at the Conference on International Debt held at the World Bank in April 1984. Comments on the conference draft by Francis Colaco, Constantine Michalopoulos, Ernest Stern, and T.N. Srinivasan are gratefully acknowledged. Nicholas Hope not only provided valuable comments, but also suggested far better data than had been used in the earlier version, and David McMurray assisted with data preparation.

prospects, some observers thought that, without some extraordinary measures, many countries would be unable to service their debt and would be forced to default, some regarded the difficulties as likely to reduce prospective growth rates but manageable, and still others re-. garded future prospects for growth as only temporarily impaired.

These analyses were widely at variance with earlier held conclusions. During the 1970s, most economists observing the international economy had viewed the emergence of the middle-income countries as borrowers in the private international capital market as a sign of success in the development effort. Prior to that decade, most capital flows to developing countries had originated from official sources as those countries were not regarded as creditworthy in private markets. As more and more developing countries attained economic structures and levels of income that rendered them creditworthy, the increased importance of private capital flows seemed to mark progress in the international economy. Indeed, it appeared that more and more developing countries would attain levels of development at which they could access private markets. That increased access, in turn, was regarded as signifying progress in raising living standards and making economies more productive. Although individual countries occasionally had debt-servicing difficulties in the 1960s and 1970s, these were viewed as temporary and emanating from the particular circumstances of the country. Recent developments, however, have called that view into question, and observers have questioned whether the issue is not more systemic.

In this paper, I set forth a simple framework for understanding capital flows and debt, and to use that framework to assess the often conflicting assertions made with respect to the origins and consequences of the 'debt problem', and the policy prescriptions that emerge. A natural way to proceed is to review the simple theory of capital flows in a world with efficient resource allocation, and then to examine the consequences of various phenomena that might impair efficiency. This permits a typography of 'debt problems' with different countries falling into different categories with respect to causation of difficulties. It also provides a framework within which the policy lessons arising from the experience of the past decade can be assessed.

Section 14.1 sets forth the simplest possible framework, in which the international capital market functions efficiently and resource allocation in the borrowing country is efficient. Within that framework, ways in which international lending might differ from national lending are discussed, and the analysis is extended to cover more than one kind of financial instrument. Section 14.2 then considers ways in which, in the context of a well-functioning international market, domestic economic conditions might lead to difficulties with respect to debt servicing.

Section 14.3 contains an assessment of the effects of various inefficiencies in the international capital market.[1] Section 14.4 part then addresses the debt difficulties of the developing countries in light of the analysis and the available empirical evidence. Section 14.5 draws some tentative conclusions, both with respect to policy and with respect to further needed research.

14.1 CAPITAL FLOWS IN A WELL-FUNCTIONING INTERNATIONAL ECONOMY

It is simplest to start by assuming that international lending is the only means by which savings in one country can finance investment in another.[2] Recall that we start with the assumption that both domestic markets and international capital markets function smoothly. In a static framework, theory is then straightforward: at a uniform real rate of interest there will be more savings than investment opportunities in some countries and more investment opportunities than savings in others. Capital flows will be from countries with an excess of savings over investment at the prevailing world real rate of interest to those with an excess of profitable investment opportunities over domestic savings. It is natural to suppose that in reality, labor-abundant, capital-poor developing countries would be net capital importers from labor-scarce, capital-abundant developed countries.

A number of complications to this simple proposition immediately arise that need not be dealt with here: in a dynamic setting, a theory of the determinants of investment would be required; there might be 'corner solutions' in which some countries had higher rates of return than others even after capital flows if there was no new investment in the low-return countries; and so on.

14.1.1 Differences between Foreign and Domestic Lending in the Simple Case

For present purposes, the questions at issue pertain to why international lending might differ from domestic lending. It is widely recognized that investors might demand a premium for investing abroad as contrasted with acquiring domestic assets because of sovereign risk. This risk arises because investors are protected within their own countries by laws which may not protect foreigners. In the literature, this has been taken to mean that a government might find it in its self-interest to fail to honor the overseas obligations of its citizens simply in the sense that the present value of future repayment streams would outweigh the present value of expected future net inflows of capital (Eaton and Gersovitz, 1981). In practice, it is doubtful whether any country which has achieved a state of development sufficient to be creditworthy to any major degree would ever find it in its self-interest to default: the gains from trade and normal financing (as contrasted with the loss of trade credits and costs of restoring to barter that would arise as a consequence of deliberate default) and the willingness of lenders to 'reschedule' are probably sufficiently large to preclude the default option. Rescheduling itself is a continuum, in that the present value of repayment obligations can be reduced; because of this the extreme case of 'no rescheduling and no payment' seems unlikely.

If 'wilful' default, in the sense of deciding not to pay when the present value of the future flow of capital and interest will be negative, is ruled out, the question arises as to whether there are differences between domestic and international lending under the simple assumptions made so far. At first glance, it would at first sight appear that if laws protecting creditors are enforced equally for foreigners and for domestic residents, then any project yielding an income stream which the creditor can appropriate, which is sufficient to service the debt, will be viewed equally by potential lenders regardless of the location of the project or the financial condition of the debtor. That this is overly simplistic can immediately be seen by noting two interrelated propositions: (1) even within countries, borrowers with greater earning ability and assets are more likely to repay in the event a specific investment goes sour and, therefore, typically receive more favorable terms than the small investor whose assets and other sources of income are limited; and (2) even if a project in a foreign country generates the anticipated income stream, the borrower must convert the domestic currency earnings into foreign exchange in order to service the debt.

Turning to the first proposition, the fact that large firms can use their generalized earning and asset position to permit them to borrow on more favorable terms suggests that even within domestic markets, lenders may prefer to have the borrower share the risk associated with his activities (for moral hazard, possibly, as well as other reasons). Internationally, small investors are probably even more disadvantaged due to the lenders' lack of information, costs of evaluating projects, and related reasons than they are in domestic markets. This implies that international lending is likely to take place largely through financial intermediaries, known to foreign borrowers, whose role may be largely that of knowing local conditions, and presenting an asset and earnings position that provides foreign lenders the same sorts of assurances that larger size may provide domestically. For present purposes, the important point is that, when lending is to intermediaries (or, more generally when claims are backed by an earnings stream other than the individual project financed), it is not only the prospective rate of return on potential new investments that will be relevant to the lender, but also the existing asset and income position of the borrowing entity. Thus, the volume of outstanding debt and debt-service obligations, as well as the prospective earnings stream from past investments, will be relevant to determinations of creditworthiness. As will be seen below, creditworthiness may then be impaired when earnings streams from existing assets decline.

The second proposition is that there is need for additional assurance about convertibility of a repayments stream into foreign exchange. In all cases where there is any question whatever about the government's commitments to full convertibility of its currency, there is an additional risk associated with foreign lending that is absent within a unified currency area: even if the realized earnings stream from a project was satisfactory, the lenders might be unable to purchase foreign exchange. Hence, for countries where there is some degree of exchange control, lenders might be well advised to seek government guarantees of convertibility, or otherwise attempt to reduce this risk.

As will be discussed below, these two propositions would in any event lead lenders to distinguish risks between lending to domestic residents and lending to foreigners even under conditions of efficient resource allocation. If, for whatever set of reasons, a series of past investments had yielded lower rates of return than anticipated, the debt-servicing obligations already existing would necessarily be a factor of some importance in lenders' willingness to extend new credit. When, however, there are also domestic inefficiencies, the situation would be substantially confounded.

14.1.2 Role of Uncertainties

The complications described thus far pertain to the degree to which there are risks inherent in lending abroad that exceed the risks associated with generating the same earnings stream in the lender's home country. A second type of risk arises because the phenomena described in Section 14.1.1 can interact with floating interest-rate obligations.

This can be most easily seen by assuming a very simple world in which the earnings streams from future investments are known with certainty. If the income stream from a given investment project is known with certainty and the investment can be financed by fixed-rate lending, the income stream from the project can finance the loan when the investment constitutes the sole activity of the borrower. The lender would not need to concern himself with any broader aspects of macroeconomic policy, the likely generation of foreign-exchange earnings, or other phenomena within the borrowing country provided only that he had assurances that his claim against the earnings stream would be honored.

With variable-rate lending (or with unexpected fluctuations in earnings streams due, for example, to terms-of-trade changes), the situation could differ significantly. In particular, with an increase in the real interest rate, the yield on past investment might not adequately finance the debt-service obligation. In so far as default on past lending would affect the borrower's ability to finance future investments, it could be rational to honor the obligation. Clearly, however, part of some other income streams would need to be diverted to financing the obligation. If new income streams are among those against which the claim is exercised, then additional borrowing which just equated the rate of return on investment with the real cost of the borrowing would not be warranted.[3]

Once the possibility of variable-rate borrowing (or fluctuations in terms of trade) is taken into account, it is immediately apparent that the economically efficient capital inflow does not depend only on the real interest rate. It is also a function of. (1) the prospective earnings stream in the economy that is potentially capturable to service debt in the event of a rise in interest obligations; (2) the outstanding stock of variable-rate debt; (3) and the expected variability in earnings streams and interest rates.

14.1.3 Relevance for the Debt Problem

The potential relevance of the above considerations for analysis of the debt difficulties of the developing countries should be immediately apparent. First and foremost, both because expected earnings streams dropped and because the cost of servicing the outstanding volume of debt rose, countries became less creditworthy than they had been. Even when a country had followed a 'prudent' borrowing strategy, it is quite possible that higher real interest rates and reduced export earnings might have rendered it 'uncreditworthy' as a reduced income stream was available to finance a larger debt-service burden.

Second, as will be elaborated further below, the additional step of converting a domestic income stream into foreign exchange could cause difficulties with a sharp and unexpected deterioration in the terms of trade, even if the domestic income stream itself was of the expected magnitude. The ease of substitution in production between non-tradables and tradables therefore becomes a critical issue in examining creditworthiness.

14.2   IMPERFECT DOMESTIC MARKETS

To this point, discussion has been couched in terms of an efficiently functioning domestic economy in which private incentives appropriately reflect the relevant trade-offs and in which levels of saving and investment are optimal. Since the optimal rate of capital inflow is really the optimal rate of investment less the optimal rate of savings, evaluation of actual flows can be undertaken only by assessing the overall macroeconomic policy stance within a country. This in itself raises a host of difficulties which must be briefly analyzed here (issue 1). Second, other inappropriate domestic signals (exchange rate, interest rate, non-uniformity of incentives for imports and exports) may create a major wedge between rates of return in domestic currency and those in foreign currency (issue 2). Third, and closely related to the second issue, when markets are imperfect, there are questions, additional to those already raised in Section 14.1.2, about the ease with which returns denominated in domestic currency can be transformed into foreign exchange (issue 3). Finally (issue 4), it is widely recognized that markets do not always adjust instantaneously. This may be particularly important when there are large shifts. In this section, these four issues are discussed in turn.

14.2.1   Optimality of Domestic Savings and Investment

In Section 14.1, it was assumed that domestic savings and investment were both at appropriate levels. Since the optimal amount of foreign borrowing (or, more generally, capital inflow) is the difference between domestic savings and investment at the prevailing world real interest rate, it is apparent that anything which makes either of those aggregates inappropriate will affect the amount of foreign borrowing.

There are two sets of interrelated, but distinct, reasons why these domestic aggregates might be inappropriate. One, discussed here, concerns the interaction between the public sector budget and private expenditure decisions. The other, discussed in Section 14.2.2, concerns the extent to which inappropriate incentives to the private sector may influence investment and savings decisions in ways that make foreign borrowing privately profitable but economically unwarranted when the true trade-offs are recognized.

Turning, then, to the overall stance of macroeconomic policy, it is widely recognized that a public sector deficit can be financed either through 'crowding out' of private investment or through some combination of increased private and foreign savings. Since governmental borrowing is usually backed by its ability to tax the individual, activities financed by additional borrowing (even if one could identify the marginal activities) need not necessarily be productive. It is the entire array of activities encompassed within the government budget that needs to be reasonably economic if a capital inflow financing a public sector deficit is to generate the earnings stream to finance it.

A rational consumer, confronted with an unexpected downward shift in his expected future earnings stream, may gradually adjust his consumption pattern downward, borrowing or drawing down assets in the short run in full knowledge that future consumption will be even lower on that account. An irrational consumer, by contrast, might choose to run down all his assets or borrow until no further credit was available, failing to adjust until various sanctions forced it upon him. There is, however, nothing in economic theory that explains apparently irrational individual behavior.[4]

For countries, however, individuals may behave rationally while the outcome is none the less analogous to the irrational consumer: after 1973 and 1979, for example, some oil-importing countries failed to alter domestic energy prices, incurring larger public sector deficits to finance the additional costs of imports or incurring larger current-account deficits when the exchange rate was maintained at its earlier level in altered circumstances. Consumers, behaving rationally (given the incentives with which they were confronted), continued their earlier expenditure patterns.[5] For the country as a whole, however, this continuation resulted in dissaving (or a reduction in saving) contrasted with the earlier situation. The resulting current-account deficits, financed by borrowing abroad, would have been smaller had appropriate trade-offs been reflected to domestic residents.

Borrowing of this type – to avoid adjusting to altered circumstances – is clearly very different from borrowing to finance investments in new income streams. While a consumer could, in principle, rationally decide that, given his time preference, he would consume more than his income now, it is hard to believe that decisions taken in the 1970s to maintain oil imports and pre-1973 energy price levels were based on rational consideration of alternate future time paths of consumption. While even those countries that did alter their internal relative prices in 1973 and 1979 none the less incurred current-account deficits in 1974 and 1980, those deficits appear to have been of proportionately smaller magnitude and were diminishing almost from the outset (see Table 14.2 below).

In summary, one way in which the model of efficient borrowing set forth in Section 14.1 might be violated is through the incurring of public sector deficits financed by borrowing abroad. Such a capital inflow, if used to finance current consumption expenditures (or, for that matter, investment expenditures with rates of return lower than the real interest rate), could clearly fail to generate the additional income stream that would service the debt. If repeated for a sufficient period of time (presumably because it is the totality of governmental receipts that back any borrowing), debt-servicing problems might well arise. In addition, adjustment would be required simply in order to reduce capital inflows, the topic of Section 14.2.4.

14.2.2 Domestic Distortions

Given the large existing literature on the effects of domestic distortions on resource allocation, little analysis is required here. Suffice it to say that in many developing countries, credit is rationed at artificially low interest rates, scarce foreign exchange is allocated by license to the fortunate recipients at far less than its scarcity value, and automatically prohibitive protection is granted to new industries which produce import substitutes for the domestic market. In these circumstances, it is readily demonstrable that some capital inflows that finance privately profitable investments may none the less have a much lower or even negative 'true' rate of return (see Bhagwati and Brecher, 1979, and Bhagwati and Srinivasan, 1978, for demonstration of this result).

Moreover, there is some presumption that policies that encourage substitution of domestic production for imports without due regard to cost may result in increasing divergences between economic and private rates of return over time. If that happens, mounting debt-service obligations with ever smaller average actual returns could lead to debt-servicing difficulties. In the absence of a reversal of underlying economic policies, one would anticipate that a 'debt problem' would ultimately arise.

Another source of difficulty might arise in circumstances in which rates of return were adequate but non-capturable. Suppose, for example, that a government borrowed to finance elementary education. It could recapture only that fraction of the additional earnings stream that was reflected in its tax structure. In this case, the 'distortion' is in the financing of the investment. For developing countries where transport, education, agricultural extension, and related activities are a major part of total investment, this 'distortion' may be quantitatively significant.

14.2.3 Transforming Domestic Currency into Foreign Exchange

Many highly profitable investments in developing countries are in 'home goods' – education, transport, power generation, communications, and so on. These investments typically have a very long payout period and could, on that account alone, result in debt-servicing difficulties under some conditions (see Section 14.3.2) if financed by foreign borrowing of shorter maturity structure.

Otherwise, assuming that capital markets are sufficiently flexible, there is no reason in principle why problems should arise if domestic markets are reasonably efficient: the real exchange rate would appropriately reflect the marginal rate of transformation of home goods into tradables and hence the relevant costs and returns to investment in home goods would be adequately reflected via the price mechanism.

When exchange rates are overvalued, there is a major market distortion: the overvaluation of the exchange rate penalizes export activities. This raises the possibility that, while rates of return to investments in home goods activities might be at or above the rate of interest on foreign borrowing, there would be no commensurate increase in foreign-exchange earnings. Under these conditions, rates of return (on some investments in home goods) might yield at least the international borrowing rate in domestic currency, yet the foreign exchange to service the debt which financed the investments might simply not be available.

14.2.4   Speed of Adjustment

It is often assumed that adjustments can be undertaken instantaneously and costlessly. In reality, it is widely recognized that adjustments take time and that large shifts in macroeconomic variables in short periods of time may entail high economic, as well as social and political, costs.

Since a net capital inflow permits an increase in expenditure relative to income, a change in the size of the capital inflow requires an adjustment of commensurate size in other macroeconomic aggregates. If, for example, the warranted capital inflow fell to zero, the required shift in domestic aggregates would be the magnitude of the earlier inflow as a percentage of GNP. When this percentage becomes sizeable (as it has in many countries, as will be seen in Section 14.4), the macroeconomic magnitudes of potential shifts will also be large. This is more likely to be the case, the more activities financed by inflows employ both home goods and traded goods. If, for example, half the cost of a new investment project typically consists of imports, then the cutback of such a project will entail the reallocation of half the (home goods) resources employed in the project to the production of other tradables (since the capital inflow would presumably have freed the home goods from other activities).

It is readily apparent that, when capital inflows drop, domestic adjustment will be warranted. Combining this proposition with the theory set forth in Section 14.1, two questions arise: (1) What is the magnitude of the shift in the warranted inflow when the real interest rate rises? (2) Given that there are costs of adjustment, is not the rate of inflow itself a variable to be monitored?

With respect to the first, it is arguable that the higher real interest rate confronting borrowers with variable-rate debt probably implied that the outstanding level of indebtedness, although economically desirable at a real rate of interest of 3 per cent, was not justified or sustainable at real rates of interest of 6, 8, or 10 per cent. In those circumstances, economically justified borrowing (even when domestic policies were sound) may well have shifted from positive to negative as some repayment may have become warranted (because of overall credit-worthiness considerations, discussed above). The magnitude of the required shift in the domestic economy may well have been sizeable, especially when the required additional interest payments on existing debt added to the magnitude of the necessary adjustment.

With respect to the second question, one suspects that the appropriate policy response to potential vulnerability induced by wide swings in the current account may well be to hold additional reserves, rather than to restrain current flows. When, in reality, there are adjustment costs, that is clearly reason to moderate fluctuations in the current account balance that might otherwise be required (see Harberger, 1984, on this question with respect to Chile). It will be seen in Section 14.3 that the required shifts on the part of some developing countries have been large enough to raise question as to their manageability.

14.3 IMPERFECTIONS IN INTERNATIONAL CAPITAL MARKETS

In Section 14.1, the simple theory of capital flows was examined with respect to developing countries' debt problems on the assumption that the international capital market and the economy of the borrowing country were efficient. In Section 14.2, the assumption that the domestic economy functioned efficiently was relaxed, to examine the sorts of problem that might arise with borrowing in a perfectly functioning international capital market when the domestic economy is, in one way or another, distorted.

In this section, it is assumed that the borrowing country's economy functions efficiently, but that there may be distortions in the international capital market. No effort is made to examine the possible sources of those distortions (bank regulations, political uncertainties, etc.). Rather, focus is on the potential effect of these features on the borrowing country's economy and its ability to service its debt.

Two major sources of 'distortion' come to mind: once it is recognized that there are other financing mechanisms than bank lending, the composition of a capital inflow might be inappropriate; and the maturity structure of the debt or the payback schedule may not match that of the earnings stream financed by the loan. Each of these is considered in turn.

14.3.1   Lending and Other Capital Flows

The discussion of Section 14.1 for the most part implicitly assumed certainty about future earnings streams, and paid little attention to uncertainty. In reality, the presence of uncertainty alters the analysis in an important way: unless asset markets and flow markets all function well, the portfolio composition of finance of a new project makes a difference. When the stream of returns is uncertain (whether because of project-specific features or because of uncertainty about the environment in which the project will operate), lending and equity finance have different implications for the sharing of risk. Should an investment be financed by an entrepreneur in a developing country through foreign borrowing only, the foreigners have a future claim regardless of what happens to the income stream. In that case, the proportionate variance in the entrepreneur's return will exceed that of the project itself. By contrast, should an investment be undertaken by foreign entrepreneurs, the nationals of a country (ignoring the possibility of distorted incentives discussed in Section 14.2.3) have smaller obligations in the event of an unfavorable outcome on the investment.

As these considerations suggest, an 'optimal' capital inflow undoubtedly has an 'optimal' composition, given the availability and terms of equity and debt financing on the international market. To the extent that the portfolio of the capital inflow diverges from that composition, the warranted size of the inflow will be smaller. Moreover, to the extent the portfolio is unbalanced (toward debt, and especially short-term debt, to be empirically relevant), the likelihood of debt-servicing difficulties arising under outcomes with low probabilities (prolonged and severe recession, high real interest rates, etc.) increases.

The reluctance of the developing countries to accept equity finance in the 1970s may have intensified their debt-servicing difficulties in the world-wide recession of 1980–3. Whether this is regarded as an imperfection of the international capital market, as an imperfection in the domestic economy, or as a case of inappropriate expectations about future conditions in the international economy hardly matters: the combination of adverse events which took place concurrently in the early 1980s had even more impact on the developing countries than it would have had their capital inflows been financed by a higher proportion of equity investment.[6] It may be noted, too, that equity finance implies a different time path and structure of the servicing stream than does debt financing (and is equivalent to the use of consols in that principal as such is never repaid). How much of the apparent disproportionate use of borrowing led to difficulties because of inappropriate distribution of risk and how much because the maturity structure of obligations was shorter with a higher proportion of debt-to-equity finance is difficult to judge.

For very low-income countries, the unavailability of concessional assistance (which can in large part be regarded as compensating for a market failure in that available maturities are insufficiently long – see Section 14.3.2) in the 1970s led to resort to private capital flows to a greater extent than may have been warranted by the state of development and ability to withstand cyclical fluctuations. Further discussion of that issue must, however, await consideration of factors pertaining to the maturity structure of outstanding debt.

14.3.2   Maturity Structure of Debt

It is widely recognized that unless there is to be refinancing, the time profile of debt repayment must match, or at least not be substantially shorter than, the payout period of a project. And, the greater the mismatch between the time structure of debt-service obligations and that of the project, the greater is the likelihood of difficulty.

There are two distinct ways in which mismatches probably occurred in the 1970s: the term of much private lending fell short of the structure of expected returns; and nominal interest rates rose with inflation to increase the disparity. The first, the shorter-term structure of outstanding debt, is probably more important for low-income countries, for which many of the appropriate investments have pay-out periods of decades rather than years. The average maturity of outstanding private medium- and long-term debt never exceeded eleven years, and fell to less than ten after 1973. As this happened, maturities became increasingly disconnected from expected cash flows.

Even for middle-income countries, however, the fact that nominal interest rates rose sharply in the late 1970s implicitly shortened the real maturity structure. Consider two loans, each serviced by a fixed-sum annual repayment stream over n years. In one case the rate of inflation is zero, and the real and nominal rate of interest 3 per cent. In the other case the rate of inflation is 10 per cent per year, so the nominal rate of interest is 13 per cent. In the latter case, 10 per cent of the real debt is repaid in the first year of the loan, as the higher nominal interest rate implicitly compensates for the reduced real value of the outstanding principal balance. I shall argue in Section 14.4 that a significant factor in the debt difficulties of the developing countries was the sharp shift in implicit maturity structure from the mid-1970s (when negative real rates of interest in effect lengthened maturity structures and the cost of debt) and the 1980s (when the inflation-induced premium over the real rate of interest implicitly shortened the term structure of the debt).

It seems evident that a project could realize a satisfactory rate of return, but that servicing might be difficult or impossible if the maturity structure of the debt is shorter than that of the project. Given the sorts of project that constitute a large part of investment in developing countries, the explicit and implicit shortening of the maturity structure of the debt resulting from inflation has surely resulted in an increased imperfection of the international capital market over the past decade.

14.4   THE DEBT PROBLEM IN ANALYTICAL PERSPECTIVE

The foregoing review of possible market imperfections, and their implications for analysis of the current debt situation, is far from exhaustive: it would require at a minimum further analysis of the possible interactions of domestic-market imperfections and international capital-market imperfections, and then the construction of a model within which the relative magnitudes of various contributory factors might be quantified. Such a quantification of the various phenomena and the extent that they may have contributed to the current problem is well beyond the scope of this chapter, and may not be possible at all given the current state of knowledge. Moreover, as the previous discussion indicates, debt-servicing difficulties can originate in a variety of different situations. While some factors, such as rising real interest rates, were common to all countries, others (such as macroeconomic policies) differed significantly across countries.

None the less, it is worthwhile to pull together some suggestive pieces of evidence to shed light on the current situation. To anticipate the argument and help the reader, it may be useful to summarize tentative conclusions at this stage. They are:

1.   External shocks, inappropriate domestic economic policies, and the shift in the optimal level of borrowing all contributed to the 'debt problem', but the relative importance of each component differed vastly among countries.
2.   The warranted shift in the size of the current account, with the consequent large implied shift in flows of national product and expenditure, which resulted from the change in the real interest

rate, was probably the major reason why developing countries found the adjustment so very difficult.
3. The shortened term structure of the debt, and other 'distortions' arising from international inflation have intensified the problems that would anyway have arisen.

Before turning to the implications for policy, it will be useful to examine each of these in turn.

14.4.1   Causes of the Debt Problem

It seems indisputable that both the world-wide recession and the inappropriate macroeconomic policies of some developing countries contributed to bringing about the virtually simultaneous difficulties many developing countries faced. One set of estimates of the relative importance of these two sets of factors has been presented by Enders and Mattione (1984). They have quantified the magnitude of external shocks and the degree to which domestic policies responded for a number of developing countries.[7]

Their results are reproduced in Table 14.1 for a group of Latin American debtors. The first row estimates the magnitude of the external shock facing each country, defined as the deterioration in the current-account balance brought about by increased interest payments and worsened terms of trade. It should be noted that Latin America had a high fraction of variable-rate debt, thus exacerbating the interest-rate shock. As can be seen, some countries (e.g. Mexico because of oil) experienced an improved external environment.

The second row gives the actual change in the current account. When that change is larger in magnitude than the external shock, Enders and Mattione attribute the additional deterioration to poor domestic macroeconomic policies; when it is smaller, they attribute the difference to macroeconomic policies designed to bring about adjustment. Thus, they interpret the Brazilian macroeconomic adjustments to have resulted in an improvement in current account of about $25 billion compared with what it would have been with 'neutral' macroeconomic policies, while they regard Argentine economic policies as having led to a current account over $5 billion more negative than it would have been with 'neutral' policies. The third row for each country gives the Enders–Mattione estimate of the order of magnitude of capital flight from each country, which clearly exacerbated the problems of Argentina, Mexico and Venezuela substantially.

There are a large number of qualifications that must be made to any interpretation of the Enders–Mattione results. An important assump-

Table 14.1   Enders and Mattione's calculations of overall adjustment/disadjustment to external shocks ($ billions)

Country	Results of shock	1979	1980	1981	1982	Cumulative*
Colombia	Shock	−0.8	−1.2	−2.1	−2.8	−6.8
	Current account change[†]	**	−1.1	−2.5	−3.0	−6.6
	Capital export[‡]	−0.1	0.3	0.5	**	0.7
Brazil	Shock	−3.3	−9.4	−16.5	−19.3	−48.5
	Current account change[†]	−4.1	−6.0	−4.7	−8.8	−23.6
	Capital export[†]	1.3	1.6	−0.3	−0.7	2.0
Chile	Shock	0.4	**	−2.6	−2.6	−4.8
	Current account change[†]	−0.7	−1.5	−4.3	−1.9	−8.5
	Capital export[‡]	0.4	0.5	0.9	−0.8	1.0
Argentina	Shock	**	−3.5	−4.6	−5.4	−13.4
	Current account change[†]	−2.1	−6.5	−5.9	−4.4	−18.9
	Capital export[‡]	1.7	−2.3	−8.7	−5.0	−14.3
Peru	Shock	0.3	0.5	**	−0.5	0.4
	Current account change[†]	1.5	0.9	−0.6	−0.5	1.3
	Capital export[‡]	**	0.2	0.5	0.6	1.3
Mexico	Shock	0.3	3.3	3.9	4.2	11.7
	Current account change[†]	−2.8	−4.8	−10.1	−1.0	−18.7
	Capital export[‡]	−0.8	−1.1	−4.9	−8.3	−15.2
Venezuela	Shock	2.6	5.9	6.7	3.9	19.1
	Current account change[†]	3.6	8.3	7.9	−0.2	19.5
	Capital export[‡]	2.4	−3.1	−4.9	−7.4	−13.0

* Figures may not add because of rounding.
** Between − $0.05 billion and $0.05 billion.
[†] Adjusted for inflation.
[†] A minus sign denotes capital flight, that is, an unfavourable movement in the relevant items of the capital account
Source: Enders and Mattione (1984).

tion is that, once terms-of-trade and interest-rate changes are accounted for, the current account would remain unchanged in the absence of deliberate policy changes. Despite the necessary qualifications, however, the estimates give an idea of both the relative orders of magnitude for that particular group of countries. Enders and Mattione (1984, p. 33) interpret their results to show that,

> for this group of Latin American countries as a whole, internal causes of the crisis predominated over external. The net total shock was $42.3 billion for the seven countries. But the total incremental financing requirement came to $96.9 billion, $55.7 billion in increased current account deficits after correcting for inflation, and $41.2 billion in increased capital export.

While this general conclusion holds when summing over the seven countries, perhaps the most striking aspect of their findings, as they themselves note, is the major differences between countries. At one extreme, Mexico experienced a favorable external environment and yet experienced a sharp deterioration in her current account; the explanation must lie largely in domestic macroeconomic policies. At the other extreme (of this group) Brazil adopted policies which offset some of the negative external shock.

As one would expect, the countries that were most adversely affected were those whose domestic policies were initially inappropriate and for whom the external environment turned most sharply unfavorable. The apparent coincidence of timing of debt difficulties probably arose at least as much because a world-wide recession would be expected to impact most heavily on those with underlying economic problems as because of the incidence of the recession itself.

14.4.2   Extreme Adjustment Difficulties

It is self-evident that higher interest rates, all else equal, intensify the difficulties of the developing countries. In fact, about three-quarters of the middle-income countries' outstanding medium- and long-term debt to private lenders has been at variable interest rates so that debt-servicing obligations on existing loans have increased. And the average interest rate paid on all LDC medium- and long-term debt to private lenders rose from 9.7 per cent in 1978 to a peak of 14.6 per cent in 1981, falling to 13.1 per cent in 1982 and probably a little further in 1983.

Obviously, increased interest payments combined with reduced prices for exports and shrinking international markets made developing countries' situations more difficult than they would otherwise have been. Some countries would in any event have been unable to continue on their existing paths – Turkey is an example of a country which, before the effects of higher real interest rates or world-wide recession anyway was confronted with an impossible situation due largely to earlier failures to adjust. Even without the oil-price increase of 1979, Turkish economic policy would have required major reforms during 1980. The question arises, however, as to whether the orders of magnitude so obtained even begin to capture the nature of the problem. If one takes $500 billion as the total outstanding debt of developing countries in 1980, the increase in interest rates from 9.7 per cent to 14.6 per cent would have accounted for about $25 billion. While this is certainly a sizeable amount, it cannot be the major reason for difficulty.

A more plausible interpretation has to do with the magnitude of the shift in the optimal size of outstanding debt and desirable amount of capital inflows. A shift in the real interest rate of the order of magnitude experienced between 1978 (when export unit values were rising at a rate almost equal to the interest rate) and 1981, when export unit values fell 5 per cent, is enormous. Warranted borrowing in 1981 and 1982, along the lines of reasoning of Section 14.2.4, must have been negligible, if not negative, abstracting from the question of an optimal speed of adjustment. However, many developing countries had been running net current account deficits ranging from 2 to 10 per cent of GNP (see Table 14.2), delaying the needed adjustment to the changes of the 1970s. When the oil price rose in 1979 and the real interest rate rose sharply, the required shift in domestic expenditure and resources was too massive, both because debt was already sizeable and because adjustment to earlier changes had been too long delayed.

Table 14.2 gives the net capital inflow less interest payments for seven large debtor countries as a percentage of GNP. As can be seen, the swings in their inflows were massive. For Chile, the shift amounted to 8 per cent of GNP in one year, and for Mexico over 6 per cent. For Venezuela, a shift of more than 23 per cent took place over two years. Moreover, the recorded shifts are those that countries were able to effect: clearly in some cases, the adjustment (in the absence of adjustment costs) simply could not be made as quickly as would have been desirable.

Seen in this light, much of the pain arising from the debt situation from the perspective of the developing countries may be interpreted as emanating not from the height of interest payments *per se*, but from the difficulties associated with adjusting to any large change in the current account balance. If decisions were based on the expectation that real interest rates would remain negative or barely positive, then the warranted shift when the real rate was in excess of 10 per cent was massive. Such a shift entailed not only a real reduction in growth prospects (for those countries that were adopting policies that permitted efficient use of capital inflows) but also a massive adjustment in macroeconomic aggregates. And, given the height of real interest rates, countries could not quickly begin to work down their variable–rate debt so that total real debt was rising while the serviceable level of outstanding debt was falling.

Given the unobservability of the magnitude of the warranted outstanding debt of developing countries, there is no way of verifying this interpretation of the debt problem. Some more inferential evidence is available, however, and presented in Table 14.3. Column 1 gives the medium- and long-term debt of all developing countries as of the end of each year. Column 2 gives net medium- and long-term borrowing (i.e. the difference between years in column 1 adjusted for valuation changes in outstanding debt). Column 3 then gives the real debt outstanding at the end of each year, calculated by deflating nominal debt by the index

Table 14.2 Current-account deficits less interest payments as percentage of GNP, selected countries, 1970–82

	1970	1971	1972	1973	1974	1975	1976	1977	1978	1979	1980	1981	1982	1983
Brazil	1.4	2.6	2.1	1.7	5.6	3.9	3.1	1.8	1.9	2.5	2.7	1.4	2.5	-0.5
Chile	-0.1	0.9	3.6	2.2	1.7	4.4	-4.0	2.3	4.9	3.1	4.1	10.9	2.2	-1.7
Colombia	4.0	5.6	1.6	-0.3	2.0	-0.1	-2.3	-3.1	-2.1	-2.7	-0.4	3.6	4.1	5.5
Korea	7.3	8.6	2.6	0.7	10.2	8.0	0.2	-1.2	0.9	5.5	7.2	4.9	1.3	-0.4
Mexico	2.3	1.4	1.3	1.7	2.9	3.4	2.4	0.3	1.1	1.7	2.1	3.5	-2.9	-2.6
Philippines	1.2	0.4	0.3	-4.0	1.7	6.1	5.9	3.4	4.0	4.1	4.8	4.4	6.2	4.7
Venezuela	0.4	-0.5	0.1	-6.2	-23.3	-8.4	-1.4	7.9	13.2	-2.5	-10.5	-9.0	2.2	-8.1

Note: Current account deficits exclude official transfers. Interest payments are for public and private guaranteed and non-guaranteed long-term debt. GNP data are derived from local currency estimates converted to US dollars at official exchange rates. Data for 1983 are estimates.

Source: World Bank, Economic Analysis and Projections Department; *Balance of Payments Handbook*; World Bank, *World Debt Tables*, 1983–84.

Table 14.3 Change in developing countries' real inflows and liabilities, 1972–83

	Debt ($ bn) (1)	Net borrowing ($ bn) (2)	Real debt (Constant 1980 prices) ($ bn) (3)	Net borrowing less interest ($ bn) (4)	Real transfer (Constant 1980 prices) ($ bn) (5)	Debt/ GNP (%) (6)	Index of export unit value (1980 = 100)	GNP ($ bn)
1970	66.3	7.8	203.4	5.2	16.0	17.3	32.6	382.3
1971	77.4	8.8	243.4	5.9	18.6	18.3	31.8	422.7
1972	90.8	12.8	271.0	9.4	28.1	19.3	33.5	469.3
1973	109.2	15.7	246.5	10.8	24.4	18.6	44.3	587.0
1974	135.6	23.4	225.0	16.8	28.0	18.0	60.0	753.5
1975	161.5	29.0	272.8	20.8	35.1	19.2	59.2	839.8
1976	194.9	32.8	311.8	23.8	38.1	20.4	62.5	955.0
1977	239.5	39.4	333.1	28.4	39.5	22.2	71.9	1079.7
1978	299.9	48.2	402.0	32.8	44.0	23.9	74.6	1254.9
1979	353.0	53.7	405.3	31.2	35.8	23.2	87.1	1521.8
1980	406.5	55.5	406.5	24.9	24.9	22.3	100.0	1825.9
1981	464.6	69.4	489.6	30.4	32.0	24.1	94.9	1924.0
1982	517.8	52.9	583.8	6.6	7.4	29.0	88.7	1783.8
1983	575.0	35.0	672.5	–11.0	–12.9	n.a.	85.5	n.a.

Notes: The debt figures for 1983 are preliminary and subject to revision. The index of export unit value for 1983 is an average of the first two quarters only. GNP data are derived from local currency estimates. and then converted at official exchange rates. Debt is public and private, medium- and long-term; short-term is excluded.

Source: World Bank, *World Debt Tables*, 1983–84 (and related data files); International Monetary Fund, *International Financial Statistics* (various issues).

of export unit values of non-oil developing countries. As can be seen, during the burst of borrowing after the 1973 oil-price increase, world-wide inflation implied that real debt was falling in 1974. By contrast, after the 1979 oil-price increase, total real medium- and long-term debt outstanding rose sharply. Column 4 gives the net borrowing of each year less interest paid on the debt during that interval (it may be noted that interest payments as a percentage of debt are less than the average interest rate on outstanding private borrowing because of concessional assistance and grace periods on longer term loans).

Column 5 gives the 'real transfer', that is net borrowing less interest payments. This number most closely reflects the additional resources available for domestic utilization over and above domestic production. As can be seen, the real values of these net transfers were smaller in the early 1980s than ten years earlier. Column 6 gives debt outstanding relative to all developing countries' GNPs.

Several observations are in order. First, in the 1970s, there was a significant positive transfer of resources *and* the real value of outstand-ing debt was falling, thus in effect providing resources as a pure transfer from the viewpoint of the borrowing country. By contrast, in the 1980s, a smaller real transfer was accompanied by a much larger increase in real debt outstanding (at a higher real interest rate). Second, debt as a percentage of developing countries' GNP was no higher in 1980 than it had been in 1970. By contrast, the percentage rose sharply in 1981 and 1982.

All economic considerations therefore suggest that borrowing in the 1970s was economically warranted from the viewpoint of those develop-ing countries that had adjusted to altered international conditions; their outstanding indebtedness was not increasing relative to their incomes; their cost of borrowing was low if not negative; and the real outstanding debt was growing relatively slowly. In the early 1980s, the cost of new borrowing was much higher, and the ratio of debt to GNP was rising. It is not unreasonable to interpret the developing countries' anguish as a consequence of their inability to shift expenditures relative to income sharply enough. They, therefore, had to borrow more, thereby increas-ing outstanding debt when the sustainable level of outstanding debt was in fact falling.

I conclude, therefore, that if one calculates only the increased interest payments on outstanding variable-rate debt, the orders of magnitude do not appear overwhelming. But if, instead, the shift in the warranted size of the current account less interest payments is examined relative to real income in developing countries, the implied orders of magnitude of needed adjustments in the domestic economy in many developing countries are truly staggering.

14.4.3 Shortened Term Structure of Debt

As discussed in Section 14.3, when the nominal rate of interest increases at a constant real interest rate, the economic time profile of scheduled repayments of principal is shortened. The premium of the nominal over the real interest rate implicitly is a payment of principal.

The rise in nominal interest rates in the late 1970s may therefore be interpreted as having increased a distortion in international capital markets due to developing countries' inability to match the schedule of repayments against the payout period for investment projects. Because world-wide inflation resulted in a greater implicit principal repayment in early years of loans, more debt rollover was needed.

That this problem is not inconsequential for the debt difficulties of the developing countries is evidenced by two statistics: the ratio of debt-servicing obligations to principal payments and the maturity structure of currently outstanding debt. With respect to the first, interest payments are estimated to have been $46 billion in 1983, contrasted with scheduled principal repayments on medium- and long-term debt of $50 billion. Since no interest payments are supposed to roll over during debt rescheduling, it is actually rescheduling of principal payments that has been in the headlines (although new credits have been extended partially or entirely covering interest payments in some cases). The second statistic even more vividly illustrates the nature of the problem: over 70 per cent of all medium- and long-term debt of developing countries outstanding at the end of 1983 was repayable in the years 1985–7. Clearly, if developing countries were to repay according to that schedule, the magnitude of the shift in macroeconomic aggregates would be beyond the reasonable adjustment range of either developed or developing countries.

14.5 POLICY IMPLICATIONS AND CONCLUSIONS

Perhaps the biggest single question confronting policy-makers in developing countries is the likely future path of the real interest rate in international private capital markets. Should the real rate of interest remain at or above its range of 1982–3, it is questionable whether many developing countries would find it in their rational economic self-interest to borrow very much to finance new investments, once the current readjustment phase was over. The outstanding level of real debt, which may have been comfortable at the levels of real interest rates prevailing in the late 1970s, clearly caused servicing difficulties in the early 1980s.

Should high real interest rates continue, and if there is no other change in the international economy that makes debt-service less onerous than it now is, policy-makers might continue to undertake measures to increase their current-account surpluses and hence reduce outstanding debt. This would, naturally, mean that resources available for new domestic investment would be reduced relative to what they would otherwise be, although the considerable scope for increased efficiency in resource allocation (via improvement in domestic economic policy regimes) may provide an offset.

However, given the difficulties associated with adjustments of the magnitude called for in reversing the direction of capital flows (and the consequently lessened prospects for growth that result), there will be high costs for continuing those adjustments should the real interest rate return to more historical levels. For, at real rates of interest at 3–5 per cent, there is little question but that those developing countries whose internal incentive structure is appropriate and whose macro-economic policies are conducive to growth can benefit substantially from augmenting their domestic savings with foreign savings.

From the viewpoint of policy-makers in developing countries, this conclusion is somewhat uncomfortable: there will be high costs entailed in failing to adjust further should the real interest rate remain very high, and there will be high costs of adjusting further should the real interest rate return to more usual levels in the near future. If wide variability in real interest rates is likely to persist, that in itself would require flexible economic policies capable of adapting to fluctuations.

Whatever the future, however, the cries of anguish from developing countries' politicians over high interest rates may be heard much more sympathetically when seen in light of the role of the real interest rate in affecting their long-term development path and the appropriate role of international capital flows in it.

Regardless of the level of the real interest rate, however, three major lessons emerge from the experience of the past decade. One is the importance of domestic economic policies in affecting rates of return on all investments. As the analysis of Section 14.2 indicated, this may be especially important in the context of countries relying on the international capital market, as the costs of inappropriate economic policies may be magnified in so far as foreign financing is employed. If there is a lesson from the experience of the 1970s and early 1980s, it is the overriding importance of the overall macroeconomic policy framework including the trade and payments regime and the efficiency of public sector investment, that is important in determining ability to device debt. The second, which is closely related to the first, is that the marginal–average distinction in rates of return is important. Even if a particular investment project is sound, it is the average rate of return on all investments that will influence a country's ability to finance its outstanding debt. This is especially important for countries at very low levels of income. For them, the fact that gestation periods of investment are very long, combined with the length of available private lending, strongly suggests that the world was too quick to reduce concessional assistance to low-income countries. The third lesson relates to the role of foreign equity financing in development. The trade-off between borrowing and equity may have been appropriately perceived in the 1970s when the real rate of interest was very low. For the foreseeable future, however, it seems unlikely that that regime will return. In the presence of positive real interest rates (whether in the 3–5 per cent range or 10 per cent or more), developing countries' policy-makers might be wise to re-evaluate their policies with respect to equity investment. While there are clearly trade-offs, and hence political judgements to be made, greater reliance on equity-financed capital inflows in the 1970s would have eased some of the difficulties encountered in the early 1980s.

For the medium term, there seems little doubt that the pressing policy issue pertains to finding ways to restructure the scheduled principal payments on developing countries' debts. The implausibility of the currently scheduled principal repayments in itself suggests the crucial importance of finding ways to reschedule without year-to-year efforts. For new borrowing, putting a cap on nominal interest payments with any excess added to the outstanding principal balance regardless of the nominal interest rate, would stretch out the maturity structure of the debt. For debt currently outstanding, however, other mechanisms will have to be found.

A final policy lesson of some importance will be relevant if real interest rates resume more normal levels. Under those circumstances, many developing countries might find that the economically warranted level of borrowing rose sharply. They might do well to consider mechanisms to smooth the swings in the size of capital inflows, to avoid the need in future for abrupt shifts in the current-account balance. If, indeed, there are sizeable costs of adjustment, and especially if those costs increase with the magnitude of the required adjustment, policies that dampen those swings may be economically warranted. Clearly, larger holdings of international reserves might serve this function.

NOTES

1. Focus is on capital flows entirely from the viewpoint of borrowing countries. Therefore, only difficulties in the international capital market that affect the

borrowers are discussed here. That rules out consideration of ways in which bank regulation, taxation, and other policies in lender countries may affect the supply of capital in ways detrimental to efficient resource allocation in the international economy. For purposes of analyzing the origins of the debt problems and the policy lessons that arise, this limitation is probably not important. There are two ways in which supply-side phenomena may affect the ease of ameliorating the situation, however: regulations on lending institutions clearly inhibit the development of a secondary market in debt and also may affect banks' willingness to resume lending and their portfolio choices. Those issues are not discussed here, as they take the analysis into an entirely different field.

2. The simple theory of capital flows essentially addresses the issue of net flows. In the evolution of the debt difficulties of the developing countries, two aspects of gross flows have been relevant: first, countries have simultaneously borrowed to augment reserves; and, second, there have been a number of situations in which private capital outflows, motivated by concern over monetary stability, have been offset by public borrowing. The public-indebtedness, private-asset problem is discussed in Section 14.2, and both issues are dealt with in assessing the origins of the debt problem. Reviewing the theory underlying the demand for reserves would take the analysis far from the main theme of the chapter and is not attempted here.

3. The capturability of income streams to finance obligations has serveral other aspects. One pertains to the situation where private capital flight has been financed by public borrowing. The inability of the authorities to tax earnings of the private assets may in itself present a major debt-service problem. Another pertains to the situation in which the government has financed high-yielding investments but cannot capture a sufficient portion of the return, e.g. with investments in primary education in rural areas.

4. Of course, even that behavior could be rational if the consumer expected never to have to repay his obligations, but as stated in Section 14.1, that seems unlikely in the case considered here.

5. If consumers know that government price and borrowing policies are unsustainable, that will affect their behavior but not in the same way as would alternative macroeconomic policies.

6. This statement assumes that profits would have fallen during the recession. In circumstances where equity financing is devoted to highly protected domestic industries, high profitability may not have any counterpart in real rates of return, and difficulties in financing profit repatriation could be severe.

7. Capital flight is separately estimated as a third factor because this made gross borrowing larger than net borrowing. Capital flight is normally symptomatic of underlying difficulties in macroeconomic policy.

REFERENCES

Bhagwati, J. and R. Brecher (1979). 'National Welfare in an Open Economy in the Presence of Foreign-Owned Factors of Production', *Journal of International Economics*.

Bhagwati, J. and T.N. Srinivasan (1978). 'Shadow Prices for Project Selection in the Presence of Distortions: Effective Rates of Protection and Domestic

Resources Costs', *Journal of Political Economy*, vol. 86, no. 1, pp. 97–116.
Eaton, Jonathan and Mark Gersovitz (1981). 'Debt with Potential Repudiation: Theoretical and Empirical Analysis', *Review of Economic Studies*, vol. 48, pp. 289–309.
Enders, Thomas O. and Richard P. Mattione (1984). *Latin America: The Crisis of Debt and Growth*. Washington, DC: The Brookings Institution.
Harberger, Arnold C. (1984). 'Lessons for Debtor Country Managers and Policymarkers', paper presented at Conference on International Debt, World Bank, Washington, DC, April.
Swoboda, Alexander K. (1984). 'Debt and the Efficiency and Stability of the International Financial System', paper presented at Conference on International Debt, World Bank, Washington, DC, April.

15 · DEVELOPMENT THOUGHT AND DEVELOPMENT ASSISTANCE

Anne O. Krueger and Vernon W. Ruttan

Donor agencies have extended foreign assistance from one country to another for a variety of motives. Recipients also have had different motives for seeking assistance. In both cases, the motives sometimes have not been consistent with developmental purposes. The analysis in this chapter is directed to assessing how effectively aid has supported development and examines donors' motives only in so far as they impinge on effectiveness.

The evaluation of aid effectiveness is possible only if the underlying development process is understood. There are two reasons for this. Without such an understanding, assessment of the contribution of aid would be impossible. Furthermore, aid constitutes but a small portion even of most poor countries' resources and is highly fungible. Hence, aid effectiveness must be considered within a country's overall growth framework. Our starting point in this chapter is the evolution of development thought in relation to development policy.

Until the Second World War, growth was not a conscious policy objective even in most industrial countries.[1] In so far as some governments attempted consciously to stimulate economic growth, little or no systematic body of knowledge was available to guide their efforts. Furthermore, many now-developing countries were colonies until after 1945. As they attained independence and set economic development as a prime objective, economists turned their attention to what seemed to be at the time relevant issues and policies. The early development theories were relatively simplistic.[2] As experience mounted theory and policy were altered and they interacted with experience to build a knowledge base for understanding the development process.

The purpose of tracing the evolution of thought about the development process is to assess how far thinking about development has progressed.

First printed in 1988. The authors are indebted to T.N. Srinivasan and Ramon Marimon for comments and suggestions on an earlier draft of this chapter.

It would be unfair to assess the effectiveness of aid in earlier years without some understanding of the thinking about the development process that was then prevalent.

Economic development – even economic growth – was not a major theme in modern economic thought until well into the 1950s. Development thought, however, has been strongly influenced by the 'magnificent dynamics' of the classicals, particularly Malthus and Ricardo. Other precursors were the members of the German historical school, from List to Sombart, who outlined a series of stages of economic development. These stages were little more than simple expository devices and had only a minor impact on economic policy. When Marx invested his growth-stage sequence with a sense of historical inevitability, he provided the ideology for the forced-draft industrialization policies pursued by the Soviet Union. Schumpeter's (1934) brilliant speculations on the roles of technical change and the entrepreneur in economic growth, of course, were formulated in 1912 to apply primarily to the already advanced capitalist economies. Three particularly important landmarks in the problems of developing economies were Colin Clark's (1940) massive statistical study, *The Conditions of Economic Progress*; and the studies by Paul Rosenstein-Rodan (1943) and Kurt Mandelbaum (1947) on problems of industrial development in eastern and southeastern Europe.

In the five sections of this chapter, the history of development assistance is necessarily presented in brief. Section 15.1 sketches the state of thought as of the early 1950s when attention was turning to the economic objectives of developing countries and how foreign assistance might facilitate their achievement. Section 15.2 identifies some of the early lessons and insights. Section 15.3 indicates how the simple early paradigms led to a more complex appreciation of the development process. Because foreign assistance is essentially government-to-government and development policy is inherently government policy, Section 15.4 addresses the role of government in development as it is presently understood. To sum up, section 15.5 provides a broad picture of where development economics stands now and some of the important questions that stem from our current understandings.

15.1   EARLY POST-WAR DEVELOPMENT THOUGHT: THE SIMPLE SOLUTIONS

The most striking aspects of 'underdevelopment', as it was then known, were the extremely low income accruing to workers and the remarkable similarity of economic structures across the developing countries. Substantial proportions of their populations depended upon subsistence agriculture, and only relatively small proportions of their labor forces were engaged in industrial activities. Exports were limited to a few primary commodities and imports met the demand for most manufactured goods. Although many observers commented on, for example, the needs for public health, education, and technical assistance in those countries, emphasis was placed on two factors as primarily responsible for low incomes: very little capital stock per person and what were widely believed to be significant 'market failures'.

Undoubtedly, the capital stock of developing countries was low relative to that of the developed countries. Even casual observation confirmed the lack of roads, irrigation, electrical power-generating capacity, communications facilities, buildings, and machinery and equipment. Because incomes were low, it was believed that only relatively low savings rates could be expected. Low savings rates, in turn, seemed to imply low rates of investment. The explanation of underdevelopment as the result of a vicious circle in which low incomes led to low savings, which led to low rates of capital formation and small amounts of capital for each person to work with and hence low productivity, which in turn kept incomes low, generated a policy prescription: find the means to raise the rate of capital accumulation.

A closely related observation, later largely discredited, tended to reinforce the idea that a significant segment of the labor force in developing countries was idle. This phenomenon was referred to as 'disguised' unemployment, meaning that farm workers were less than fully employed and would willingly work more hours and days were opportunities available. By implication, the marginal product of labor was zero, either because some workers could leave agriculture and others would work more hours to maintain total output or because idle household members would willingly undertake tasks with positive marginal products (Eckaus, 1955). Thus, it was thought that not only was capital scarce, but, also, the resources complementary to capital were, in effect, free goods. Capital accumulation, therefore, should have a very high return.

When the observation that developing countries were predominantly rural and agricultural was combined with the perceived lack of capital, the development process was reviewed as one of 'structural transformation', that is, to find means to increase the rate of capital accumulation so the structure of economic activity would shift from rural-agricultural to urban-industrial activities. Clark (1940) had provocatively and painstakingly classified economic activities as primary, secondary, and tertiary: primary being farming and mining, secondary being industrial (manufacturing, construction, and electric power generation), and tertiary being service activities (e.g., health care, education, wholesale and retail trade, finance, and other sources). Growth was envisioned to take place as capital stock increased and capital was allocated largely to secondary activities and labor (according to this line of reasoning, labor was essentially costless) migrating from primary to secondary employment.

Given such a view of the development process, the question was how it could be achieved. This brought into focus the second factor thought to be responsible for low incomes: the premise that many more significant market failures occur in developing than in developed countries. It was based in part on the belief in the existence of disguised unemployment and, in part, on the belief that in most developing countries the majority of the poor follow traditional patterns of behavior and are unresponsive to incentives. The economic behavior of peasants was assumed to be essentially irrational. Also, some commentators even asserted that peasants' utility of income was limited and, should returns to labor increase, that the number of hours per days worked would diminish at least proportionately. The belief in pervasive market failure gained support from the apparent power of a number of economic agents: rural landlords who held monopsony power over their tenants and were also moneylenders which made the credit market seem highly imperfect; monopsonistic traders; and industrialists who were the sole producers of goods. Entrepreneurship appeared to be lacking. Distrust of the market and of market mechanisms was buttressed by the view that the demand for exports of primary commodities was income- and price-inelastic and, therefore, that the prospects were dim for developing countries' export earnings to grow rapidly. This 'elasticity pessimism' was widespread, especially when commodity prices fell sharply at the end of the Korean War.

If accelerated capital accumulation is thought to lead to the structural transformation that is the essence of development, and markets cannot be relied on to function well enough to do the job, the policy prescription seems to be straightforward: government must become a major actor in the economy. In this role, it has the responsibility not only to intervene to raise the savings rate but, also, to allocate the resulting investable resources among different economic activities. Thus, private economic activity must be regulated by government because monopolists cannot be relied upon to behave in socially valuable ways. The attention of development economists, consequently, focused on (a) devising analytical techniques to determine investment allocations across economic activities, and (b) developing planning methods and models that could be used as analytical instruments to support the policy-makers charged with the mobilization and allocation of resources.[3]

India's prominence among developing countries made it the focus of much development thought. Several plans – one by the colonial government and one by leaders of the movement for independence[4] – were drawn up before independence. Subsequently, a Planning Commission was put in place by the new government. At the core of the Commission's work were the policy measures that were widely believed in the 1950s to be conducive to development. They included an outline of planned government expenditures on infrastructural activities, macroeconomic objectives and projections, and somewhat detailed specific industry and commodity output targets for the entire economy. 'Investment' licenses regulated the expansion of productive capacity to ensure that over-expansion in some industries did not occur at the expense of others.

Several points should be noted here, however, because they relate to the beliefs about development policy current at the time. (1) Had the Indian planners trusted the international market, they need not have been so concerned with detailed output levels. They could have exported those goods for which 'overcapacity' had been built. (2) The planners envisaged savings as being within the government's power to raise. (3) The underlying belief was that the government would have to carry out or enforce its plans; incentives to induce the types of economic activity desired received minor attention. In fact, import prohibitions provided powerful incentives for domestic production, but the planners did not envisage the successful encouragement of exports through exchange-rate policy, or the liberalization of the financial system as a major means of inducing savings increases. Incentives were given major attention only in those areas in which the government thought it could correct market failure; for example, to implement a 'small savers' scheme, the government established outlets that paid interest to attract rural savings, though the interest rates were usually low.

In sum, Indian planning, reflecting the views of the time, relied on government to raise and allocate resources and to control private economic activity. The economists or policy-makers who were concerned with development never considered the fact that these activities might overtax the administrative capabilities of the government and/or divert its attention from essential tasks and from tasks for which government had a clear competitive advantage.

During the 1950s a number of attempts were made to extract the lessons from the initial implementation of development programs by the developing countries and from the financial and technical assistance endeavors of the developed countries. Two of these programs – one centered at the Massachusetts Institute of Technology Center for International Studies (MIT-CENIS), the other at the National Planning Association and the University of Chicago (NPA-Chicago) – substantially influenced development thought and development policy in the late 1950s and the 1960s.

The perspective that characterized the MIT-CENIS study was that the economic development of underdeveloped areas requires a deliberate, guided, and intense effort over one or two decades to move an economy from stagnation to development. This view was encapsulated in metaphors such as 'big push', 'take-off', and 'minimum critical effort' (Hirschman, 1982; Rostow, 1985, pp. 36–56).

The implications of the MIT perspectives were embodied in a series of proposals for a dramatic increase in the level of capital transfers to the countries of South Asia and Latin America (Millikan and Rostow, 1957).[5] If the amount of aid to all countries were to be sufficiently large to remove lack of capital as a bottleneck to growth, then a commitment of $10–12 billion ($42–50 billion in 1985 dollars) would be required, in the form of loans or grants, over a five-year period. The MIT proposals were influential in shaping the thinking of the Eisenhower and Kennedy administrations on the role of economic assistance in foreign policy (Rostow, 1985, pp. 3–12, 84–196; Rosen, 1985, pp. 101–7).

During the mid-1950s, Theodore W. Schultz of the University of Chicago directed an ambitious study[6] for the National Planning Association on the organization and impact of technical assistance in Latin America. The authors of the individual studies took the value of technical assistance as self-evident; and focused on the policy and administrative reforms needed by recipients and donors to make technical assistance more effective. A more coherent view did emerge, however, in Schultz's (1956a, p. 17) own writing in which he argued that 'for poor countries, and for rich countries as well, much and probably most economic growth does not come from additional inputs of the conventional types'. He saw it as coming instead from two neglected variables: (a) the quality of people as productive agents, and (b) the level of the productive arts – of technology (Schultz, 1956a, p. 19). Investment in these non-conventional inputs, rather than additional conventional inputs, he argued, has permitted some countries to grow rapidly. By the early 1960s Schultz's insights were beginning to be articulated by others at Chicago, particularly Harry G. Johnson (1963) and Gary S. Becker (1964), in what Johnson termed a 'generalized human capital' approach.[7] These ideas were formulated more precisely with respect to agricultural development by Schultz (1964; see especially p. 145).

By the mid-1960s the Chicago and MIT perspectives were beginning to converge, largely because of the crises associated with the lagging growth of agricultural production in South Asia. A landmark in the convergent perspective was the 1964 conference, sponsored by CENIS, on Productivity and Innovation in Agriculture in Underdeveloped Countries (Millikan and Hapgood, 1967). After the conference knowledgeable development theorists or practitioners could no longer assume that a combination of massive capital transfers and simple technical assistance was sufficient to generate growth, particularly in the agricultural sector, without investment in human capital, the development of technology consistent with resource endowments, and appropriate economic incentives.

It was not until two decades later, however, that the insights into the role of human capital began to be effectively incorporated into growth theory. In his 1985 Marshall Lectures, Robert E. Lucas (1986) incorporated human capital into a Solow-like growth model that lent itself to the quantification of both formal education and learning-by-doing as well as technical change.[8] He went on to show that human-capital formation occurs most rapidly in an environment in which new goods are continuously being introduced and then argued that an export-oriented economy provides the most favorable environment for the continuous introduction of new goods and, hence, for the formation of human capital.

15.2 COMPLICATIONS TO THE SIMPLE MODEL

Throughout the 1950s the simple capital-accumulation-cum-market-failure view of development was the predominant intellectual basis for development policy and foreign assistance (see Krueger and Ruttan, forthcoming). Many countries experienced accelerated rates of growth, especially in contrast with the 1930s and 1940s. In most, savings rates rose surprisingly rapidly, thereby permitting a fairly sharp increase in the rate of capital accumulation. None the less, a number of problems arose. In trying to understand what was happening, development economists articulated new insights, although they were not directly integrated into the simple model until well into the 1960s.

Four lines of the new thinking deserve mention here. First, one cannot simply 'transfer resources out of agriculture and into industry'. Evidence had mounted that the neglect of agricultural production could severely constrain development. Lewis (1954), Ranis and Fei (1961), and Jorgenson (1961) developed 'dual-economy' theories in which a 'marketed surplus' from agriculture had to increase if development was not to falter (Krishna, 1967). Increased agricultural output was necessary to support the out-migration of labor from agriculture. Early studies of supply response demonstrated that production was not so inelastic with respect to price as had earlier been thought. Careful analysis of peasant households in developing countries had revealed little 'disguised unemployment' in case after case; productivity was painfully low, and peaks and troughs occurred, but to 'transfer labor out of agriculture' without a loss in output was simply not possible (Krishna, 1967; Behrman, 1968; and Askari and Cummings, 1976). In other words, agricultural production had to increase in the course of development. Therefore, resolving problems associated with agricultural development was a prerequisite for satisfactory and sustained industrial growth.

Second, employment issues are at once different from those previously considered and somewhat less readily amenable to quick resolution by government policy. Most developing countries achieved fairly rapid rates of increase in industrial output in the first years of a conscious development strategy. Although the starting base was very low, the annual rates of growth (at domestic prices – an important provision) exceeded 5 per cent and often 10 per cent in a number of countries for sustained periods. Surprisingly, however, industrial employment failed to grow at anywhere near the rate of industrial growth, and urban employment growth often lagged behind even the natural rate of increase of urban population, which did not permit significant out-migration from rural areas. Thus it was recognized that capital accumulation alone could not increase employment or living standards for most of the population.

Third, the belief in structural rigidities was questioned. The views of the Latin American 'structuralist' school, led by Prebisch (1959), that 'structural transformation' was a prerequisite for economic development were especially important in contributing to skepticism about the functioning of markets in developing countries. However, empirical examination failed to support the structuralist interpretation of inflation. Evidence mounted that by and large inflation can be explained by the same monetary phenomena and budgetary deficits in Latin America as in other parts of the world.

Fourth, when country after country encountered balance-of-payments difficulties, a model of growth was formulated in which foreign exchange, alongside capital, was seen as a scarce factor in development. The balance-of-payments difficulties experienced in country after country were generated, in large measure, by planners' underestimation of the future growth of imports and the overestimation of the rate of growth of exports. Carlos Díaz-Alejandro (1965) aptly noted that import substitution turned out to be import-intensive.

The pervasive 'foreign exchange shortage' that became a stylized fact of development by the early 1960s led to the development of the influential 'two-gap' model of development (Chenery and Bruno, 1962; Chenery and Strout, 1966). In this formulation, labor remained essentially a free good and capital was still needed for growth; but, instead of focusing only on capital accumulation, the two-gap model posited a second constraint on output growth: imports were needed in fixed proportion to both investment and output of import-substitution industries because newly-established factories could not operate without the inter-mediate goods and raw materials that were not produced at home. In the two-gap model, export growth was exogenous at a predetermined rate and the domestic savings rate was taken as given. Output expansion could occur only with new capital and imports. Depending on the para-meters for a particular country, either the savings or foreign-exchange constraint was the limiting factor to growth. Hence, the term 'two-gap' model: a gap existed between domestic savings and investment or be-tween foreign exchange demand and supply. At early stages of develop-ment, foreign exchange, rather than savings, was conjectured to be the binding constraint. (The use of the two-gap model in the programming of economic assistance is discussed in Krueger and Ruttan, forthcoming.)

Each of the preceding lines of thought pointed toward a sector or an issue that had been overlooked in the simple models of the early post-war years and focused attention on factors that were important in development in addition to capital accumulation. Subsequently, the implications for aid policy in the two-gap and the Ranis–Fei and Jorgenson models were recognized (see Krueger and Ruttan, forth-coming Chapter 3).

15.3   TOWARD A MORE COMPLEX PERSPECTIVE: PRIVATE BEHAVIOR

If early development thought implicitly or explicitly assumed market failure and irrational behavior by individual economic agents, the thrust of development economics ever since has been the recognition that private behavior is much more rational and responsive to the incentives in the economic environment than was earlier thought. When con-fronted with an apparent failure of markets to function as forecast in the 1950s, almost all development economists instinctually ascribed the failure to irrational behavior, non-responsiveness to price, or monopoly behavior of one sort or another (including inequality of asset holdings). In contrast, the development economist of the 1980s is far more likely to enquire why people are behaving as they are, on the assumption that their behavior is most likely a rational response to current incentives.

This change in perspective draws on seven interrelated advances in the understanding of development processes:

1. The development of the theory of human capital: it provides an economic rationale for various phenomena previously regarded as 'cultural'.
2. The mounting evidence that peasant responses to market incentives

and technical opportunities are more significant than had been anticipated.

3. The response of entrepreneurs to incentives for industrialization in country after country has eroded the belief in a lack of entrepreneurship.

4. If technical change is to become an efficient source of new income streams, the new technology must be consistent with the factor endowments in the country or region in which it will be used.

5. Institutional innovation also represents an important source of new income streams.

6. The development of the economics of information reveals that the apparent anomalies of interconnected factor markets can, in fact, be efficient market responses to the costs of acquiring information; thus, even tenancy and share-cropping that earlier had appeared to be inefficient and, hence, probably irrational traditional arrangements, may be rational responses to the difficulties associated with the high costs of obtaining information or the lack of it.

7. Experience with alternative trade regimes indicates that 'elasticity pessimism' is unfounded and slow export growth is attributable more to supply difficulties than to foreign demand.

Each of these seven advances is briefly considered in turn.

15.3.1   Human Capital

In early development economics, low levels of literacy, short life expectancies, poor health, and rapid population growth rates, which made the challenge of development and raising living standards difficult, were basically regarded as non-economic phenomena. This view began to change in the early 1960s with the new understanding of the role of human capital in economic development (Schultz, 1961; Becker, 1964). The initial simple assertion was that acquiring education is an investment, as is the allocation of time and effort to job-search, migration, or improvement in health. Investment in education covers both the amount of income foregone and the direct costs of schooling. A choice to make this investment, under economically rational behavior, depends on the higher future income a person might expect to receive by virtue of the additional education.

The human-capital approach is not inconsistent with the view that many people will choose more education regardless of the return. But the founders of the human-capital school insisted that for most people a positive real rate of return is needed to induce more investment in themselves. Thus, the higher the return the greater is the number or proportion of an eligible population who will make such investments and the higher is the investment per person.

The early work on human capital and its focus largely on individual decisions was highly influential in affecting thinking about development. Subsequent work (see Binswanger and Rosenzweig, 1984) has extended the analysis to family decision-making (e.g. choice of family size). Such choices are recognized now as far more rational economic responses to circumstances than was assumed earlier. Policies that ignore the existing incentive framework are likely to be ineffective, quite aside from their welfare implications.

The other insight that emerges from the human-capital literature is that people are as important a resource as physical capital. Even people in developed countries who are regarded as 'unskilled' have sizeable amounts of human capital. Literacy is a virtual prerequisite for most 'unskilled labor' and the rate of return even to primary schooling is high (Psacharopoulos and Woodhall, 1985, pp. 29–71). An efficient means to resource accumulation, then, is to invest in both humans and machines to the point where the rates of return are approximately equal.

15.3.2 Peasant Responses

The rationality of peasant behavior began to be recognized during the 1950s. Their responses to changes in the prices of individual agricultural commodities and to prices confronting producers could not be ignored. Schultz's (1964) work on traditional agriculture eventually persuaded many development economists that small peasants usually respond rapidly to incentives. Peasants who refuse to adopt new techniques often have good reasons: risks are unacceptably high; soil erosion would quickly result; or a technique is not as productive in a local region as officials assume. On the other hand, when a potential for change has a demonstrated pay-off and acceptable levels of risk, peasants adapt very quickly. Thus, when agricultural extension agents fail to persuade peasants to undertake the new techniques they are recommending, Schultz's presumption is that the agents are ignorant of the conditions confronting the peasants, the exact opposite of the earlier presumption of peasant irrationality. Thus a very different role for government in fostering economic development is implied (see Section 15.4).

15.3.3 Entrepreneurs' Responses

Although no systematic body of theory was formulated with respect to entrepreneurship,[9] it was the experience in country after country, none the less, that whatever the incentive structure erected by the government, private entrepreneurs respond to it. When governmental controls are designed to prohibit profitable private undertakings, smuggling, gray markets, and other mechanisms for avoiding the controls quickly spring up. When import-substitution activities are made highly profitable, investment in the protected industries increases. And when incentive structures are dramatically altered (e.g. in Korea after 1960), the rapidity and magnitude of the response surprises all observers.

15.3.4 Technical Change

Technical change also has come to be seen as largely an endogenous economic phenomenon. During the initial period when capital accumulation was the focus, emphasis was placed on the direct transfer of technology (capital-intensive 'turnkey plants' and large scale farming systems) from developed to developing countries. In environments with widely different factor endowments the borrowed technology often was commercially viable only when it was protected by high tariffs or other barriers, which made it a burden on development rather than a source of economic growth. In the case of agriculture it became apparent that peasant farmers in the tropics had access to more productive crop and animal technologies only when the new technologies were developed in the same agroclimatic and socioeconomic environments as that in which the technology would be used.[10]

Hayami and Ruttan (1985), for example, demonstrated that major differences exist between the types of technical change developed for American land-abundant agriculture (basically mechanical to augment scarce labor on abundant land) and those adopted in land-poor Japan (mostly new technologies that essentially enhances the productivity of land). Teece (1977) investigated the costs of adopting existing patents in foreign locations and demonstrated that the costs are a very significant barrier and often are almost equal to those in the initial location. The clear implication of this entire line of work is that most technical change to increase future earnings streams requires the investment of resources and is seldom possible as a 'free' or almost free good.

15.3.5 Institutional Innovation

Greater recognition has been given the role of institutions. Both the American institutional school and Marxian ideology had emphasized the constraints on development associated with traditional property, market, and government institutions (Zingler, 1974). This perspective was pervasive in development economics during the 1950s and 1960s. Beginning in the mid-1960s a new view began to emerge: institutional innovations, along with changing resource or factor endowments, are a productive source of new income streams (Schultz, 1968; North and Thomas, 1970), and modern technical change is dependent on the invention of new institutions – the industrial-research laboratory and the agricultural-experiment station. In both the Schultz and North–Thomas works, differences and changes in resource endowments play a role in the efficient evolution or design of institutional innovations in a manner analogous to the design of efficient technical change.

Access to knowledge and technology in the developed world requires investment in scientific and technical education and in the institutionalization of agricultural- and industrial-research capacity. This institutionalization usually must be calculated in terms of decades rather than the traditional three- or five-year project cycles of bilateral and multilateral assistance agencies. But the developed countries and the assistance agencies must be prepared to make the required investments so that developing countries can have access to the very large income streams that become available as the technological disequilibria with the developed world is narrowed.

15.3.6   Economics of Information

From the perspective of economics of information, the apparently irrational market structures observed in many developing countries, as well as tenancy and share-cropping arrangements, can be interpreted as rational responses to uncertainty and the high costs of information.[11] For example, providing a share-cropper fertilizer may not improve the landlord's return because the cost of monitoring its use may be excessive. If, however, the landlord can make a tie-in arrangement with the share-cropper, as a money-lender or as a marketer, the result may be advantageous to both parties.

Not all decisions are entirely rational from an economic perspective nor are all individuals equally responsive to changes in economic incentives. However, enough evidence has emerged that people act in their own self-interest to cast doubt on the extent of market failure in developing countries and to indicate that failure is certainly less pervasive than was earlier thought. Much remains to be learned about economic behavior in both developed and developing countries, of course, but there is far less basis in the 1980s than in the 1950s and 1960s to presume that policies for growth should differ significantly between developed and developing countries because of differences in the degree of market imperfection.

15.3.7 Experience with Alternative Trade Regimes

Experience with alternative trade regimes led to another advance in development economics. When commodity prices fell sharply in the mid-1950s the typical policy response was to intensify protection for balance-of-payments reasons, often with little regard for the original 'industrialization' or infant-industry aims. The alternative – adjusting incentives to encourage exports – was not adopted, partly because of 'elasticity pessimism'. Three things – domestic inflation rates exceeding the world rate with fixed nominal exchange rates; rising costs of inputs (as imports were prohibited once domestic production started); and sharp increases in demand for imports because of the 'import intensity' of import substitution (Díaz-Alejandro, 1965) – resulted in the slow growth of export earnings, thus making elasticity pessimism a self-fulfilling prophecy.

Meanwhile, articulation of the concept of the effective rate of protection, and empirical estimates of high and variable rates of protection in a large number of developing countries, demonstrated that highly protected industries are usually high-cost and inefficient and that growth based upon them cannot long be sustained (Krueger, 1978). Moreover, the rates of growth measured at domestic (protected) prices greatly overstated actual industrial growth because of the heavy weight given to protected industries. Conceptual developments may by themselves have challenged the dominance of the two-gap model later but, in fact, the challenge came from evidence derived from the analysis of both cross-country and individual country experience, on the effectiveness of incentives, and a move to 'outer-oriented' trade strategies. The latter actually consisted of providing incentives to sell on the international market at least as great as the incentives for selling on the domestic market.

The Korean experience was perhaps the most dramatic. Exports indeed were responsive to incentives; their failure to grow in the 1950s was due more to normal supply responses (emanating from overvalued exchange rates and strong inducements to pull resources into import-substituting industries) than to any failure of world demand or structural rigidity (Mason et al., 1980). The subsequent institution of a series of macroeconomic and trade policy reforms, combined with implicit export-promotion policies, was followed by rapid growth in industrial output, rapid growth in total factor productivity, and rapid growth of exports.

By the 1970s, the developing countries as a group were markedly increasing their share of world exports of manufactures – the most rapidly growing segment of the market – and the 'elasticity pessimism' hypothesis was discredited by experience. The success of the countries that switched strategies also provided evidence of the importance of incentives and the responsiveness of individuals to them (see Krueger, 1984).

15.4 TOWARD A MORE COMPLEX PERSPECTIVE: GOVERNMENT BEHAVIOR

In early development thinking, 'the government' was assumed to be an instrument that could be readily used to promote social welfare without imposing large costs on economic growth. It was seen as a selfless monolithic entity whose objective function was simply to promote the cause of development (on the assumption that that was what people wanted) consistent with the social good.[12]

Experience and analysis demonstrated that this view is far too simple. 'Government' consists of various decision-makers, many of whom have particular interests (rather than some vaguely defined common good) at heart; laws and regulations are not automatically and costlessly implemented and enforced; pressure groups emerge and divert resources to their own favorable ends; and resource constraints narrow the choices available to governments.

When the understanding of individual behavior improved, the question arose as to whether market failure is as pervasive as was initially believed. As long as it was assumed that governments could effortlessly implement a correction for market failure, the presumption of government responsibility for economic activity in all its dimensions remained. No one was about to assert that any market functions perfectly (in the textbook competitive sense).

Experience demonstrated, however, that governments are not the perfect and costless economic agents that had been implicitly assumed; government intervention is often perverse and often has a negative impact on economic growth. The considerable analysis of how trade policy actually works in contrast with the textbook theory of how it might be implemented led some trade theorists to enunciate the theory of economic policy in the presence of distortions, noting in particular that not all policy interventions improve welfare when contrasted with the distorted situation; and to recognize that other manifestations of government failure (e.g. high-cost parastatals, inconsistent and contradictory policies, and rent-seeking as a major economic activity) cast doubt on earlier assumptions about government behavior.

The combination of these insights with growing appreciation of individuals' responsiveness to incentives began a re-examination of the role of government in the development process.[13]

The first line of research (e.g. Krueger, 1978) focused on how policy actually worked as opposed to intentions. Trade interventions were so visible and costly that estimates of effective rates of protection, domestic resource costs, and other analyses of trade regimes convinced most observers that existing policies were irrational: nothing in the infant-industry argument (or in optimal tariff theory) could justify the prevalence over several decades of rates of effective protection ranging up to over 1,000 per cent.

Experience with costly trade regimes led a number of trade theorists to develop the second important line of research: the theory of first- and second-best policy (see Bhagwati, 1971). In essence, the types of policy instruments that had been employed in trade regimes were found to be frequently second or third best, or even ineffective, in terms of achieving desired results. Among the externalities that might justify encouragement to infant industries, protection in most cases was likely to be inferior to the direct encouragement of an activity such as workers' training, or to fail completely (Baldwin, 1969).

Bhagwati demonstrated the same sorts of principles for other perceived distortions: if a factor-market distortion was believed to exist, first best policy would be to intervene in the factor market; second best would be a production subsidy; and third best, a tariff. Not only were these instruments unequivocally ranked but it could be demonstrated also that the highest attainable level of welfare with a tariff (even at the optimal rate) is below the attainable level with a production tax, which, in turn, is below that achievable with the first best intervention (see Krueger, 1986). Production externalities and other rationales for intervention could be similarly analyzed; only in the case of trade-monopoly power was trade intervention a first best instrument.

When the theory of optimal policy is contrasted with the highly protectionist trade policies adopted by many developing countries, it is hard not to conclude that motives other than the improvement of welfare, as assumed in the theory, guided policy formulation and, at best, that the theory of optimal policy conveniently legitimizes the measures adopted for other reasons.

Experience with technological transfer led to recognition of the importance of institutional changes. But other factors also contributed. Motivated by the spread of smuggling, tax evasion, and economic activity designed to profit by controls, the economics of rent-seeking, or 'directly unproductive activities', was developed. Resources allocated to increasing a claim against fixed government licenses were costly and yielded no social (but possibly a high private) return. The positive and welfare economics of the economics of policy-making, in which public agents are considered to be self-serving, is less advanced than is the theory of optimal policy design. To date, most development economists are convinced that reassessment of many propositions earlier taken as givens is in order. One can no longer assume that any textbook policy (e.g. tariff, quantitative restriction, food subsidy, credit rationing, or tax) works as intended. Nor can it be assumed that they will not in themselves set in motion political forces to amend such policies. This view of developing countries in which the government is an independent actor, bureaucrats pursue personal interests, and private interests exchange economic for political resources, led to the rise of a more sophisticated perspective on government behavior.

Economists working primarily on problems of the developed economies in the 1960s and 1970s generated a new 'political-economy' literature that explored the effectiveness with which legislative bodies and bureaucracies translated individual preferences into public policy.[14] Hence, it became clear that public-sector enterprises (e.g. government bureaus, regional and local development authorities, and nationalized industries) could not be expected to follow the maximization rules implied by enabling or funding legislation or by planning agencies. The behavior of managers of such institutions is influenced by their individual objective functions and by the economic and political structure and product markets in which they generate and allocate resources.

Beginning in the early 1970s economists and political scientists in the field of international development began to explore the implications of 'rent-seeking' (Krueger, 1974; Tollison, 1982), corruption (Bhagwati and Hansen, 1973; Pitt, 1981) and institutional organization (Bates, 1981) for the implementation of public policy and the behavior of public institutions. Economic historians (North and Thomas, 1970) and development economists (Ruttan, 1978; Ruttan and Hayami, 1984) explored the implications of differences or changes in resource endowments and in levels and rates of growth in demand for institutional innovation and development.

The effect of this new body of theoretical and empirical research was to interpret institutional change as largely endogenous, rather than exogenous, to national economic and political systems. Institutional innovation and reform influence resource acquisition and, at the same time, are resource-using activities. It is no longer possible to treat institutional change or technical change as disembodied manna from heaven, or as a costless transfer arising out of technical assistance or policy dialogue. In both developed and developing economies property rights are costly to design and enforce, market development and exchange consume resources, information is scarce and expensive to acquire, and policy decisions and implementation draw heavily on both political and economic resources. The view that 'getting policies right' involves little more than an exercise of careful analytical skill by planning commissions combined with the enlightened application of 'political will' by legislative and executive bodies, has given way to a more sophisticated understanding of the forces that bear on the formulation and implementation of economic policy.[15]

15.5   THE ROLE OF POLICY IN DEVELOPMENT

The preceding lines of thought leave many questions unresolved and lead to a general rethinking of the role of government in development. The conclusions that stand out clearly, however, center on the importance of policy, and especially on the avoidance of policies that may have large negative consequences for development.

In this section, the implications of current understandings of individual and governmental behavior on economic policy in support of development are reviewed and then some of the unanswered questions (on which we hope future research will shed light) are briefly sketched.

As to the role of policy, both the insights into behavior (Section 15.4) and the distinctly different experiences of countries with entirely different policy stances have convinced all observers of the overriding importance of 'policy framework' in determining the success of development efforts. To be sure, any 'policy framework' will appear more successful in an environment of the world economy's rapid growth in which more concessional flows and other resources are available for augmenting domestic resources. None the less, the differences in performance between, for example, Far Eastern exporters and heavily inward-oriented Latin American countries during both times of rapid growth in the international economy and the world-wide recession of the 1980s, are testimony to this difference.

The process of development can be viewed as one of accumulating productive resources (both quantitatively and qualitatively, including human capital) per capita and of increasing the efficiency of resource use. Initially, development thought focused on the problem of resource accumulation, on the implicit assumption that the resources would be efficiently used. Theory and practice demonstrated, however, that the efficiency with which resources are employed depends heavily on the economic environment in which private and public decisions are made.

That environment has three major, albeit interrelated, components: (a) the physical, institutional, and human infrastructure; (b) the macroeconomic framework; and (c) the microeconomic incentive structure. Clearly, growth cannot proceed without the simultaneous development of the physical, institutional, and human infrastructure necessary to support it. Early insights into the necessity for better transport facilities, a more effective communication system, a reliable power supply, widespread access to education, public health, enforcement of contract with respect to financial agreements, and so on, were valid, but their importance, relative to the seemingly more directly productive investments in industrial development, was often underestimated. The available infrastructure at any moment sets an upper limit on economic activity; below that limit a weak infrastructure may impose sharply rising costs of additional output. No development program can proceed for long if it does not provide for expansion of infrastructural capacity. And for some purposes (e.g., development of new export industries), neglecting the development of reasonably efficient communications, transport, and financial facilities can effectively foredoom whatever efforts may be made. See, for example, Morawetz's (1981) revealing description and analysis of the competitive advantages of the Far Eastern textile and clothing exporters over their Colombian counterparts.

If the importance of infrastructure was recognized but unappreciated, the role of macroeconomic policy was almost entirely neglected. High and fluctuating rates of inflation (especially when nominal exchange rates are held constant and only reluctantly altered), low nominal and negative real interest rates, and large fiscal deficits that either drain resources from the private sector or result in buildups of foreign debt, are all deceptive insofar as growth apparently can continue for periods of several years even with such policies in place. Yet they are inherently unsustainable and their costs mount. When the time comes, a balance of payments crisis, a debt crisis, or a rate of inflation that is regarded by all segments of society as intolerable can wipe out the apparent gains of past growth over through several years of stagnation or even declines in output.

Finally, microeconomic incentives clearly matter, and matter greatly. If the macroeconomic environment is neglected and the infrastructure underappreciated, analysts may be positively wrong about the responsiveness of individuals to incentives. Price controls (often imposed to contain inflation) lead to gray markets, resource misallocation, and worse. When the controls are sustained, savings rates fall and capital takes flight. Where producer prices of agricultural commodities have been suppressed, negative output responses are much greater than expected

(Ghana's loss of share in cocoa and Sudan's loss in cotton are but two cases in point of a much more general phenomenon). Appreciating real exchange rates result not only in the failure of new export activities to grow but also in the decline in exports even of traditional commodities when economic rents make continuing production at least possible. Credit rationing and implicit subsidies to capital goods imports result in the use of capital-intensive techniques and in the failure of productive employment opportunities to increase, even in countries in which rapidly growing labor forces make such employment growth a political necessity.

Several lessons, consequently, are clear. The first is to avoid making big policy mistakes. This dictum applies as much to large public-sector infrastructure schemes as it does to the key macroeconomic variables set by governments. Although neoclassical economics may not be 'right', it provides a reasonable guide for many purposes; also, there needs to be presumption against deviations, and especially large ones. The hallmark of successful developing countries that have made policy mistakes along the way has not been the perfection of policy but the avoidance of (and willingness to correct) large mistakes.

The second is that a foremost consideration for policy-makers is to avoid letting a key policy instrument generate large conflicts between government regulations and private profitability. When government policies are put in place to prevent profitable endeavors or to require unprofitable courses of action by individuals, the policies are likely to be ineffective. People are always ready to seize opportunities for evasion, whether legal or illegal, but they in turn generate additional government efforts at containment. The result is more complex administrative regimes and more profitable opportunities for bureaucrats and private agents. Thus, the exchange-rate regime must be realistic enough to keep exchange controls and import licensing unnecessary or at least insufficiently restrictive. Too high a rate of inflation induces significant difficulties with regard to savings and often results in capital flight. Suppression of producer prices in agriculture leads to urban food shortages and negative supply responses. Credit rationing, where effective, leads to incentives for the use of capital-intensive techniques for those to whom credit is allocated and large decreases in the efficiency with which new resources are employed. And encouragement of infant industries with high walls of protection and the conferral of monopoly positions induces monopolistic behavior, including a mismatch between consumer demand and types and varieties of output offered, inattention to quality, and pricing outputs that lower levels of demand.

Implicit in these lessons, but important enough to mention in its own right, is the growing appreciation of trade and trade policy to further development. High walls of protection not only fail to induce sustainable rapid growth (for the reasons cited above) but also become a stronger disincentive to the development of exports than was earlier recognized. Development of exports is perhaps the most promising path for rapid growth for most developing countries: it permits them to use their scarce capital and abundant labor to concentrate on the production of those goods (industrial and otherwise) which they can produce relatively efficiently; and, given their relatively small domestic markets, the international marketplace becomes a competitive environment that simultaneously permits rapid expansion of efficient entrepreneurs, encourages plants of adequate size to allow economies of scale, and spurs all to better performance.

That much said, there are many areas where understanding is still highly imperfect. A first concern is how to achieve better governmental performance in those areas such as infrastructure where government has a clear comparative advantage. Here, the key, perhaps, is understanding the types of institutional arrangements that induce behavior consistent with good performance. When government officials derive power and income from the ability to withhold or delay valuable licenses and permits, they are likely to be less concerned with the growth objectives intended by the policy-makers. An important question then is how to create incentive frameworks more consistent with the underlying objectives. Research is greatly needed for answers. In fact, our understanding of how effective institutions arise and are maintained is still very limited. Some degree of professional ethic seems essential in a number of activities, for example, when teachers evaluate students only on the basis of performance. Greater understanding of such issues will inform the design of development policy enormously.

A second major area of concern relates to the 'economics of transition': granting that we know a reasonable amount about an appropriate policy framework for development, how does one design a policy for transition? To what extent can the dislocations associated with adjustment be minimized, and how costly and long-lasting are such adjustments? When politicians are unwilling or unable to reform all policy instruments simultaneously, are there particular policies that require reform before others? Although some insights have come from research and experience (see Krueger, Michalopoulos and Ruttan, forthcoming), a number of reform efforts have floundered for one reason or another.

Analysis of lessons learned to date cannot, however, await further developments. The implications of the lessons thus far learned for aid and aid effectiveness are discussed in Krueger and Ruttan (forthcoming).

NOTES

1. One notable exception was Turkey where economic development became a major objective of government policy in the 1930s. The Soviet Union was the most dramatic example, during the inter-war period, of a nation attempting to mobilize its economic and political resources to generate economic growth. Other developing countries, in Latin America and Thailand, for example, were not colonies, but the conscious pursuit of development there was not a primary objective of government until after World War II.

2. Two very useful sources of development thought in the 1940s and 1950s are Williamson and Buttrick (1954) and Agarwala and Singh (1958). The origins of academic interest in foreign economic development have been reviewed by Simpson (1976) and Arndt (1981; 1987).

3. For a review of development planning theory and practice, as viewed from the early 1960s, see Waterston (1965). His book was commissioned by the World Bank to evaluate the methodology and experience of plan formation and implementation at the time when the 'planning ideology' still dominated much of development practice. However, Waterston (1965, p. 4) warned: 'Even a casual examination of the results achieved from development planning in most less developed countries indicates that they are falling short of what is reasonable to expect. The record is so poor – it has been worsening in fact – that it has sometimes led to disillusionment with planning and the abandonment of plans.'

4. For a fuller account of Indian planning experience see Sukhatme (forthcoming); Bhagwati and Desai (1970); and Bhagwati and Srinivasan (1975).

5. The MIT perspective was first articulated by Millikan and Rostow in a paper prepared for a small foreign policy conference of thinkers associated with the Eisenhower administration in 1954. That draft was subsequently enlarged and published in 1957 (Millikan and Rostow, 1957).

6. For the published results, see the monographs by Maddox (1956), Glick (1957), Rottenberg (1957), Mosher (1957), Maddox and Tolley (1957), Samper (1957) and Schultz (1956b).

7. The generalized human capital approach reflects, in part, a dissatisfaction with the treatment of technical change in the growth-accounting approach of the mid-1950s. Schmookler (1952), Ruttan (1956), Solow (1957), and Denison (1962) had demonstrated that a very large part of output growth in the developed market economies could be accounted for not by the growth of labor and capital inputs but, rather, by productivity growth – growth in output per unit of total input, termed 'total factor productivity'.

8. For an earlier attempt to incorporate human capital investment into growth theory see Uzawa (1965). His was a two-sector model in which one sector produced capital goods, including human capital, and a second sector produced consumption goods. Uzawa assumed a linear technology in the education sector and constant returns to scale in the consumer-goods sector. The model has no tendency for growth rates to converge. The Lucas model, in contrast, incorporates a positive externality in the education sector and increasing returns to education in the production of consumer goods. We are indebted to Stephen L. Parente for the comparison between Uzawa and Lucas.

9. Numerous studies were conducted during this period of the ethnic and religious origins and psychological and educational characteristics of entrepreneurs. Schumpeter placed entrepreneurship, along with technical change, at the center of the development process. Influenced largely by the literature from psychology, sociology, and anthropology, many development economists during the 1950s viewed lack of entrepreneurship as a major constraint on the development process (Brozen, 1954). The most ambitious attempt to incorporate the factors contributing to the development of entrepreneurship in development theory was by Hagen (1962). He did not, however, contribute much more than a checklist of social and psychological attributes that characterize entrepreneurs in different societies at different times. Subsequently, he implied that little can be said beyond the fact that a disproportional number of entrepreneurs emerged from cultural minorities who were excluded from elite roles in traditional societies (Hagen, 1980, pp. 215–31).

10. Hayami and Ruttan (1985, pp. 260–2) identified three levels of technology transfer: (a) *material transfer*: the simple transfer of new materials such as seeds, machines, and techniques; (b) *design transfer*: the transfer of designs, blueprints, and formulae; and (c) *capacity transfer*: the transfer of scientific and technical knowledge and personnel and the development of domestic research and development capacity. A country finds it difficult to capture more than a small share of the gains from technical change until it has achieved substantial capacity to adapt, redesign, and design technology suited to its own factor endowments and socioeconomic environment.

11. See Stiglitz (1986) for an excellent survey of the current state of the economics-of-information literature as it applies to development.

12. This view is a direct extension of the welfare-economics approach to the reform of public policy in the 1940s and 1950s. It is illustrated by Abba P. Lerner (1944, p. 6) and reinforced by Samuelson (1948).

13. For a fuller discussion of the changing perception of the role of government, see Lal (1983) and Srinivasan (1985).

14. Within welfare economics itself an 'institutional design' perspective began to emerge in the work of economists such as Hurwicz (1972) and Reiter (1977). Initial contributions to the new political economy literature included work by Downs (1957), Buchanan and Tullock (1962), Olson (1965), and Niskanen (1971).

15. In the 1960s the US Agency for International Development funded several major research projects that were designed to provide insight into the process of institution-building and political development (e.g. land tenure, agricultural credit markets, international trade regimes, and rural development). The two major institution building research projects were centered at (a) the Universities of Pittsburgh and Indiana and (b) Purdue University, North Carolina State University, and the University of Missouri. For an early conceptual paper see Esman (1962) and Thomas *et al.* (1972). A major weakness of the institution-building approach is that it focuses on bringing about institutional innovations with the guidance of technicians and planners. It is 'an elitist theory with an implicit social engineering bias' (Esman, 1962, p. 2). The literature on political development gave greater attention to endogenous development in politics and administration. By the late 1960s, however, much of the intellectual excitement and scholarly

commitment of the field had evaporated. Much of the political development literature of the 1960s is brought together in Braibanti (1969).

REFERENCES

Agarwala, A.N. and S.P. Singh (1958). *The Economics of Underdevelopment.* New York: Oxford University Press.

Arndt, Hans W. (1981). 'Economic Development: A Semantic History', *Economic Development and Cultural Change*, vol. 29, pp. 457–66.

Arndt, Hans W. (1987). *Economic Development: The History of an Idea.* Chicago: University of Chicago Press.

Askari, Hossein and John T. Cummings (1976). *Agricultural Supply Response: A Survey of the Econometric Evidence.* New York: Praeger.

Baldwin, Robert E. (1969). 'The Case against Infant-Industry Tariff Protection', *Journal of Political Economy*, vol. 77, pp. 295–305.

Bates, Robert H. (1981). *Markets and States in Tropical Africa.* Berkeley: University of California Press.

Becker, Gary S. (1964). *Human Capital.* Princeton, NJ: Princeton University Press.

Behrman, Jere R. (1968). *Supply Response in Underdeveloped Agriculture: A Case Study of Four Major Annual Crops in Thailand, 1937–1963.* Amsterdam: North-Holland.

Bhagwati, Jagdish (1971). 'The Generalized Theory of Distortions and Welfare' in J.N. Bhagwati *et al.* (eds), *Trade, Balance of Payments and Growth.* Amsterdam: North-Holland.

Bhagwati, Jagdish and Padma Desai (1970). *India: Planning for Industrialization.* London: Oxford University Press.

Bhagwati, Jagdish and Bert Hansen (1973). 'A Theoretical Analysis of Smuggling', *Quarterly Journal of Economics*, vol 87, pp. 172–87.

Bhagwati, Jagdish and T.N. Srinivasan (1975). *Foreign Trade Regimes and Economic Development: India.* New York: Columbia University Press, for the National Bureau of Economic Research.

Binswanger, Hans P. and Mark R. Rosenzweig (1984). 'Contractual Arrangements, Employment and Wages in Rural Labor Markets: A Critical Review' in Hans. P. Binswanger and Mark R. Rosenzweig (eds), *Contractural Arrangements, Employment and Rural Labor Markets in Asia.* New Haven, CT: Yale University Press, pp. 1–40.

Braibanti, Ralph (1969). *Political and Administrative Development.* Durham, NC: Duke University Press.

Brozen, Yale (1954). 'Entrepreneurship and Technological Change' in Herold F. Williamson and John A. Buttrick (eds) *Economic Development, Principles and Patterns.* New York: Prentice Hall.

Buchanan, James M. and Gordon Tullock (1962). *The Calculus of Consent.* Ann Arbor: University of Michigan Press.

Chenery, Hollis B. and Michael Bruno (1962). 'Development Alternatives in an Open Economy: The Case of Israel', *Economic Journal*, pp. 79–103.

Chenery, Hollis B. and Alan Strout (1966). 'Foreign Assistance and Economic Development', *American Economic Review*, pp. 679–733.

Clark, Colin (1940). *The Conditions of Economic Progress*. London: Macmillan.

Denison, Edward F. (1962). *The Sources of Economic Growth in the United States and the Alternatives before Us*. Washington, DC: Committee for Economic Development.

Diaz-Alejandro, Carlos (1965). 'On the Import Intensity of Import Substitution', *Kyklos* 18 (Fasc. 3), pp. 495–511.

Downs, Anthony (1957). *An Economic Theory of Democracy*. New York: Harper & Row.

Eckaus, Richard (1955). 'The Factor Proportion Problem in Underdeveloped Areas', *American Economic Review*, pp. 539–565.

Esman, Milton J. (1962). 'Institution Building in National Development', *International Development Review*, pp. 27–30.

Glick, Philip M. (1957). *The Administration of Technical Assistance*. Chicago: University of Chicago Press.

Hagen, Everett E. (1962). *On the Theory of Social Change*. Homewood, IL: Dorsey Press.

Hagen, Everett E. (1980). *The Economics of Development*, 3rd edn. Homewood, IL: Irwin, pp. 215–31.

Hayami, Yujiro and Vernon Ruttan (1985). *Agricultural Development: An International Perspective*. Baltimore, MD: Johns Hopkins University Press.

Hirschman, Albert O. (1982). 'The Rise and Decline of Development Economics' in Mark Gersovitz, Carlos F. Díaz-Alejandro, Gustav Ranis and Mark R. Rosenzweig (eds) *The Theory and Experience of Economic Development: Essays in Honor of Sir W. Arthur Lewis*. London: Allen & Unwin, pp. 372–90.

Hurwicz, Leonid (1972). 'Organizational Structures for Joint Decision Making: A Designer's Point of View' in Matthew Tuite, Roger Chisholm and Michael Radnor (eds) *Interorganizational Decision Making*. Chicago: Aldine, pp. 37–44.

Johnson, Harry G. (1963). 'Towards a Generalized Capital Accumulation Approach to Economic Development' in Harry G. Johnson (ed.) *The Canadian Quandary: Economic Problems and Policies*. Toronto: McGraw-Hill, pp. 227–52.

Jorgenson, Dale (1961). 'The Development of a Dual Economy', *Economic Journal*, vol. 71, pp. 309–31.

Krishna, Raj (1967). 'Agricultural Price Policy and Economic Development' in Herman M. Southworth and Bruce F. Johnston (eds) *Agricultural Development and Economic Growth*. Ithaca, NY: Cornell University Press, pp. 497–540.

Krueger, Anne O. (1974). 'The Political Economy of the Rent-Seeking Society', *American Economic Review*, vol. 64, pp. 291–303 (see also Chapter 7, this volume).

Krueger, Anne O. (1978). *Foreign Trade Regimes and Economic Development: Liberalization Attempts and Consequences*. Cambridge, MA: Ballinger, for National Bureau of Economic Research.

Krueger, Anne O. (1984). 'Comparative Advantage and Development Policy Twenty Years Later' in Moshe Syrquin, Lance Taylor, and Larry Westphal (eds), *Economic Structure and Performance*. New York: Academic Press (see also Chapter 3, this volume).

Krueger, Anne O. (1986). 'Aid in the Development Process', *Research Observer*, vol. 1, no. 1, pp. 57–78.

Krueger, Anne O., Constantine Michalopoulos and Vernon W. Ruttan (forthcoming). *Aid and Development*. Baltimore: Johns Hopkins University Press.

Krueger, Anne O. and Vernon W. Ruttan (forthcoming). 'Toward a Theory of Development Assistance' in Krueger, Michalopoulos and Ruttan (forthcoming), Chapter 3.

Lal, Deepak (1983). *The Poverty of Development Economics*. London: Institute of Economic Affairs.

Lerner, Abba P. (1944). *The Economics of Control*. New York: Macmillan.

Lewis, W. Arthur (1954). 'Economic Development with Unlimited Supplies of Labor', *Manchester School of Economic and Social Studies*, vol. 22, pp. 139–91.

Lucas, Robert F. (1986). *On the Mechanics of Economic Development*. Nankong, Taipei, Taiwan: The Institute of Economics, Academia Sinica (original presented as the 1985 Marshall Lectures, Cambridge, England).

Maddox, James G. (1956). *Technical Assistance by Religious Agencies in Latin America*. Chicago: University of Chicago Press.

Maddox, James G. and Howard R. Tolley (1957). *Case Studies of Training through Technical Cooperation*. Washington, DC: National Planning Association.

Mandelbaum, Kurt (1947). *The Industrialisation of Backward Areas*, Oxford University Institute of Statistics Monograph no. 2. Oxford: Basil Blackwell.

Mason, Edward S., Mahn Je Kim, Douglas S. Perkins, Kwang Suk Kim and David C. Cole (1980). *The Economic and Social Modernization of the Republic of Korea*. Cambridge, MA: Harvard University Press.

Millikan, Max F. and David Hapgood (1967). *No Easy Harvest: the Dilemma of Agriculture in Underdeveloped Countries*. Boston: Little, Brown.

Millikan, Max F. and W.E. Rostow (1957). *A Proposal: A Key to Effective Foreign Policy*. New York: Harper.

Morawetz, David (1981). *Why the Emperor's New Clothes Are Not Made in Colombia: A Case Study in Latin American and East Asian Manufactured Exports*. London: Oxford University Press.

Mosher, Arthur T. (1957). *Technical Cooperation in Latin-American Agriculture*. Chicago: University of Chicago Press.

Niskanen, William A., Jr (1971). *Bureaucracy and Representative Government*. Chicago: Aldine-Alberton.

North, Douglass C. and Robert Paul Thomas (1970). 'An Economic Theory of the Growth of the Western World', *Economic History Review*, vol. 23, pp. 1–17.

Olson, Mancur, Jr (1965). *The Logic of Collective Action: Public Goods and the Theory of Groups*. Cambridge, MA: Harvard University Press.

Psacharopoulos, George and Maureen Woodhall (1985). *Education for Development: An Analysis of Investment Choices*. New York: Oxford University Press.

Pitt, Mark M. (1981). 'Smuggling and Price Disparity', *Journal of International Economics*, vol 11, no. 4, pp. 447–58.

Prebisch, Raúl (1959). 'Commercial Policy in the Underdeveloped Countries', *American Economic Review*, vol. 40, pp. 251–73.

Ranis, Gustav and J.C.H. Fei (1961). 'A Theory of Economic Development', *American Economic Review*, vol. 51, pp. 533–61.

Reiter, Stanley (1977). 'Information and Performance in the (New) Welfare Economics', *American Economic Review*, vol. 67, pp. 226–34.

Rosen, George (1985). *Western Economists and Eastern Societies: Agents of Change in South Asia, 1950–1979*. Baltimore, MD: Johns Hopkins University Press.

Rosenstein-Rodan, Paul (1943). 'Problems of Industrialization in Eastern and

Southeastern Europe', *Economic Journal*, vol. 53, pp. 201–11.

Rostow, W.W. (1985). *Eisenhower, Kennedy and Foreign Aid*. Austin: University of Texas Press.

Rottenberg, Simon (1957). *How U.S. Business Firms Promote Technological Progress*. Washington, DC: National Planning Association.

Ruttan, Vernon W. (1956). 'The Contribution of Technological Progress to Farm Output: 1950–75', *Review of Economics and Statistics*, vol. 38, pp. 61–9.

Ruttan, Vernon W. (1978). 'Induced Institutional Change' in Vernon W. Ruttan and Hans P. Binswanger (eds), *Induced Innovation: Technology, Institutions and Development*. Minneapolis: University of Minnesota Press, pp. 327–57.

Ruttan, Vernon W. and Yujiro Hayami (1984). 'Toward a Theory of Induced Institutional Innovation', *Journal of Development Studies*, vol. 20, pp. 203–23.

Samper, Armando (1957). *Secondary Education in Chile*. Washington, DC: National Planning Association.

Samuelson, Paul A. (1948). *Foundations of Economic Analysis*. Cambridge, MA: Harvard University Press.

Schmookler, Jacob (1952). 'The Changing Efficiency of the American Economy', *Review of Economics and Statistics*, vol. 34, pp. 214–32.

Schultz, Theodore W. (1956a). *The Economic Test in Latin America*, Bulletin 35. Ithaca, NY: New York State School of Industrial and Labor Relations, Cornell University, August.

Schultz, Theodore W. (1956b). 'Latin America Economic Policy Lessons'. Washington, DC: National Planning Association.

Schultz, Theodore W. (1961). 'Investment in Human Capital', *American Economic Review*, pp. 1–17.

Schultz, Theodore W. (1964). *Transforming Traditional Agriculture*. New Haven, CT: Yale University Press.

Schultz, Theodore W. (1968). 'Institutions and the Rising Economic Value of Man', *American Journal of Agricultural Economics*, vol. 50, pp. 1113–22.

Schumpeter, Joseph A. (1934). *The Theory of Economic Development*. Cambridge, MA: Harvard University Press (first published in 1912).

Simpson, James R. (1976). 'The Origin of United States' Academic Interest in Foreign Economic Development', *Economic Development and Cultural Change*, vol. 24, pp. 633–44.

Solow, Robert M. (1957). 'Technical Change and the Aggregate Production Function', *Review of Economics and Statistics*, vol. 39, pp. 313–20.

Srinivasan, T.N. (1985). 'Neoclassical Political Economy, the State and Economic Development', *Asian Development Review*, vol. 3, no. 2, pp. 38–58.

Stiglitz, Joseph E. (1986). 'The New Development Economics', *World Development*, vol. 14, no. 2, pp. 257–65.

Sukhatme, Vasant (forthcoming). 'Assistance to India', in Krueger, Michalopoulos and Ruttan (forthcoming), Chapter 12.

Teece, David J. (1977). 'Technology Transfer by Multinational Firms: The Resource Cost of Transferring Technological Know-how', *Economic Journal*, vol. 37, pp. 242–61.

Tollison, Robert (1982). 'Rent Seeking: A Survey', *Kyklos*, 35 (Fasc. 4, 1982), pp. 575–602.

Uzawa, Hirofumi (1965). 'Optimal Technical Change in an Aggregate Model of Economic Growth', *International Economic Review*, vol. 6, pp. 18–31.

Waterston, Albert (1965). *Development Planning: Lessons of Experience*. Baltimore, MD: Johns Hopkins University Press.

Williamson, Harold F. and John A. Buttrick (1954). *Economic Development: Principles and Patterns*. New York: Prentice Hall.

Woods, Thomas, D., Harry R. Potter, William L. Miller, and Adrian F. Aveni (eds) (1972). *Institution Building: A Model for Applied Social Change*. Cambridge, MA: Schenkman.

Zingler, Ervin K. (1974). 'Veblen vs. Commons: A Comparative Evaluation', *Kyklos*, 17 (Fasc 2), pp. 322–44.

16 · THE DEVELOPING COUNTRIES' ROLE IN THE WORLD ECONOMY

Since 1960 the developing countries as a group have achieved growth in real income and living standards at rates never previously attained over sustained periods in world history. Those gains in and of themselves represent a major achievement of the international economy over the post-war period. Possibly even more important for future prospects, a great deal has been learned about the development process and factors which accelerate or retard it.

Those lessons, in turn, provide a basis for optimism about the future of the developing countries (and the prospects for those developing countries) which have not as yet achieved major gains in real per capita income levels. Should the trends of the 1970s continue or further accelerate, the developing countries will become increasingly important in the international economy. That optimism, however, must be dampened by concern about the reaction by the OECD countries to the increased role of the developing countries. If the trends of the 1970s continue, the 'adaptation problems' associated with the increased relative importance of the developing countries in the international economy will be no less severe in the future than they have been in the past, and they may even intensify.

In this chapter, I propose, first, to sketch the enormity of the achievements of the developing countries in raising their living standards. Second, it will be well to review development experience and development thinking over the past three decades. Thereafter, some of the major lessons that have emerged from that experience are reviewed, including the role of aid and international capital flows and the importance of an open and growing international economy for the growth prospects of the developing countries. Next, the emergence of some

First printed in 1984. I am indebted to Constantine Michalopoulos. Sarath Rajapatirana, Richard Snape, and Juan Ying for helpful comments on an earlier draft of this chapter.

developing countries as exporters of manufactured products, and the reactions they have engendered, is considered. The origins of the 'protectionist' threat to the liberal international economy are then assessed. Next, consideration is given to the role of the developing countries in international capital markets, both official and private. Those topics then set the stage for considering, finally, the prospects for the developing countries in the international economy in the 1980s.

16.1   THE GROWTH OF THE DEVELOPING COUNTRIES, 1950–80

It is difficult to realize that many of today's developing countries had not yet achieved independence in 1950.[1] Even those that had, with rare exceptions had failed to that date to achieve increases in living standards at rates even equal to those of the developed countries. Mexico, for example, is regarded as having had one of the better growth performances prior to 1950, yet Mexican per capita income growth is estimated to have been 1.2 per cent annually from 1877 to 1950 (Maddison, 1970, p. 32) compared to 2.0 per cent annually for the United States over a roughly comparable period. In the early 1950s, observers questioned whether sustained growth of the developing countries was even feasible. Indeed, development textbooks of that period focused on the possibility that 'cultural factors' or a 'tropical climate' led to 'underdevelopment'; there were even questions as to whether Japan should be regarded as a developed or developing country.

The impediments to growth in the early 1950s appeared enormous. The similarity among developing countries in the early 1950s was great enough that it was probably accurate to regard most developing countries as having much the same economic structure. Since few meaningful aggregate figures for the early years are available, let me illustrate the point with data from two countries, Korea and India. These two represent, respectively, a country whose growth performance has been spectacular and a country where growth performance has been considered disappointing. In the 1950s, it is estimated that the infant mortality rate was about 173 per thousand births in India and 86 in Korea. Life expectancy is estimated to have been 42 and 53 years, respectively. The literacy rate is estimated to have been 27.8 per cent of the adult Indian population and 70.6 per cent of the adult Korean population. In 1955, an estimated 75 per cent of the Indian population was engaged in the agricultural sector, which generated 42.3 per cent of Indian national income. In Korea, 70 per cent of the population and 44.5 per cent of income is estimated to have originated in agriculture. At 1980 prices,

Indian per capita income in 1950 is estimated to have been $147.10, while in Korea it was about $348.80. The litany of statistics indicating the extent to which poverty was a nation-wide phenomenon in each country which no amount of redistribution could single-handedly have solved could be continued, but only one further indicator requires mention: the estimated rate of savings as a proportion of GNP was 0.08 in Korea and 0.12 in India.

Under these circumstances, it is small wonder that observers were pessimistic about prospects for the improvement of living standards at rates that might permit a 'closing of the gap', even proportionately, in incomes. In the mid-1950s, there was even a debate in the American administration as to whether it would be possible for the Korean economy to generate any increases in living standards, or whether US policy ought not to be predicated upon the proposition that 'sustaining aid' would be required in order simply to maintain living standards.

Understandable as these views may have been in light of initial conditions, events have belied them. The growth of the developing countries has been considerably more rapid than even optimistic observers expected (see the discussion of early projections of growth rates in Morawetz, 1977, p. 21). For India, per capita income is estimated to have increased at a rate of 1.6 per cent annually from 1950 to 1980, compared with the rate of less than 0.5 per cent annually in the preceeding 80 years. Moreover, life expectancy is estimated to have risen from 38.7 in the early 1950s to 51.8 years, literacy of the adult population has reached 36 per cent, and the infant mortality rate has fallen to 123 per thousand. Although India is one of the more slowly-growing countries, its savings rate rose from 12.1 to 20.2 per cent and the percentage of national income originating in agriculture has declined from 48.5 in 1950 to 33.2 in 1980.

The Korean figures are even more striking. Per capita income in constant prices is estimated to be $1479.30 in 1980 compared to the $348.80 figure for 1950, giving an annual average rate of growth of 4.9 per cent despite relatively slow growth in the 1950s and the impact of the Korean war. Life expectancy has risen to 65 years; infant mortality is now 34 per thousand, and literacy is virtually universal (93 per cent).

Korea, of course, represents in many ways the most successful of the developing countries, at least over the fifteen years from 1960. Among other things, the Korean experience has taught the world that, under appropriate circumstances, high rates of growth and a closing of the gap are feasible and can deliver rising levels of economic well-being to all groups in society. The fundamental, and first, point I wish to make, therefore, is that many of the developing countries have come a long way since the early days of focus on development. Even those countries which have been unable to date to achieve sustained increases in output and living standards have the benefit of the demonstration effect from the successful developers.

16.2 THREE DECADES OF DEVELOPMENT EXPERIENCE

In the early 1950s, it was reasonable for most analysts to regard developing countries as very much alike. By the early 1980s, that situation changed completely. Broadly speaking, a minimum classification would have to include as separate groups the sparsely populated oil exporters (such as Saudi Arabia and Kuwait), the other oil exporters (such as Nigeria and Indonesia), low-income African countries (which have generally failed to achieve satisfactory rates of growth per capita income and many of which in fact experienced declining living standards in the 1970s), other low-income countries (primarily South Asia, where growth rates have been somewhat more satisfactory but where initial levels of poverty were extreme), and the middle-income developing countries (almost all of Latin America, East Asia, Southeast Asia, and Turkey). To be sure, the middle-income countries have higher levels of income in large part because they have experienced satisfactory rates of economic growth. None the less, domestic economic structures and policy problems, and interests in the international economy, differ significantly between the various groups. Thus, a major change in the past thirty years has been the differentiation among developing countries. That differentiation, in turn, has permitted us to learn a number of lessons about the development process.

Analysts of development in the 1950s, noting the severity of the poverty levels, assumed that the underlying 'cause' of poverty was the absence of complementary resources with which workers could increase their productivity. It followed that low savings rates due to poverty made prospects for growth relatively poor in the absence of a 'transfer of resources' from richer countries. Hence, attention in the 1950s was given to incremental capital–output ratios, savings ratios, and planning agencies. The task of development, as seen from that perspective, was to raise savings rates, identify projects with relatively low incremental capital–output ratios, and hence accelerate the development process.

In early 1950s and early 1960s, almost all developing countries adopted a variety of economic policies that can most aptly be characterized as direct interventions and attempts to regulate and control private economic activity. Not only were many 'public-sector enterprises' established, but imports were usually strictly rationed, new investments often required licenses, credit was rationed, wages and conditions of employment were regulated, prices were often controlled with frequent efforts to ration 'essential' commodities, and so on. These policies proved economically detrimental and unadministerable over large segments of the economy. The consequence was that, for the 1950s as a whole, the share of almost every single developing country in world GNP and international trade fell. In part, this was due to the extraordinarily high growth rates of the OECD countries. In part, however, growth rates of the developing countries were relatively low. The proportionate, as well as the absolute, gap in living standards between developed and developing countries increased.

During the 1960s, some developing areas began switching policies. By the late 1950s, Taiwan and Hong Kong had begun to increase real income rapidly, based on a rapid expansion in their exports of manufactured commodities. In the early 1960s, Korea sharply reversed her policies which had earlier been typical of the direct controls employed throughout the developing world. Her real per capita income and exports began rising sharply, as did Singapore's after the mid-1960s. In the late 1960s, Brazil and Colombia also reversed policies with similar results.

Those countries which altered their policies met with great success in increasing growth rates and living standards for the majority of their peoples. In the development world as a whole, they were too small a proportion to be reflected in aggregate statistics: in 1970s, the exports of developing countries represented 19.2 per cent of the world exports, contrasted with 23 per cent in 1960. However, the East Asian exporters were beginning to attract notice as their shares grew rapidly, albeit from a very small base.

The 1970s represented a major watershed in the history of the world. In that decade, developing countries as a group, despite the failures in sub-Saharan Africa, increased their share of the world GNP and of world trade. Even if one abstracts from the oil exporters and examines only world trade in manufactures, the developing countries' share, which was a minimal 6.7 per cent in 1960 (and that mostly processed raw materials), remained 6.7 per cent in 1970 and rose to 11.6 per cent in 1980. Even those numbers, however, obscure the trend: the middle-income oil-importing developing countries, whose share of world trade in manufactures stood at 4.0 per cent in 1960, experienced an increase in their share to 4.8 per cent in 1970 and 9.6 per cent by 1980. By 1980, that relatively small group of developing countries had increased its share of various commodity-group markets significantly: it is estimated that the middle-income non-oil exporting countries had 30.3 per cent of the world exports of clothing and apparel, 15.2 per cent of world exports of footwear and leather products, and 11.5 per cent of electronic exports.

While the emergence of these middle-income, rapidly growing developing countries as significant competitors was a major shift in the international economy, it is worth pausing to note that their success was sufficient so that, for the decade as a whole, developing countries increased their share of world GNP from 20.4 to 22.5 per cent. World GNP is estimated (excluding centrally planned economies) to have grown at a rate of 3.7 per cent annually during the decade. For the developing countries, that rate was exceeded for every region except low-income Africa. Moreover, every region of the developing world except low-income Africa is estimated to have achieved a growth rate of per capita income in excess of that realized in the developing world: oil-exporting countries grew at 10.1 per cent annually, due in large part to the oil-price increase; but non-oil and oil-exporting middle-income countries grew at 5.7 per cent (contrasted with 5.9 per cent in the 1960s) and even low-income Asia (including China) experienced 5.0 per cent growth.

16.3   LESSONS FOR SUCCESSFUL GROWTH

In assessing the future of the developing countries, it is necessary, first, to examine some of the lessons that have been learned about how satis-factory growth is attainable. For, in all the countries that have markedly accelerated their growth, an important part of their transformation has involved their increased openness and participation in the international economy. Future prospects for development hinge in part on the extent to which the international economy resumes its earlier growth path and to which developed countries maintain open liberal trading systems. Here I focus on links between domestic policies and international trade, leaving to later a discussion of the role of capital flows to LDCs in their growth and in the international economy.

As I already mentioned, early efforts to encourage more rapid growth were intervention-oriented. Among the most visible of interventions were those relating to foreign trade. Exports usually stagnated or grew slowly despite the rapid expansion in the international economy because of the highly skewed incentive structure toward production for the domestic market. Exchange rates were overvalued, import licenses were tightly controlled, and very heavy tariffs and surcharges were utilized in an effort to restrain foreign expenditures to the level of foreign exchange receipts. Estimates of effective rates of protection as high as 1,000 per cent were not infrequent. This protection, and the incentives it provided for 'import substitution', was sometimes rationalized on 'infant industry' grounds, although more frequently protection increased far beyond any level conceivably warranted on those grounds because of 'shortage of foreign exchange'.

For reasons that have been widely analyzed (see Krueger, 1983, for a full discussion), the policies that accompanied protection were not only directly detrimental to growth but they also contributed to incentives within the domestic economy that were not conducive to rapid increases in output and productivity. To name just a few, import-licensing regimes led to inefficiencies in obtaining intermediate goods and raw materials, provided incentives for the installation of capital-intensive methods of production, yielded quasi-monopoly positions for many domestic producers, and led to smaller scales of plant and equipment than were economically efficient because of the limited size of the domestic market. The sheltered domestic market also provided few incentives for quality control, and opportunities to learn from the world were greatly diminished by 'foreign exchange shortage'. Meanwhile, the slow growth of foreign-exchange earnings led to period payment crises, to which macroeconomic policy responded with 'stop-go' cycles, with further deleterious effects on output, productivity, and growth.

By contrast, those countries which revised their economic policies often started by reducing the level of protection and simultaneously increasing incentives for export by adjusting the exchange rate to more realistic levels, permitting relatively free importation of intermediate goods and raw materials, and removing controls over production. These so-called 'export-promotion' policies usually entailed fairly uniform incentives for producing a wide variety of goods; there was little of the discrimination between exportable commodities that was inherent among import-competing goods in import-substitution regimes. Simultaneously, the degree to which there were special incentives for export was usually much lower than had been the earlier extent of inducement for import substitution; and the policies that necessarily accompanied successful pursuit of an open-oriented trade-and-growth strategy were far less restrictive than were those often imposed in the course of import substitution. Highly restrictive wage and employment regulation, for example, proved infeasible in the presence of an export orientation.

In passing, it must be noted that preferential trading arrangements among developing countries have failed to yield the benefits that have been realized by the genuinely outer-oriented countries. In part, this has been because those arrangements simply enlarged the area of import substitution. In part, political difficulties prevented realization of the gains that might have been. But it is also the case that trade between developed and developing countries offers much greater scope for gain because of bigger differences in comparative advantage.

For present purposes, several points are important. First, the policy transition from an inner-oriented restrictive trade regime to a more open, liberal economic order was necessarily politically difficult. The task was rendered substantially easier by a rapidly expanding international market. Rapid economic growth in the international marketplace meant newcomers could enter new markets by competing for the increments in demand rather than having to take sales away from other competitors. That ensured more success for a given effort on the part of the new exporters, and simultaneously meant that the industrial countries could absorb additional imports with less dislocation than there would have been in an era of slow growth. Second, although there are always gains to be had by reallocation of resources in line with the international prices, the gains are greater when exports can in fact increase rapidly. As such, the rate of growth of the successful new exporters would have been lower had there been less growth of their exports for the same policy stances. Thus, while a necessary condition for rapid economic growth was appropriate domestic economic policies, the rapidly expanding international economy facilitated the installation of those policies and increased the benefits from them.

16.4   DEVELOPING COUNTRIES' MANUFACTURED EXPORTS

Reorientation of incentives in line with international prices has led to major increases in output and employment in most lines of economic activity in developing countries. More rapid rates of overall growth have been associated with higher sectoral expansion rates in agriculture, mining, manufacturing, and services. But, in terms of the international economy, the most visible aspect of the emergence of the rapidly growing developing countries has been their entry as significant competitors in the international market for a number of manufactured commodities. As already mentioned, developing countries as a group increased their share of the world's manufactured exports from less than 7 per cent in the 1950s and 1960s to about 12 per cent in the early 1980s.

Some salient aspects of this increase should be noted. For, while the share has risen (albeit from a small base), it has evoked protectionist cries of alarm in the developed countries out of all proportion to the magnitude of the increase. The evidence reviewed below, while indicative of the success of the NICs, does not support the notion that imports from LDCs have been the major source of difficulty for the affected industries in developed countries. Indeed, there is every reason to believe that most of these industries would in any event be experiencing rising costs (due to their intensity in the use of unskilled labor) and below average rates of growth of output and employment (due to relatively low income elasticities of demand for such items as footwear and apparel). In the United States, for example, the proportion of consumer expenditures devoted to clothing and footwear fell continuously from 1929 until the 1970s, from 12.2 per cent to 6.8 per cent. It was already down to 8.2 per cent in 1960 – long before imports from developing countries were quantitatively significant.

The real rate of growth of manufactured exports from developing countries is estimated to have been 21.8 per cent annually over the 1970–80 decade (the data in this and the following several paragraphs are drawn from Hughes and Krueger, 1984, Table 3 and 4). This compares with a rate of growth of all imports of manufactures into developed countries of 4.3 per cent over the comparable period. There can be little doubt of the success of the developing countries as a group.

It is important, however, to recognize three things. First, as late as 1980, the share of imports from developing countries in apparent consumption of manufactures in the developed countries was about 3.4 per cent. Even among two-digit commodities, the highest shares of apparent consumption in 1980 were 17.3 per cent for leather products and 16.3 per cent each for clothing and footwear. For such heavily publicized and allegedly 'disruptive' imports as radio and television sets, the share of imports in apparent consumption was 7.2 per cent, while it was 5.4 per cent in textiles. Thus, while growth of imports from LDCs was very rapid, it was from a sufficiently small base that its quantitative impact on developed-country markets was surely less than alleged by groups calling for protection.

The second phenomenon calling for attention is that the increase in manufactured exports originated predominantly from a relatively small group of developing countries. The four largest Far Eastern exporters accounted for 44.5 per cent of all textile, wearing apparel, and leather exports of LDCs by 1980; the comparable figure for miscellaneous manufactures was 70.7 per cent, and that for fabricated metal products, machinery and equipment was 43.7 per cent. If the newly industrializing countries of Latin America are added to the picture, the concentration of imports by origin in fact increases.

Third, and equally significantly, some of the increase in exports of manufactures from developing countries (and especially the Far East 'super-exporters') was offset by declining exports from Japan. While the net exports of the 'super-exporters' of textiles, wearing apparel, and leather goods rose from $1.42 billion in 1970 to $13.97 billion in 1980, Japanese exports of those same commodities rose by $1.65 billion and Japanese imports rose by $2.31 billion. Thus, the net shift in Japan's trade balance – a natural consequence of her rising real wages and shifting comparative advantage – offset at least 5 per cent of the increment in exports from other Far Eastern countries, and undoubtedly would have offset more had voluntary export restraints not been imposed.

These three considerations, put together, have important implications for the future role of the developing countries in the international economy. First, cries of 'damage' in the developed countries were surely overdone. While rising imports undoubtedly added to the adjustment difficulties of the labor-intensive industries in developed countries, most of the difficulties would in any event have been present. Second, despite the increase in protectionist pressure, the available data suggest that protection did not appreciably retard the growth of LDC imports, except possibly of textiles and apparel (see Hughes and Krueger, 1984). Most of the costs of protection were undoubtedly borne by the countries imposing non-tariff barriers and other impediments to trade expansion. It is probably no coincidence that developed countries which were protectionist experienced relatively slower rates of growth in the 1970s, while the developing countries experiencing protectionist measures against them never the less managed relatively better to maintain their growth rates. There is thus a harmony of interests between developed and developing countries: open trading systems are vital to the health of the developed countries, while access to markets will permit significantly more rapid growth for developing countries following growth-oriented policies.

Third, an open international economy is vital to permit successful exporters to shift their export base and make room for other developing countries in the international market for labor-intensive manufactures. Those developing countries which have prospered under outer-oriented trade strategies and appropriate domestic incentives have experienced rapid increases in real wages. As such, their comparative advantage is shifting away from the labor-intensive commodities which initiated their rapid growth, just as Japan's did. Despite that, many of them have relatively high trade barriers against imports of these labor-intensive commodities. There is thus an opportunity for the NICs to open their markets to imports from countries which have to date been less successful than they in raising living standards and accelerating growth. Should they do so, they would absorb part of the output and export expansion of a new generation of rapidly growing developing countries, while simultaneously releasing scarce resources for more productive uses in their own economies. The fact that the successful exporters are allocated market shares under the Multi-Fiber Agreement unquestionably slows down this process, as it has prevented a more rapid shift in Japan's commodity composition of trade.

There are thus two possible paths the developing countries and the international economy can take. On the one hand, rising protectionist pressures can be accommodated: this would reverse the trend toward increasing liberalization that has been such a pronounced characteristic of the entire post-war period. It would also result in poorer growth prospects for developing countries, both because policy shifts would become more difficult and because the benefits derived from successful shifts would be reduced. The newly industrializing countries would experience retardation in their growth rates as resources were locked into industries in which comparative advantage no longer lay. And the developed countries would lose the contribution to growth that increased competition and international specialization have permitted over the past three decades.

On the other hand, it may, and I believe more likely will, be that the mutuality of interests in a liberal international economic order are recognized by all. Should that be the case, the share of the developing countries in international trade will undoubtedly continue to increase in the future as they become integrated into the international economy.

16.5 DEVELOPING COUNTRIES AND THE INTERNATIONAL CAPITAL MARKET

One of the more remarkable phenomena of the post-war period has been the emergence of official capital flows to developing countries. These flows – foreign economic aid, or official development assistance – differed significantly from earlier capital flows to newly settled regions, which had been either equity investments, bond financing (in the more affluent settled regions), or not forthcoming at all.

Official development assistance was the predominant flow of capital to the developing countries in the 1950s, the only other significant source of funds being equity investments in primary commodity projects. In 1956, for example, developing countries experienced a net capital inflow of $6.3 billion. Of that total, $3.3 billion was official development assistance, $2.3 billion represented direct investment, and export credits were $500 million. Private lending and borrowing was negligible (Pearson, 1969, Table 15).

Interestingly, many of the countries that were large recipients of official development assistance in the 1950s are now among the more prosperous, middle-income countries. Investments financed by official development assistance in the 1950s – in developing educational systems, transport and communications networks, irrigation, and so on – laid the basis for expanded economic production that permitted countries to become sufficiently economically viable to attract private capital. In the 1980s, most of the middle-income countries are no longer dependent on official development assistance, although low-income Asia and most of Africa are still too poor to be able to rely on the private-capital market.

The emergence of the developing countries as major borrowers (as contrasted with equity participation) in the international capital market is relatively recent and largely confined to the successful middle-income countries. If the 1950s could be characterized as an era of trade liberalization for the OECD countries, the 1960s can be regarded as the decade which witnessed the rapid integration of the international capital market among the developed countries. The Eurodollar market, the emergence of multinational corporations, and the expansion of international banking were all part of this underlying trend.

In each of the liberalizations (trade and capital flows), the developing countries were a decade behind. As already mentioned, the 1960s were the decade in which some developing countries emerged as significant participants in trade in manufactures, although from such a small share that it took until the 1970s for that to be reflected in their share of world markets. Similarly, private capital flows to developing countries emerged in the 1970s as a significant component of the international capital market, predominately to the same group of countries. For the years 1978–80, private non-concessional flows to developing countries accounted for 53 per cent of net capital flows, compared with 34 per cent for the years 1960–2, while official development assistance fell from 59 per cent to 34 per cent.

This emergence was natural and economic: until developing countries had realigned their incentives to assure export growth, their reliability as debtors was subject to severe skepticism. Earlier official development assistance had helped lay the basis for growth and contributed to pressures for policy changes. Once rapid growth had started, however, high rates of return were available, and it constituted a rational allocation of world resources for additional private capital flows to supplement rising domestic savings as sources of funds for highly profitable investments. The roles of the World Bank and International Monetary Fund in bringing about policy changes and providing information to private capital markets should not be underestimated.

Indeed, it can be forcefully argued (see Branson, 1980) that the middle-income developing countries buffered the international economy against many of the effects of the oil-price increase of 1973–4: they adapted their own domestic economies relatively rapidly to the new relative prices, and thus were able to sustain their rapid growth. Accompanying that, their profitable investment opportunities remained in excess of domestic savings at a time when international banks were accepting large deposits from the Middle East oil-exporting countries.

While that development represented, up to a point, an economically efficient response to an altered geographic distribution of savings, some other developing countries which had failed to adapt their domestic economies also resorted to the international capital market. As with the successful countries, those countries had experienced fairly satisfactory growth during the 1960s and were regarded as 'creditworthy' by commercial banks. Unlike those which had adapted, however, the lending to this latter group of countries (of which Turkey may have been the most visible and obvious case) served to permit them to delay adjustment measures.

Meanwhile, in the latter part of the 1970s, the rapid world-wide inflation, combined with negative real rates of interest, served to reduce the real value of debt for most developing countries. With the oil-price increase of 1979–80, most developing countries tried to adjust and, as in 1973–4, borrowed to smooth over the adjustment process.

However, four circumstances were different in the later period: first, the real value of the initial debt was substantially higher in 1979–80 than it had been in 1973–4; second, the real rate of interest was highly positive, contrasted with its earlier negative level; third, world-wide inflation decelerated so much that export prices for developing countries as a group remained constant over the 1980–2 period, thus effectively making the nominal rate of interest the real rate of interest; and fourth, the recession following 1979–80 was substantially more protracted and severe than that following 1973–4 with industrial country growth estimated to have averaged only 0.5 per cent annually over the period 1980–2.

Given the magnitude of these differences, it is small wonder that the world became concerned with the debt to commercial banks of the developing countries in mid-1982. In a sense, the fact that Mexico was the first highly visible victim was unfortunate; in the Mexican case, it was evident that macroeconomic policies in 1981 had been a major factor contributing to the rapid build up of debt. For many developing countries, debt and debt-servicing difficulties arose for reasons less directly associable with their own macroeconomic policies, although countries which had earlier followed appropriate domestic policies have generally fared better than those which persisted in price setting and direct allocations.

The concerns popularly voiced about developing countries' debts in the latter half of 1982 and 1983 were largely misdirected: the developing countries with high levels of indebtedness to the private banks were precisely those which had earlier been successful, at least to a fair degree, in opening up their economies and providing appropriate signals and incentives to domestic producers and consumers. They were so integrated into the international economy that default was unthinkable. The cost to those countries of abnormally high debt-servicing obligations probably lies in prospectively reduced rates of economic growth (and possibly the political difficulties that may arise in consequence) rather than in debt repudiation. While there are some smaller debtors whose interests in the international economy are less dominant and where the viability of the economy may be more questionable, their outstanding private debts are substantially smaller and could not significantly affect the international financial system.

Hence, while levels of indebtedness and debt-service constitute major problems for most developing countries at the present time, those problems lie more in the costs to the economies of servicing the debt (and possibly the costs of rescheduling) than in a threat to the international system (the perception of which appears, in any event, to have receded).

As recovery takes place, the heavy burden of debt-service payments is likely to diminish, while net lending to the developing countries will in all likelihood once again increase. Indeed, in view of the prospects outlined above – that the lessons about appropriate policies for growth have been learned and that more and more countries will succeed – it is likely that developing countries will become even more major actors in the international capital market in the future than they have been in the past. At present, there are only about fifteen developing countries with sufficient standing in the world capital markets to have been deriving more than half their capital inflow from private sources. With a resumption of growth in the international economy and the adoption of rational growth-promoting policies in more and more developing countries, it is quite possible that there will be forty-five developing countries relying primarily on commercial credit sources by the year 2000.

As this discussion suggests, the headlines focusing on developing country debt may have been misplaced during 1982 and early 1983, but the developing countries will in all likelihood become increasingly important actors in the world capital market over the next several decades. Given the high rates of return that are achievable under appropriate incentives, this development could constitute a rational allocation of world investment. While there are undoubtedly risks associated with the increased exposure of the international financial system to the political and economic growing pains of the developing countries, those risks are probably no larger than those accepted by London in the nineteenth century when it was the financial center and investing heavily in the then-developing countries of the Western Hemisphere.

16.6   PROSPECTS FOR THE 1980s

The potential for rapid improvements in productivity and living standards in the developing countries is greater now than at any earlier point in the post-war period. The lessons that have been learned about the importance of appropriate policies and incentives are gaining ever wider acceptance, and the international institutions focusing on development issues – most notably the World Bank – as well as bilateral agencies are increasingly focusing upon the policy environment in the countries with which they are concerned.

Even with the lessons already learned, however, the fortunes and future prospects of the developing countries are intimately related to the prospects of the developed countries. For, as I have tried to argue in this chapter, a healthy, open and growing international economy is at least as much in the interests of the developing countries as it is in the interests of the developed. A major lesson of the past thirty years has been the importance of access to the international economy for the developing countries.

Whether the economies of the industrial countries will continue in the stagflation of 1980–82 in the years ahead is still an open question, and one that will have been evaluated elsewhere. Prospects of the world-wide 'stop-go' cycle for the 1980s cannot be ruled out. This dismal prospect would inevitably be associated with heightened protectionist pressures, a reversal of the trend toward increasing interdependence and multilateralism, and relatively low rates of growth of output and living standards in the developed countries.

For the developing countries, that prospect is inimical. It would almost inevitably imply that fewer countries will be able to adapt their domestic policies successfully, and even those that did succeed would be confronted with far less satisfactory prospects than were open to those realigning their policies in the 1960s (although it must be noted that many countries at that time did not alter policies because they were pessimistic about the future of the international economy). To be sure, countries which do not realign their economic policies will be in even worse difficulties than those that do: the early 1980s have demonstrated that the countries with the greatest ability to adapt have been those which earlier had adopted outer-oriented strategies.

However, it is to be hoped that the present international economic difficulties represent instead a turning point at which countries have successfully reduced inflation rates, realigned their domestic incentive structures, and laid the basis for a sustained expansion without the re-emergence of rapid inflation. Should that occur, the developing countries' prospects will be vastly better. Those that are already outer-oriented middle-income countries will be the first to benefit. But even the low-income countries of South Asia and Africa will be vastly better off with improved prospects for their exports and terms of trade.

In the medium term, with resumed expansion of the international economy, the real questions center on the avoidance of protection against imports from developing countries – a more likely phenomenon with growth – and on the ability of governments in developing countries to move toward policies that are compatible with economic growth.

To the extent that they are successful, the rate at which developing countries are able to start closing the gap should increase markedly. While some sub-Saharan African countries have not yet been able to realign their domestic policies and may therefore continue to face severe difficulties, most other developing countries show prospects of increasingly rational policies and improved performance. While that 'structural change' in the international economy is bound to call for adjustments in the developed countries, those adjustments will be more readily manageable in the context of resumed growth than they have been in the period since 1973. Just as Japan first emerged in the international economy in the 1950s and 1960s, and then eased the adjustment of the other OECD countries to the newly industrializing countries, it is to be hoped and expected that the successful middle-income countries will themselves emerge as major markets.

One must conclude, overall, that the 1980s will represent something of a crossroads. Either the international economy will remain relatively stagnant, protection will increase, and the developing countries will fall further behind in their development efforts, or resumed expansion and liberalization of international trade in goods and services and of capital flows will permit an acceleration of the trend toward closing the gap that emerged in the 1970s. For political, economic, and humanitarian reasons, it is devoutly to be hoped that the world follows the latter path.

NOTE

1. A few countries, such as Argentina and Uruguay, that are today regarded as developing, were regarded as being similar to Australia, New Zealand, and other high-income, land-rich countries after the Second World War. Their retrogression must stand as a qualification to the generalization presented in this section, although their experience conforms with the lesson discussed in Section 16.3.

REFERENCES

Branson, William H. (1980). 'Trends in United States International Trade and Investment since World War II' in Martin Feldstein (ed.), *The American Economy in Transition*. Chicago: University of Chicago Press, pp. 183–257.

Hershlag, Z.Y. (1968). *Turkey: The Challenge of Economic Growth*. Leiden: E.J. Brill.

Hughes, H. and A.O. Krueger (1984). 'Effects of Protection in Developed Countries on Developing Countries' Exports of Manufactures' in R. Baldwin and A.O. Krueger (eds), *American Trade Relations*. Chicago: University of Chicago Press.

Krueger, Anne O. (1983). 'Comparative Advantage and Development Policy Twenty Years Later' in M. Syrquin, L. Taylor and L. Westphal (eds), *Economic Structure and Performance, Essays in Honor of Hollis B. Chenery*. New York: Academic Press (see also Chapter 3, this volume).

Maddison, Angus (1970). *Economic Progress and Policy in Developing Countries*. London: George Allen & Unwin.

Morawetz, David (1977). *Twenty-Five Years of Economic Development, 1950 to 1975*. Washington, DC: World Bank.

Pearson, Lester B. (1969). *Partners in Development*. New York: Praeger.

INDEX